LITERATURE AND CULTURE

IN MODERN BRITAIN

Volume Three: 1956–1

Literature and Culture in Modern Britain

Series Editors:
Clive Bloom, Professor in English and American Studies, Middlesex University
Gary Day, Lecturer, De Montfort University

Already published:
Literature and Culture in Modern Britain, Volume One: 1900–1929
Literature and Culture in Modern Britain, Volume Two: 1930–1955

Literature and Culture in Modern Britain

Volume Three: 1956–1999

Edited by Clive Bloom *and* Gary Day

An imprint of **Pearson Education**

Harlow, England · London · New York · Reading, Massachusetts · San Francisco
Toronto · Don Mills, Ontario · Sydney · Tokyo · Singapore · Hong Kong · Seoul
Taipei · Cape Town · Madrid · Mexico City · Amsterdam · Munich · Paris · Milan

Pearson Education Limited
Edinburgh Gate
Harlow
Essex CM20 2JE
England

and Associated Companies throughout the World.

Visit us on the World Wide Web at:
www.pearsoneduc.com

First published 2000

ISBN 0 582 07552 1 PPR
ISBN 0 582 07553 X CSD

British Library Cataloguing-in-Publication Data
A catalogue record for this book is available from the British Library

Library of Congress Cataloging-in-Publication Data
A catalog entry for this title is available from the Library of Congress

10 9 8 7 6 5 4 3 2 1
05 04 03 02 01 00

Typeset by 35 in 10/12pt Bembo
Produced by Pearson Education Asia Pte Ltd.,
Printed in Singapore

Contents

Acknowledgements	viii
Series Preface	ix
List of Contributors	x
Chronology	xii

Introduction   *Gary Day*   1
Economic and social policy   1
Culture   11
Conclusion   18

1. British Poetry 1956–99   *Jessica Maynard*   25
The poetics of cliché   25
Chance encounters: Larkin, Tomlinson   28
Metamorphoses: Fisher, Clark   32
Autobiographies: Betjeman, Bunting, Prynne   37
Two varieties of irony   45

2. Novel Voices   *Steven Earnshaw*   51
Rogue males   53
Lone voices   54
From the middle-brow to the high forehead:
    women-centred fiction   56
The dark gods   58
Empire   60
Experimental literature   62
Genre fiction   63
The postmodern   64
'There's no such thing as society . . .'   68
Martin Amis   70
Voice projections   71

3. **Popular Fiction**   *Michael Hayes*   76
   Market stall to global market   78
   Fictions galore   81
   Consuming passions   86
   Popular fiction: *The Legacy*   89

4. **Lifting the Lid: Theatre 1956–99**   *Michael Woolf*   94
   Prologue   94
   What is 'theatre'?   96
   Beyond censorship   100
   Lost Edens: politics and nostalgia   105
   A humanist theatre   107
   The music hall   109
   Joe Orton and the outrage of Mrs Edna Welthorpe   110
   The presence of Harold Pinter   113
   Ayckbourn: a singular exception   115
   Conclusion: theatre and the segmented society   117

5. **British Newspapers**   *Nicholas Rance*   125
   'A dreadful, long-running detective story': reporting the
      case of the Yorkshire Ripper   135
   Conclusion   139

6. **British Cinema: A Struggle for Identity**   *Lez Cooke*   143
   The British 'new wave'   146
   The social problem film   149
   Hammer horror: the return of the repressed   151
   Carry On and the 'carnivalesque'   155
   The Empire strikes back?   156
   'Swinging London'   158
   The 1970s: mainstream decline and the rise of
      independent cinema   162
   British cinema and Thatcherism   165
   The British film renaissance of the 1990s   170

7. **Television**   *Lez Cooke*   177
   The impact of ITV on the BBC   178
   The 'Golden Age' of British television   181
   British television in the 1970s: a mirror to society?   185
   The 1980s: Channel 4, competition and deregulation   190
   British television in the 1990s   197

8. **British Art**   *David Masters*   204
   The avant-garde moves home: Paris to New York   204
   'The situation in London now'   205

Abstraction − a new realism?   206
. . . and the situation in St Ives   208
IG, TIT and pop   209
Later pop   210
Challenging modernism: artists with attitude   212
When concept replaced the unique art object   215
A crisis of modernity? The emergence of postmodernism
    and anti-modernism   217
'Nostalgia for the unattainable'   218
Some went mad . . . some ran away   219

 9. **Popular Music since the 1950s** *Andrew Blake*   224
Popular music before pop   224
Aspects of amateurism: folk roots and r 'n' b   226
Professionalism and pop   227
The 1960s and after   228
The ambivalence of broadcasting   230
Youth and music   231
The urban soundscape   233
Let's mix again   235

10. **Technology 1956–99** *John Morris*   239
What is technology and where is it taking us?   239
The information explosion   242
Genetic engineering   246
Outcomes of the high tech. process   252
Final thoughts   255

11. **Epilogue and Overture** *Clive Bloom*   259
The role of the university   262
Criticism at the end of the century   263
New and future approaches   264
British culture at the Millennium   265

Index   268

Acknowledgements

The editors would like to thank Margaret Griffiths and Libby Di Niro for their help with the chronology.

Series Preface

LITERATURE AND CULTURE IN MODERN BRITAIN

As literary and cultural studies expand into new areas of enquiry, the aim of this three-volume sequence is to give the reader the intertextual cultural history of modern Britain, one in which literary, cultural and historical processes are intimately connected. It is a history in which literature is neither seen as mere reflection of social forces nor as separate from such forces, but rather as a participating and moulding factor in the history of perception in this country over the century.

List of Contributors

Andrew Blake lectures at Winchester University College

Clive Bloom is Professor of English and American Studies at Middlesex University

Lez Cooke lectures at University of North Staffordshire

Gary Day is principal lecturer in English at De Montfort University

Steven Earnshaw lectures at Sheffield Hallam University

Michael Hayes lectures at the University of Central Lancashire

David Masters is a Tutor at the Open University

Jessica Maynard lectures at King's College, London

John Morris lectures at Brunel University

Nicholas Rance lectures at Middlesex University

Michael Woolf is director of Syracuse University (London)

For Charlotte, Jonathan and James
who will inherit the next century.

Chronology

YEAR	LITERARY EVENTS	OTHER CULTURAL EVENTS	POLITICAL AND OTHER EVENTS
1956	John Osborne, *Look Back in Anger* Robert Conquest, *New Lines*	Alexander Korda dies First television appearance of Elvis Presley	Hungarian Uprising Suez Crisis
1957	*Grace Metalious, Peyton Place* Alan Sillitoe, *Saturday Night and Sunday Morning* Ian Fleming, *From Russia With Love* John Braine, *Room at the Top* Richard Hoggart, *The Uses of Literacy*	Sibelius dies Bill Haley arrives in UK	Malayan Independence
1958	Shelagh Delaney, *A Taste of Honey*	Manchester United air crash First Atlantic jet travel Ralph Vaughan Williams dies	CND mass rally Notting Hill riots

YEAR	LITERARY EVENTS	OTHER CULTURAL EVENTS	POLITICAL AND OTHER EVENTS
1959	William Burroughs, *The Naked Lunch* (first UK publication, 1964) Colin MacInnes, *Absolute Beginners* Alain Robbe-Grillet, *The Voyeur* (first UK publication)	The Mini car invented First hovercraft built	Fidel Castro comes to power in Cuba Tibet invaded by China
1960	–	Albert Camus dies Royal Shakespeare Company formed First showing of *Coronation Street*	Sharpeville Massacre in South Africa
1961	Allen Ginsberg, *Kaddish and Other Poems* Harold Robbins, *The Carpet Baggers* (first UK publication)	Dashiell Hammett dies Carl Jung dies Ernest Hemingway dies Yuri Gagarin is first man in space	Construction of the Berlin Wall Bay of Pigs crisis
1962	Ken Kesey, *One Flew Over the Cuckoo's Nest* Anthony Burgess, *A Clockwork Orange* A. Alvarez, *The New Poetry*	Francis Crick and James Watson win Nobel Prize for Medicine for the discovery of DNA Marilyn Monro dies First James Bond film, *Dr No*	Cuban Missile crisis Algerian Independence Nelson Mandela jailed
1963	Sylvia Plath, *The Bell Jar* Nell Dunn, *Up the Junction* John Le Carré, *The Spy Who Came In from the Cold*	–	Assassination of John F. Kennedy Great Britain refused entry to the Common Market Martin Luther King makes 'I have a Dream' speech Profumo affair

YEAR	LITERARY EVENTS	OTHER CULTURAL EVENTS	POLITICAL AND OTHER EVENTS
1964	–	Herbert Marcuse, *One-Dimensional Man* Ian Fleming dies	–
1965	John Lennon, *A Spaniard in the Works*	T.S. Eliot dies Le Corbusier dies	First US offensive in Vietnam Rhodesia declares UDI
1966	Jacqueline Susann, *The Valley of the Dolls* Frank Herbert, *Dune*	England beat Germany 4–2 in the World Cup Final Walt Disney dies André Breton dies	Cultural Revolution in China
1967	–	*Sergeant Pepper* recorded by the Beatles Festival of Flower Power at Woburn Abbey Marshall McLuhan, *The Medium is the Message*	Death of Che Guevara
1968	Booker Prize created	–	Assassination of Martin Luther King Assassination of Robert Kennedy Invasion of Czechoslovakia Riots in Paris Grosvenor Square riot
1969	Germaine Greer, *The Female Eunuch*	Woodstock	Yasser Arafat takes over Palestine Liberation Organisation First troops in Northern Ireland

YEAR	LITERARY EVENTS	OTHER CULTURAL EVENTS	POLITICAL AND OTHER EVENTS
1970	Antonin Artaud, *The Theatre and its Double* (first UK publication)	E.M. Forster dies New English Bible published	–
1971	A. Alvarez, *The Savage God* Richard Allen, *Boot Boys*	–	Introduction of decimal currency Internment introduced in Northern Ireland
1972	Ted Hughes, *Crow* George Steiner, *Extraterritorial* (first UK publication)	–	Bloody Sunday massacre in Northern Ireland
1973	J.G. Ballard, *Crash*	Picasso dies Noel Coward dies J.R.R. Tolkien dies W.H. Auden dies	Britain joins EEC
1974	James Herbert, *The Rats* Stephen King, *Carrie*	–	Sir Keith Joseph makes first speech on monetarism (Preston)
1975	–	–	Margaret Thatcher becomes leader of the Conservative Party
1976	Anne Rice, *Interview with a Vampire*	The Sex Pistols appear on television	Israeli raid on Entebbe Mao Zedong dies
1977	John Fowles, *The French Lieutenant's Woman*	The Queen's Silver Jubilee Elvis Presley dies Maria Callas dies Charlie Chaplin dies	–
1978	Ian McEwen, *The Cement Garden*	F.R. Leavis dies	–

YEAR	LITERARY EVENTS	OTHER CULTURAL EVENTS	POLITICAL AND OTHER EVENTS
1979	–	–	Fall of Shah of Iran Iran Hostage crisis Russia invades Afghanistan 'Winter of Discontent'
1980	–	John Lennon shot	Rhodesia becomes Zimbabwe SAS storm Iranian Embassy Solidarity created in Poland Sir Oswald Mosley dies Ronald Reagan becomes US President
1981	Salman Rushdie, *Midnight's Children* D.M. Thomas, *The White Hotel*	Royal Wedding between Lady Diana Spencer and Prince Charles	Social Democratic Party (SDP) formed Liberal–SDP alliance Black People's Day of Action Toxteth and Brixton riots
1982	Blake Morrison and Andrew Motion, *Contemporary British Poetry*	–	Falklands War Anti-missile protestors camp at Greenham Common Unemployment rises to 3 million
1983	Graham Swift, *Waterland*	William Walton dies	US Star Wars strategy
1984	William Gibson, *Neuromancer* Iain Banks, *The Wasp Factory*	Richard Burton dies J.B. Priestley dies Ted Hughes made Poet Laureate	IRA bomb Conservative Party at Brighton Bhopal disaster The Miners' Strike

YEAR	LITERARY EVENTS	OTHER CULTURAL EVENTS	POLITICAL AND OTHER EVENTS
1985	Timothy Mo, *Sweet Sour*	Orson Welles dies Marc Chagall dies First compact disc (CD) introduced	Broadwater Farm riot Mikhail Gorbachev new leader of Soviet Union
1986	Clive Barker, *The Hellbound Heart* Jeanette Winterson, *Oranges are not the Only Fruit* J.M. Coetzee, *Foe*	Henry Moore dies	First cases of Aids reported Miners' Strike ends Chernobyl disaster
1987	Liz Lochhead, *Mary Queen of Scots got her Head Chopped Off*	Andy Warhol dies	Black Monday Stock Market crash
1988	James Ellroy, *The Black Dahlia* (first UK publication) Salman Rushdie, *The Satanic Verses*	–	Lockerbie disaster
1989	Kazuo Ishiguro, *The Remains of the Day* Julian Barnes, *A History of the World in 10½ Chapters* James Kelman, *A Disaffection* Fatwa declared against Salman Rushdie	–	Fall of the Berlin Wall
1990	Martin Amis, *London Fields* A.S. Byatt, *Possession*	Space Shuttle *Discovery* places Hubble Telescope in Earth orbit First surgery on baby in its mother's womb A.J.P. Taylor dies	Reunification of Germany Social Democratic Party wound up Anti Poll Tax riots in Trafalgar Square BSE crisis Margaret Thatcher loses leadership of Conservative Party

YEAR	LITERARY EVENTS	OTHER CULTURAL EVENTS	POLITICAL AND OTHER EVENTS
1991	Bret Easton Ellis, *American Psycho* Angela Carter, *Wise Children* Derek Walcott, *Omeros*	Helen Sharman is the first Briton to go into space *Listener* magazine closes down Robert Maxwell dies Graham Greene dies	Invasion of Kuwait by Iraq Gulf War begins End of Apartheid in South Africa Release of Birmingham Six Croatia and Slovakia declare independence from Yugoslavia
1992	Jung Chang, *Wild Swans* Ian McEwan, *Black Dogs* Michael Ondaatje, *The English Patient* Alasdair Gray, *Poor Things*	Foundation of the British Literature Prize UN Conference on Environment and Development in Rio de Janeiro: convention binding countries to the protection of biodiversity and awareness of climate change Church of England Synod votes to allow women to be ordained to the priesthood Francis Bacon dies	Serbia announces plan to create new Yugoslavian state British Muslims inaugurate first Muslim Parliament in London Rodney King affair
1993	Roddy Doyle, *Paddy Clarke Ha, Ha, Ha* Nick Hornby, *Fever Pitch* Robert Swindell, *Stone Cold*	New Tate Gallery opens in St Ives, Cornwall British Sky Broadcasting multi-channel satellite television launched	Murder of Stephen Lawrence IRA bombing campaign on mainland England Murder of Jamie Bulger

YEAR	LITERARY EVENTS	OTHER CULTURAL EVENTS	POLITICAL AND OTHER EVENTS
1994	Michael Hulse, David Kennedy and David Morley, *The New Poetry*	–	–
1995	–	Seamus Heaney receives Nobel Prize for Literature	Labour Party delegates vote to change Clause 4 Riots in Bradford, Luton and Brixton Sir Paul Condon, Commissioner of Metropolitan Police, says 'most muggings are carried out by black men'
1996	Arundhati Roy, *The God of Small Things*	Completion of Shakespeare's Globe in Southwark, London Stone of Scone returned to Scotland	Scott enquiry into Arms to Iraq
1997	Louis de Bernières, *Captain Corelli's Mandolin*	Princess Diana dies in car crash *Sensation* Exhibition	Scots vote for their own Parliament Welsh vote for their own Assembly Election of Labour government under Tony Blair
1998	–	–	Northern Ireland peace plan

YEAR	LITERARY EVENTS	OTHER CULTURAL EVENTS	POLITICAL AND OTHER EVENTS
1999	–	Millennium Dome built Lionel Bart dies Ted Hughes dies	War with Serbia over ethnic cleansing of Kosovo NATO begins bombing of Serbia Millennium Dome built Stephen Lawrence Inquiry Report notes 'institutional racism in Metropolitan Police' London terror campaign by 'lone' racist bomber Worries over genetically modified foods East Timor votes for independence from Indonesia

Introduction

Gary Day

The aim of this series is to give the reader a real sense of the breadth, complexity and exuberance of British literary and cultural history across the twentieth century. The previous volume took the story to 1955 and the present work takes us from the Suez crisis to the Millennium Dome with its hopes for the twenty-first century. Any history of the last 43 years, from 1956 to 1999, will be confronted with an extraordinary array of complex and conflicting cultural and political messages. No such history can hope to be definitive. Our volume lays out the many strands of the period and defines some of the questions to be asked. It may be another century before the definitive volume on this period is written. The present volume, like its two companions, integrates literary and cultural concerns in order to produce both a sociological analysis and a social history, taking into account not only artistic problems but also their complex and often forgotten relationship with economics and industrialism, the changing social role of literature and the influence of the other media.

ECONOMIC AND SOCIAL POLICY

It is a matter of debate how far the late 1950s differ from the late 1990s. Then, as now, there was felt to be little difference between Labour and Conservative policies. What has changed is their attitude towards the economy and the welfare state. In the former period both Labour and Conservative were committed to a mixed economy, full employment and the welfare state; today they are committed to the free market, flexible labour and welfare to work. Both parties now believe that it is the free play of market forces rather than state regulation which will lead to wealth creation and international competitiveness. This represents a rejection of the post-war consensus which was based on the belief that governments had a responsibility to ensure that the poverty and unemployment of the 1930s did not recur. However, the costs of maintaining that responsibility, spiralling wage demands and inflation, were deemed too high a price to pay and it was effectively abandoned with the election of Margaret Thatcher's Conservative government in 1979. Her monetary policies were seen to provide the answer to the question 'what's wrong with the British economy?' which, since the late 1950s, 'has been at the very heart of political debate'.[1]

The first problem facing Harold Macmillan's Conservative government was how to rebuild and restore confidence in the economy after the Suez debacle. The new Chancellor, Peter Thorneycroft, advised that in order to reverse the fall in sterling there needed to be a reduction in the subsidies to nationalised industries, a curb on wages and substantial cuts in defence and welfare. Iain Macleod, the Minister of Labour, and who had been personally responsible for a massive programme of hospital building, strongly opposed these proposals on the grounds that 'it would imply the withdrawal of more than half the only post-war social service which a Conservative government could claim to have created.'[2] Indeed, throughout their term of office, the Conservatives had steadily increased expenditure on education, housing and the National Health Service. Political considerations therefore prevailed over economic ones and Thorneycroft resigned, 'an early martyr for monetarism.'[3]

Derick Heathcoat-Amery succeeded Thorneycroft as Chancellor. A balance of payments surplus in 1958 meant that he was able to give away £370 million in tax relief in his 1959 budget. This accelerated consumer spending which, since the relaxation of hire purchase restrictions in 1954, had been growing steadily throughout the 1950s. It was against this background that Macmillan reputedly silenced a Bedford heckler with his assertion, 'You've never had it so good.'

The demand for consumer goods was met not by increased production at home but by imports from abroad, causing a series of balance of payments crises between 1961 and 1964. In 1961 the new Chancellor of the Exchequer, Selwyn Lloyd, attempted to dampen demand by raising interest rates and indirect taxes and, most controversially, by introducing a 'pay pause' which froze the pay of public sector employees for nearly a year. In addition, he set up the National Economic Development Council which stipulated productivity targets and which provided information to help arbitrators determine the level of pay increases. These measures had the desired effect in that the balance of payments was back in surplus by 1962, but they failed to either stimulate production or improve exports. In 1962

Selwyn Lloyd was replaced by Reginald Maudling whose tax cuts and abandonment of the pay pause effectively reversed the measures of his predecessor. Britain was once again faced with a balance of payments problem, amounting to almost £800 million, which Labour inherited when it was elected in 1964.

Harold Wilson, the leader of the Labour Party, brought his party to power with the promise that it would embrace the new technology and use it to harness 'the white heat of a second industrial revolution'.[4] Before the government could implement its modernisation programme, however, it had to deal with the balance of payments problem left by Maudling. The Chancellor of the Exchequer, James Callaghan, raised income tax and imposed a 15 per cent surcharge on imported goods. He also began negotiations for a loan from the International Monetary Fund. These measures alarmed the City, particularly as the tax rises were in part designed to pay for increases in pensions and health and social insurance benefits. A run on the pound followed and was only stopped by a combination of interest rate rises and another massive loan from the US Federal Reserve and the European central banks.

A prolonged seamen's strike in 1966 caused another sterling crisis which was exacerbated by the temporary embargo on oil following the Six Day war between Egypt and Israel. The result was that the pound was devalued on the 18 of November 1967 from $2.80 to $2.40. Callaghan was replaced as Chancellor by Roy Jenkins whose budget of March 1968 'rained blows on the consumer and industry alike.'[5] Taxes were raised, duties were imposed on petrol, cigarettes, betting and drink and £923 million was taken out of public expenditure. These and other measures put the balance of payments back into the black by the end of 1969.

Labour's promise to plan economic development was embodied in the drawing up of a National Plan and the creation of the Department of Economic Affairs. The aim was to increase the national output by 25 per cent between 1964 and 1970, tying this to an incomes policy that would restrict the growth of wages and salaries. Since the National Plan and the Department of Economic Affairs had neither legal status nor coercive powers, they were seen as merely a public relations exercise and both were abandoned in 1966. Thereafter, Labour pursued the traditional economic policy of maintaining the pound rather than modernising the economy. One obstacle to modernisation were the unions. The problem was the inability of the TUC general council to control what happened at a local level where the demands of shop stewards and plant representatives on pay and working conditions 'made a mockery of the rhetoric of national unity and consensus.'[6] In order to deal with this issue Barbara Castle drafted a White Paper called *In Place of Strife*. Union opposition, together with division in the cabinet, meant that the Bill was dropped. Wilson was seen as having surrendered to the unions and *The Economist* derisively described the episode as 'In Place of Government'.[7]

Although Labour maintained its commitment to full employment and the welfare state, the latter evident in the establishment of the giant Department of Health and Social Security (1968), this was not enough to save it from electoral defeat in 1970. Neither were Labour's notable achievements such as the abolition of capital punishment (1965), the decriminalisation of homosexuality (1967), the expansion of higher education and the creation of the Open University (1966). What counted with the electorate was Labour's failure to modernise the economy and its inability to deal with the unions. Edward Heath began his period of office as Prime Minister of a Conservative government as an adherent of free enterprise. The Conservatives pledged to end support for 'lame ducks', whether these were nationalised industries or welfare claimants.[8] Accordingly, subsidies were reduced and the government's first budget instituted massive cuts in public spending including the controversial ending of free school milk. The government also adopted an anti-interventionist approach to industrial relations. When a dock strike broke out shortly after the election, Robert Carr, the new Minister of Labour, refused to mediate between the two parties.

These measures, however, failed to revive the economy. Inflation and unemployment were rising while industrial production remained static. Accordingly the government changed course, nationalising the ailing Rolls-Royce in 1971 and, in the same year, granted a £35 million subsidy to the Upper Clyde Shipbuilders. The Chancellor, Anthony Barber, reversed his previous budget by increasing public expenditure. Indeed, between 1970 and 1974, the Heath government proved to be bigger spenders than the previous Labour administration. Education, for example, was transformed by a schools building programme, the extension of the comprehensive system and the raising of the school leaving age to 16. In the same budget Barber also cut taxes and relaxed credit controls in an attempt to encourage investment in industry; instead they fuelled a property boom and overseas speculation. They also had the effect of stimulating consumer demand which in turn led to an increase in imports that damaged the balance of payments.

In an attempt to control the unions, whose wage claims were threatening to drive up inflation, the government introduced its ill-fated Industrial Relations Bill in 1971, but the TUC was hostile and threatened to expel any union that complied with the Act. The government's chief confrontation, however, was with the miners who resented the curb on wages and whose pay, in recent years, had fallen behind that of other industrial workers. They rejected the National Coal Board's offer of 8 per cent and began a national strike on 9 January 1972. The use of flying pickets to prevent coal from being delivered to power stations meant that existing stocks had to be rationed, and so industry was put on a three-day week and homes went short of coal. After prolonged negotiations with miners' leaders, a Committee of Inquiry under Lord Wilberforce recommended a pay rise of between 17 and 24 per cent which the government had little option but to accept.

In 1972 the government introduced a Prices and Incomes Bill which aimed to freeze wage increases for a six-month period. Again, the miners were defiant, demanding large minimum increases of between £8 and £13 a week. This came at the time, 1973, when the Yom Kippur war between Israel and Egypt led to an oil embargo and a four-fold increase in its price. The miners went on strike and Heath declared a national emergency as, on 13 December, Britain again was put on a three-day week. Unable to make headway against the miners Heath called a general election for February 1974 on the theme of 'Who governs Britain?' The answer was neither Heath nor the miners. Harold Wilson was returned at the head of a minority Labour government.

The new administration continued its previous endeavour to make society more egalitarian. Labour had passed the Equal Pay Act in 1970 and followed it up in 1975 with a Sex Discrimination Act while, in 1976, the Labour MP Jo Richardson piloted through the Domestic Violence and Matrimonial Proceedings Act. The first task facing the new administration, however, was to deal with the effects of the increase in oil prices which had led to a deficit in the nation's finances. Denis Healey, the new Chancellor of the Exchequer, sought to reduce it by overseas borrowing and raising taxes, though he also made provision for higher pensions and increased food subsidies. Although these measures, together with Britain's income from North Sea oil, led to a rise in the reserves, they did not address the problem of inflation which, aggravated by excessive wage demands from the unions, reached 20 per cent by the end of 1974. These claims put the unions in breach of the 'social contract' (1972) whereby the unions pledged a policy of voluntary restraint on wages if Labour promised not to introduce the law into the area of free collective bargaining. In 1975, alarmed at the level of some settlements, Jack Jones, the Secretary of the Transport and General Workers' Union, proposed a flat-rate rise of no more than £6 a week for everyone. This helped to rein back inflation, as did the tax rises and cuts in public spending in Healey's budget of April 1975, the fourth in rapid succession. This new industrial peace was shattered, however, by a strike by the National Union of Seamen in 1976. The pound sank to a low point of $1.70 and interest rates climbed to 15 per cent. There seemed no alternative but to apply to the International Monetary Fund (IMF) which insisted on a package of public spending cuts as a condition of its loan.

The immediate effects of the IMF loan were a rise in unemployment and a drop in the standard of living. By the summer of 1977, however, the economy was stable and even showing signs of a modest recovery aided by the flow of North Sea oil. This enabled the government to maintain payment of unemployment benefit, the 'social wage', give a Christmas bonus to old age pensioners and increase spending on schools. The rate of inflation also fell from 25 per cent at the end of 1975 to around 7 per cent by mid-1978. This was partly attributable to the 'flat-rate' formula which was abandoned in 1977 when the TUC conference called for a return to free collective bargaining. The firemen and the ambulancemen both went on strike for higher wages, prompting the government to call a state of emergency. It was in this context that the Prime Minister, James Callaghan, imposed a pay increase norm of 5 per cent. The unions refused to accept what seemed an arbitrary figure and, in January 1979, public sector workers began a national strike. Schools were closed, rubbish piled up in the streets and the dead remained unburied. The government eventually negotiated a 9 per cent increase, giving the impression that it was unable to control unruly unions, and the Labour administration was voted out of office on 28 March.

The election, in May 1979, of a Conservative government led by Margaret Thatcher represented an end to support for the welfare state, which was accused of creating a 'dependency culture,' and an abandonment of the Keynesian approach to the economy. Broadly speaking, Keynesianism was a means of maintaining full employment by stimulating demand, usually in the form of tax cuts or increased public spending to create jobs. The problem was that increased demand was not met by increased production and this led to greater imports which had to be paid for out of the foreign exchange reserves of the Bank of England. Whenever the foreign reserves were found to be flowing out too fast a crisis was created, necessitating tax and interest rate rises, a tightening of credit and a reduction in government spending. While the Keynesian approach had undoubtedly contributed to the growing affluence in the twenty years after 1945, it nevertheless failed to address the fundamental problems of the British economy: a declining manufacturing base and a growing service sector, low investment and productivity, and poorly trained managers and workers. A more radical approach was needed and this was provided by the doctrine of monetarism.

Monetarism aimed to eliminate inflation by control of the money supply. Hence there could be no borrowing or printing of money to meet wage claims. The money for these had to be found out of increased revenue arising from a more competitive economy. Mrs Thatcher illustrated the central point of monetarism, that national expenditure could not exceed national income, by the using the metaphor of the household budget where the housewife could not spend more than her husband earned. This figure of speech encapsulated the Thatcherite appeal to traditional values, namely the nation and the family.[9] However, this appeal to tradition existed in some tension with monetarist philosophy which, in its criticism of the planned economy and the welfare state, undermined ideas of society that underpinned conceptions of the nation and the family. These were further eroded by the insistent emphasis on the individual who was defined in economic terms of thrift, self-reliance and enterprise rather than social ones of interdependency, care and co-operation. This culminated in Mrs Thatcher's notorious assertion that 'there is no such thing as society, only individual men and women'.[10]

The first budget of Geoffrey Howe, the Chancellor of the Exchequer, exemplified monetarist principles. He raised interest rates, reduced public spending and sold public assets to finance the public sector borrowing requirement, that is the gap between what a government raises in taxes and what it spends. However, the increase in interest rates fuelled inflation, which received a further boost from the government's decision to honour the recommendations of the Clegg Commission on public sector pay. Nevertheless, by the end of Mrs Thatcher's first term of office, inflation had fallen from 22 per cent in 1980 to 5 per cent in 1983. This was achieved less by control of the money supply than by the loss of manufacturing output and rising unemployment. In addition to these hardships, the government imposed the first real cuts in social security benefits since the 1930s. The unemployed, strikers, pensioners, pregnant women, the disabled and the victims of industrial accidents all had their benefits cut.[11] This policy was continued in Mrs Thatcher's second term where one of the most controversial measures was the replacement of grants to the very poor with loans from the Social Fund. By 1992, the Department of Social Security found that almost 70 per cent of those in receipt of the fund did not have enough to live on after their weekly repayments.[12]

Mrs Thatcher's second administration was also characterised by a relaxation of one part of monetarist doctrine, control of the money supply, and an intensification of another, commitment to the free market. The government saw the power of the unions as an obstacle to the free market and so sought to diminish their influence. High unemployment had already weakened the unions, making it easier for the government to drive home anti-union legislation concerning, among other things, secondary picketing and the seizure of union funds. The miners, who had been so successful against Heath, were comprehensively beaten by Mrs Thatcher.[13] Another key to establishing the free market was the privatisation of state industries such as coal, steel, water and electricity. The belief was that privatisation would bring more competition, a better service and cheaper prices. It was also a means of raising money. This was then used to pay for tax cuts which were intended as a spur to enterprise; in fact Conservative tax policy merely transferred money from the poor to the rich without a corresponding increase in productivity. Will Hutton makes the further point that 'the distribution of incomes after tax has been made more unequal by cutting top marginal rates of income tax and switching from direct to indirect taxation, with those on lower incomes having to pay the same for any given purchase as those on higher incomes.'[14]

Privatisation really got under way with the sale of British Telecom in 1984 which earned the government almost £4 billion. This, however, has to be set against the fact that the sale cost over £3 billion as a result of under-pricing the shares and a lavish advertising campaign. The privatisation of the nationalised industries put the needs of shareholders above those of the community at large. Despite the rhetoric, profits mattered more than service. Furthermore, privatisation did not necessarily mean the withdrawal of the state from the economic sphere, since the newly formed companies required regulation by official bodies. This increase in regulation was at variance with government deregulation of the economy exemplified in such measures as the removal of controls of long- and short-distance bus routes. One of the most important was the deregulation of the finance sector in 1986, known as the Big Bang, which opened trading to a wide range of financial institutions including foreign banks. This added to the already massive expansion of credit based largely on rising house prices and, on 14 October 1987, later known as Black Monday, the Stock Market crashed, wiping billions off shares. The Conservative boom had turned into a spectacular bust. Mrs Thatcher, like her predecessors, had failed to solve the problems of the British economy. Indeed, it can be argued that her government intensified them.

The abolition of the exchange rate in 1979 meant that the value of the pound was determined by international money markets. North Sea oil made sterling a good investment and its value soared.[15] This made exports very expensive, causing orders for them to drop with a consequent rise in unemployment. By 1986 there were 3.13 million people without work and Britain had lost 25 per cent of its manufacturing capacity.[16] In 1976 the Oxford economists, Roger Bacon and Walter Eltis, proclaimed that Britain had too few people producing wealth and too many working in administration, finance or the professions.[17] This trend continued under Mrs Thatcher with the exponential growth of the financial sector and the massive expansion of the leisure 'industry'. Nor did Mrs Thatcher's government address the problem of low investment, using the money from privatisation and North Sea oil to subsidise tax cuts and current spending. A 1987 House of Lords Select Committee Report on Science and Technology concluded that the government 'was not spending enough to restore our present position in world markets.'[18]

Mrs Thatcher's legacy was not, then, a revitalised economy. When she was voted out of office in 1990 the country was more sharply divided between rich and poor than when she had been elected in 1979. As early as 1985, the top 6 per cent of the population received 25 per cent of the national income while the share of the poorest 20 per cent had actually fallen from even the 5.9 per cent they had in 1979. Between 1979 and 1993, poverty increased from 6 to 24 per cent among couples with young children and from 19 to 58 per cent among lone parents.[19] These figures can be directly related to the increase in unemployment, the abolition of the minimum wage, the 'casualisation' of labour and the cuts in welfare benefit.[20] The growing gap between rich and poor was a consequence of Mrs Thatcher's belief that the most important values in a society were not communal but commercial. As Morgan notes, the key characteristic of her premiership was the 'sustained attempt . . . to inject the institutional and cultural life of the nation with market philosophies and business values.'[21] It is here that Mrs Thatcher's influence was most apparent.

John Major's government continued the Thatcherite programme of sound money, privatisation and the importation of commercial considerations into more and more areas of national life. In an attempt to maintain the exchange rate of the pound Major, as Mrs Thatcher's Chancellor, entered Britain into the European Exchange Rate Mechanism (ERM) headed by the Deutchsmark, but at a time, 1990, when the British inflation rate was three times that of Germany. By 1993 the markets were deserting sterling and, despite a massive expenditure of the currency reserves to prop up the pound, Britain was forced to withdraw from the ERM and devalue the pound by some 20 per cent.[22]

There was no relaxation of the drive to privatisation. The government floated British Rail and the nuclear power industry and even prisons were put into private hands. This latter was yet another instance of how the Conservatives were introducing market values into public services. The National Health Service was reorganised to create an internal market with general practitioners in direct control of their own budgets, while league tables were established for schools. Even the police were not immune from this trend, with the Sheehy Committee recommending the introduction of appraisal and performance-related pay as part of their career structure.[23] Nor has the process shown any signs of abatement with the election, in 1997, of New Labour led by Tony Blair. Not content with league tables for schools, David Blunkett, the Education Secretary, also plans to link teachers' pay to pupils' results.

New Labour is so called to distinguish it from old Labour. At the heart of old Labour was Clause 4 of the party constitution which aimed to 'secure for the workers the full fruits of their industry and the most equitable distribution thereof . . . and the best obtainable system of popular administration and control of each industry or service.' At the heart of New Labour is the new Clause 4 which commits the party 'to the enterprise of the market and the rigour of competition.'[24] Unlike old Labour, New Labour is not interested in addressing the problem of inequality. According to Stephen Byers, the Secretary of State for Trade and Industry, 'wealth creation is more important than wealth distribution.'[25] This is the language of Thatcherism and New Labour is Thatcherite to the extent that it is committed to free trade, flexible labour markets, sound money and the spirit of entrepreneurial capitalism. It believes that a government's main function in a global economy is to maintain investors' confidence or capital will flow out of the country. Hence taxation levels, spending programmes and inflation cannot differ too widely from competitor countries. It is for this reason that one of the first acts of the New Labour Chancellor, Gordon Brown, was to hand control of interest rates to the Bank of England. In addition to a sound financial policy, New Labour is committed to the development of a trained and flexible workforce which will attract investors. In contrast to old Labour, which was identified with the unions, New Labour courts the business community, appointing figures such as Martin Taylor from Barclays Bank and Sir David Simon from British Petroleum (BP) as consultants on welfare and European trade respectively. It is true that New Labour has reintroduced the minimum wage[26] but it is also true that there are plans to withdraw employment rights from workers in small firms and this is consistent with the non-repeal of Conservative industrial legislation.[27]

On welfare too New Labour shows its Thatcherite principles. The rhetoric is of self-reliance more than state support, of responsibilities more than rights. The New Labour programme of welfare to work is an extension of the Conservative Job Seekers' Allowance which, among other things, pressured claimants to accept low-paid jobs or lose their 'allowance', a term with quite different connotations from the old 'entitlement'. New Labour's Welfare and Pensions Bill, described by the Social Security Secretary Alistair Darling as 'harsh but justifiable', compels lone parents and the disabled to attend repeated job advice interviews or forfeit benefit.[28] This hardening of attitudes to welfare is underlined by the abolition in 1998 of the single parent's supplement. It also represents a further break with the principles of old Labour. Tony Blair's administration is the first example of a Labour government which did not increase benefits on coming to office, and this at a time when poverty is worse now than it was in 1964 or 1974.[29]

Like the Conservatives, New Labour favours a strong state. Mrs Thatcher's premiership was characterised by the contradiction between market freedom and state centralisation. Under her government, for example, local authorities lost a great deal of their power and autonomy.[30] Michael Howard, the Home Secretary in John Major's government, 'restricted the rights of free assembly, gave the police draconian powers to control ravers and travellers, abolished the right to silence and obliged the courts to impose fixed sentences for certain crimes.'[31] The incorporation of the European Convention of Human Rights and the extension of the Race Relations Act to the police would seem to suggest that New Labour is more liberal than its predecessors.[32] In fact, the anti-social behaviour orders designed to contain nuisance neighbours can also, according to the Home Office, be used against protestors. Similarly, the government is seeking to expand the definition of terrorism to cover 'political, religious and ideological protest' and it has also opened a National Public Order Intelligence Unit whose job is to monitor and compile profiles of protestors. 'Nothing Michael Howard did', opines George Monbiot, 'compares to these new assaults on civil liberties.'[33]

CULTURE

It is tempting to see a direct relation between ideas of culture and the economic and social developments of the last half-century. For example, it seems reasonable to claim that a common culture existed before 1979, but then became increasingly diversified until it was better to talk about different and conflicting cultures rather than a single, unifying one. In Patricia Waugh's words:

> [t]he cultural ideal of welfare capitalism was the maintenance of a common culture through education, good literature and state subsidies for the Arts. The eighties, however, saw the emergence of a plurality of voices, the acceptance of irreconcilable difference, the acknowledgement of a multiplicity of cultures each with its own order of value and social and aesthetic norms.[34]

Thus a common culture would be the expression of the Keynesian economy and the welfare state while a diversity of cultures would be consistent with the competitive market, at the same time posing some challenge to a centralised state.

The problem with this description is that its emphasis on difference hides similarities which persist across the ostensible divide of 1979. For example, the distinction between Keynesianism and monetarism is not an absolute one. All governments in this period were monetarist to the extent that they cut public spending to help maintain the value of the pound.

And, as Peter Riddell has noted, the monetarist policies of Mrs Thatcher 'were in line with those which had been practised by the Labour government.'[35] The reason for such continuities is because both Keynesianism and monetarism represent different facets of capitalism: both are committed to the maintenance of private property and profit as the mainspring of the economy.[36]

The continuities in the economic sphere are reflected in the cultural one. The term 'culture' was as problematic in the late 1950s as it is in the late 1990s. Culture may seem to be fragmenting now, but it is a mistake to suppose that it was more uniform earlier in the period. As C.P. Snow remarked in his Reith Lecture of 1959, 'we have lost even the pretence of a common culture.'[37] One context for the problem of culture in the late 1950s was the recognition that, after Suez, Britain was no longer a world power. This necessitated a reconsideration of what it meant to be British as well of Britain's role in the world. The problem of culture, in other words, was bound up with the crisis of national identity. It is ironic that one of the most celebrated accounts of Englishness, as opposed to Britishness, in this period came from the German-born art critic Nikolaus Pevsner. His list of characteristics – ability to compromise, fair play, queuing, reasonableness and conservatism – represented a diminished view of 'Great' Britain but one which was gaining increasing acceptance through the work of the Movement.[38]

The work of this group was part of that tension between metropolitan and provincial values which was another context for the problem of culture in the late 1950s. What was at issue was metropolitan artifice against provincial authenticity, formal experiment against traditional form and the grand theory against the empirical fact. There was also the matter of class. Movement writers like Kingsley Amis, Philip Larkin and John Wain were predominantly *petit bourgeois*, a class that had been empowered by the new welfare state. Although it defined itself against the established middle class, it aspired to join them, hence the ambiguous attitude of Movement writers to 'high' culture: on the one hand they were scornful of its pretensions, on the other they were respectful of its achievements. What they especially objected to was its cosmopolitan character. Jim Dixon in Kingsley Amis's novel *Lucky Jim* finds the cultural evening at the Welches unbearable because there is a reading of Anouilh. 'Why', he moans, 'couldn't they have chosen an English play?'[39] The Movement aimed to replace the Modernism of the metropolis with a distinctively English art of irony and understatement. The Movement, then, was a focus for a number of ideas about culture. First, it called into question the right of London to legislate on cultural matters; second, it sought access to culture and third it sought to reassert a particularly English idea of culture.

The Movement was the expression of welfare capitalism. The arts, like state benefits, should be available to all. Furthermore, the Movement's characteristic distrust of big ideas was a fair reflection of the consensus between the two main parties, summed up in the word 'Butskellism' (a term coined by *The Economist* in 1954 to describe the lack of real difference between the economic policies of the Conservative Chancellor R.A. Butler and the Shadow Chancellor Hugh Gaitskell). In this respect, the late 1950s is like the late 1990s. Then, as now, there was a sense that ideology was dead and government was accordingly a purely pragmatic affair. This proved a source of deep dissatisfaction for many and Jimmy Porter's outburst in John Osborne's play *Look Back in Anger* (1956), that there were no great causes anymore, came to typify the attitude of the 'angry young man' to the narrowed horizons of post-war Britain; horizons which found their consummate expression in Movement writers.

The achievement of the Movement was to confer a sense of cultural worth on the ordinary things of life. The meaning of culture was no longer quite so strongly identified with the sort of 'high' culture that was characteristic of Modernist art. This idea of culture as 'ordinary' was explored at length by Raymond Williams. He began by pointing out that the idea of culture was forged in opposition to the *laissez-faire* society emerging in the nineteenth century. 'Against mechanism, the amassing of fortunes and the proposition of utility as the source of value, it offered a different and superior social idea.'[40] From the mid-nineteenth century, Williams continues, culture offered a standard of perfection, 'the harmonious development of those qualities and faculties that characterise our humanity', which was available 'not merely to influence society, but to judge it.'[41]

This understanding of culture, however, was closely tied to a class-based view of the social formation. It originated with Coleridge who divided society into three estates – the landowners, the manufacturers and the clerisy – who were 'the ground' and 'necessary antecedent condition of both the former.'[42] The purpose of the clerisy was 'to preserve the stores and guard the treasures of past civilisation' and 'to diffuse through the whole community . . . that quantity and quality of knowledge which was indispensable . . . for the performance of the duties correspondent [to their station].'[43] A concept of 'high' culture was thus implicated in the maintenance of social divisions and so had little to offer to the new welfare society where everyone was equal, in principle if not in fact.

Any new concept of culture had, therefore, to address the problem of the changed condition of society. The difficulty was that class differences persisted despite the attempt to establish a more fair and inclusive society.[44] It is not surprising, then, to find different understandings of culture brought to bear on this problem. One favoured response was that conventional 'high' culture should be available for all. This was the principle behind state funding for the arts. 'Culture', as T.R. Fyvel declared in 1956, 'is no longer for a minority.'[45] There were both right-wing and left-wing objections to this approach. The right-wing view was that in trying to disseminate culture to as wide an audience as possible, it would inevitably be diluted.[46] The left-wing view was that the whole process would benefit the middle class but alienate the working class who were being asked to jettison their own culture in favour of something 'better'.[47] State subsidy of the arts, then, was an attempt to use 'high' culture as a unifying force, but it could not succeed in this because it took too much account of the middle classes and not enough of the working classes. Williams criticised both Labour and Conservative governments for choosing to reconstruct 'the cultural field in capitalist terms [instead of] funding institutions of popular culture and popular education.'[48]

This is not to imply that the working class were ignored. On the contrary, they received a great deal of attention. This was partly because they had been excluded in the past, partly because the new consumerism was threatening to blur class distinctions, and partly because working-class culture seemed to offer a better model of community for the ostensibly egalitarian ethos of post-war Britain than 'high' culture. A key work here is Richard Hoggart's *The Uses of Literacy* which appeared in 1957. This described the pattern of friendliness and co-operation of working-class life based on the extended family and the neighbourhood. It was a vision that informed *Coronation Street* which was first broadcast in December 1960. The programme offered an image of community and a reference point for a range of personal and social concerns.⋆ What *Coronation Street* did not reflect, however, and this was the thrust of Hoggart's analysis, was how traditional working-class culture was succumbing to the pressures of the consumer society.

Hoggart's argument was that the long-established characteristics of working-class culture were being degraded by the 'candy floss world' of popular culture. One of the many examples he gives is popular songs. Traditionally, Hoggart argues, these drew their strength from 'neighbourliness' and were addressed to working-class people 'laughing at themselves and their troubles.'[49] But in 1950s Britain, he continues, this was being replaced by 'a drumming mass call' where 'the fibre of personal oddity and positive group sense are both missing.'[50] Indeed, *The Uses of Literacy* can be regarded as a forerunner of current anxieties about whether or not culture is being 'dumbed down'. On one side there are laments about 'the deliberate neglect of history, the trashing of works which do not fit contemporary fads and

---

⋆ Indeed it still does. At the time of writing one couple in the *Street*, Nick and Leanne, are contemplating whether or not to go ahead with an abortion. At the end of the episode (7. 4. 99), a helpline number was given for those who were in similar circumstances.

prejudices, the loss of biblical and poetic memory and the truly remarkable enmity to the ideas of standards.'[51] On the other, there are the findings of the cultural trends study by the Policy Studies Institute 'that the British are becoming more cultured and more active.'[52]

The impact of popular culture meant that the capacity of working-class culture to provide a model of community that could be adapted for British society was severely undermined. Although some writers, such as Arnold Wesker, criticised the usurption of working-class communities by a 'candy floss' culture others, such as John Braine, saw these same communities as a prison from which the ambitious struggled to escape. The problem with both high culture and working-class culture was that they were both too limited to represent the complexities of the whole society. What was needed was a common culture and this, as already mentioned, was the particular interest of Williams. He argued that culture is common to the extent that it describes our 'common inquiry'. This does not mean that it is uniform, for 'our conclusions are as diverse as our starting points.'[53] Similarly, in a common culture, there is equality of being but not equality of skill or knowledge; such inequalities are necessary to maintain the diversity essential to the health of the common culture. In Williams's words, '[t]he kind of respect for one's self and one's work is a different matter from a claim to inequality of being . . . which lead[s] to denial or domination.'[54] For culture to be common it has to embrace the whole range of activities which make up a society, but since culture is also an 'effort at total qualitative assessment'[55] it does not simply respect those activities, it also judges them. The concept of a common culture, then, has to balance two opposed elements; culture 'as a whole way of life' and culture as 'a body of intellectual and imaginative work.'[56] The former implies an acceptance for what is, the latter that it might be improved. This conceptual difficulty is matched by more practical ones, the main one being the existence of economic inequality. There is also the problem of identifying what counts as common experience in a highly complex and multicultural society.

For these and other reasons, the ideal of the common culture failed to materialise. What emerged in its place was 'mass' or 'popular' culture. This, more than 'high', working-class or common culture, came to provide the co-ordinates for shared experience. Sport, advertising, the soap-opera and the game show were, and still are, some of the key ways in which Britain was represented to itself. This entailed certain consequences for literature. F.R. Leavis had argued that an understanding of literature was crucial not just for a sense of cultural continuity but also as a testament to the 'creative reality of significances, values and non measurable ends' which were ignored by what he called 'our technologico-Benthamite civilisation'.[57] This argument appealed to the idea of culture as the development of our human faculties or, in Arnold's famous phrase, 'the best that is known and thought in the world' against which industrialism was found wanting.[58] It also informed the conception of literature which was formulated in opposition to popular culture. The explicit aim of literary training was to preserve the individual against the blandishments of popular culture which was 'replacing our national culture with a synthetic substance.'[59] Furthermore, so the argument went, entertainment was 'a form of propaganda for things as they are, relentlessly pressing us to be good conformers and avid consumers.'[60]

It has already been shown that such a conception of culture, resting as it does on a strictly hierarchical view of society, was unsuited to the temper of the times. In addition, its appeal to a national culture begged the question of what exactly the national culture was in post-empire Britain. These problems, together with the challenge posed by popular culture, provoked a crisis in the humanities. Writing about the crisis in literary studies, Graham Hough made the point that 'much English literature has dropped below the horizon because England is no longer the centre of literary creation.'[61] Hough identified African, Australian, Indian and West Indian writing as the important areas of development, thus anticipating the advent of post-colonial criticism which is a now key feature of many university English departments.

Hough also claimed that the ideal of literary education, a socially unifying force based on the study of great national writers, was no longer viable because literature 'has become a game played by professionals according to professional rules' and this has alienated the general reader.[62] Waugh makes the same point about theory, that is, the various discourses of post-structuralism, when she writes that it represents an intensification of the professionalisation of literary criticism but at the cost of withdrawing it from the 'ordinary' reader's experience of literature.[63] Hough's essay was published in 1964, the year that Wilson was elected on the promise of creating a second industrial revolution. It is therefore not surprising to read his suggestion that another reason for the crisis in the humanities was the nebulousness of their claim to enhance the quality of life, compared to the demonstrably beneficial effects of science. It seemed that scientific culture had eclipsed literary culture despite Leavis's assertion, in his bilious response to Snow's Reith Lecture, that it failed to address the need of human beings to feel that life was significant.

In the late 1960s and early 1970s, literary criticism sought to imitate the rigour of science by adopting the methodology of structuralism. Structuralists studied 'the relations between mutually conditioned elements of a system and not between self-contained essences.'[64] They were heavily influenced by the Swiss linguist Ferdinand Saussure's view that language was 'a system of differences without positive terms.'[65] This was a challenge to the traditional literary critical assumption that a work was a sensuous enactment of experience, a concrete realising of its potential. Consequently, there was a move away from the consideration of a work's significance, how it enhanced or diminished the possibilities of 'life', towards how it produced meaning.[66] This necessitated a change in the perception of literary works. In particular, more attention was given to their formal properties and the part these played in the production of meaning.[67]

The idea that meaning was the effect of a relation suggested that a full understanding of literary works was not just a matter of understanding their internal relationships but also of situating them in the wider contexts of their production and consumption. Again, this was in contrast to conventional literary criticism where truly significant works were seen as part of a tradition of representative human experiences which transcended the contingencies of the period in which they were written. Marxist structuralists especially aimed to analyse literature in relation to the social formation. Of particular relevance here is the work of Louis Althusser and Pierre Macherey, both of whom were interested in the relationship of literature and ideology.[68] The structuralist claim that meaning was conventional was also important in changing ideas about literature. The structuralist argument was that since the relation between the signifier - the sound or written form of the word – and the signified – the idea or concept associated with it – is arbitrary, it is possible to alter it. In other words, the way we use language determines our perceptions, which in turn determine the kind of society in which we live. The application of this to literature is that criticism is no longer about revealing the meaning of a work but using it to produce meanings which can then help to change the way we live.

Structuralism was a method which could be applied to almost every kind of signification system, from food and clothes to music and art. If there was no common culture, there was a common method which made sense of its diverse forms. There were various problems with structuralism. One was that structuralism was more concerned with the abstract system of rules rather than the concrete individual events to which they gave rise. A second problem was that the stress on the self-regulatory nature of systems seemed to leave little room for human agency. The dissolution of the structuralist enterprise saw the emergence of two overlapping critical movements, post-structuralism and cultural studies.

Post-structuralism is an umbrella term that describes movements such as deconstruction, psychoanalysis, feminism, post-colonialism and cultural materialism as they apply to literary works. It was a reaction to the structuralist conception of the work as a regulated and unified whole, stressing, instead, its multiple and conflicting meanings.[69] Apart from the common effort to tease out 'the warring significations'[70] of a text, these various approaches are also united by their interest in how a text participates in power structures and in how it constructs subjectivity, race, gender and sexuality. Since these are features of popular as well as literary texts little distinction is made between the two. Indeed little distinction is made between criticism and literature, though it has to be said that Arnold made a similar point in the nineteenth century.[71] The post-structuralist endeavour is to intervene in the way that meaning is constructed in society and, especially in the case of some feminist and post-colonial writing, to recover repressed histories that will empower those who are marginalised because of their gender or their race.

The history of cultural studies can be traced back to the work of Williams and Hoggart. Apart from an interest in the development of the term culture, cultural studies was also concerned, in the early days, to win respect for the variety and integrity of working-class culture. It borrowed its method and terminology from literary criticism; phrases such as 'felt life' and 'concrete particularity' abound in both writers. Unfortunately, these militated against a proper understanding of that culture precisely because they derived from a discourse which valued hierarchy. Hoggart went on to found, in 1964, the Centre for Contemporary Cultural Studies at Birmingham. A key figure here was Stuart Hall who later moved to the Open University and was influential in setting up its famous Popular Culture course, U203. Apart from advocating the virtues of cultural difference and diversity, cultural studies developed a concept of culture as struggle. The inspiration for this was the Italian philosopher Antonio Gramsci's concept of hegemony. Briefly, hegemony describes how the dominant group in society seeks to maintain control of its rule by consent rather than coercion; a process which involves constant struggle, negotiation and compromise.[72] An example would be the mass media which produces a set of meanings that have 'the political and ideological order imprinted on them' but which can be interpreted by the viewer according to his or her own priorities or ends.[73] What this view of culture does not tell us, however, is what is at stake in the struggle. Without some sort of ideal, struggle is in danger of being absorbed into the system. It is, after all, a commonplace that capitalism is able not only to accommodate opposition but even to turn it to its advantage. The recent shift in cultural studies from a rhetoric of resistance to a rhetoric of pleasure suggests that it is even now becoming an apologist for the very order it set out to oppose.[74]

CONCLUSION

The period 1956 to 1999 has seen the decline of the category of literature and the expansion of the category of culture. The latter term no longer refers to 'the best that is known and thought in the world' or to 'the harmonious development of those qualities and faculties that characterise our humanity.' Instead it denotes the anthropological sense of culture, culture as a way of life, and this, in turn, has led to an appreciation of cultural relativity which makes it difficult to accept the idea that there are standards which can apply to everyone everywhere.

The predominantly economic character of culture has received little recognition in either cultural studies or literary theory where the emphasis is on culture as identity, gender, race and sexuality; and yet economics is central to all these. It is ironic that cultural studies, which had its origins in an awareness of class difference, should have so little to say about the growth of economic inequality that has led to a sharpening of those differences. One reason for this lies in the reaction in the late 1970s and early 1980s to a vulgar Marxism which reduced cultural phenomena to a reflex of economics. The work of Althusser and Gramsci was important in establishing the idea that culture was 'relatively autonomous' in respect of the economic base but, today, it seems to be regarded as a totally separate sphere. Such a view is consistent with the post-modernist antipathy to the concept of totality which discourages analysis of society in terms of an organised whole, but it is legitimate to ask whether we can really understand the nature of culture without some reference to economics. From Edmund Burke through to George Steiner, the history of culture has been a protest against the effects of economics and now, more than ever, we need to consider the relation between the two, from the simple question of funding for the arts, which has steadily declined since the 1960s,[75] to the more complex one of whether society has any other end than that of wealth accumulation.

The rise of British post-structuralism, in the early 1980s, also eclipsed economic considerations and, with them, the issue of class. Waugh, for example, has argued that British post-structuralism's theoretical critique of the Leavisian canon may have revolutionised the reading of earlier texts, 'but it withdrew academic interest from contemporary writing.'[76] Consequently, British post-structuralism had little to say about literature that engaged with the poverty and inequality caused by the operation of market forces. At the same time, however, the very idioms and assumptions of British post-structuralism seemed, unconsciously, to endorse market ideology.[77] For example, the post-structuralist critique of the integrity of the text coincided, in the early 1980s, with the deregulation of the economy and the dismantling of the welfare state: the free play of market forces found its counterpart in the free play of meaning. Similarly, the post-structuralist resistance to closure in literary analysis mirrored the essentially open nature of capitalism, its endless quest to accumulate. There were also parallels between the post-structuralist claim that the signifier was always in excess of the signified, and the credit boom of the mid-1980s. Finally, the market emphasis on performance was matched by the image of the critic or reader as producer. Originally this was seen in politically progressive terms, the critic intervening in the construction of meaning to alter perceptions of the past and identify possibilities for the future,[78] but the changes in the university system have meant that the critic increasingly produces for government targets rather than to enrich our understanding of culture, a fact reflected in the increasingly diminished and specialised audiences for his or her work.

The reason for this unwitting complicity between British post-structuralism and the ideology of the market is the intimate relation between culture and economics. This is particularly clear in Leavis's work against which British post-structuralism partly defined itself. On the one hand, Leavis concedes that economic assumptions pervade the language, making the task of criticism one of 'wresting meaning from the economist.'[79] On the other hand, he describes literary valuations as 'paper currency based upon a very small proportion of gold',[80] thereby endorsing the very economism he is struggling to resist.

The economic idiom of British post-structuralism derives from its adoption of Saussure's conception of language, which rests on a metaphor of money.

> To determine what a five-franc piece is worth one must know: (1) that it can be exchanged for a fixed quantity of a different thing, e.g. bread; and (2) that it can be compared with a similar value of the same system, e.g. a one-franc piece, or with coins of another system (a dollar, etc.). In the same way a word can be exchanged for something dissimilar, an idea; besides, it can be compared with something of the same nature, another word. Its value is therefore not fixed so long as one simply states that it can be 'exchanged' for a given concept, i.e. that it has this or that signification: one must also compare it with similar values, with other words that stand in opposition to it.[81]

Leavis believes that money has a fixed value, Saussure that it has a relative one. The consequence for Leavis's literary criticism is that language can sustain the idea of firm standards; the consequence for followers of Saussure is that standards are flexible; an idea that goes a long way to undermining the idea of standards altogether. Leavis's metaphor of money cannot be divorced from Britain's anxieties about the gold standard in the late 1920s and early 1930s, Saussure's metaphor cannot be divorced from the abolition of exchange controls and the deregulation of the financial market in the late 1970s and the mid-1980s, the very time when his influence on British post-structuralism was most marked.

The argument, then, is that post-structuralism has facilitated the decline of literary culture as an expression of values other than those of the market. Furthermore, the economic metaphor has eased the transition of the university from a transmitter of cultural heritage to servicing the needs of industry; a change which has also entailed the importation into academic culture of practices such as appraisal and productivity targets. Humanities departments have paved the way for this change by embracing post-structuralism, which is suffused with market values. It is therefore not surprising to find that writers on management theory use post-structuralist ideas to improve efficiency and performance in the workplace. To this end, the management theorist Paul Bates declares that 'the struggle for words is the struggle for meaning', a phrase that could serve as an epithet for the whole post-structuralist enterprise, while Gareth Morgan, another management theorist, refers to Derrida's 'White Mythology' to support his claim that 'metaphor has a formative impact on language, on the construction and the embellishment of meaning.' He then goes on to say that if managers can find useful metaphors for tasks this will motivate workers and improve production.[82]

As we stand on the verge of a new millennium we can look back over the last twenty years and say that a particular conception of culture has been finally laid to rest; the irony is that it has participated in its own demise. Our common culture is now consumerism. The old idea of culture may be dead but Williams's declaration that '[w]e need a common culture, not for the sake of an abstraction, but because we shall not survive without it'[83] still rings true in a world where difference remains a cause of persecution, instead of a means of diversifying our common life.

NOTES

1. Dilwyn Porter, ' "Never-Never Land": Britain Under the Conservatives 1951–1964' in Nick Tiratsoo, *From Blitz to Blair: A New History of Britain Since 1939* (London, 1997).
2. Cited in Kenneth O. Morgan, *The People's Peace: British History 1945–1989* (Oxford, 1990), p. 174. I am indebted to this comprehensive book for much of the information in this chapter.
3. Morgan, op. cit., p. 174.
4. *The Times*, 2 October 1963.
5. Morgan, op. cit., p. 279.
6. Kevin Hawkins, *Trade Unions* (London, 1981), p. 236.
7. *The Economist*, 21 June 1969.
8. Cited in Nick Tiratsoo, ' "You've never had it so bad"?: Britain in the 1970s' in Tiratsoo, op. cit., pp. 163–90, p. 164.
9. For a good analysis of the many facets of Thatcherism see Stuart Hall and Martin Jacques (eds.), *The Politics of Thatcherism* (London, 1983). See also Robert Skidelsky (ed.), *Thatcherism* (Oxford, 1989).

10. Interview with *Woman's Own*, 26 May 1987.
11. Nick Davies, *Dark Heart: The Shocking Truth About Hidden Britain* (London, 1997), p. 289.
12. Ibid., p. 291.
13. For details see Morgan, op. cit., pp. 472–5. For the miners' point of view see Raphael Samuel et al., *The Enemy Within: Pit Villages and the Miners' Strike of 1984–5* (London, 1986).
14. Will Hutton, *The State We're In* (London, 1995), p. 170.
15. For a comprehensive account of this and Mrs Thatcher's other economic policies, see Hutton *passim*.
16. Paul Hirst, 'Miracle or Mirage? The Thatcher Years' in Tiratsoo, op. cit., pp. 191–217, p. 201.
17. Roger Bacon and Walter Eltis, *Britain's Economic Problems: Too Few Producers* (Oxford, 1976).
18. Cited in Peter Riddell, *The Thatcher Decade* (Oxford, 1989), p. 85.
19. 'Britain's Exclusion Zone', *Observer*, 13 April 1997.
20. For an example which draws all these together, see 'Thatcher's old boast rings hollow', *Guardian*, 18 April 1997. For a graphic account of the effect of cuts in welfare benefit see Davies, op. cit., pp. 286–94 and also Nick Danziger, *Danziger's Britain: A Journey to the Edge* (London, 1997).
21. Morgan, op. cit., p. 491.
22. For details, see Hutton, op. cit., pp. 75–6.
23. Patrick Sheehy, 'Case of the Hostile Cops', *Guardian*, 26 June 1993.
24. Cited in Stephen Driver and Luke Martell, *New Labour: Politics After Thatcherism* (Cambridge, 1998), p. 67. This book provides a sympathetic introduction to the nature of New Labour.
25. Cited in Paul Foot's column, *Guardian*, 16 February 1999.
26. Not, though, for young people between 18 and 21. Rodney Bickerstaffe of NALGO was reported as saying that a minimum wage is not the same as a living wage. The Six O'-Clock News, Radio 4, 8 April 1999.
27. 'Ministers target workers' rights', *Guardian*, 29 March 1999.
28. '"Harsh" rules to benefit poor', *Guardian*, 2 February 1999.
29. See Roy Hattersley, 'Why I'm no longer loyal to Labour', *Guardian*, 26 July 1997.
30. See Morgan, op. cit., pp. 475–82.
31. See Hirst, op. cit., p. 207.
32. According to a recent report, however, the Human Rights Act 'is being put off once again.' See John Griffith, 'Not getting it right', *Guardian*, 9 April 1999.
33. George Monbiot, 'Protest at your peril', *Guardian*, 26 March 1999.
34. Patricia Waugh, *Harvest of the Sixties: English Literature and its Background 1960–1990* (Oxford, 1995), p. 208.
35. Riddell, op. cit., pp. 8–9.
36. For an account of how Keynesianism contributes to the maintenance of capitalism, see John Westergaard and Henrietta Resler, *Class in a Capitalist Society: A Study of Contemporary Britain* (London, 1976), pp. 198–221.
37. C.P. Snow, *The Two Cultures* (Cambridge, 1959), p. 60.
38. Nikolaus Pevsner, *The Englishness of English Art* (Harmondsworth, 1956).
39. Cited in Blake Morrison, *The Movement: English Poetry and Fiction of the 1950s* (London, 1980), p. 59.
40. Raymond Williams, *Culture and Society 1780–1950* (London, 1958), p. 77.

41. Ibid.
42. Samuel Taylor Coleridge, cited in Williams, op. cit., p. 78.
43. Ibid.
44. A.H. Halsey, 'British Universities and Intellectual Life' in A.H. Halsey, J. Floud and C.A. Anderson (eds.), *Education, Economy and Society* (London, 1961), pp. 497–514.
45. Cited in Alan Sinfield, *Literature, Politics and Culture in Postwar Britain* (London, 1997), p. 53.
46. See Robert Hewison, *Culture and Consensus: England, Art and Politics since 1940* (London, 1995), pp. 52–7.
47. See Sinfield, op. cit., p. 55.
48. Raymond Williams, *Politics and Letters* (London, 1979), p. 73.
49. Richard Hoggart, *The Uses of Literacy* (London, 1957), p. 226.
50. Ibid.
51. Henry Porter, 'Trivial Pursuit', *Guardian*, 1 February 1996.
52. 'Bye-bye Baywatch, hello Herodotus', *Observer*, 26 June 1997.
53. Williams, *Culture and Society*, op. cit., p. 285.
54. Ibid., p. 305.
55. Ibid., p. 285.
56. Ibid., p. 311.
57. F.R. Leavis, *Nor Shall My Sword: Discourses on Pluralism, Compassion and Social Hope* (London, 1972), p. 110.
58. Matthew Arnold, *Culture and Anarchy and Other Writings* (Cambridge, 1993), p. 36.
59. Denys Thompson 'Introduction' in Denys Thompson (ed.), *Discrimination and Popular Culture* (Harmondsworth, 1964), p. 16.
60. Ibid., p. 15.
61. Graham Hough, 'Crisis in Literary Education' in J.H. Plumb (ed.), *Crisis in the Humanities* (Harmondsworth, 1964), p. 104.
62. Ibid., p. 102.
63. Waugh, op. cit., pp. 39–40.
64. John Sturrock, 'Introduction' in John Sturrock (ed.), *Structuralism and Since: From Lévi-Strauss to Derrida* (Oxford, 1979), p. 10.
65. Ferdinand Saussure, *Course in General Linguistics*, trans. Wade Baskin (London, 1974).
66. See ibid., pp. 277–9.
67. For a brief overview of these developments, see Tony Bennett, *Formalism and Marxism* (London, 1979).
68. Louis Althusser, 'A Letter on Art in Reply to André Daspré' in Louis Althusser, *Lenin and Philosophy and Other Essays*, trans. Ben Brewster (London, 1971), and Pierre Macherey, *A Theory of Literary Production,* trans. Geoff Wall (London, 1978).
69. For a good introduction to post-structuralism see Peter Barry, *Beginning Theory* (London, 1996).
70. Barbara Johnson, *The Critical Difference: Essays in the Rhetoric of Contemporary Reading* (Baltimore, 1985), p. 5.
71. Arnold, op. cit., pp. 28–30. For a twentieth-century example, see Paul de Mann, *Blindness and Insight: Essays in the Rhetoric of Contemporary Criticism* (London, 1983), pp. 3–19, 277–89.
72. Antonio Gramsci, *Selections from the Prison Notebooks*, trans. Quintin Hoare and Geoffrey Nowell Smith (London, 1972), pp. 261–4.

73. David Harris, *From Class Struggle to the Politics of Pleasure: The Effects of Gramscianism on Cultural Studies* (London, 1992), p. 118.
74. See, for example, John Fiske, *Understanding Popular Culture* (London, 1989) and Barbara Kruger, *Remote Control: Power, Culture and the World of Appearances* (Massachusetts, 1994).
75. Morgan, op. cit., p. 395.
76. Waugh, op. cit., p. 40.
77. I say 'unconsciously' because although the economic idiom pervades British post-structuralist writing, there is little awareness of that fact on the part of the writers themselves. See, for example, one of the most influential histories of British post-structuralism, Antony Easthope, *British Post-Structuralism Since 1968* (London, 1991).
78. See the last chapter of Catherine Belsey, *Critical Practice* (London, 1980).
79. F.R. Leavis, *For Continuity* (Cambridge, 1933), p. 17.
80. Ibid.
81. Saussure, op. cit., p. 83.
82. Paul Bates, *Strategies for Cultural Change* (Oxford, 1995), p. 4 and Gareth Morgan, *Imaginization: The Art of Creative Management* (London, 1993), p. 52.
83. Williams, *Culture and Society*, op. cit., p. 304.

CHAPTER ONE

British Poetry 1956–99

Jessica Maynard

[I]t is possible to interpret the information carried by the message as essentially the negative of its entropy, and the negative algorithm of its probability. That is, the more probable the message, the less information it gives. Clichés, for example, are less illuminating than great poems.

Norbert Wiener, *The Human Use of Human Beings*

Where do these
Innate assumptions come from? Not from what
We think truest, or most want to do:
Those warp tight-shut, like doors. They're more a style
Our lives bring with them: habit for a while,
Suddenly they harden into all we've got

And how we got it . . .

Philip Larkin, 'Dockery and Son'

THE POETICS OF CLICHÉ

The poem's superiority to the cliché, according to Wiener's formulation, lies in its ability to transmit a meaning unadulterated by repetition. Whatever truth may once have informed the cliché has long since been defused by force of habit, custom and recognition. The great poem, on the other hand, retains its communicative power in its commitment to innovation over familiarity, its refusal to rely on preformulated language and, by extension, preformulated ways of seeing. It might rather be described as engaged in a reformulation or revaluation of language that attempts to transcend the debased currency of cliché, if cliché is taken to its furthest limits to denote the linguistic and social contract that underwrites everyday communication. This question, essentially another way of asking to what extent poetry differs from other forms of discourse, and in what sense it can be taken to be 'about' anything or 'mean' anything, is fundamental to any investigation of the development of British poetry in the latter part of the twentieth century, not least because consideration of this issue has in some cases become inseparable from poetic practice itself. The question is one that has elicited a variety of responses from poets, critics and readers, according to affiliation. This fact alone testifies to the challenge faced in the 1950s and after by those seeking to find for poetry a social and political significance beyond the wry comment and neo-classical restraint offered by the Movement generation of Davie, Larkin, Amis and Wain.

For Philip Larkin, for instance, 'one of the great criticisms of poets of the past is that they said one thing and did another, a false relation between art and life.' Rather, the relation between poetry and experience should be a stable and transparent one that conformed to realist expectations.[1] On the other hand, it was this very assumption – that poetic discourse could be converted into a readily paraphrasable 'meaning' originating in the external world – that Veronica Forrest-Thomson, both practitioner and theorist, sought to correct in *Poetic Artifice* (1978). In promoting the primacy of conventional and formal techniques ('internal relations') as key to poetic interpretation, and, correspondingly, resisting the temptation to look at a poem as if it were a cipher in need of decoding, Forrest-Thomson was not necessarily reverting to New Critical axioms of aesthetic autonomy, the poem as self-supporting mechanism, 'well-wrought urn' and so on. She was putting the case, quite simply, for the difference, the strangeness of poetic discourse, or, as she put it, its 'artifice'. To accept the particularity of language as it was used poetically was not to abandon meaning, or the outside world, or relevance, but to gain an understanding of external relationships through a committed reading of internal relations. Forrest-Thomson accepted that the task of criticism was inevitably to endow a poem with some measure of intelligibility (a process she termed 'naturalisation'), but a 'bad naturalisation' would always use the thematic as a lens through which to refract its reading, while a 'good naturalisation' would arrive at the thematic via, first and foremost, the patterns yielded by the poem itself. At a time when the poetry of Ted Hughes, distinguished by the banality of its diction, looseness of form and propensity for allegory, above all the kind of poetry likely to attract the bad naturalisers, Forrest-Thomson's book was something of a corrective, an appeal against a certain *laissez-faire* trend in poetry criticism. It is not surprising, then, that Hughes's *Crow* (1970) does not correspond to Forrest-Thomson's criteria:

the discourse is that of everyday language. The descriptive lines – 'he saw the sea/Dark spined, with the whole earth in its coils./He saw the stars, fuming away into the black, mushrooms of the nothing forest, clouding their spores, the virus of God' – work tiredly like worn out tunes. There is no clue as to where they come from; does Crow make these formulations or the poet? Nor . . . are these questions interesting clues as to the disruption of our everyday world through disruptions of syntax; the syntax is quite correct. The lines are an indication of complicity between poet and reader, an indication that they share the common clichés of the 'poetical'; and these clichés are not parodied or distanced by the conventional level as they would have to be in order to form the basis for a new technique.[2]

For all its superficial shock effects – a rugged natural environment which docile students of Hughes, a staple of the school English curriculum, soon learned to identify with the brutalities of Western capitalist society itself – the tendency of this kind of poetry was to reinforce what was already known instead of forcing open new avenues of knowledge and enquiry. And for all the liberties it took with form – an unequivocally unpoetic register, for instance – the poetry assuaged the liberal conscience in representing the chaos of modernity, and leaving it at that. Or, to return for a moment to Wiener on the inevitable degeneration of certain overworked modes of expression, on closer inspection a poem like *Crow* didn't carry much information that was new. In 1970, in the midst of Vietnam, on the brink of economic recession and a decade that was to usher in a three-day week, one and a half million unemployed and, finally, in 1979, a Conservative administration committed to dismantling the social and economic responsibilities of the state, to look at the world and conclude that it was lacking could hardly be said to constitute radical critique. The self-conscious naïveté of tone in *Crow* may in part be traced to the oral narrative and creation myths of non-Western cultures which Hughes believes to be 'as vital for our literature as they were for their own, alive with possibilities'. His choice of words bears attention here. He bemoans the 'emasculations . . . prettifications . . . denaturings' to which such tales have traditionally been subject by bowdlerising abridgers and continues: 'It is in the elemental autonomy of these pieces that we can detect the seminal thing that in primitive sculpture and primitive music has already operated on us.'[3] In other words, anthropological materials become yet another site of authenticity to which weary sophisticates may turn. *Crow* itself denounces the psychopathology of the West as rapacious, all-consuming (materially, technologically, intellectually) –

Crow thought 'Alas
Alas ought I
To stop eating
And try to become the light'?[4]

('Crow Tyrannosaurus')

– and as gorging itself on waste:

> Crow spraddled head-down in the beach-garbage
> guzzling a dropped ice-cream[5]

('Crow and the Birds')

Yet it also engages in its own form of consumption, looking to recoup the real from other cultures.

It is no coincidence, in the late-1970s, when a sense of cultural failure could endorse *laissez-faire* monetarism, an economic policy harking back not so much to one-nation Toryism as to nineteenth-century free market liberalism, that Forrest-Thomson should appear to look inwards, towards aesthetic autonomy and non-referentiality as dissent. If monetarist, deregulationist politics offered a riposte to state intervention, then Forrest-Thomson's insistence that poetry's future 'lies in the exploitation of non-meaningful levels of language'[6] was another, admittedly very different rebellion against stagnant forms of rational organisation. This much she has in common with Ted Hughes. But where Hughes looked for renovation essentially from relapse into the world of instinct, Forrest-Thomson believed that by responding to the innovatory linguistic practices of poetry it should be possible to view the world anew.

There is, therefore, an ideological dimension to the choice sketched here – between approaching language as a medium for reflecting and reinforcing a reality already presumed known, and as an instrument for exposing what may not necessarily be known about that reality, but which may nonetheless be immanent. Philip Larkin's prominence throughout this period up to his death as the nation's representative poetic voice (though, typically, he resisted the full poetic professionalisation that the office of Poet Laureate would have conferred) suggests that the choice apparently foisted upon the poetry-reading public was for familiarity over challenge, for cliché over what Wiener, with refreshing quaintness, calls 'great poems'. It is possible, therefore, for Larkin to confront the consequences of this capitulation to a clichéd culture in a poem such as 'Dockery and Son' ('what/ We think truest, or most want to do:/ Those warp tight-shut, like doors'[7]), and yet at the same time remain in paralysed contemplation of this predicament, aware that those 'innate assumptions' sooner or later petrify into moribund habit but unable to believe in positive alternatives.

CHANCE ENCOUNTERS: LARKIN, TOMLINSON

Larkin's insistent privileging of content over technique, his preference for working within an established poetic legacy with the traditional resources of rhyme and metre (most obviously identifiable with the work of Hardy), and his well-publicised disdain for anything that smacks of the modernist 'myth kitty', account at once for the appeal and the limitations of his poetry. The persona of 'The Whitsun Weddings', for example, shifts easily and almost imperceptibly from 'I' to 'we', confident of a more generalised complicity in a poem that might be said to be about complicity itself. 'The Whitsun Weddings', the title poem of Larkin's 1964 collection, in both tone and subject matter, is concerned with a number of collusions or contractions: that between 'I' and 'we'; the momentary convergence of multiple lives as newly-weds board the train en route to London; and the compression of space (geographical and personal) enabled by the rail travel-ler's transient point of view. The wedding parties are united by an act of witnessing and, in the same vein as Auden's 'Night Mail' (written, it should be remembered, as a commentary for part of a GPO film documentary aimed at a national audience), by technological contingency. However, in 1960s Britain, this 'frail/Travelling coincidence', a volatile collectivity at best, seems the closest this poem can come to an idea of community. Chance, for Larkin, is what forges civic identity, and this by its very nature is an ephemeral experience, subject to the same dissipation as 'an arrow-shower/ Sent out of sight, somewhere becoming rain.' If the Larkinesque landscape is only too recognisable – from the windows of the train, a blurring of country and city, an amorphous agri-industrial hinterland – then this is because Larkin's poetic vision locates national culture in the customary, the familiar, the clichéd: the wedding guests who 'settle hats and say/ *I nearly died*', the 'uncle shouting smut', 'the perms,/The nylon gloves and jewellery-substitutes.'[8] Such a neutral persona is ideally suited to the mechanical registration of the mass-produced, merely prompting the vicarious viewer into seeing what he or she has doubtless already seen on numerous occasions: on television, on advertising hoardings, on provincial high streets. In realist vein, the working method here is that of the repres-entative glimpse, snatched by accident from the carriage window and all the more authentic for it, or the eavesdropping that is sufficiently telling to denote an entire social context. Apart from the images towards the end of the poem ('postal districts packed like squares of wheat' and the 'arrow-shower/ . . . somewhere becoming rain.'), the technique is more suggestive of the metonymies of the novel, perhaps not surprising in a poet who professes he 'wanted to be a novelist . . . I've never felt as interested in poetry as I used to feel in novels.'[9]

The chance encounter, then, in 'The Whitsun Weddings' is a kind of default principle of social organisation ('none/ Thought of the others they would never meet/ Or how their lives would all contain this hour') and a means of representation. It is also, at the moment of impending dispersion, an opportunity for speculation on 'the power/ That being changed can give'. The poem closes with a glimpse of plural potentialities, a moment of release certainly, but one in which destinations are, of necessity, unknown, and one which might just as well speak of dissipated energy as of targets attained.

Charles Tomlinson's 'The Chances of Rhyme', which appeared in his 1969 collection *The Way of a World*, in a comparable though not strictly speaking analogous spirit to Larkin's poem, takes on the creative possibilities of chance. However, it is the conjunctions of internal poetic form rather than those of the external world that, at least initially, take precedence. If 'The Whitsun Weddings' has been read as indebted, despite the protests, to *The Waste Land* for its hints of regenerative ritual,[10] then in Tomlinson's case the generative mechanism begins with syntactic and phonetic collisions:

> The chances of rhyme are like the chances of meeting –
>   In the finding fortuitous, but once found, binding:
> They say, they signify and they succeed, where to succeed
>   Means not success, but a way forward
> If unmapped, a literal, not a royal succession;[11]

This is not to say that the aural and visual conjunction of 'finding' and 'binding', or the semantic conjunction presented by the sequence of 'succeed', 'success' and 'succession', remain nothing more than a mechanism for indulging the free play of language. Like 'The Whitsun Weddings', this is a poem about accident and possibility, how the former engenders the latter, though, unlike 'The Whitsun Weddings', it is prepared to entertain new prospects, to take risks. If Larkin, legitimately enough, finds pathos in randomness, then Tomlinson's poem chooses to find scope for development. The difference perhaps is that one poet begins with the haphazard encounter of social atoms and transmutes this with an almost Augustan finesse (via Eliot?) into mock heroic verbal order (see, for example, the zeugma of 'The last confetti and advice were thrown'), while the other begins with the encounter of verbal components and attempts to use this as the basis for the elaboration of some kind of human order. This is perhaps another way of saying that the unexpected, what doesn't necessarily fit the pattern, also at that moment inaugurates a new structure. For Tomlinson, chance shades into determinism, and back again:

> [C]hance occurrences, chance meetings invade what we do everyday
> and yet they are drawn into and out of patterns, as they criss-cross with
> our feeling of what we are, as they remind us of other happenings, or
> strengthen our sense of future possibility. Poetry is rather like this, also.[12]

Hence, 'the chances of rhyme' become 'continuities of thought'.[13] Or, in the poem's terms, the idea of 'success' becomes permeated with the related sense of 'succession', a following on, or a meaning '[t]hat we . . . are led into'. There is qualification (this is 'not a royal succession') but that very qualification, through the etymological and cultural connotations of the words royalty and region (a province ruled over; both words traceable back to *rex*, 'king') breeds new thought: 'Though royal (it may be) is the adjective or region/That we, nature's royalty, are led into.' Through these verbal transmutations, the poem takes the reader into 'unmapped' regions, suggesting also this agility of consciousness as exhibiting a sovereignty of its own (we, in our capacity to think, as 'nature's royalty'). The apparently inexhaustible reciprocity between form and content both demonstrated and thematised in this poem undermines Larkin's proposition that art remain in mimetic subservience to life: '. . . why should we speak/ Of art, of life, as if the one were all form/ And the other all Sturm-und-Drang?'

Tomlinson's four-stress lines (occasionally, he points out, 'dancing' into five stresses[14]) resist absorption into normal speech patterns, their cumbrousness necessary to the sense of thought evolving through deviation. By means of slippages in both sound (internal rhyme and assonance) and sense (the conversion of 'rest-in-peace' into a 're-lease' of more vital connotations) the poem makes the particles of the words themselves synthesise an argument for the capacity of language to shape experience:

> And between
> Rest-in-peace and precipice,
>   Inertia and perversion, come the varieties
>   Increase, lease, re-lease . . .

It should be stressed that language for Tomlinson here is not necessarily a medium for challenging reality. Tomlinson in fact repeatedly refers to an exterior creation that, contrary to the post-Wittgensteinian view that the world cannot but be mediated by language, has its own autonomous, prior existence. This is all the more reason, in Tomlinson's poetic, for a near-ascetic devotion to objective detail, a sustained attentiveness that Donald Davie finds 'not normal'[15] and that is traceable, in part at least, to the influence of William Carlos Williams ('no ideas but in things').

Descriptive precision, as with the chances of rhyme, is a matter of generating meanings, 'the beauty of a world of fact ramifying out into that of imaginative possibility,' says Tomlinson.[16] This is always a dynamic, open-ended operation, which, for all his formal decorum, may make Tomlinson something of a *bricoleur*. Bricolage, in fact, is a cultural practice that interests Tomlinson a good deal. He comes to it by way of anthropology, through Claude Lévi-Strauss's *The Savage Mind*, first published in 1962 and translated into English in 1966, and, in particular, through what Lévi-Strauss designates the 'science of the concrete'.[17] For those cultures which do not follow Western empirical procedures in ordering and harnessing the natural

31

world, there may well exist alternative systems for naming, understanding and exploiting the environment and, significantly, such procedures depend on close attention – perhaps, to Western eyes, an almost preternatural, hair-splitting degree of attention. But what is most telling is that such scrupulous habits of perception *precede* what will eventually be considered useful; they *yield* and do not merely reflect what will constitute valuable cultural knowledge. Abstract propositions have no place here. Random accumulation is the condition for the acquisition of understanding. Or, another way of putting this, the future application of data collated here and now is unforeseeable.

This, essentially, is the meaning of bricolage: an *ad hoc* making-do, a cobbling together, an ingenuity in the face of the resources readily to hand. At the heart of the word, and the activity, is the sense of deviation, a redistribution of energy, an unpredictable swerve away from the usual course of things, and also, it should not be forgotten, a sense of constraint or circumscription.[18] Bricolage, to return to that preliminary question of whether or not art should stand in opposition to what is habitual, is the art of redeploying the everyday in an unexpected way:

> In its old sense the verb 'bricoler' applied to ball games and billiards, to hunting, shooting and riding. It was however always used with reference to some extraneous movement: a ball rebounding, a dog straying or a horse swerving from its direct course to avoid an obstacle. And in our time the 'bricoleur' is still someone who works with his hands and uses devious means compared to those of a craftsman. The characteristic feature of mythical thought is that it expresses itself by means of a heterogeneous repertoire which, even if extensive, is nevertheless limited. It has to use this repertoire, however, whatever the task in hand because it has nothing else at its disposal.[19]

The successful *bricoleur* responds with a certain measure of guile to the contingencies of what is available. Chance becomes a resource, where for Larkin in 'The Whitsun Weddings' it seemed to remain neither more nor less than randomness.[20]

METAMORPHOSES: FISHER, CLARK

As a poet whose earlier material could be regarded by some as occupying a similar post-industrial territory to that of Larkin and yet who has chosen to take up European and American aesthetic precedents (see the influence, for example, of Russian avant-garde art and the open forms of Charles

Olson), Roy Fisher suggests some alternatives to Larkinesque resignation, or Hughesian primitivism.[21] In a sense, the ravaged landscape of *City* (1961), an assemblage of prose and poem fragments, in which the great works of a municipal past jostle up against the 'speciously democratic'[22] good intentions of post-war urban planning, calls up the very issues of modernisation entailed in Fisher's compositional technique: whether to proceed into the future by centralised edict, or by a more subversive route. *City* is not to be equated with Fisher's native Birmingham, a critical reductiveness which he deplores, but should be approached as an amalgam of locations, none of them necessarily real, geographically identifiable. 'Pithead gears thrust out above the hawthorn bushes'[23] may, on the one hand, present a contemporary ruination upon which to meditate, a romantic reassimilation of culture into nature. On the other hand, it is more reliably viewed as the opportunity for creative synthesis in which something *other* is generated by such a collocation of industrial and pastoral. In the same way, the architectural detail of 'slaughterhouse campanile'[24] in 'The Sun Hacks' has the surrealist effect of dignifying the local abattoir with Italian Renaissance splendour, effectively reshuffling the categories of sacred and profane. The issue of naming an environment for which no adequate vocabulary or syntax exists is central here, and places Fisher's work in the context of a post-structuralist concern regarding the fit between world and language – though only to the extent that, as Antony Easthope comments, 'poststructuralism as a conceptual movement . . . caught up with what was inherent in the aesthetic practices of modernism a generation after the event':[25]

> in things like street layouts, domestic architecture, where the schools were, how anything happened – all these things were left all over the place as a sort of script, an indecipherable script with no key. And the interesting thing for me was that the culture, particularly the metropolitan culture, the literary culture, had no alphabet to offer for simply talking about what I saw all the time, I mean when I say in *City*, 'most of it's never been seen,' it's a provocative phrase; it wasn't verbalized, it wasn't talked about. And there I wasn't interested really at all in the particular city, but in the phenomenon of having a perceptual environment which was taken as read, which was taken as to be assumed and not a thing for which any vocabulary needed to exist.[26]

This is not an outright rejection of the objective world but a movement towards accommodating subjective states as indissociable from an apprehension of world, suggesting a correspondence between Fisher's poetics and the practice of ethnography as described by James Clifford: 'a characteristic attitude of participant observation among the artifacts of a defamiliarised cultural reality.'[27] This ethnographic attitude is, above all, a critical one which, through the unexpected juxtapositionings of its collages, offers alternative realities:

not the prevailing modes of ordering the world, but salvaged objects, flotsam and jetsam, things perhaps neglected or overlooked, or which the viewer may have become habituated to regarding in a certain prescribed context. It is a way, as Clifford argues, of valuing the unclassified and excluded, of refusing to take things 'as read' and of challenging the stable subject position of the

> Sadist-voyeur,
> stalled and stricken, fallen
> into that way from the conviction of
> not doing but
> only looking;

(*A Furnace*)[28]

To propose Fisher as ethnographer of his own culture, then, is to find the exotic and unfamiliar, improbably perhaps, amongst the derelict infrastructure of post-war Britain, an estrangement only conceivable when the self and the self's cognitive processes become *part* of the investigation. Once the 'sadist-voyeur' is dethroned from his authoritative vantage point, and relegated, as in *A Furnace* (1986), to bus or car, implicated in 'doing' and moving as well as 'looking', even the most everyday, as Walter Benjamin observed, can become impenetrable.[29] The distance is an epistemological rather than a specifically geographical one, hence Fisher's resistance to thinking about *City* as a particular place.

As Clifford explains, an emphasis in ethnographic practices on collecting, collage and juxtaposition militates against traditional narrative exposition:

> By excess of subjectivity, a kind of objectivity is guaranteed – that
> (paradoxically) of a personal ethnography. The realist imagination,
> fabricator of the *vraisemblable* is refused in favor of an impossibly sincere
> record of the real: perceptions, moods, facts.[30]

Similarly, Fisher maintains a commitment to the real ('I feel it's facile to let your writing run free, just not necessarily refer to anything') but a wariness of plans or programmes imposed upon reality ('at the same time I won't simply produce a photo album'[31]). Particularity of experience and observation are clearly important to a poet with enough reverence for twentieth-century material culture to render 'the alloy/ fenders that edge the deck' of a trolley-bus or, with a line-break that reinforces the discordant note of this urban detail, 'cafés in the style of lit/ drains' (*A Furnace*). Fisher's poetic self remains resolutely the pedestrian, the passenger on public transport, the car-driving commuter down at street level:

> I'm obsessed
> with cambered tarmacs, concretes,
> the washings of rain.[32]

('Wonders of Obligation')

When Fisher talks of his compositional methods, he champions that same sense of movement or fluidity implied in the above instance, continually returning to the need to avoid what he calls the 'dangers of setting',[33] or, as Larkin intimated, of allowing habit to 'harden into all we've got'. In 'Wonders of Obligation', for example, the poet acknowledges the temptation to submit to meanings as they are already set by forces beyond us:

> The things we make up out of language
> turn into common property.
> To feel responsible
> I put my poor footprint back in.[34]

Fisher's strategies for breaking out of such prescribed paths emphasise the role of chance, fragments (newspaper clippings, movie stills, isolated anecdotes), anything that will lead his poetry in new and unforeseeable directions. This leads Fisher to stress natural rhythms that follow their own laws ('I work on the assumption that life has . . . its own tides'[35]), to point out that perception always follows what in *A Furnace* he calls a 'pulse-beat'. 'Whatever/ approaches my passive taking-in' will be understood 'only/ phase upon phase' ('Introit').[36] Sensory apprehension happens

> the way in cold air
> ice-crystals, guessed at, come densely
> falling from where they were not;[37]

> ('The Return')

The exterior world descends on the perceiver unannounced, like ice-crystals 'falling from where they were not'. This is why the method is cumulative, driven by accident not design, arriving at its material by circuitous rather than direct means. Poems come to Fisher, he says, 'by devious ways',[38] by the variations thrown up by improvisational techniques:

> The aim in the improvisations was to give the words as much relief as
> possible from serving in planned situations; and the work was taken
> forward with no programme beyond the principle that it should not know
> where its next meal was coming from. It was unable to anticipate, but it
> could have on the spot whatever it could manage to ask for. This method
> produced very rapid changes of direction.[39]

Fisher is referring here to the evolution of *The Cut Pages*, which even entitles a sequence of prose fragments 'Metamorphoses', metamorphosis being what keeps perception on its toes. This, essentially, is Fisher's justification for poetry: that it does a kind of violence to or rearranges one's perceptions: 'The poem is always capable of being a subversive agent, psychologically, sensuously, however you like.'[40]

Choosing to work with whatever fortune throws in one's way, then, is not self-indulgent perversity, but an act of critique. Making the peripheral a principle of composition is a way of undermining the truths that cultural, educational and political institutions may choose to promote as centrally important. It's always crucial, says Fisher, 'to try to see what is outside the range of vision',[41] an attempt that is central to the work of another poet who deals in metamorphoses, Thomas A. Clark, 'supremely the poet of variation,' as Clive Bush observes.[42] Clark's *Sixteen Sonnets* (1981), again, present poetic consciousness at the continually renewing moment of its adaptation to the environment:

> as I stepped out bravely
> the very camber of the road
> turned me to its purpose
> it was on a morning early
> I put design behind me
> hear us and deliver us
> to the hazard of the road[43]

In sonnet seven, poetic discourse becomes more explicitly a matter for concern, self-consciously romantic vocabulary seeming to elude the poet, replaced instead with banal, 'unpoetic' alternatives:

> in place of forest glades
> I was given only clearings
> when I searched for pebbles
> I found nothing but stones

But the poetic 'clarity' that proves so elusive is, after all, only a clarity that emerges on the poet's recognition of these difficulties: that clearings resist poetic formulation as 'forest glades', that stones resist reduction to the cliché of 'pebbles'. Finally, clarity can be nothing more nor less than 'my pencil moving on the paper',[44] an activity that significantly remains open and unending. In Fisher's 'The Poplars', clarity seems to lie in the formal abstraction of the trees and, on the part of the perceiver, in a reticence regarding self comparable to Clark's:

> To know these tall pointers
> I need to withdraw
> From what is called my life
> And from my net
> Of achievable desires.[45]

(*City*)

Clark's more recent work, such as *Of Shade and Shadow* (1992), has continued this modification of the pastoral, using the eclogue's mood of retreat from 'heat of noon' into the 'coolness which the shadow spreads at the foot of the tree' to investigate what Clark terms 'reticence'. Reticence stands in opposition to a Western cultural preoccupation with 'measurement, logic and purpose', and is another manifestation of the spirit of *praxis* which that first sonnet announces with its invocation to 'deliver us/ to the hazard of the road'. The poem, then, invites us to 'cherish all forms of delay, of arrestment, or digression', to cultivate 'a waiting that renounces every path'. Though Clark works rather differently to Fisher, invoking romantic and classical poetic precedents, his preference, too, is for a critical position which derives its force from a willingness to take to the road without knowing where the next meal is coming from. And, as with Fisher, the mutability of forms means that they can never be summarily stated or 'set'. Reticence, or shade, or shadow, or waiting – for these are all part of the complex of metaphors that Clark uses to express this state of consciousness – is an attitude of deferral (of fully stating the world) and deference (to the complexity of the world):

> In every assumption we make, in any energetic movement of thought,
> we should remember shade, the obscured connections, the mitigating
> circumstance, the shelter one thing lends another.[46]

In *Larch Covert* (1994), a kind of chiaroscuro, a flickering play between light and shade, is enacted through the very displacements, the delicate shifts of the second and third lines over four five-line stanzas which otherwise remain constant: in the first stanza, 'spots of light on branches/ patches of light on tree trunks'; in the second, 'flecks of light on branches/ patterns of light on tree trunks'; in the third, 'stains of light on branches/ pauses of light on tree trunks'; and in the fourth, 'points of light on branches/ touches of light on tree trunks'.[47] This succeeds in being both conventional nature poetry which registers continual adjustments in the apprehension of a physical landscape and a poetry which also records the changes brought about by the minutest deviations in vocabulary. Here, Clark brings the faltering of linguistic and natural illuminations together. It is this same air of provisionality that is evident in a series of metamorphoses in *Of Shade and Shadow* where the transmutations of mythology, causality and visual association are brought together:

> To avoid the scrutiny of light, forms in shade are constantly changing –
> mist into smoke, fox into scent, girl into laurel.[48]

AUTOBIOGRAPHIES: BETJEMAN, BUNTING, PRYNNE

Clark's emphasis on transmutation is also an emphasis on connection, on the inevitability with which consciousness is located in the world, adapting at each instant to the 'very camber of the road'. Throughout the 1960s, a number of very different poets, whose working methods and aesthetic affiliations might at first glance seem to have little in common, confronted similar questions in what can roughly be described as autobiographical ventures. However, it should become clear that when autobiography is pressed as far as Basil Bunting and Jeremy Prynne (for whom Bunting is an acknowledged influence) wish to take it, it becomes less of a subsidiary genre of poetry and rather more of an investigation into the fundamentals of poetic expression.

Summoned by Bells (1960) is John Betjeman's account of his poetic evolution against a background of North London suburbia. It records, with the usual melancholic cadences, a developing taste for High Anglican ritual; a dalliance with aestheticism at Oxford; the reassurances of Early English architecture, buttered toast and Cornish holidays; and a topography that is always meticulously named (West Hill, Chetwynd Road, 'sylvan' Highbury). However, poetic impulse for Betjeman is defined in opposition to a family in trade (an industrial pedigree that goes back further than the Great Exhibition itself, where '[t]he Betjemann device for hansom cabs'[49] was displayed; the expectation that Betjeman would succeed his father in the family furniture business; his guilt at refusing to do so). Or is it quite so simple as this? For Donald Davie, the machine culture apparently so reviled lives on in the 'rigidity and intricacy of Hardy's metrical procedures' which Betjeman expertly adopts.[50] It is this disjunction between form and content, a *knowing*, stubborn insistence on anachronism, that yields the tone of rueful irony. In this, Betjeman's procedure may be said to have much in common with those self-conscious or parodic practices designated 'postmodern'. Innocence, whether of the textual or the suburban-utopian variety, is no longer possible.

However, it is for its particular refusal to be 'poetic' that *Summoned by Bells* is of significance here. Betjeman's rebellion against industrial despoliation takes the form of refuge in what are essentially another set of national clichés, and in a medium that, like Larkin's determination to renounce the mystical bombast of the 1940s in favour of the prosaic, quite expressly avoids the burden of being distinctively poetic. An introductory note explains:

> Why is this account of some moments in the sheltered life of a middle-class youth not written in prose? The author has gone as near prose as he dare. He chose blank verse, for all but the more hilarious moments, because he found it best suited to the brevity and the rapid changes of mood and subject.[51]

There is no lack of evidence elsewhere in Betjeman's work of his accomplishment and skill in exploiting traditional verse forms, but this statement nonetheless draws attention to what Donald Davie has regarded as the decline of the compact between poet and reader which depended on tacit assumptions concerning metre, rhythm, sound (even if such assumptions were ultimately defied, as in free verse, for instance). *Summoned by Bells*, says Davie, 'satisfies only the minimal requirements [Betjeman] has contracted for, so that the metronomic recurrence of the pentameter shape only distracts us from the narrative, which would have been more interesting written in prose.'[52] This seems a curious contradiction in a work which, after all, sets out to make an argument for a poetic rather than commercial destiny:

> Atlantic rollers bursting in my ears,
> And pealing church-bells and the puff of trains,
> The sight of sailing clouds, the smell of grass –
> Were always calling out to me for words.
> I caught at them and missed and missed again.
> 'Catch hold,' my father said, 'catch hold like this!',
> Trying to teach me to be a carpenter,
> 'Not *that* way, boy! When will you ever learn?' –
> I dug the chisel deep into my hand.[53]

As with another long autobiographical poem of the 1960s, Basil Bunting's *Briggflatts*, published in 1966 by Fulcrum Press, the possibilities, limited or otherwise, of mimetic representation are a central issue here. Betjeman fails at the family craft, and this same gaucherie is used to express a sense of the difficulty of another craft: that of the poet, who must learn to shape words into forms that will do justice to the world.

For Bunting, equally, poetry is a vocation, but one which ultimately might be said to thrive on such experiences of failure, clumsiness, dissatisfaction even. This is perhaps why the figure of the mason-poet occupies such a central position in *Briggflatts*, offering a form of inscription that resists the smooth reproducibility of paper and ink, suggesting instead an affinity with the rough edges, the incompletion of the material world:

> Words!
> Pens are too light.
> Take a chisel to write.[54]

To look for perfection, for 'finish', for finely honed rhythms which hum to the same tune as machine tools, is the error: similar quarrels with modernity as Betjeman, then, but different forms of protest. In fact, in his promotion of so unwieldy a writing implement as a chisel, Bunting might be situated in the same mode of romantic cultural critique as Ruskin, who promoted gothic architecture for the similar reason that modernity's drive to eliminate every flaw entailed a certain slavery: 'Rather choose rough work than smooth work, so only that the practical purpose may be answered, and never imagine there is reason to be proud of anything that may be accomplished by patience and sandpaper.'[55]

In his lectures on prosody, Bunting explains that he finds the rigid arithmetic of text-book scansion both constrictive and untrue to a long-standing spirit in English verse which depends on an appreciation of the deviation from the norm. Bunting would trace this sense of rhythmic give-and-take back to Wyatt, who should be understood not as a poet who couldn't count, but one who composed with the latitude and flexibility of musical accompaniment in mind.[56] The shaping of words in *Briggflatts*, correspondingly, is continually aligned with shapes that occur in music or in dance or in the natural world: always with other *things*. The convergence between the polyphonic complexity of late sixteenth-century music and other similarly kaleidoscopic forms[57] is evident, for instance, in the imagistic juxtapositions of 'Starfish, poinsettia on a half-tide crag,/ a galliard by Byrd' where the influence of Ezra Pound is clear.[58] And a convergence between natural and artistic processes is evident here:

> Silver blades of surf
> fall crisp on rustling grit
> shaping the shore as a mason
> fondles and shapes his stone.[59]

Briggflatts, says Bunting, is an autobiography 'but not a record of fact'.[60] Hence the provisionality of words or marks etched on seashore and stone; hence the recognition of the inadequacy of tombstone's inscription to repres-ent a life in its infinite complexity ('the stone spells a name/ naming none,/ a man is abolished'[61]); hence the slipperiness of attempted memorials:

> It is easier to die than to remember.
> Name and date
> Split in soft slate
> a few months obliterate.[62]

Part of the autobiographical task is to trace, however difficult ('Hounds falter and stray/ Shame deflects the pen'), the memory of love squandered, opportunities wasted, to consider, yet again, botched jobs. In many ways, Bunting's concern with both artistic and personal evasions, and the com-plex interaction between, recalls the work of a poet he is known to have admired, Robert Browning. Like Fra Lippo Lippi, a painter whose artistic apprenticeship is served out in the gutters, quite literally amongst rubbish, the poet of *Briggflatts* 'dare not decline/ to walk among the bogus',[63] while, in the persona of slowworm, a creature defying easy categorisation, he con-fesses 'I prosper lying low'.[64] Unlike Andrea del Sarto, another of Browning's Renaissance autobiographers, this poet resists the trap of a sterile perfec-tionism. *Briggflatts*, it could be said, emerges as a monument to many forms of waste and dissipation, as witness repeated references: 'Dung will not soil the slowworm's/ mosaic'; 'Wind writes in foam on the sea'; the mason who

> shaping evasive
> > ornament
> litters his yard
> > with flawed fragments[65]

and the poet who admits

> Where rats go go I,
> accustomed to penury,
> filth, disgust and fury;[66]

But this familiarity with what is thrown away, whether love or anything else, and with the exorbitancies of 'fury', is also a condition for production, just as for the bricoleur a certain excessive and futile accumulation could give way to usefulness. *Briggflatts* accepts such evasions, failures and privations to the extent that these, too, will give on to something useful, in a way in which abstract theorising, or a more concerted search for value will not. In other words, *Briggflatts* supports the obliquity of the bricoleur or the mason-poet's methods, putting starfish, poinsettia, galliard by Byrd side by side to produce something different, something that otherwise might remain unsaid. Of the claim that 'Love murdered . . . / . . . jogs the draughtsman's elbow', Bunting himself comments:

> It does, you know, damnably. Perhaps if it didn't we would have no need to write: and perhaps again as in my poem, it is the need to write which comes first, and engenders the things it hardly dares handle.[67]

The strategy is, above all, an adaptive one, content to wait and see what happens, wise enough not to demand programmatic logic. Or, as it is expressed in the poem, 'Follow the clue patiently and you will understand nothing.' This respect for adaptation, of course, has its counterpart in the natural history of Charles Darwin, where it is precisely genetic deviations that take an organism in new directions. 'I have tried off and on to get English departments to make *The Origin of Species* a set book,' Bunting complains, 'but they scoff.'[68]

There is much of the paradoxical in this: accidents that are somehow transformed into new possibilities; the throwaway detail that becomes fundamental. Towards the end of the fifth section of *Briggflatts* (or perhaps 'recapitulation' would be more faithful to Bunting's borrowing of sonata form in the poem) we are presented with a further paradox, and a further instance of a form of dissipation that yet remains productive. 'The star you steer by is gone' but its light nevertheless guides the helmsman here and now. The same paradox might well be applied to the deflections of language as they are perceived in *Briggflatts*. Words, despite their deficiencies, and despite their tendency, through their very place in an arbitrary system of signification built on repeatability, to disperse the singularity of the

person, the experience, the thing that they name, are also the poet's working materials, dead maybe in some ways, like the guiding star, but still
affording their illumination.[69]

This same contradiction, and this same image, lie at the heart of Jeremy
Prynne's 'Sketch for a Financial Theory of the Self', a poem included in
Andrew Crozier and Tim Longville's anthology, *A Various Art*. This was
first published by Carcanet Press in 1987 and attempted to present a profile
of contemporary English poetry that had been suppressed by the dominance
of, in Crozier's words, 'the constructed totalities that represent national
culture'.[70] Much of the work, correspondingly, was published throughout the
1960s, 70s and 80s by small presses (Fulcrum, Trigram, Goliard, Grosseteste,
for example) and little magazines administered along less commercial lines
than mainstream publishers, often with the more immediate involvement
of poets. The role of anthologies, and those major publishers which still
maintain active poetry lists in defining and perpetuating a dominant 'British'
poetic should not, in fact, be underestimated. And though striking a
polemical attitude is permissible, it is only more widely sanctioned if it does
not stray beyond certain preordained boundaries. A. Alvarez's *The New
Poetry* (1962) could quite acceptably inveigh against 'gentility, decency and
all the other social totems' which for Alvarez marred so much poetry of the
time, but the 'new seriousness' promoted in the place of English reticence
presented its own set of conventionalities: this time, the commonplace that
depth of experience, married to the appropriate technical skills of course,
produced good poetry. Under the criteria advanced by Alvarez in his
introduction, 'The New Poetry or Beyond the Gentility Principle', Hughes
is preferable to Larkin, the obduracy of nature more 'serious' and poetic
than a trip by British Rail, an assumption which may be just as limited in
its own way.[71] Poets such as Prynne, and others mentioned here who,
contrary to the prevailing anti-modernism ushered in during the 1930s and
confirmed by the Movement, have persevered in experimental and innovative poetic practices, on the other hand, may be characterised as wilfully
seeking out the margins (Prynne as Cambridge academic with a very particular following), when there is, in fact, a more mundane market explanation for their obscurity.[72] Bunting, for example, was unpublished in Britain
until *Briggflatts* was taken up by Fulcrum Press.

'Sketch for a Financial Theory of the Self', published originally in *Kitchen
Poems* by Cape Goliard Press in 1968, might perhaps be described as closer
to autobiographical writing as conceived by Paul de Man: 'a figure of
reading or of understanding that occurs, to some degree, in all texts.'[73] By
this, de Man means that autobiographical writing raises questions, albeit in
bolder relief, that apply to any text claiming to be 'by' someone or other
and which therefore assert a corresponding authority or validity as reliable

representation. The autobiographical problem – how far does a text faithfully reflect a life and, conversely, how far does a text actually produce that life? – becomes the double-bind (or what de Man compares to being caught in a revolving door) that extends to all writing. Does the apposite figure of speech respond to pre-existent circumstances, or does it, in directing a reader's interpretation, actually create those circumstances? This quandary, argues de Man, is 'part of all understanding . . . [and] . . . underlies all cognitions, including knowledge of self.'[74] It is with this kind of circumspection that Prynne also approaches his own particular 'theory of the self'.

Stanzas numbered rather bureaucratically 1–8 may seem to pay homage to the tone of rigorous enquiry already established in the title. 'Sketch', on the other hand, suggests something rather less assured, and certainly not complete. Accordingly, the poem launches into a discussion of 'qualities', the exact nature of which only becomes apparent (and even then, not quite) by the fifth stanza. Prynne's poetry moves through a number of verbal registers, here, for example, through those derived from science, economics, philosophical argument and theological dogma. Linguistic, social, religious and monetary compacts become continuous with another, united by the idea of trust. It is trust, or a cultural undertaking to take certain things on faith, that drives all these systems (a word, a banknote, a social ritual is taken to denote a certain value), and this is what is hinted at in the title. Though in its metaphysical density and non-realism it may seem to have little in common with 'The Whitsun Weddings', this poem nevertheless is deeply concerned with social collectivities, and with the contractual nature of personal identity within these systems. These obscure 'qualities', as slippery and as precious as 'silk', then, emerge as those beliefs or, to reinforce Prynne's economic metaphors, *investments* that are necessary to the functioning of social life, yet cannot necessarily be proven or redeemed. There may, as the last stanza suggests, be no 'return' on such investments, but there still remains 'the primacy/ of *count*', the latter making more explicit the sceptical spirit in which Prynne numbers his own paragraphs. This is a poem, it seems, about the ubiquity of many kinds of organisation (naming, numbering) in modern culture, and yet which views such structures through recourse to the diaphanousness of silk, or the insubstantiality of starlight:

> The name is the sidereal display, it
> is what we *know* we cannot now have.
> The last light is the name it carries,
> it is this binds us to our unbroken trust.[75]

The commodity of silk, calling up histories of trade routes and exchange, the activities of nascent Western capitalism itself, is paralleled to those qualities to be hoped for – to whatever ideals we invest in. But, as the poem proceeds in its reasoning – and there is always a sense of *emergent* thought here – the thing itself is shown not to correspond so easily to the name it is given. This is why, to justify the comparison with *Briggflatts*, '[t]he name is the sidereal display', lost or invalid as soon as it reaches its target, as soon as it is applied. Our trust, then, is founded on the illumination of doomed stars, and is, for that reason, 'absurd'. On the other hand, such a lack is necessary or constitutive:

> And we should
> have what the city does need,
> the sky, if we did not so
> want the need.

Lack, or having some gap to fill in with an investment of faith, is fundamental to the 'pattern of / bond and contract and interest' that Prynne then shifts from market to individual context:

> we give the name of
> our selves to our needs.
> We want what we are.

It should be clear by now that this is a poem that does not lend itself to rapid 'naturalisation', but, then, nor do the speculations on the nature of subjectivity that concern the poet here. These, by their nature, make any reliance on transparent modes of expression inappropriate, contradictory and untenable. Our very selves, the name we use to think about ourselves as individuals, depend, paradoxically, on what we do not have, what may be outside or beyond us, what we may perhaps have to imagine. We need a name, a fiction, what may well be an 'absurd trust in value', or, another expression used in the poem, a variety of 'tricks'. 'Quality is habit' is an elliptical way of saying that the beliefs and absolutes on which we rely are sustained by custom and assumption. This quality is exorbitant (like silk, for instance) in that it takes the individual beyond the scope of immediate empirical knowledge: 'I have squandered so much life & good nature I could hardly/ guess the account.' Ultimately, it seems, these processes of investment and expenditure are what being social is all about. Again, there is the suggestion of an investment of energy that is, necessarily, excess to requirement. Trust may be squandered or misapplied and, in fact, this indeterminacy of outcome or 'return' is in the very nature of trust, which is something of a gamble. The great difficulty that emerges is that of finding an adequate way of conceptualising a 'self' so caught up in the endless range of economies suggested by the poem, a self which must take many things on trust in order to live, and which must therefore be seen to be engaged in another form of hazard or risk.

TWO VARIETIES OF IRONY

It is customary to cite a certain ironic sensibility as distinctive of the Movement poets – a defensive, educated but nonetheless populist tone of voice which disparaged pretension and abstraction. Tomlinson's review of Robert Conquest's anthology, *New Lines* (1956), is frequently cited as one of the more caustic accounts of a poetic attitude that combined the scepticism of the man on the Clapham omnibus and the secular smartness of post-Education Act generation:

> Thus Mr. Amis, according to *The Express*, opts for blondes, billiards, bars and progressive jazz-bands. Mr. Larkin abominates Mozart, never goes abroad, is a mild xenophobe. The beer-mug (we learn from the *Educational Supplement*) 'is never far from Mr. Wain's hand'.[76]

Tomlinson goes on to add 'self-caricature'; 'intense parochialism'; 'suburban mental ratio' and 'watered-down democratic culture' to the list of charges on the indictment.[77] It is an attitude which must be set in the context of a sense of wider cultural failure throughout the post-war period, attributable to a loss of faith in forms of radical modernisation (notwithstanding various cross-party claims for radicalism). Roy Fisher sees the degeneration of 'Joe/ Chamberlain's sense of the corporate' in Birmingham into a 'headless/ relativity of zones', a dream of a benignly administered society in which the state still carries responsibility for its citizens (and vice versa it is to be supposed) now reduced to a heterogeneous topography:

> unstable, dividing, grouping again
> differently; giving the slip to being
> counted, mapped or ever recognised
> by more than one head at a time.[78]

('Authorities')

In the face of such heterogeneity, an ironic sensibility may seem to provide some manner of refuge. This form of irony, contemporary beneficiaries of which might include Simon Armitage, whose favoured province is that of the bus-stop gossip, the pub raconteur and the witty recycler of everyday experiences, reclaims the illusion of consensus by positing a reality upon which we are all agreed, however dispiriting, absurd and grubby it may be. Armitage's first collection, *Zoom!*, appeared in 1988, almost contemporaneously with Alan Bennett's *Talking Heads*, a commercially successful and critically acclaimed BBC television series of 1987 consisting of dramatic monologues which Bennett himself describes as 'stripped-down' short stories.[79] The comparison illuminates Armitage's own particular exploitation of dramatic irony which, as every English undergraduate knows, steers an audience towards a complacent and privileged knowledge of what the truth really is. Irony, in other words, becomes merely something else to be decoded in the text.

But there is another, more subversive form of irony which cultivates a permanent state of disruption, an irony which continually insists on the reversal of our expectations and which therefore, unlike the mode of dramatic irony outlined above, is not easily assimilable into a pre-existing referent. It deals in disillusion of a different order: the shocking defamiliarisations of surrealist art; Walter Benjamin's revision of the everyday as impenetrable, the impenetrable as everyday; the discontinuity that Forrest-Thomson argued was produced by specifically poetic conventions; Fisher's technique of estrangement. The distinction that emerges might be described as that between familiarising and defamiliarising ironies. The former makes poetry itself the object of ironic devaluation (Betjeman, Larkin), and a sense of vocation rather ludicrous, as Fisher observes:

In barbarous times
all such callings
come through as rank parodies,

refracted by whatever murk
hangs in the air.[80]

(*A Furnace*: 'On Fennel Stalks')

The latter form of irony would see poetry itself as subversively ironic, refusing to commit itself to a stable point of view, exhibiting 'detachment,' as Paul de Man has described it, 'in relation to everything, and also in relation to the self and to the writer's own work'.[81] In this guise, poetry is anti-realist, anti-narrative, anti-teleological, perpetually variable and deviant, always favouring obliquity over direct statement. Realism, narrative and history, for their part, cannot be adequate to a culture in which migrations, technological developments and the range of social and political oppressions acknowledged by poets of this period produce dislocated selves. More recently, this seems to be a problem that a poet commanding mainstream approval such as Seamus Heaney has approached halfway – halfway because, though the problem is admitted, it is still contained. 'From the Frontier of Writing' in Heaney's 1987 collection, *The Haw Lantern*, moves from the subjugation of individual to state imperative (a checkpoint incident typifies the British military occupation of Northern Ireland), to the various subjugations that occur at 'the frontier of writing' where the self is similarly targeted, asked to present identity papers. The point is made, but only at the cost of a lyrical voice reasserting itself, a resolution out of keeping with a world in which 'everything is pure interrogation'.[82]

Opting for art that emphasises emergence rather than historical completion, fragments rather than totalities, is not a backward step into obscurantism but expresses the hope that language may be capable of saying something new, unthinkable perhaps. The close-ups enabled by the camera but unavailable to the naked human eye, says Benjamin, enhance 'our comprehension of the necessities that rule our lives' but also 'assure us of an immense and unexpected field of action.'[83] This willingness to do violence to familiar surfaces through an intensification of perspective (mechanical perspectives enabling a view of the 'unconscious' of our culture that optical physiology cannot hope to capture) is not an abdication of responsibility to the real, but a confirmation or intensification of it. It reveals reality anew, reveals what may have been obscured by habit, by cliché.

The tension between the official and, for want of a better term, hidden cultures of the poetry world has its counterpart in a society which, lacking the consensus of the 1950s, finds itself casting about for new conceptions of collective identity. Throughout a period of consumer prosperity and economic boom, the communal compensations of purchasing power, television or fashion could perhaps serve as an ersatz form of identity. This, coupled with the liberalising legislation of the 1964–70 Labour government on matters such as divorce, abortion and homosexuality, could make possible Larkin's petulant complaint in 'Annus Mirabilis' that: 'Sexual intercourse began/ In nineteen sixty-three/ (Which was rather late for me)'.[84] This recreational, permissive culture, it seemed, was the best that modern improvement had to show for itself and, to that extent, it would be unfair to represent Larkin's complaint as nothing more than the spleen of the excluded.

The importance of poetry that resists the 'official version' lies in its attempt, however incomplete it must be, to endow each individual with some degree of social and political agency. Roy Fisher's techniques, for example, in embracing the unforeseeable also resist programmes which 'set' reality and therefore reduce the opportunities for disputing that reality. His words, which suggest an approach to history sceptical of the claims of liberal democratic progress, and prepared to resist the particular story that it tells, provide an appropriate note on which to end:

> If you have your attention, and this is what you *have* got, it is up to you
> to make a world to which you can attend. . . . If you decide to accept
> history – well, if it gives you a kick to be carried along screaming, that is
> your privilege. If you don't want to be carried along by your own invention,
> or the invention you accept, then you use some other invention.[85]

NOTES

1. Ian Hamilton, 'Interviews with Philip Larkin and Christopher Middleton', in Graham Martin and P.N. Furbank (eds), *Twentieth Century Poetry: Critical Essays and Documents* (Milton Keynes, 1975), p. 247.

2. Veronica Forrest-Thomson, *Poetic Artifice: A Theory of Twentieth-Century Poetry* (Manchester, 1978), p. 149.

3. Ted Hughes, 'Tricksters and Tar Babies', in *Winter Pollen: Occasional Prose* (London, 1994), pp. 74–8.

4. Ted Hughes, *Crow: From the Life and Songs of the Crow* (London, 1970), p. 19.

5. Ibid., p. 31.

6. Forrest-Thomson, op. cit., p. xiv.

7. Philip Larkin, *Collected Poems*, Anthony Thwaite (ed.) (London, 1988), p. 153.

8. Ibid., pp. 115–16.

9. Hamilton, op. cit., p. 247.

10. Ian Gregson in *Contemporary Poetry and Postmodernism: Dialogue and Estrangement* (Basingstoke, 1996) describes 'The Whitsun Weddings' as 'a realist rereading of *The Waste Land*'s fertility metaphor' (p. 4). Donald Davie on the same lines comments that 'the human value suffuses the abstractly schematized with the grace of an organic fertility', *Thomas Hardy and British Poetry* (London, 1973), p. 66.

11. Charles Tomlinson, *Collected Poems* (Oxford, 1985), p. 194.

12. Charles Tomlinson, 'The Poet as Painter', *Poetry Review*, December 1986, vol. 76, no. X, p. 14.

13. Ibid., p. 14.

14. Ibid., p. 14.

15. Donald Davie, 'Bunting, Tomlinson and Hughes', in Davie, *Under Briggflatts: A History of Poetry in Great Britain 1960–1988* (Manchester, 1989), p. 129.

16. Charles Tomlinson (ed.), Preface to *Marianne Moore: A Collection of Critical Essays* (Englewood Cliffs, New Jersey 1969), p. 4.

17. Claude Lévi-Strauss, *The Savage Mind* (London, 1972), p. 16. First published as *La Pensée Sauvage* (Paris, 1962). Calvin Bedient cites Tomlinson's own use of Lévi-Strauss's term. See Bedient, *Eight Contemporary Poets* (Oxford, 1974), p. 3.

18. According to *Robert*, a *bricole* was originally a catapult-like engine of war, propelling its missiles via a ricochet effect. Hence, the sense of a slightly off-kilter trajectory that survives in the word as applied in the sense of 'odd-job man', someone who turns things round, and so on.

19. Lévi-Strauss, op. cit., p. 16.

20. Tomlinson also finds himself drawn to chance as a compositional principle in his visual art, using techniques of collage and surrealist decalcomania: 'This latter consists of crushing diluted paint between two surfaces, then using the chance forms of the pigment as a suggestive basis for a new picture', 'The Poet as Painter', p. 15.

21. Davie, rather prematurely, puts Fisher alongside Larkin in his 'bitter distaste' for the outcomes of post-war social democracy and Hardyesque resignation to a world of 'reduced expectations.' See *Thomas Hardy and British Poetry*, p. 165; p. 172.

22. Roy Fisher, *The Dow Low Drop: New and Selected Poems* (Newcastle upon Tyne, 1996), p. 20.

23. Ibid., p. 19.

24. Ibid., p. 21.

25. Antony Easthope, 'Donald Davie and the Failure of Englishness', in James Acheson and Romana Huk (eds), *Contemporary British Poetry: Essays in Theory and Criticism* (New York, 1996), p. 28.

26. Jed Rasula and Mike Erwin, 'An Interview with Roy Fisher', in Roy Fisher, *19 Poems and An Interview* (Staffordshire, 1975), p. 18.
27. James Clifford, *The Predicament of Culture: Twentieth-Century Ethnography, Literature and Art* (Cambridge, Mass., 1988), p. 121.
28. Roy Fisher, op. cit., p. 169.
29. Walter Benjamin, 'Surrealism: The Last Snapshot of the European Intelligentsia', in *One Way Street and Other Writings*, tr. Edmund Jephcott and Kingsley Shorter (London, 1985), p. 237. The title of Fisher's poem alludes to Heraclitan philosophy, 'furnace' suggesting, amongst other things, change and conversion, the difficulty of separating subject from object, and therefore a kind of ceaseless reciprocity which appears in the image of the double spiral throughout the poem.
30. Clifford, op. cit., p. 167.
31. Rasula and Erwin, op. cit., p. 32.
32. Fisher, op. cit., p. 136.
33. Rasula and Erwin, op. cit., p. 21.
34. Fisher, op. cit., p. 130.
35. Roy Fisher, 'Poet on Writing', in Denise Riley (ed.), *Poets on Writing: Britain, 1970–1991* (Basingstoke, 1992), p. 273.
36. Fisher, op. cit., p. 151.
37. Ibid., p. 159.
38. Ibid., p. 274.
39. Roy Fisher, *The Cut Pages* (London, 1971), p. 6.
40. Rasula and Erwin, op. cit., p. 23.
41. Ibid., p. 33.
42. Clive Bush (ed.), *Worlds of New Measure: An Anthology of Five Contemporary British Poets* (London, 1997), p. 5. For a more detailed discussion of Clark's work see Clive Bush, *Out of Dissent: A Study of Five Contemporary British Poets* (London, 1997).
43. Bush, *Worlds of New Measure*, op. cit., p. 34.
44. Ibid., p. 40.
45. Fisher, op. cit., p. 24.
46. Bush, *Worlds of New Measure*, op. cit., p. 82.
47. Ibid., pp. 86–9.
48. Ibid., p. 84.
49. John Betjeman, *Summoned by Bells* (London, 1960), p. 12.
50. *Thomas Hardy and British Poetry*, p. 106.
51. Betjeman, op. cit., n.p.
52. Donald Davie, 'Prosody', *Under Briggflatts*, pp. 124–5.
53. Betjeman, op. cit., p. 20.
54. Basil Bunting, *Collected Poems* (Oxford, 1978), p. 41.
55. John Ruskin, *The Stones of Venice* (1851–3), vol. II (London, 1906), p. 165.
56. Basil Bunting, '"Thumps" and "Wyat": Two Lectures on Prosody', in Richard Caddell (ed.), *Sharp Study and Long Toil: Basil Bunting Special Issue* (Durham, 1995), pp. 13–35, Durham University Journal Supplement.
57. See Bunting's own use of the word in a letter of 1953 to the American poet Louis Zukofsky with reference to flute music 'as kaleidoscopic as the shadow pattern, getting in a single line that extreme multiplicity that Byrd gets in many parts, and that is nearer to reflecting life than in any simpler art.' Quoted by Eric Mottram in 'Basil Bunting: Human Framework and "Nature"', Caddell, op. cit., pp. 73–4.

58. Basil Bunting, *Collected Poems*, p. 47. See Pound in the *ABC of Reading* on the Chinese ideogram, which works by juxtaposing things in order to conjure up that property they have in common. For 'red', for example, the symbols for flamingo, cherry, iron rust and rose might be juxtaposed. In James Scully (ed.), *Modern Poets on Modern Poetry* (London, 1966), p. 46.

59. Bunting, *Collected Poems*, p. 57.

60. Ibid., p. 148.

61. Ibid., p. 39.

62. Ibid., p. 42.

63. Ibid., p. 43.

64. Ibid., p. 51.

65. Ibid., pp. 42–6.

66. Ibid., p. 55.

67. Letter of 13 January 1965, quoted by Peter Makin in *Bunting: The Shaping of His Verse* (Oxford, 1992), p. 157.

68. Interview in *Scripsi*, 1: 3&4, Summer/Autumn 1982. Quoted by Eric Mottram in 'Basil Bunting: Human Framework and "Nature"', Caddell, op. cit., p. 81.

69. See Jacques Derrida on this point in 'Shibboleth: For Paul Celan', tr. Joshua Willner, in Aris Fioretos (ed.), *Word Traces* (Baltimore, 1994), p. 22. 'A date gets carried away . . . and thus effaces itself in its very readability.' A date (or equally a word) is both unique and endlessly reproducible.

70. Andrew Crozier and Tim Longville (eds), *A Various Art* (London, 1990), p. 13. See also another anthology, now out of print, which similarly aimed to present an alternative range of contemporary work, Fred D'Aguiar, Gillian Allnutt, Eric Mottram and Ken Edwards (eds), *The New British Poetry 1968–1988* (London, 1988).

71. *The New Poetry: An Anthology Selected and Introduced by A. Alvarez* (London, 1962), p. 28.

72. Prynne's work has recently been made more widely available through the publication of his *Collected Poems* by Bloodaxe (Newcastle upon Tyne, 1998).

73. Paul de Man, 'Autobiography as De-Facement', in *The Rhetoric of Romanticism* (New York, 1984), p. 70.

74. Ibid., p. 71.

75. Crozier and Longville, op. cit., p. 233.

76. Charles Tomlinson, 'The Middlebrow Muse', in *Essays in Criticism*, vol. 7, 1957, p. 208.

77. Ibid., pp. 214–15.

78. Fisher, op. cit., p. 171.

79. Simon Armitage, *Zoom!* (Newcastle upon Tyne, 1989). Alan Bennett, *Talking Heads* (London, 1988), p. 7.

80. Fisher, op. cit., p. 186.

81. Paul de Man, 'The Concept of Irony', in Andrzej Warminski (ed.), *Aesthetic Ideology* (Minneapolis, 1996), p. 177.

82. Seamus Heaney, *The Haw Lantern* (London, 1987), p. 6.

83. Walter Benjamin, 'The Work of Art in the Age of Mechanical Reproduction', in Hannah Arendt (ed.), *Illuminations*, tr. Harry Zohn (London, 1992), p. 229.

84. Larkin, op. cit., p. 167.

85. Rasula and Erwin, op. cit., p. 36.

CHAPTER TWO
Novel Voices

Steven Earnshaw

The 1956 Suez debacle has long been taken as the symbol of Britain's demise as a front-line world power, and the fortunes of the British novel have often been seen to mirror this downward path after the Second World War.[1] Conversely, the novel has been in the ascendant elsewhere: the literary legerdemain of the early American postmodernists (Pynchon, Vonnegut, Barthelme, Coover); the magical realism of the South Americans, most notably Gabriel García Márquez; and the new literatures in English, that is, English literature produced anywhere except Britain.[2] Whilst this assessment is fair in that there is no single grouping in the period of writers with the stature of the American postmodernists, on the other hand there are British novelists of such international standing as Doris Lessing, John Fowles, Angela Carter, Muriel Spark, Salman Rushdie and Martin Amis, who have come to prominence during this time.

All writers after modernism have been aware that changes in technique have placed them in a certain relationship to modernism, whether they liked it or not, and the debate of how to respond to modernism, and more recently how to respond to 'postmodernist literature', has often been tied up with questions surrounding 'the death of the novel'. The majority of British writers have deferred to the dominant tradition of the English novel which stretches from Fielding, Defoe and Richardson in the eighteenth century, through Austen, the Brontës, Dickens and George Eliot, up to Conrad and Lawrence in the twentieth century. For most novelists writing for a contemporary audience, their craft has entailed manipulating the varieties of realism found within this canon. Others have looked for a more accessible, attenuated modernism, shorn of experimental extremes and often compatible with realism. In both modes the British novel has continued to play to its strengths: subtle analyses of society, history and, with novel sequences such as Anthony Powell's *A Dance to the Music of Time* (1951–75), social change. But such nuanced observation within a conservative tradition has not gained an international audience. From the late 1970s onwards, however, postmodernist innovations in novel form and technique have become more widespread in the English novel. With the critical and popular success of Salman Rushdie's *Midnight's Children* in 1981, a Booker Prize winner that year, the English novel could be said to have been brought up-to-date, at least in the formalist narrative outlined here.

Beyond this narrative the image is one of the addition of new voices, both single and collective, a natural consequence of the change in Britain's social complexion. The arrival of people from the West Indies and Africa, and from India, Pakistan and Bangladesh, has turned Britain into a multicultural society. These experiences, as well as knowledge of different artistic traditions, have fed directly and indirectly into British fiction, although, Rushdie aside, the impact has arguably been greater in poetry than in prose. Access to education for those previously excluded, from the grammar school boys of the 1950s to the expansion of higher education in the 1960s and after, has also meant new realms of experience have become familiar territory in the novel (although a self-conscious promotion of 'working-class writing' had begun in the 1930s). The impact of feminism, particularly in the 1960s and 1970s, has equally found the novel a congenial medium for expression in the shape of fictionalised autobiography, from Margaret Drabble through to Jeanette Winterson. Theories of literary interpretation have been encountered with increasing frequency by writers from the late 1960s onwards, theories that often overlap with social theories, and these have informed the way some novelists structure their narratives. Without openness to these inputs, the British novel would most likely have become moribund.

The broader base of social groups contributing to the novel has meant that 'Britain', once the literary preserve of white, middle-aged, middle-class English males, has been replaced by more 'local' versions less willing to lay claim to speak for the whole nation. The previous cultural hegemony has itself had to come to terms with a changed society, and has often provided an acute commentary upon its own relegation. However, to say that British identity has dissolved altogether into an incompatible plurality ignores the fact that nationality and identity are dynamic concepts, constantly redefined to accommodate and position contesting voices whenever necessary.

Other writers have felt the need to look beyond Britain's shores to include more global matters: the aftermath of the Holocaust, the threat of 'mutually assured destruction' (MAD) throughout the Cold War period, the Cold War itself, increased secularisation of Western society, threats to the environment, modern alienation as understood by psychology, Marxist politics, and existentialist philosophy, the turn to 'the market' in the 1980s.

All of which is to say that the novel in Britain has expanded its range considerably in both technique and subject matter during this period.

ROGUE MALES

In Britain in the 1950s there was a desperate search to find a collection of writers who could take their place on the international scene.[3] It was a sign, perhaps, not only of economic decline, but also of an anxiety that Britain was facing cultural decay as a result of the loss of its empire, coupled with the deleterious inroads made by Americanisation. Critics and the media managed to find two bodies of writers which they could at least attempt to promote. The first literary grouping was the Movement, coined in 1954 to describe a loose association of writers who were mainly poets, and which included Kingsley Amis, Donald Davie, D.J. Enright, Thom Gunn, Elizabeth Jennings and Philip Larkin. What allowed J.D. Scott to place them together was their sense of poetic craft, irony, rationalism, academicism, and a certain 'Englishness', a return to artistic values presumed to be in force before the mistake of modernism in the first third of the twentieth century.

The second group was known as 'the angry young men', and gained wider media attention. The phrase described the lowest common denominator of a variety of exciting new literary productions. It referred to a type of hero, or 'anti-hero', who was usually working-class – Joe Lampton the ruthless social climber in *Room at the Top* (1957); factory worker Arthur Seaton the hedonist each weekend in Alan Sillitoe's *Saturday Night and Sunday Morning* (1958) – although Jim Dixon, the pinched lecturer in Kingsley Amis's *Lucky Jim* (1954), is lower middle class ('class' remained a crucial point of contention). The new brand of hero was an opportunist, a sexual predator, and resented authority as a matter of course. This male protagonist could be found in drama as well as fiction – Jimmy Porter in John Osborne's *Look Back in Anger* (1956) for example – and extended to the public's perception of the authors themselves. The writing was not innovative, turning its back on the more experimental writing of the previous decades. It was a prosaic, realistic mode best defined as 'anti-modernist', since it eschewed the intense psychologism of the modernist novel, and continued the reaction against modernism begun in the 1930s.[4] The 1950s novel characteristically concentrated upon recognisable people in ordinary environments living everyday lives in the Midlands and the North.

However, most of these writers are now remembered for their first novels only. This suggests that they caught the mood of the time, an empty rebellion against the conformity of the new welfare state, carried out in the comfort of an increasingly prosperous Britain – Arthur Seaton has a wardrobe full of Teddy Boy suits and his father has a television. What was new was the class base of these authors, mainly working-class men who could portray provincial working-class life 'from the inside'. 'Insider' status gave a first-hand 'authenticity' to the depiction of the new Britain, in contrast to the treatment of the Midlands and the North by writers in the 1930s who had believed these areas were dark jungles to be explored, their inhabitants observed, exhibited and explained sociologically. *Saturday Night and Sunday Morning* opens with Arthur Seaton blind drunk, falling down the stairs at the local social club. Although the narrative voice is in the third person, there is a clear identification with the character and his weekly ritual of binge drinking: 'You followed the motto of "be drunk and be happy", kept your crafty arms around female waists, and felt the beer going beneficially down into the elastic capacity of your guts.'[5] This narrative technique of free indirect discourse, whereby the narrator appears to be privy to the thoughts and emotions of the characters, was a dominant feature of the modernists. Here, instead of using it to describe unique psychological individuals, Sillitoe subordinates it to the ends of social realism. The aim is anti-modernist in that it offers a readily accessible picture of shared worlds and shared values.

Novels at the beginning of the 1960s continued along the realist/anti-modernist track, novels such as Stan Barstow's *A Kind of Loving* (1960), and David Storey's *This Sporting Life* (1960). Yet the impression that these novelists were radicals, on the political left and a coherent grouping, was soon dissipated. Kingsley Amis's *One Fat Englishman* (1963), which details the adventures of an overweight, obnoxious, middle-aged Anglo-Saxon in America, a country he despises with all the Little Englander mentality he can muster, might appear an apt epitaph for the angry young man. The only thing that hadn't changed was the misogynistic world depicted. However, the well-observed tale of 'ordinary' lives has remained a staple feature of the British novel to the present day and this style has proved flexible enough for other groups wishing to provide a realistic fictionalised account of experience, such as the women-centred fiction that emerged in the 1960s.

LONE VOICES

Outside the major groupings there were a number of writers ploughing their own furrows in the 1950s, both in terms of style and subject matter.

One of the most remarkable debut novels was Muriel Spark's *The Comforters*, published in 1957. If the 1950s were a time for first novels, startling because of their brash voices from newly empowered classes, Spark's first novel is remarkable because many of its techniques would become standard fare for the postmodernist style of writing that emerged in America in the 1960s, a type of fiction characterised by disrupted plot lines, a blurring of the distinction between fiction and reality, narrators passing from self-contained fictional worlds into the reader's world, and peopled by characters without stable identities or psychologies. In Spark's novel, one of the main characters, Caroline Rose, keeps hearing a single voice tapping out messages on a typewriter in a number of different tones. These messages are her thoughts, rendered in the past tense, so that they appear to form the very novel we are reading: 'At this point in the narrative, it might be as well to state that the characters in this novel are all fictitious, and do not refer to any living persons whatsoever./ *Tap-tappity-tap. At this point in the narrative. . . .*'[6]

But not only is Caroline haunted by the awareness that she is a character in a novel that is currently being written (read), she is working on a book called *Form in the Modern Novel*. A couple of times the joke is made that she is both living in a book and writing one.[7] This provides the 'short-circuit': she is living in the book she is writing, whilst the book we are reading is itself a shining example of 'form in the modern novel', and so the voice she hears is also that of a new mode of writing. Other postmodern trickery includes a character who literally disappears as a character in the novel when she has no public life (going to her room; falling asleep),[8] and Caroline's anticipation that the book she is in (we are reading) is about to end because certain events in the plot appear to be drawing to a close (the somewhat implausible mystery of a diamond smuggling racket is solved). For all its stylistic innovations the environment portrayed in the novel is thoroughly recognisable, and the satirical edge close to Evelyn Waugh. The various forms of 'comfort' available involve the Catholic religion, diabolism, psychoanalysis and fiction itself. Caroline's 'voice' can be explained away according to 'insanity', if the reader wishes to remain within the 'real world' rather than the slippery fictional one Spark half offers.

Equally concerned with the form of the modern novel was Lawrence Durrell, whose *Justine* was also published in 1957. This was the first novel in the sequence known as the *Alexandria Quartet*, which proclaimed itself 'an investigation of modern love' in its charting of the emotional lives of a fixed group of characters. In a note to the second volume, *Balthazar* (1958) Durrell informs us that he has used science's 'relativity proposition' of time-space as the unifying concept for the quartet. Space has three dimensions, and three of the novels correspond in the sense that they 'interlap, interweave, in a purely spatial relation'. The odd one out, *Mountolive*, covers the 'time' aspect and is thus more straightforwardly realist. In the books themselves a novelist called Pursewarden hovers in the background and is quoted from time to time as if giving a running commentary on the problems faced by the modern writer: 'He was at that moment trying to escape from the absurd dictates of narrative form in prose: "He said" "She said" "He cocked an eye, shot a cuff, lifted a lazy head, etc." Was it possible, had he succeeded in "realizing" character without the help of such props?'[9] The attempt at spatialisation might set it apart from other novels of the period, since British novel sequences are usually historical, although it also gives the *Quartet* a feeling of stasis. Its sheer sensuousness and impressionism, its erotic lyricism, is unusual for the British novel, and not evident again until some of the work of Angela Carter, who was also interested in de Sade.

Yet Durrell is obviously anxious that these theoretical and structural ideas might sound 'immodest' and 'pompous' to his British audience.[10] His caution is indicative of the problems that have faced any British novelist wishing to depart from the main tradition. As Doris Lessing stated in the 1971 introduction to *The Golden Notebook* with respect to the English novel tradition: 'there is no doubt that to attempt a novel of ideas is to give oneself a handicap: the parochialism of our culture is intense.'[11] Both Durrell and Spark are examples of writers wishing to experiment without losing accessibility to a wider audience.

One writer who has continued to follow his own fictional direction is Wilson Harris, a Guyanese who moved to London in 1959. His first four novels, beginning with *Palace of the Peacock* in 1960, were published collectively as *The Guyana Quartet* in 1985. They are 'poetic' and as such tend to proceed along metaphorical rather than plot lines, concerned with the impact of technology and greed upon a mythologised Guyana. The world is a complex mixture of survival, dreams and symbolically-charged landscape, and formally a self-conscious enterprise to move away from 'the canons of realism'.[12] His later work has become more difficult and obscure, but throughout Harris has remained one of the most individually-voiced novelists writing in Britain.

FROM THE MIDDLE-BROW TO THE HIGH FOREHEAD: WOMEN-CENTRED FICTION

After the predominantly masculine culture of the 1950s novel, the 1960s showed the growing confidence of women writers to voice their own concerns. And just as the novels of the angry young men had opted for a style firmly within the domain of realism, women writers too found the more traditional-looking anti-modernist stance the most congenial one for their objectives. In both cases it is the subject matter of the novels and social position of the authors which are understood to be new, rather than any innovations in writing technique. Margaret Drabble's first novel, *A Summer Bird-Cage* (1963), is a fair example of the 'women on the brink of liberation' novel, and of what the standard, good, middle-brow British novel was (and is) believed to be.

The novel concerns two sisters, Louise and Sarah Bennett, and is about 'the twisted motives of middle-class girls 'with no sense of vocation'.[13] It thus explores the problems of well-educated women who face the prospect of not being able to get suitable jobs, and of having to work out an attitude towards the bird-cage of marriage: 'the birds that are without despair to get in, and the birds that are within despair and are in a consumption for fear they shall never get out'.[14] The novel charts the relationship between the two sisters, as Louise, the sister who has it all, makes an unhappy marriage. Sarah's own decision is held in suspense because the man she might marry is out of the country. The novel itself is caught in the same dilemma, aware of the same old traps but uncertain of the new possibilities for women, that is, if there are any: it ends with two cheers for Louise's adulterous relationship.

Drabble's fictional world is one of relationships and interiors, the kind of cosy provincialism that has given British fiction a bad name and from which it has often felt obliged to free itself. Her second novel, *The Garrick Year* (1964) has a central female character married to a philandering actor. She herself engages in adultery, the major thematic of cosy provincialism, with its modern-day racier equivalent, 'shopping and fucking' novels. Although Drabble herself has moved in later fiction to deal with wider social issues, writing 'condition of England' novels, the social territory she began with has continued to provide the material for many women novelists.

Fay Weldon evinces a sharper attitude to relationships than Drabble, female to female in particular: 'Down among the women. What a place to be! Yet here we all are by accident of birth, sprouted breast and bellies, as cyclical of nature as our timekeeper the moon – and down here among the women we have no option but to stay' states one of her characters.[15] The emphasis on biology as a major determinant for gender has been a central thread of Weldon's work, as in *Puffball* (1980) which contrasts deterministic medical descriptions of the female body during menstruation, taking 'the pill', and pregnancy, with a typical 'infidelities' storyline. Later feminist authors however have tended to focus on gender as a cultural construct rather than a biological given, seeing the latter view as too restrictive and unhelpfully keeping the binary opposition of male/female in place.

The limitations of such writing as Drabble's – the novel as reportage – were exposed in Doris Lessing's *The Golden Notebook* (1962), an immense and immensely complex book.[16] Its centre-piece is a middle-brow novel called *Free Women*: it could easily be a pastiche of a Drabble novel, concerned as it is with the relationship between two close female friends, in which the title is both an injunction and an ironical description. The nested novel is then juxtaposed with four notebooks as kept by Anna Wulf, a character in *Free Women*, who needs to compartmentalise facets of her life into manageable portions to provide some sort of order, and thus avoid her own disintegration. The notebooks are colour-coded and cover different aspects of her life: the Black Notebook is her time in Africa; the Red Notebook is her relationship with the Communist Party; the Yellow Notebook is partly a novel itself, *The Shadow of the Third*, and contains ideas for other novels; the Blue Notebook is part diary, part newspaper clippings, and part psycho-analysis. The Golden Notebook of the title is the 'something new' that can emerge from the 'fragments' of the notebooks. Taken together the novel is a critique of the 'sex war', Women's Liberation, commitment to political action, socialism in England, art, and mental breakdown – a novel of ideas as well as a condition of England novel, ambitious and comprehensive in a way which distinguishes it from most novels of this period.

THE DARK GODS

With religious belief still fading in the aftershocks of Hiroshima and Auschwitz, other types of explanation were required to say why human nature functioned as it did. Freudian psychology still had its followers, and psychology in general, which had received a huge boost thanks to American military confidence in psychometric testing, seemed to hold out answers. Lessing's concern with mental breakdown is visible throughout her five-novel *Children of Violence* sequence (1952–69) and in *Briefing for a Descent into Hell* (1971), which is scathing of medical psychology, yet still obviously concerned with the hidden workings of the mind as the prime mover in human behaviour.[17] 'Into hell' also suggests that the little-understood mental phenomenon of madness is the site for a new metaphysics which can fill the vacuum left by the departure of religious belief. Anthony Burgess's *A Clockwork Orange* (1962) has a central character who truly is an 'angry young man', regarded as mad because of his extremely violent, anti-social behaviour. But the message of this book seemed to be that such dark gods are necessary for great art, since once he is cured of his addiction to 'horrorshow' violence he no longer appreciates Beethoven.

Iris Murdoch's *A Severed Head* (1961) deals with similar themes to those of the middle-brow woman's novel, but it attempts to give itself a gravitas and meaning beyond realistic social description by hinting at mythological and psychological undercurrents (a technique favoured by modernist writers). The narrator of Murdoch's novel feels that Frazer's *The Golden Bough* (the anthropological tome that props up T.S. Eliot's *The Waste Land*) is the best model to understand an incestuous relationship between an American psychoanalyst and his sister. As to the novel's own stance on how the 'dark gods' of irrational behaviour are to be defeated – either through therapy (unlikely) or mythemes (more promising) – there is ultimately an ambivalence which had been evident in her earlier *The Bell* (1958), about a lay religious community comprised of people spiritually unfulfilled in the modern world.

Murdoch's gesture towards the dark side of human nature has been one way of escaping the insularity of British fiction. With deeper forces at work than straightforward realist narrative will allow, the depiction of a universe constructed upon quasi-religious lines now that the world is supposedly secular has been the mainstay of two of Britain's major post-war novelists: William Golding and Muriel Spark.

Nobel Prize winner for Literature in 1983, William Golding's *Lord of the Flies* (1954) set the pattern for his later work: human nature is stripped of its gloss of civilisation to show the 'heart of darkness' beneath, and his subsequent novels continued to evoke a sense of a Manichean world of good and evil, as in *Pincher Martin* (1956), *The Spire* (1964) and *Darkness Visible* (1979). Although predominantly realist, the invisible world is called up through a symbolic schema reminiscent of the modernists.

Spark too has found the dark gods fruitful: *Memento Mori* (1959) concerns a group of elderly people who are phoned up by death; *The Ballad of Peckham Rye* (1960) follows the impact on a small group of people when a stranger arrives who might be the devil – he has two bumps on the top of his head; and in *The Driver's Seat* (1961) the protagonist appears to foresee and/or arrange her own death. But not everyone has been convinced of the importance of Spark's writing,[18] and it is true that the slimmer novels can sometimes appear like extended short stories. Her best work is *The Prime of Miss Jean Brodie* (1961) and *The Girls of Slender Means* (1963), which benefit from a greater focus on characterisation and less mobilisation of a metaphysical framework.

The urgency for British writers to deal with the 'dark gods' was outlined in A. Alvarez's introduction to *The New Poetry* (1962), where he noted that in the aftermath of Dachau and Buchenwald the English empire mentality of 'gentility' could no longer regard 'evil' as something so completely alien it could be ignored.[19] How successful British writers have been in coming to terms with such areas is questionable, as with D.M. Thomas's *The White*

Hotel (1981). Lisa Erdman is a patient of Freud's, and her neuroses and sexual fantasies which constitute a majority of the book give no indication that the reader will later see her as a victim in the Babi Yar massacre. The novel shows the impossibility of describing even one life in all its rich variety, but the use of Freudian sexual fantasy as the background to genocide, was (is) controversial. It is unclear whether Thomas's evocation of the constant, suppressed battle between eros and thanatos is meant to reveal the underlying mechanism that led to the event or whether such psychomachia is confined to the hidden lives of each person regardless of the horrors they suffer.

Perhaps the most audacious attempt to deal with the Holocaust in the British novel has come in the shape of Martin Amis's *Time's Arrow* (1991). It works backwards in time, tracing the life of a successful American doctor through to his life as a Nazi doctor in Auschwitz. The novel itself has provoked mixed reactions: for some its technique allows for psychological and historical insight, for others it is a case of 'Holocaust chic'. Amis himself took the 'reversal of events' idea from a short passage in Kurt Vonnegut's novel *Slaughterhouse Five* (1969), where bombs are miraculously sucked into planes and returned to their workshops instead of causing the wholesale destruction of Dresden in the Second World War. Amis's 'Afterword' makes it clear that the narrative problem of 'telling the story of a man's life backwards in time' came first, and the subject matter was subsequent to this, which does suggest that the novel's *raison d'être* was primarily an experiment in narrative ingenuity rather than increased under-standing of the Holocaust.[20] This remains a problem for writers using the Holocaust for fictional material – seriousness is automatically granted to areas of experience that can only be second-hand at best, and the issue of whether or not those who are not 'witnesses' should thus leave the area alone continues to be contentious.[21]

EMPIRE

Reactions to the decline of formal empire have produced some of the best literature. Paul Scott's *The Raj Quartet* (1966–74) is the most well-known, in large part thanks to its lavish dramatisation on television in the 1970s. Rather like Durrell's *Alexandria Quartet*, the overall structure is 'spatial' rather than chronological, viewing the same events from different characters' viewpoints in the years from 1942 up to India's independence in 1947. This leads to some stunning psychological perspectivism of the type opened up by the modernists and their use of interior monologue, although it also leads to some clumsy plot re-capping in order to grant the books autonomy if read singly. Some of the historical background is also poorly integrated in novelistic terms, as when characters give extended speeches to explain the political context.

With a definite nod to E.M. Forster's *Passage to India* and the consequences of a white woman's claim that she has been raped by an Indian, *The Raj Quartet* has at its centre the rape of gawky Daphne Manners. Her relationship with the English-educated Indian Hari Kumar is frowned upon by the ex-pat community. The bigoted policeman Ronald Merrick believes Kumar to be one of the rapists and imprisons him. When Merrick tortures Kumar to extract a confession, he self-consciously re-enacts his view of the relationship between England (Britain) and India as one of master-servant imbued with sado-masochism. As a whole the sequence is an example of the British novel successfully using a number of modes to provide a nominally complete and realistic picture of a particular social and historic period as seen, mainly, from the British point of view.

J.G. Farrell's *Empire Trilogy* finds presentiments of the decline of empire in three historical events, each of which is depicted through the story of a group of people under siege. *Troubles* (1969) is set in Ireland in 1919 in the Hotel Majestic, a decaying symbol of the Anglo-Irish aristocracy. The good-natured Major Brendan Archer holds together a number of eccentrics oblivious to the momentous political events occurring outside their enclave, which Farrell indicates by flashing up contemporary newspaper reports. *The Siege of Krishnapur* (1973) conflates two sieges from the time of the Indian Mutiny in 1857, and *The Singapore Grip* (1978) follows the fortunes of another besieged group in the events leading up to the fall of Singapore in 1942. The books are all suffused with an original humour, as in *The Siege of Krishnapur* when the people under attack run out of cannon balls and are reduced to using busts of famous figures for ammunition: Shakespeare's head is the most lethal missile because bald, flying through the air with the greatest of ease. The last of the trilogy shows a greater density of economic and historic factual material, as if Farrell were working toward something more in the line of Scott. Farrell died in 1979 in a boating accident, cutting short one of the more original voices of post-war British fiction.

Another feature of post-war Britain has been the place of the formerly colonised as they articulate experiences of emigration and independence. It has also meant the rewriting of empire history. George Lamming's *The Emigrants* (1954), opened up the world of West Indian immigration to Britain for fiction.[22] Colin MacInnes's *London Trilogy* – *City of Spades* (1957), *Absolute Beginners* (1959) and *Mr Love and Mr Justice* (1960) also gave some insight into the 'meeting' of these two cultures, although from a current perspective this work can look rather patronising. From a different angle, the Trinidadian V.S. Naipaul has written of a sense of dislocation for Indians in the colonial world and twentieth century in general, using a balanced prose which for some critics has marked him out as the natural successor to Conrad. *A House for Mr Biswas* (1961) makes an epic hero out of a weak personality, and in doing so makes for one of the great comic novels of the period. It also hints at a more threatening side to life, as when Mr Biswas is put in isolated charge of a plantation and begins to live a nightmarish, paranoid existence. Such a section looks forward to Naipaul's *Guerillas* (1975), a novel about the desperate politics of a small tropical island, where England remains firmly in the distant background as an invisible, distorting force.

Like Jean Rhys's *Wide Sargasso Sea* (1966) before it, *Guerillas* partly deals with the legacy of colonialism through reference to Charlotte Brontë's *Jane Eyre*.[23] Rhys's novel has certainly been one of the most influential critiques of empire in the canons of the post-war British novel. An established writer in the 1920s and 1930s, she was generally assumed to be dead until a 1958 radio broadcast of her novel *Good Morning, Midnight* (1939) entailed that 'she was finally traced to an address in Cornwall'.[24] *Wide Sargasso Sea* focuses upon Bertha Mason, here called Antoinette Cosway, the madwoman in the attic in *Jane Eyre*. The novel is set in Jamaica, relegating England to nothing more than a remote spot on a map. Although never named, Rochester is a symbol of the blustering empire, destructive of a culture he makes no effort to understand, yet is attracted to and repelled by. The novel itself is split into three sections: the first is Antoinette's narrative as a girl, the second section shuttles between Rochester's and Antoinette's points-of-view, and the last section belongs to Grace Pool, Bertha's gaoler-come-nurse when in England. The novel has its own dream quality, achieved through symbolic leitmotifs, limited perspectives, and a highly-charged poetics. By taking *Jane Eyre* as its founding text, *Wide Sargasso Sea* acknowledges the power this most-favoured novel has had within the literary canon, which thus enables it to make plain the received prejudices the canon and its cultural power have continued to foster: Rochester's wealth is built upon West Indian plantations and slavery; Bertha Mason is not white enough for England's heritage; she is also a woman who is too passionate, and so through male eyes is deemed to be mad. Rhys's singular work manages to expose all these targets by way of a carefully engineered intertextuality.

EXPERIMENTAL LITERATURE

There was a determinedly avant-garde nature about modernism, one branch of which foregrounded the experimental nature of its work. A number of writers continued this tradition in Britain. Their distinction from writers such as Spark, Lessing and Carter is perhaps one of degree rather than category, since all these writers have also experimented with one or more of the various constituents of the novel: plot, character, genre, form and language. However, as with the Dadaists and Surrealists, the more avowedly 'experimental' writers produced work regardless of whether there was an audience for it or not. B.S. Johnson may have baulked at the term 'experimental' since it was usually synonymous with 'unsuccessful', yet he was fully aware of the consequences for his explorations of fiction. When he considered who the public for his novels might be, he concluded that 'I write perforce for myself'.[25] Others of his ilk, Christine Brooke-Rose, Eva Figes and Giles Gordon for instance, also pushed (and still push) against 'the novel' as traditionally understood, in a way which continues the more extreme attacks by modernists on plot, character and language, and partakes of similar attacks from more virulent postmodernists. The title of one of Christine Brooke-Rose's more recent novels, *Textermination* (1992), is apt for some of the material here. B.S. Johnson's work was perhaps the most notorious. One novel, *Albert Angelo* (1964) had a hole in the middle representing a knife cut whereby later (and previous) pages could be glimpsed. Another novel, *The Unfortunates* (1969) was published in loose-leaf format for the readers to assemble as they saw fit – to mimic the way the mind (supposedly) works.[26] Both in a way are reminiscent of the shock tactics of the avant-garde.

Other novels have been experimental without being so demonstrative. John Berger's *G.* was Booker Prize winner in 1972. The initial stands for a number of characters: Italian national hero Garibaldi, the aviator Geo Chavez, and Don Giovanni. The novel disorientates the reader through shifts in narrative style and address, as well as consistent mystification of who the protagonist might be. But even here there is a sense that the 'experiment' is not so original, for Thomas Pynchon had used such a disjunctive framing device for a historical narrative in *V.* (1963), whereby the initial stands for a variety of characters throughout the twentieth century.

GENRE FICTION

If some writers have cared little for an audience, others have written within established modes to large niche markets. Barbara Cartland's 'romances' and Catherine Cookson's historical novels have achieved huge sales whilst remaining highly formulaic. British writers have been highly successful in other genres: science fiction (Michael Moorcock, John Wyndham, J.G. Ballard, Terry Pratchett), who-dunnits – Ruth Rendell; thrillers – Frederick Forsyth; sagas – Jeffrey Archer. When critics talk of 'the novel', what is meant is the 'literary' novel, or non-genre fiction, and so such 'genre' novels are usually excluded. However, some of these writers have come to be regarded with critical acclaim, such as John Le Carré and Len Deighton. These latter authors depict a world of down-at-heel spies, in direct contrast to Ian Fleming's James Bond. The novels are tightly structured in terms of plot, and it has been claimed that the dominant theme is that of 'betrayal', the code of honour on offer in public school education. This might be so in the earlier novels, such as *The Spy Who Came in from the Cold* (1963), and Deighton's *Funeral in Berlin* (1964). But in the later *Smiley's People* (1980), Le Carré is concerned to register how a new political ethos has affected MI6 rather than recreate schoolboy ethics. Both writers can observe social and political environments as well as any of the more self-conscious 'literary' authors. However, if 'the novel' depends upon innovation to remain 'alive', it must be admitted that such genre writing only occasionally achieves this.

THE POSTMODERN

As already suggested, description of the post-war British novel fits in with assessments of the novel in general, that is, the most significant event in its recent history is the displacement of realist and modernist modes by writing commonly termed 'postmodern' and, slightly later, 'magic realism'. In this time line modernism ousts realism some time at the beginning of the twentieth century, to be superseded in its turn by American postmodernism some time in the late 1950s/early 1960s, and by 'magic realism' in the late 1960s and early 1970s.[27]

This shift to a different mode only occurs in the British novel some time in the 1970s. The sense of belatedness may indeed be due to the fact that the British novel has at bottom remained attached to empirical reality. For the novel written in England, modernism was never so much in opposition to realism as in fact instantiating a new realism, with detailed psychological description replacing external social observation, and consequently available to the empirical tradition. Postmodernist writing requires a different ontological base-line from either social or psychological realism since it is the epistemological notion of reality which is at issue from the very outset. The American novel is seen to be more suited to postmodern modes since its own novel tradition is usually regarded to favour 'romance' rather than realism, and is therefore initially closer to narrative styles that are not dependent upon descriptions of familiar social events and environments. Thus, although writers in Britain from the 1950s onwards align themselves with either the realist pole or the experimental modernist pole of fiction, Andrzej Gasiorek in *Post-War British Fiction: Realism and After* (1995), maintains that the majority of British novelists have found a middle ground that renders such a division between 'realist' and 'experimental' redundant.

In addition to this view, it could also be said that although discussion of 'morality' is no longer fashionable in relation to the novel, since it smacks of Victorian didacticism, the attachment to some version of realism bespeaks a moral sense on the part of these writers which is often taken as absent (because also outmoded) from other fiction. It is true that a philosophical and political belief in 'realism' does not necessitate any particular type of fiction, as is sometimes claimed, but there does appear in the British novel a clear connection between a particular type of world we inhabit, one that is taken to be empirically verifiable, and the evaluation of moral behaviour. In the British novel the tradition is one where the novel is a laboratory for analysis of manners and mores within a liberal humanist framework, and it is this, as much as any empirical turn of mind, which constrains the British novel post Second World War to steer a middle course in reaction to modernist and postmodernist dominance. Gasiorek affirms that most British novelists were still intent on addressing a real world. Some of the writers he cites are Doris Lessing, V.S. Naipaul, George Lamming and Angus Wilson. Gasiorek is also prepared to find such middle ground in the work of Angela Carter, Graham Swift and other postmodern writers who are usually described as working predominantly outside the realist tradition.

Postmodern thought claims that the ability to represent reality is always compromised because reality is not 'out there' to be discovered and described, but is a construct of language and narration. If, however, there is a commitment to some version of reality on the part of all post-war British novels, even ones so compromised as the postmodern novels, this might be down to an empirical tradition which other literatures do not have or abide by, and would mark British fiction out from contemporary fiction elsewhere. Further, whilst there is an argument that American writers attenuated the extremes of modernist fiction by making it accessible to a general audience, in other words, F. Scott Fitzgerald's readable *The Great Gatsby* (1925) rather than James Joyce's difficult *Ulysses* (1922), the argument might be applied in reverse to postmodernism: that British postmodern fiction has attenuated the wilder excesses of American postmodern novels to make such a mode more accessible (the advantage of belatedness).

A good example is John Fowles's *The French Lieutenant's Woman* (1969) which was highly praised on its publication, and perhaps ushered in the possibility of a type of British novel that was both popular and postmodern. Set in the Victorian period, Charles Smithson is engaged to Ernestina Freeman, but captivated by Sarah Woodruff when he sees her standing alone at the end of Lyme Regis Cob. She is an outcast from the community because she is believed to have had an affair with a French sailor. Fowles juxtaposes this fraught tangle with disquisitions upon the nature of the Victorian period (Marx, Arnold, Darwin, prostitution, the Reform Acts, etc.), and the nature of history and narrative. It takes a knowing attitude to its own material and the process of writing a novel. The (in)famous Chapter Thirteen breaks the relatively straightforward narrative flow to demonstrate that it is fully aware of contemporary literary theory: 'I do not know. This story I am telling is all imagination. These characters I create never existed outside my own mind. . . . But I live in the age of Alain Robbe-Grillet and Roland Barthes; if this is a novel, it cannot be a novel in the modern sense of the word.'[28] The novel also supplies the reader with two endings, one happy, one sad. The questioning of the role of the author, the representation of characters as coherent entities, the relationship between fact and fiction, truth and narrative, are standard pointers for this type of novel, but its popularity has more likely depended upon its romantic element than its incorporation of metafictional self-questioning. It undoubtedly made some features of postmodern fiction workable for the British tradition. A.S. Byatt's 1990 novel *Possession*, enjoys a similar interplay to that of *The French Lieutenant's Woman* between past and present, literary theory and literary practice, whilst again using a strong romantic element to drive the narrative. In doing this, neither novel strays too far from the British realist tradition. The deconstructive seepage of separate worlds into each other, such as that of fact and fiction, history and plot, has since become commonplace: for instance in Peter Ackroyd's *Chatterton* (1987) and *Hawksmoor* (1985), Graham Swift's *Waterland* (1983), Julian Barnes's *Flaubert's Parrot* (1984), and the work of Angela Carter and Salman Rushdie. Bruce Chatwin's *The Songlines* (1987) uses the Aboriginal notion of time and space to connect apparently discontinuous cultures and ideas of world history.

Carter and Rushdie have felt least constrained by the literary tradition that ties the British novel to the empirical. Carter's penchant for the artificial and the grotesque, allied to her interest in de Sade and magic realism, has provided some of the most original writing. As early as her first novel, *Shadow Dance* (1966), one of Carter's themes is evident – the character Honeybuzzard manipulates other people much as a 'puppet master' might, and such control is obviously analogous to the role of the author. In addition, the use of a character who is both beautiful yet horribly scarred is a typical Carteresque touch.[29] Carter's feminist concerns became more evident in *The Passion of New Eve* (1977), exploring the constructed nature of gender. But her relationship with feminism, like that of Doris Lessing's, was one which always had a critical distance. Her reworkings of fairy stories and folk tales in *The Bloody Chamber* (1979) relies on de Sadean philosophy as much as feminist theory. In *Nights at the Circus* (1984) the influence of magical realism is also very much to the fore – the reader is never sure if the wings of the protagonist and *aeraliste* Fevvers are real or not – and at one point the novel makes a knowing reference to its own magical realist mode.[30] Carter's love of the carnivalesque and theatre, their liminal relationship with 'reality', was further explored in her last novel, *Wise Children* (1991), a tumbling narrative that rips its way through Shakespearean plots of mistaken identities and doubtful parentage. Carter has perhaps been the one writer who has created her own literary milieu over and beyond her sources.

Whether the same can be said of Salman Rushdie is another matter. His debt to Gabriel García Márquez is obviously great, as is his admiration for Laurence Sterne's *Tristram Shandy* (1759–67). Within this context his immensely ambitious works can appear laboured. *Midnight's Children* (1981), the book that brought Rushdie to international fame, deals with the consequences following on from Indian independence on 15 August 1947. The narrator Saleem Sinai is one of those children born on 'the stroke of midnight' of independence. He tells his family's story, constantly reminding the reader that the stories he himself tells are as much constructed as they are 'natural', and that there are thousands of such stories that go up to make the lives of all 'midnight's children'. In such a way is the folk history of India to be told, with family anecdotes charted alongside public historical events.[31] *Shame* (1983) has a similar imaginative trajectory, again working within the magical realist mode. This time Pakistan is the focal point, and the novel is particularly critical of the ruling elite: 'So-called Islamic "fundamentalism" does not spring, in Pakistan, from the people. It is imposed on them from above. Autocratic regimes find it useful to espouse the rhetoric of faith, because people respect that language, are reluctant to oppose it.'[32]

In retrospect, such comments appear to set the scene for the hostile reception of *The Satanic Verses* by Islamic regimes and sympathisers. Published in September 1988, and explicitly critical of Islam, it was banned in India in the following October, and there were protests in Britain which included 'book burning'. On 14 February 1989, the Ayatollah Khomeini of Iran proclaimed a *fatwa* (religious edict) against Rushdie:

> I would like to inform all the intrepid Muslims in the world that the
> author of the book entitled *The Satanic Verses*, which has been compiled,
> printed and published in opposition to Islam, the Prophet and the Koran,
> as well as those publishers who were aware of its contents, have been
> sentenced to death.
> I call on all zealous Muslims to execute them quickly. . . .[33]

From that day onwards Rushdie's life has been under threat, and indeed
some of those involved in publication of the book have been killed. Rushdie
apologised soon after the *fatwa* was declared (the apology was rejected) and
he later confirmed himself to be Muslim, to no avail. The whole affair
raised issues of censorship, blasphemy, 'the rise of fundamentalism', all of
which served to overshadow the book's literary worth. Along with Carter,
Rushdie has been one of the most crucial writers in opening up the British
novel to wider influences by demonstrating the possibilities of refusing
empiricism as the foundation for narrative.

'THERE'S NO SUCH THING AS SOCIETY . . .'

Whilst the South-East and parts of the Midlands benefited from policies
designed to make the British economy 'meaner and leaner' during the
Thatcher years (1979–90), the South-West, North of England, Scotland and
Wales bore the brunt of these stringent measures through huge increases in
unemployment. However, causal linking of novels and their styles to the
highly charged social context of the 1980s still requires some circumspection.

In particular Scotland produced some of the most interesting and inventive fiction within the Thatcher period. James Kelman's work has dealt with
the lives of (part of) the working classes. *The Busconductor Hines* (1984)
shows the strains on a Glasgow family unit – 'man woman and wean' –
living in a 'no-bedroomed' tenement. Rab Hines is frustrated by his job,
defiant and depressed by turns. An argument could be made that the ever-
present threat of bringing in one-man operated buses at the expense of
conductors typified the erosion of public services and a commitment to
anything called society, although it should also be noted that Hines is no
good at his job. In a typically bravura passage, Hines awaits the return of
his wife Sandra, desperately free-associating on theories of colour in order
to get a grip on the situation and his own mind:

> So what is to be done. The rude ticket dished from the pleasant machine
> while the replete suit of the colour bottle green on lucid days. He does hanker,
> however, after primaries. Let the reds also appear, and where are the blues.

It is the subtractives.
The magenta, the yellow the cyan. The black. It has to be the
black. To fuck with the white it's no good. The items to be being
produced.[34]

Alasdair Gray articulated a similar Scottish (Glasgow) harshness, this time
through a postmodern gothic narrative, in *Lanark: A Life in 4 Books* (1981,
revised 1985).[35] The book is split into four sections, and, in typical
postmodern fashion, starts at Book Three. Book Two's frontispiece is an
illustration incorporating the logo: 'Let Glasgow flourish by telling the
truth' and the novel is self-consciously designed to put Glasgow on the
map.[36] The central character/s, Lanark/Duncan Thaw finds himself flitting
between Glasgow and the fantastical city of Unthank, but ultimately this
latter hell is more a question of being an unpaid artist than anything else.
There are discourses on the centrality of money[37] and the belief that profit
is at the expense of the people,[38] but the book itself was clearly a long time
in the writing, with some of the material dating as far back as 1958. Its
contemporary relevance may well have been opportunistic chiming with
contemporary criticisms of monetarist economics. In one of the sections
the novel introduces footnotes and a list of sources from which its material
is derived. One of the notes claims: 'But the fact remains that the plots of
the Thaw and Lanark sections are independent of each other and cemented
by typographical contrivances rather than formal necessity. A possible
explanation is that the author thinks a heavy book will make a bigger
splash than two light ones.'[39]

The gothic and grotesque were familiar modes in the 1980s. One of the
most controversial was Iain Banks's *The Wasp Factory* (1984). The plot concerns an isolated patch of Scotland where Frank, a dysfunctional sixteen-
year-old, and his father, live together in disharmony. Frank, unbeknown to
anyone else, has been responsible for the death of three people. 'The wasp
factory' is a system of his own devising whereby certain future desired
outcomes are pre-determined, but the final choice is left to the contingency of a wasp's movements caught in the fatalistic mechanism. As with
Lanark, amidst the gothic humour it takes time out to make political points
about the regime the novel finds itself under: 'It has always seemed to me
that people vote in a new government not because they actually agree with
their politics but just because they want a change. Somehow they think
that things will be better under the new lot. Well, people are stupid. . . .'[40]
The novel is adept at suggesting political and philosophical depths without
bothering to explore them. The imminent return of Frank's mad brother
keeps the plot going, culminating in the revelation of Frank's twisted
childhood – he has been brought up as the wrong gender – as a possible
explanation for the humorous nastiness that pervades the novel.

With the rejection during the period of Conservative governance that there is such a thing as society, the turn to modes that prefer the socially atypical could be said to reflect this. Yet Ian McEwan, scriptwriter of the politically astute film *The Ploughman's Lunch* (1983), had already shown a fascination before the 1980s kicked in for the more perverse side of human natures in his first two short story collections, *First Love, Last Rites* (1975) and *In Between the Sheets* (1977), and in his first novel *The Cement Garden* (1978). In this novel two brothers and two sisters avoid being split up after the death of their mother by burying her body in cement. Incest gives the novel its sexual frisson, and it is usually the use of socially risqué material which is the most prominent feature of McEwan's earlier work. *The Comfort of Strangers* (1981), set in Venice and with echoes of Thomas Mann's *Death in Venice* and the film *Don't Look Now*, is a tale of psychosexual unease. Later work, such as *The Child in Time* (1987) about parental grief at the loss of their child, and *Black Dogs* (1992), about the enduring influence of Holocaust memories, suggest a shift in concerns.

Jeanette Winterson found use for the grotesque in *Sexing the Cherry* (1989). The central character is the gigantic Dog-Woman, who runs entertainments and looks after the foundling Jordan in London at the time of the Civil War. This is a novel firmly underwritten by a feminism that regards gender as constructed. It is wilfully ahistorical, and the fantastical elements of it, for example, the story of the Twelve Dancing Princesses, are overdetermined to show women coming out on top: one of the twelve princesses comments that they all lived happily after their marriages, 'but not with our husbands.'[41] It forms an interesting contrast with Fay Weldon's *The Life and Loves of a She-Devil* (1983). Both novels have a giantess as the central character and both decide to re-write the mythical trope of 'the princess' in a feminist language. For Winterson princesses remain much as they were, but live in an all-female utopia. Weldon's grotesque she-devil heroine decides that it is Mary Fisher, the princess who 'lives in a High Tower' and who has stolen her husband, who must be destroyed. However, the she-devil ends up having drastic plastic surgery, described with some gusto, in order to look exactly like Mary Fisher.

MARTIN AMIS

Looming large over the later part of this period has been the work and persona of Martin Amis. The son of Kingsley Amis, he showed an adolescent talent for humour in *The Rachel Papers* (1973), following a young man's attempts to get the girl of his fantasy, a type of humour which has stood him in good stead for set pieces in other works. *Dead Babies* (1975) shows a similar cruel satirical streak, targeting contemporary decadence with relish. The phrase 'dead babies' is shorthand for the kind of emotional blackmail people use and which is here ridiculed by a set of characters whose main activity is drug-taking. With *Success* (1978) Amis continued to map out the terrain of the modern male's psyche: basically, the getting of sex. It also seems prophetic of the 1980s self-image with its emphasis on money and power, yet this in itself shows the continuity across the two decades. The lives of two men are contrasted, one going from apparent success in all the necessary departments of life (women, money, social status, more women) to abject failure, whilst the other's life takes the opposite direction at his expense. The three books, when taken together, describe a type of male that later came to be defined as 'the new lad', quite at ease with his overt sexual interests and not to be cowed by politically-correct feminisms.

With *Other People* (1981) Amis demonstrated his interest in the thriller genre, which he would return to in *London Fields* (1989) and *Night Train* (1997), as well as the complexities of narrative voicing. A novel that has left most readers simply bemused, *Other People* remains one of Amis's most challenging narrative experiments. A female tries to regain her memory, which involves more than mere recall; it also requires the comprehension of what 'self' is amidst the role of narrative and interpersonal relationships (the 'other people' of the title). *Money* (1984) continued the fascination with all things financial and sexual, although this time Amis drew more upon his acquaintance with America. The comedy is based on excess and farce, and fitted easily into the dominant critique of the greedy 1980s.

VOICE PROJECTIONS

British novelists have become adept at using once-foreign modes of writing, none more so than Louis de Bernières, whose *The War of Don Emmanuel's Nether Parts* (1991) and *Captain Corelli's Mandolin* (1994) are consummate achievements firmly within the Marquez style: a military man dominates in a cruel world of fantastic happenings and immense beauty. The latter novel is set on Cephallonia in 1941, and maintains a realistic base. It might be expected that such anchorings will continue to function within the British novel, with notions of realism continuing to pull fiction into the dominant tradition, whilst experimental extremes define its limits and expand its possibilities. The growth of creative writing courses in Higher Education in Britain will undoubtedly continue to produce highly polished items such as Kazuo Ishiguro's *The Remains of the Day* (1990), a novel which makes the life of a dutiful, sycophantic/stoic servant synonymous with Britain's policy of appeasement in the 1930s. These courses will also, hopefully, pave the way for more adventurous narratives.

Currently the market for overtly 'literary' fiction depends much on the success of first novels, which in themselves tend to depend upon fictionalised autobiography (or the appearance of autobiography) and thus the sense of new 'voices' coming through. A typical example would be Esther Freud's *Hideous Kinky* (1992). It covers a childhood spent in Morocco with a hippie mother, told from the point of view of her five-year-old daughter: it is well-crafted, engaging, witty, and it has a distinct style without being flashy or wilful.

Novels recording the experience of women in a changing social environment will continue to be popular, whether mediated through straightforward realist modes or newer narrative styles. Middle-brow fiction, such as that of Anita Brookner and Stanley Middleton, with their well-trodden grounds of moderately dissatisfied lives, will retain their audiences. Marginalised areas of experience will continue to find the novel an excellent medium of expression: Timothy Mo's *Sour Sweet* (1982) describes the life of Hong Kong Chinese in London, and Jeanette Winterson's *Oranges are not the Only Fruit* (1985) is a lesbian *Bildungsroman* which works powerfully through disjunctions rather than the psychological continuity prevalent in realist texts.

This curiosity to read about 'new' areas of experience, which has always been a feature of the novel, will also induce the documentation of whatever is 'new' in society, particularly 'sub-cultural' experience: for example Irvine Welsh's *Trainspotting* (1993) and the subsequent rash of novels based on drug- and rave-culture. British novelists will also continue to provide perceptive, solid, social commentary – Doris Lessing's *The Good Terrorist* (1985); and imaginative historical reconstructions – Timothy Mo's *An Insular Possession* (1986) about the Opium Wars, and Pat Barker's First World War trilogy, *Regeneration* (1991), *The Eye in the Door* (1993), and *The Ghost Road* (1995). Comic writing remains popular and strong and another means of social commentary and entertainment: for example the work of David Lodge, William Boyd and Beryl Bainbridge.

For this essayist, Scottish writing continues to provide some of the most interesting reading. The Scottish poet Alison Fell's lyrical *The Pillow-Boy of the Lady Onogoru* (1994), in which an eleventh-century Japanese concubine can only achieve orgasm through the stories told to her by the blind servant hidden from her lover, may inaugurate a new genre: postmodern erotica. Another Scottish writer, A.L. Kennedy has aroused considerable enthusiasm with her quiet blend of magical realism in *So I Am Glad* (1995), where the emotionally traumatised Jennifer Wilson becomes involved with a man claiming to be Cyrano de Bergerac. The mysterious figure who drifts into her household may be a casualty of the Conservative's 'care in the community' policy whereby people with psychiatric problems were turned out of institutions into 'society'; yet his body bears the scars of a thousand duels and he speaks seventeenth-century French: the novel embraces both possibilities.[42] This preference for domestic scenarios on the cusp of realism, instead of the grand vistas and literary pyrotechnics that have been on offer from Carter, Rushdie and Winterson, may define the mode and content for fiction in the near future. Further than this, I would not like to predict which voices the British novel will offer up next.

NOTES

1. The majority view, as taken by D.J. Taylor's *After the War: The Novel and England since 1945* (London, 1994). Malcolm Bradbury takes an opposite view in *The Modern British Novel* (London, 1993), pp. 454–5. Patricia Waugh's *Harvest of the Sixties: English Literature and Its Background 1960–1990* (London, 1995), despite its over-emphasis on the 1960s as the source of all subsequent literary culture, is an excellent overview that does not, however, enter into this debate.
2. 'New literatures in English' has replaced the older term of 'Commonwealth fiction'.
3. This is discussed in detail in Harry Ritchie's *Success Stories: Literature and the Media in England, 1950–1959* (London, 1988).
4. 'Anti-modernist' is David Lodge's phrase. The early reaction against modernism is discussed in Volume 2.
5. Alan Sillitoe, *Saturday Night and Sunday Morning* (London, 1994), p. 5.
6. Muriel Spark, *The Comforters* (London, 1963), p. 69.
7. Ibid., pp. 170, 191.
8. Compare the character Slothrop in Thomas Pynchon's *Gravity's Rainbow* (1973), who literally 'fragments' and disperses.
9. Ibid., p. 97.
10. Lawrence Durrell, *Balthazar* (London, 1991), p. 7.
11. Doris Lessing, *The Golden Notebook* (London, 1989), p. 14.
12. Wilson Harris, 'A Note on the Genesis of *The Guyana Quartet*', in *The Guyana Quartet* (London, 1985), p. 7.
13. Margaret Drabble, *A Summer Bird-Cage* (London, 1967), p. 30.
14. Ibid., epigraph to the novel.

15. Fay Weldon, *Down Among the Women* (London, 1973), p. 5.
16. Op. cit., p. 79.
17. Doris Lessing, *Briefing for a Descent into Hell* (London, 1971).
18. 'They seem all surface, and a rather dry, sparsely furnished, though elegant and mannered surface at that' is how Bernard Harrison summarises the view, which he proceeds to dismantle. 'Muriel Spark and Jane Austen' in Gabriel Josipovici (ed.), *The Modern English Novel: The Reader, The Writer and the Work* (London, 1976), pp. 225–51, p. 225.
19. A. Alvarez, *The New Poetry* (London, 1962), p. 23.
20. Martin Amis, *Time's Arrow or the Nature of the Offence* (London, 1992), p. 175.
21. Ian McEwan's *Black Dogs* (1992), is another case in point.
22. The earliest novel is Jean Rhys's *Voyage in the Dark* (1934), but Lamming's novel can more readily be seen as at the start of a group of such novels, for example Sam Selvon's *The Lonely Londoners* (1956). Linton Kwesi Johnson's *Dread Beat and Blood* (1975) shifts the focus onto the generation born in Britain to West Indian parents. See Kenneth Ramchand's Introduction to *The Lonely Londoners* (Harlow, Essex, 1985), pp. 3–21.
23. Jean Rhys, *Wide Sargasso Sea* (London, 1968).
24. Ibid., Introduction by Francis Wyndham, p. 10.
25. B.S. Johnson, 'Introduction to *Aren't You Rather Young to be Writing Your Memoirs?*', reprinted in *The Novel Today*, Malcolm Bradbury (ed.), First Edition (London, 1978), pp. 151–68, 158, 166.
26. Ibid., p. 163.
27. Magic realism is historically distinct from postmodernism, and is said to have emerged from Latin America in response to social and political conditions there, particularly military regimes, whereas postmodernism can be said to arise from a different set of factors (for example, but arguably, 'globalisation'). However, the two modes have features in common, especially in their belief that 'reality' is constructed and that narratives (including, most importantly, history) are the result of artifice and manipulation. The two might have a common ancestor in the work of Jorge Luis Borges (1899–1986), which further complicates the picture, as does the fact that a more immediate European tradition might be traced back to the work of Franz Kafka. Gabriel García Márquez's *One Hundred Years of Solitude*, first published in 1967, and translated into English in 1970, is usually taken to be the magical realist text *par excellence*.
28. John Fowles, *The French Lieutenant's Woman* (London, 1977), p. 85.
29. Angela Carter, *Shadow Dance* (London, 1994).
30. 'It could be said that, for all the peoples of this region, there existed no difference between fact and fiction; instead, a sort of magic realism.' Angela Carter, *Nights at the Circus* (London, 1985), p. 260.
31. Salman Rushdie, *Midnight's Children* (London, 1995).
32. Salman Rushdie, *Shame* (London, 1995), p. 251.
33. Reprinted from *Observer*, 19 Feb. 1989, in Lisa Appignanesi and Sara Maitland (eds.), *The Rushdie File* (London, 1989).
34. James Kelman, *The Busconductor Hines* (London, 1992), p. 104.
35. Alasdair Gray, *Lanark* (London, 1994).
36. Gray's wish to make Glasgow significant imitates what Joyce did for Dublin in *Ulysses*. In a different way, the same novel stands behind Kelman's *The Busconductor Hines*, Hines appearing as an up-dated Leopold Bloom.
37. Ibid., pp. 108–9.

38. Ibid., pp. 410–11.
39. Ibid., p. 493, n. 8.
40. Iain Banks, *The Wasp Factory* (London, 1990), p. 62.
41. Jeanette Winterson, *Sexing the Cherry* (London, 1996), p. 48.
42. A.L. Kennedy, *So I Am Glad* (London, 1995).

CHAPTER THREE

Popular Fiction

Michael Hayes

> Some time between the early fifties and the early seventies a 'cultural
> revolution' took place in Britain, so that both the physical face of society
> and its deeper emotional and intellectual attitudes were profoundly
> changed.[1]

Since 1956 that heterogeneous mass of easy reading called popular fiction
has come to occupy a new cultural position. No longer is it the despised
and raucous distant cousin of literature but a group of reading genres with
a problematic and variations of its own. In production terms it is no longer
the disreputable off-shoot of otherwise respectable publishing houses nor
the domain of sleazy back-street opportunists but an integral part of a
global entertainment industry. With that industry it shares not only development and production costs but also marketing and advertising strategies.

Aesthetically there are still, understandably, problems in identifying a
satisfactory discourse distinct from that still largely controlled by the literary
establishment and the universities. But the work of articulating appropriate
judgements across the variety that constitutes popular fiction is being for-
warded by academics such as Clive Bloom, Scott McCracken and Mary
Talbot, by critical series such as Insights and by discussion groups such as
the Association for Research in Popular Fiction.

A further result of the radical changes in perspective is that readership is
no longer presumed to be a passive, corruptible mass but is rightly seen as
a multiplicity of readerships with different motives, strategies and contexts
of reading.

Of course these perspectives are in part arbitrary, as Raymond Williams
has written:

> A culture, while it is being lived, is always in part unknown, in part
> unrealised. The making of a community is always an exploration.[2]

However communities of popular fiction readers have largely emerged from obloquy to be seen as constituencies of readers engaging in various species of reading. Relieved, very largely, of the need to see themselves as low-culture readers against high-culture readers of literature, the nature of their reading can be explored through a variety of disciplines.

The perspectives chosen for this discussion might be arbitrary but they are certainly not random. Reading itself is seen as the mostly private manifestation of a social act – in any reading we become part of a community of readers. Of community there are various accounts: Rousseau and Durkheim privileged the sharing of a repertoire of moral values, while Marx privileged economic necessity. It is interesting that with the breakdown of censorship in 1960 the paternalistic moralism that once characterised publishers has given way to the economics of the market place, a market place that in England has become decidedly Anglo-American and is inclusive of other media of entertainment. Fredric Warburg's book about publishing entitled *An Occupation for Gentlemen* (1959) epitomised its era but now sounds irresistibly quaint.

The very heterogeneity of fictions, while demanding a more theoretical approach in order to escape the peremptoriness of the individual example, serves to foreground dominant themes and images. In tracing the progress of these images the concerns of society can be seen as actively engaged in conflict with the powers that mediate the images. People no longer just buy what they are given but exercise choices to ensure they are given what they will buy. This is a transformation from the first half of the century when authority very largely prescribed, through a variety of social mechanisms, what fictions were appropriate.

But this notion of conflict must not itself be used to over-simplify the process of 'trading images'. That once important figure and creator of images, the author, might have been reported dead by Barthes, a report accepted by many, but it is a death greatly exaggerated. Italo Calvino might have declared that we no longer need authors, when we can programme computers with narrative grammars, feed in lexicons of characters and events and generate all the stories we need. But his own work determines we interpret his assertion as ironic. Authors might no longer be the convenient epitome of inspirational or acceptable values but then neither are popular writers simply tour leaders of package holidays of the imagination. Catherine Cookson does not accept the past as unproblematic, Frederick Forsyth affirms the human in the interstices of technology and Minette Walters troubles the nature-nurture argument.

This is not to make exaggerated claims for popular novelists and pulp fictionists but to assert their claims on the attention of anyone interested in identifying the cultural role of popular fiction during the second half of the twentieth century.

MARKET STALL TO GLOBAL MARKET

In *Late Capitalism* Ernest Mandel identifies capitalism through the nineteenth and twentieth centuries as falling into three distinct phases. The first, market capitalism, is followed by monopoly capitalism and in our own time succeeded by consumer capitalism or the era of multinational corporations. In adopting Mandel's paradigm Frederic Jameson puts forward his own parallel aesthetic model consisting of realism, modernism and finally postmodernism.[3]

Where modernism resisted the pervasive influence of capitalism Jameson sees postmodernism as complicit with it. With reference to popular fiction the aesthetic of modernism continues to view it as the instrument of ideological indoctrination. Postmodernism unresistingly embraces the popular and surrenders to the hegemony of capitalist power. The problem with such grand narratives is that they ignore or suppress a multiplicity of narratives some of which locate very awkwardly in relation to the main thesis.

In economic terms there are various inter-connected narratives. In the first place during this period publishing moves from the control of the 'publisher as an entrepreneur of the intellect and a purveyor of knowledge and culture'[4] with roots in the nineteenth century, to publisher as international conglomerate overseen by a board of directors and run by managers. Secondly, there is a move away from the book list as the sole or even the main business of the company, as was often still the case in the 1960s, to a position where the book list is only one of many businesses and not the most important. If we take the News Corporation Limited of Rupert Murdoch, in 1981 it purchased 40 per cent of Collins, in the late 1980s it bought the other 60 per cent, and the American publisher, Harper & Row. In spite of owning two major publishing houses in 1997 books accounted for only 6 per cent of a business that owned, among others, Bart Simpson, *The Times* and a sheep farm. One of Murdoch's rivals, the London-based Pearson plc, bought stakes in Longman's in 1968 and Penguin in 1971 which by 1996 included the American Publishers Putnam and Viking.

A characteristic of this drive towards corporate mergers was what might be termed the synergy effect. Publishers were merging with the new electronic communications industry. For publishers the advantage was access to capital for development, for the communications industry, the cachet of respectability and an entrée into the knowledge market. The worst nightmares of the intelligentsia seemed to be coming to life – booksellers' lists were bound to go 'down market'.

It has not happened. Popular fiction might have a high profile through publicity-conscious authors like Jeffrey Archer, celebrity authors like Joan

Collins and the popularity consequent on TV serialisations of Catherine Cookson's books, but at the balancing of the ledgers it is still the list as a whole that determines the success of the business.

What the interest in corporate mergers did was raise the consciousness of publishers that they were engaged in a business. With this in mind division of the fiction market between high and low came to be seen as increasingly irrelevant. Books, like any other product, had to justify their existence by market share and when Jeffrey Archer sold the television serialisation right of *Not a Penny Less, Not a Penny More* for one penny exactly he knew the attendant exposure would more than repay the apparent gamble.

As fiction comes to be seen as more and more closely tied to big business the prophets of 'commodity fetishism' award themselves honorary doctorates in perspicacity. Susan Hill gets a million pounds to write a sequel to *Rebecca* called *Manderley* (1992) and in that same year what is described as 'the ultimate naff novel',[5] Susannah James's *Love Over Gold*, is published. It reveals the lives of a yuppie couple who featured in a series of Gold Blend coffee advertisements – the book of the advert. The critical assumption has to be that the 100,000 copies of James's book that Transworld published were better not published at all, and that if a writer even as respected as Susan Hill gets a million pounds for a book it has to be inferior. Behind these assumptions are propositions such as big business driving out the smaller, innovative publisher and that fewer books means better books.

Publishing always did, and still does, offer scope for the 'shoestring operator': someone with very little capital but plenty of determination. In the late 1980s a young author from Bristol published his own detective novel in the form of a newspaper which he then brought to London and sold on Paddington Station.[6] One is reminded of the tradition invoked by Walter Benjamin's article 'Detective Novels, Read on Journeys',[7] the nineteenth-century German publisher who marketed novels in a newspaper format and W.H. Smith's beginnings with railway bookstalls.

As regards 'fewer books not better' which premises the good driving out the bad, it seems highly unlikely. After book censorship collapsed in 1960 in the wake of the *Lady Chatterley's Lover* trial, even literary tradition was subverted in the interests of saucy reading matter. In 1964 the Compact Library published *Memoirs of a Coxcomb* 'By the renowned author of *Fanny Hill*' (in letters that dominate the cover) 'John Cleland', with of course a respectable introduction by the intriguingly named Peter Lingham PhD. In 1965 Luxor Press published *The Most Delectable Nights of Straparola* 'An Audacious Selection of Rare Intimate Tales of Passion' culled from the sixteenth-century *Piacevoli Nolti* and introduced by the equally intriguingly named Rufus Robespierre.

The point being made (somewhat facetiously) is that reading is a multi-farious activity served by a great variety of publishers large and small. The mergers during the 1960s and 1970s were to solve problems endemic to the business. These problems were, and still are, centred on scale of production and promotion. The scale of production is crucial, as the numbers of outlets for publishers' remainders will attest. Fortunately for book lovers 'remaindering' has very little to do with content. It concerns numbers published, numbers sold and what to do with the rest. By becoming bigger publishers are always hoping to achieve economics of scale, control of their inventories and the advantages of a broad base for marketing.

In pursuit of these goals we find political figures such as Douglas Hurd and Edwina Currie along with the foreign correspondent Gerald Seymour and newspaper proprietor Eddie Shah all filling space on booksellers' shelves; even television gardener Alan Titchmarsh has been used to fertilise the rows of fiction. But celebrity fiction along with TV series tie-ins and fictionalised accounts of world events, such as the atom bomb, are no guarantee of sales. Each book is a one-off.

There are three main ways in which the trade attempts to overcome the uniqueness of books. Publishers, such as Mills & Boon, become identified with a certain kind of fiction. If they maintain a good pricing policy and have strict control of their list they maintain a successful market position. Since 1904 they have been filling a market niche for romantic fiction which is maintained by rigorous control. Of course they have had to change with the times, but always by expanding their output rather than by neglecting their traditional market. There are now three levels of romance fiction catering for traditional through to sexually explicit romance. Their instructions to authors, that are freely available to any aspirant, are not only explicit in terms of numbers of words, balance of direct and indirect speech and description of incident, but are also given in audio-tape format. The success of the Mills & Boon imprint is identification with a certain kind of fiction and responsiveness to changes in the readership.

Once a book becomes a best-seller then both the author and the book each individually become 'money in the bank'. Eric Ambler made his name in 1936 with *The Dark Frontier*[8] published by Hodder & Stoughton. His last thriller so far was *The Care of Time* published in 1981. During all that time his name was synonymous with a certain kind of readability. Just so Jack Higgins, Ruth Rendell and Barbara Cartland are virtually guaranteed a certain level of sales. In the same way their books with their particular 'take' on the genre are followed by imitations which increasingly are given similar identifying jacket designs. No longer is it good enough to market 'yellow jackets',[9] now even the style of design through colours, images and lettering bears a remarkable family resemblance. When booksellers believe that choices are made in seconds anything which draws attention, even blank covers and cut-out covers, is worth trying.

This increased targeting of market sectors is a result of the professionalisation of the business of publishing. Until 1972 there was no bestseller list, although one had existed in America since the 1890s. Even then it was not instituted by publishers but by the *Sunday Times*. The success of the venture was followed in 1977 when the Publishers Association itself formed a Statistics Panel.[10] Its express purpose was the generating, from publishers themselves, of more precise figures of performance in various categories, so superseding the rather too general figures produced by the Board of Trade in the *Business Monitor*.

Such quantitative measures obscured popular fiction under such categories as 'Mass-Market Paperbacks', which included among others both children's and adult books, and 'General Books' which also included children's and adult books. The need for more precise data has for twenty years been filled by Alex Hamilton's list of fast-sellers, produced for the *Guardian* (last list of the millennium, Saturday 9 January 1999). The list gives details of imprint, format, price and total sales. Such details as the almost permanent residence of Catherine Cookson and Dick Francis on the list among the Americans like John Grisham (number one) is useful to the trade but equally important for grounding academic studies in accurate, quantitative data.

In the late 1950s publishing was in the hands of gentlemen with the occasional rogue for flavour, at the end of the millennium it is in the hands of big business, with the occasional rogue to be savoured.

FICTIONS GALORE

Probably the most difficult area of the publishing business is distribution and marketing. The Leavisite and Frankfurt school objection to mass culture was that it was produced by a culture industry operating under monopoly conditions, the result being that popular culture is everywhere identical with only the details endlessly interchanged to create the illusion of difference.[11] If we carry the analogy into the present day we might claim that Dillons and Waterstones are supermarkets of popular fiction. The maroon and gold lettering of Waterstones together with the characteristic layout of shelves and display tables all betray a corporate image. Since retail price maintenance was abandoned in 1995 we even get 10 per cent off select items and 'buy 2 get 1 free' offers. In the 1980s the very ridiculousness of the idea of 'Buy *Ulysses* and get *Finnegans Wake* absolutely FREE' still betrayed the high/low culture divide: not any more. If five thousand 'units' of *Ulysses* could be shifted with a clear profit margin only diminished 25 per cent to account for a free copy of *Finnegans Wake* then the 'product' would get display table space. If a 'product' moves give it shelf space commensurate with profitability.

The twentieth-century journey through popular fiction which the present series has allowed has seen a change in focus from 'penny dreadful' to 'profit margin'. And that alteration in nomenclature signals a far more profound change. It is now the classics which are in the bargain basement, following the Wordsworth imprint at 99p and Penguin who offer Jane Austen through to H.G. Wells at less than £2.00, we have texts reasonably priced not by content but by the dictates of a mainly student market. Literature has finally become a genre of fiction with its own associated reading practices and demands on the attention particular to itself. The business of fiction now offers greater variety than at any time during the last half century.

But any profound change is marked by an innate conservatism. When printing was invented the first books produced were the established reading of the time, for example Boccaccio, Boethius and Chaucer. Twentieth-century popular reading is marked through all the changes by the remarkable continuity of genres; the romance, the detective story, the thriller and science fiction all continue. Of course some genres have become less significant. Religious fiction which was so prominent in the very early years is less prominent.[12] New genres have emerged in their own right – horror fiction and science fantasy now occupy dedicated spaces in most bookshops. Even where there is apparent continuity we find quite radical new directions emerging and each of these changes and evaluations relates to the cultural context of its inception.

Probably the most despised genre is the romance, in spite of its subject being the most significant expression of our lives. We have no control over our birth, can only delay or sadly precipitate the inevitability of death, but the nature of our close relationships with others, however culturally bound, is our own choice. The existence of the romance is coterminous with the very beginnings of prose fiction, such as Samuel Richardson's *Pamela or Virtue Rewarded* (1740); and its present distribution through Mills & Boon is unrivalled: translation of titles into twenty languages and distribution in over one hundred countries. Following the destruction of the Berlin Wall the publishers distributed over three quarters of a million books free to the East Germans alone. Of this particular segment of the market Mills & Boon claim a 60 per cent share which they have maintained since taking over Silhouette in 1985.

Romance fiction accounts for some 35 per cent of the total paperback fiction sales. Why then does its down-market image still persist? Could it be because less than 1 per cent of readership is male? Could it be because Mills & Boon's avowed aim is to provide fantasy within the realms of possibility? Could it be because, as Walter Nash says of popular fiction generally, that it is outside the critical, rational and cognitive? Could it be because it presents a traditional image 'that in order to be loved one has to be young and beautiful'?[13] As the song says 'Keep young and beautiful if you want to be loved.'

Belabouring the point in relation to romance fiction is because it is an archetypal example. The image of what it is presumes to subsume all individual examples. But it is not so, actual examples offer a wide range of difference. The prepositional content may be broadly similar with girl meets boy, they fall in love, difficulties arise, they overcome them and marry. But the intentions of the texts are various. For example even the degree of explicitness with which sexual activity is dealt with has led to Mills & Boon giving a three-part colour coding to its books from very explicit to traditionally coy. We have other writers, like Fay Weldon, who openly admit to describing sex graphically as a means of freeing women from received norms of sexual behaviour.

Arising out of the new openness are imprints, such as the pioneer Black Lace, labelled 'Erotic fiction for women'. While the ideal of heterosexual love is still finally maintained the books do portray homosexual experimentation in a non-judgemental environment. The major feature of romance fiction is its articulation of the self-in-relation, the language of the heroines like their sexuality focuses not on the autonomous self but on the self and others. The preponderance of dialogue that is a common feature of popular fiction is a means of empowering readers while at the same time encouraging social stability. As sub-genres, such as medical romances and 'sex and shopping', emerge they open up new frames of reference. They evolve in response to cultural change but finally they maintain through a slow evolution the ideological system which operates in society.

This defence of the ideological is more fully exploited in family sagas where the subject matter extends beyond the inter-personal to the realms of family, work and the law. Where the tendency was to explore middle-class life, in other words the classes that predominantly produced authors, the post-second world war sagas have very much included the working class. The symbiosis with television soaps, particularly the influence of *Coronation Street*, has encouraged settings both working-class and regional. The back streets of Liverpool, the North-East and London's East End are no longer the preserve of working-class intellectuals but subject matter for popular writers like Helen Forrester, Maisie Mosco and Catherine Cookson.

While not historical novels the family sagas do go back in time, giving utterance to 'the forgotten voices' so readily marginalised by the grand narratives of history.

A whole new sense of history arose particularly in the 1980s, no doubt heightened by the experiences of that decade. It was manifest nationally in the heritage industry, individually with interest in family trees, and socially by the popularity of local history. In fiction more and more genres are colouring their narratives with often detailed and expert historical contexts, among the most notable being Cadfael the medieval monk detective of Shrewsbury.

The classic detective story tells of transgression, usually through murder, put to rights by the solving of enigmas. Mostly they are set contemporaneously. The Victorian detectives were those written about in Victorian times. In the 1930s Jeffrey Farnol's detective who was a Bow Street Runner was an exception and the tales are as much historical thrillers as detective stories. Cadfael is part of an interest in the medieval that we, like the early Victorians, identify as the uncertain source of our modern world, its economy, technology, language and national identity. The criminal transgressions are often for complex motives. We recognise that they take place in a world that for all its difference is much like ours.

In *Faith in Fakes* Umberto Eco suggests that the return in the 1980s to the middle ages is an attempt to renegotiate the beginnings of capitalism. Certainly it mirrors the Victorian attempt to see the period as the source of the present. Charles Read's *The Cloister and the Hearth* is both a model exploration as well as popular fiction, showing as it does the breakdown of the medieval world and the opening of the renaissance.

In some respects the abbey with its hierarchical structure and quietly ordered lives could be the country house of the classic detective story. But unlike those tales it is in fact more open to the world – official visits from political and religious authorities, vagabonds, delinquency of all kinds, welfare and unemployment, and the sexual abuse of women and children all figure to disturb the hours. Cadfael with his crusader past and knowledge of the medicinal effects of herbs is of the monastery but also apart, not only unravelling the puzzles but, by acting as intercessory between conflicting parties, reconciling them 'through considered and appropriate life choices concerning marriage and employment.'[14]

Not only are the texts open to the contemporary world but themselves re-enter that world through various means. When the series was first launched in the late 1970s it was not among the best-sellers. After the international success of Umberto Eco's *The Name of the Rose* its re-launch in paperback proved it was a ready-made follow-on best-seller. This was then capitalised on by a series of television specials featuring the star actor

Derek Jacobi. The best-selling status of the new edition created attention for sites featured in the books. Edith Pargiter, the real name of Ellis Peters, allowed appeals for the support of Shrewsbury Abbey's restoration fund to be appended to the back of the books. The tourist board seized the opportunity to market Shropshire, a venture taken over and accelerated by television money, which has produced the Shrewsbury Quest, a theme park complete with Brother Cadfael's herbarium and Ellis Peters's study.

The other direction in which the detective story has opened up is by exploring the psychopathology of murderers. One of the first books dealing with the mind of a murderer was Patrick Hamilton's *Hangover Square* (1941). But it was some time before the investigation of the damaged human lives that lead to murder was such as prompted Rabbi Julia Neuberger to say, in bestowing the Gold Dagger Award to Minette Walters for *The Scold's Bridle* (1995), that it represented 'the best form of moral and philosophical debate'.[15]

Another way in which popular fiction expresses its purposefulness is by adapting to new circumstances, which include changes in the landscape of fiction and changes in cultural climate. Possibly the most important characteristic of urbanised, technological societies is the sense of powers unseen. Decisions are made and we do not know by whom or even what implications they have for our lives. Horror fiction, spy thrillers and even, developing out of detective fiction, crime thrillers all deal with the unease of people who live in close proximity to virtual strangers within a society controlled by we know not whom. As Bloom says,

> gothic writing may [also] be seen to be social disturbance thereby questioning technological, scientific and social norms as well as class relations in a way unavailable to realist fiction.[16]

Horror emphasises the vulnerability of the human body and the fragility of the human psyche. Various explanations have been given to explain both the age-old appeal of being frightened and the sources of horror in particular writers. The classic account is Freud's essay on 'The Uncanny' where he proposes as a feature of 'uncanniness' (*unheimlichkeit*) that the fiction reader is led into intellectual uncertainty as to whether s/he is encountering a real or a fantastic world. By withholding information which would allow a rational decision and so a secure view as to the reality or artifice of the fictional world anxiety is protracted.[17]

As Bloom suggests, there are two possible outcomes. One is the restoration of the status quo, the other is to continue the anxiety, so deferring resolution. It is characteristic of the late twentieth century that occasions for resolution seem to reside in the exercise of power and a false closure which in itself creates further anxiety. The atom bomb has been held in check by bigger and more dangerous bombs, the doubts about genetically engineered foods struggle for a hearing against big business's powers of concealment.

The imaginative space that horror occupies has two sources. The gothic side develops out of man's metaphysical relationship with the world, that world of spirits, religions and metamorphoses that have been used in an attempt to rationalise our position in an unpredictable world. Religious fiction as a major genre began to diminish in the early twentieth century but the codes of religious writing continue to inform much of our horror fiction. Clive Barker's books can in one respect be viewed as post-modernist religious texts deploying Ovidian transformations, medieval demonology and nineteenth century spiritualism, all with a sub-text of moral argument.

The other source of horror that stresses our physical vulnerability relates to 'newsworthiness', to plagues, diseases and physical violations that we learn about from television, newsprint and the Internet. The rats, face-destroying epidemics and untameable diseases are disturbing because reality spawns the fiction but fiction creates the signifying practices that allow the expression of horror.

Probably nowhere is this late-century ambivalence between fact and fiction, between genre, gender and national boundaries more marked than in the popular treatment of serial killers. The idea of the 'motiveless' crime puts the perpetrators outside the texture of social connections: their crimes bring no familial, financial or positional gain. Derek Raymond's 'factory' novel *Dead Man Upright* (1990) is a story of detection and a thriller with elements of horror. Thomas Harris's *Silence of the Lambs* (1988) is read as avidly in England as in America and Jamie Gumb the serial killer desires, like Ed Gein, to transform himself into a parody of womanhood.

The enigma of serial killings is the revenge of the disenfranchised on the social body whose norms of communication exclude the killers. Fiction undertakes to re-define language to include the irrational, the unthinkable – real crimes inhabit the signifiers of fiction. But it is a fiction that entails the possibility of our own random, motiveless murder.

CONSUMING PASSIONS

The tremendous increase in availability of popular fictions over the last half century, combined with the expansion in further and higher education has led to a radical overhaul of ideas about how people read. The notion that all readers of popular fiction are either 'escapists' or seekers after 'cheap thrills' has very decidedly had to make way for a more realistic account.

But while there have been some attempts, like those of Janice Radway and Bridget Fowler, at ethnologies of reading there have been far too few such investigations. The essential problem, as Ien Ang discusses in *Desperately Seeking an Audience* (1991), is that the discursive construction of 'an audience' in no way constitutes the multiplicity of social experiences that 'the audience' brings. If that is true of her television audience it is even more true of the reading audience engaged in a series of individual reading acts each contextualised, as Bourdieu points out, by a range of social, educational and cultural differences.

We are not without empirical data which has improved greatly over the last half century. Publishers keep more extensive records, libraries have had to keep better records in order to pay royalties to authors whose books are most frequently borrowed. Further the computerising of library loan systems allows most areas to publish detailed records of holdings of individual libraries and the rate of borrowings in each genre. Since postal codes are now commonly used to identify socio-economic areas for advertising putting together the two pieces of information, borrowing and income, would reveal patterns of reading preferences.

The range of statistics in relation to readers and their reading is enormous, but while it gives interesting overviews it does not reveal what is happening when an individual reads a particular book in a particular context. The investigations of reading can be subsumed under four headings. Ethnographic approaches have already been mentioned, secondly linguistic approaches consider the reader as a language user who in reading fiction is engaged in a particular kind of discourse. Thirdly, traditional literary criticism in adapting to popular texts as well as adjusting to new theoretical positions looks at how texts inscribe readers and finally response theories looking at popular reading as a species of popular culture investigate the positions readers take up in relation to texts.

The linguist Mary Talbot writes that 'a reader, just like any language-user, is an active agent and simultaneously unknowingly constituted in the act of using language.'[18] This idea has already been touched on in relation to serial killers but another genre worth considering is the reading of science fiction and science fantasy. Here the propositional content of the writing is imaginary so its relation to present culture is problematic. Given that 'science fiction is enormously popular – it accounts for one in ten books sold in Britain',[19] the nature of the discourse and its function is of particular interest. The discourse itself is 'natural', but the spatio-temporal and causal logic is subject to variation through the operations of science and technology or, in the case of fantasy, magic. This ability to vary some aspect of the world, whether natural, social or technological, puts the 'neatness' of the discourse under pressure so writing a critique of language. By posing situations of redefinition we are forced to consider the nature of language and, in order to rescue its propositional meaning, to accept its symbolic existence.

In J.G. Ballard's *Crash* (1973) the nature of the erotic is problematised in order to force a critical re-thinking of its meaning. By altering the eroticised object from human to technological, the car, all the associations of the 'erotic' are called into question. By foregrounding components such as control, disfigurement, power and violence and demonstrating their teleology as a sterile wasteland Ballard is questioning not only technology but also our cultural verification of the concept of the erotic. If eroticism is to be maintained as an attribute enhancing our humanity then its propositional content has to be continually and warily re-contextualised in our changing culture.

The third group of theorists dealing with readers and their reading derives from the areas of traditional literary criticism and cultural theory. Here all texts as well as cultural objects and functions are seen as the product and transmitter of ideology. Popular texts are scrutinised from Marxist or feminist perspectives, strategies deployed are structuralist or psychoanalytic and not surprisingly each text appropriately renders up the anticipated secrets. Deconstruction opened up texts to a multiplicity of readings but still leaves open the question of how readers are inscribed in their reading.

Taking from Bourdieu the idea of cultural capital we can begin to see how for any particular group of readers that multiplicity is narrowed to a handleable range of possibilities. An interesting case is spy fiction whose hero is the voyeur isolated from all but a few and dubious human contacts residing in a web of enigmatic interconnections. Through this web the spy must negotiate a way towards knowledge which can be exchanged for power by channelling that knowledge to one side or the other.

The reading process enacts the narrative, 'the reader, alone and with restricted knowledge, shadows the protagonist.'[20] The reader's relationship with the text will be determined by the cultural capital s/he brings to it. The games played by the genre are all part of opening the gates to knowledge. The interrogations by both supposedly friendly and opposing sides, the fights, the cracking of codes, all defer the pleasure of solution and most important of all is 'the human factor', the individual weakness that can negate the logical structures of knowledge and power. The uneasy balance of ideology and narrative finally resides with the reader who out of the matrix of texts and codes must rescue a self.

The fourth area of reader research is drawn largely from communication theory. Here the interest is in the position the viewer or reader occupies in relation to the text: readers are seen to acquiesce, to resist or to negotiate.

Popular fiction affords opportunities for either social reproduction or social change but that opportunity can be resisted by the reader. Even the most conservative of texts can be carnivalised by readers generating their own rhythms within the text. Roland Barthes in *The Pleasure of the Text* (1976) likens such transgressive readings, such as defiance of authority, to the spectacular jumping on stage to tear the clothes off the stripper. Strategies, which he calls tmesis, such as jumping from passage to passage, eliding 'boring' passages and dwelling on favoured passages defy the monolithic authority of the text which surrenders itself to the reader.

POPULAR FICTION: *THE LEGACY*

As late as 1990 Winfried Fluck can write that failure in the study of popular texts is due to 'the lack of inner disciplinary progress within the field itself.'[21] The extraordinary developments in publishing, ranges of available fiction and greater awareness of reading practices had not been matched by the development of an aesthetic. Instead the progress from marginalisation to socio-cultural study of the popular almost reluctantly included print fictions – Carol M. Thurston's excellent piece on 'Popular Historical Romances',[22] took ten years from acceptance to publication.

Given the flowering of popular fiction studies in the 1990s it seems appropriate to use this case study as a prolegomenon to an aesthetic. Three propositions underlie the enquiry:

(a) whatever can be articulated or accomplished with language can be explored in fiction;
(b) the imaginative world of fiction links, however tenuously, through language to reality;
(c) given the right conditions the fictional world can become part of consciousness.

In other words popular fiction is a matrix of intertextual inclusions which can mimic their prior uses or exceptionally, to borrow from Wallace Stevens, create a new consciousness.

The method is first to identify the various intertextual constituents, second to comment on their function and finally to consider their motivation or, paraphrasing Mikhail Bakhtin, their artistic arrangement.

The book is *The Legacy* by Mary Lide published by Grafton Books in 1991. The cover consists of a coastline with rocks and old-fashioned fishing boats, foregrounded is a young woman wearing a shawl and a straw hat, old-fashioned but reminiscent of the 1920s rather than earlier. On the upper half of the cover in fashionable Day-Glo red (but not extravagantly embossed) is the title with the author's name in white letters above. Opposite the girl's face is an explanatory motto: 'An unforgettable story of love, loss and family feud' tells us that it is a family saga set against a background of socio-legal constraints.

Inside the cover we learn that the author is from Cornwall, graduated in history at Oxford and divides her time between Cornwall and America, having lived in France, Denmark and Italy. This international background together with qualifications as an historian establish her right to deploy the discourses within which the book exists. Almost at a glance we have the author's provenance established and a correlative entitlement to authenticity. We are in the terrain of Thomas Hardy, Eden Philpotts and, specific regions apart, the fiction of Catherine Cookson and Maisie Mosco.

In the foreword the narrator introduces himself as a retired barrister, the bachelor Paul Cradock. He establishes his right to narrate on the basis of his 'legal training that prompted me to keep a record of what I say' (p. 5). As the tale progresses he becomes more involved with the protagonists until at the end he actually plays a crucial role in the unfolding of the story.

The tale starts on May Day 1912, 'the whole of Tregaran was in fête' (p. 10), a local festival called 'Calling of the Pilchard Home'. The authenticity of both narrator and tale is established by reference to Frazer's *The Golden Bough*, a famous anthropological work in which the festival is 'mentioned briefly'. This reference is clearly intended to project the imaginative world onto a narrative of true events in our consciousness. But I could find no reference to pilchards nor does the reference to Frazer's 'book' ring true. The work originally appeared in parts intermittently between 1890 and 1915 and the one-volume 'book' did not appear until 1922. A narrator is entitled, as part of his persona to be mistaken or wrong – as the story progresses he is often mistaken in his own motives – but to be uncertain about so definite a reference, however marginal to this story, is motiveless and confusing.

Other voices then enter the narrative through direct speech and standard English, Cockney and Cornish dialect, even an example of Cornish. As an upper middle-class professional Cradock's natural affiliation would be with the Tregarans, the gentry who give their name to the village. Opposed to them are the Tregarns, the dispossessed leaders of the community who speak in Cornish dialect. The solitary Cockney voice is Cradock's manservant Hodges who comes with him in retirement.

The story is a Cornish Romeo and Juliet with the dialect, albeit highly conventionalised, underscoring both class and moral differences. The

Tregarans consist of the father Michael, self-important and pompously referred to as the Colonel, and his wife Evelyn, a scheming woman who married for position. Of their two sons Nigel and John she favours the elder, Nigel. The Tregarns consist of two brothers, Zack, the over-protective implacable older brother, and Tom, and their sister Alice. John loves Alice and is the constant companion of Tom whether fishing or poaching. The narrative complication is completed by the former relationship of Zack and Evelyn.

The major link between this imaginative world and the world of consciousness is Cradock's act of narration. The authentication of the narrative is, as with any speech act, dependent on the speaker. In many ways Cradock is an ideal narrator: an outsider to the society, by nature of training able to observe people and draw conclusions. Even his movement from class loyalties to the lovers can be explained by his sentimental attachment to Alice. But at the crucial point where he becomes actually implicated in the story his narration loses credibility.

Alice is raped by Nigel. Nigel meets her at night by the sea having sent a note pretending he is John. When Alice runs he grabs her and rapes her, while the narrator, Cradock, in hiding looks on.

> And when I failed her didn't she fight against Nigel until her strength was gone, until she *succumbed* to him in the *sweetness* of that night? Didn't she scream until he again stopped her mouth with his?
>
> I wasn't there to hear or see. I couldn't stay to watch what a brother did, to cuckold me a second time. Why should I stay? Wasn't he only doing what I wanted to; *wasn't it my place he was taking there in the dark?*
> (p. 170)

The confusion of sexual violence with genuine passion has a long history in romances and family sagas but in this particular telling how authentic is it from this narrator? If we look at the italicised sections nothing prepares us for the grossness of his perception. Is he claiming any 'sweetness' in her nightmare? Is he really saying he should be raping her instead of Nigel? Finally he recounts that he 'crawled away, vomit hot bile, tears of impotence' (p. 171). The use of the word 'impotence' is psychoanalytically provocative. From this point he becomes more closely engaged in the story.

He experiences guilt but it goes no further than nightmares. Eventually it falls to him to tell both Tom and John but we get no more intimation of how they were told than 'the words dragged out of me' (p. 177), words that might be an epitaph for the final sixty pages of the novel. Instead of being a 'felt' event in his life which demands he become an actor rather than merely a 'peeping Tom', the tale becomes a problem to be unravelled. In spite of the intervention of the First World War Cradock uses his money and what passes as legal knowledge to effect a happy ending.

Like so much fiction, *The Legacy* remains firmly in the world of imagination, rehearsing many of the clichés of its genre. But to claim it negligible on that account would be wrong. It may be unpleasantly, even grossly, sentimental and have too many stock characters, but then it has an interesting if sentimental narrator who deploys a variety of intertextual origins. It has a sense of place and of time past and if it is rather blandly optimistic in its ending then it does touch on the pain of trying to express real things. 'Writing introduces division and alienation, but a higher unity as well. It intensifies the sense of self and fosters more conscious interaction between persons.'[23]

NOTES

1. Arthur Marwick, '*Room at the Top* and *Saturday Night and Sunday Morning* and the "Cultural Revolution" in Britain', *Journal of Contemporary History*, vol. IXX, no. 1 (1984), p. 129.
2. Quoted from Joseph Natoli, *Hauntings: Popular Film and American Culture, 1990–1992* (Albany, 1994), p. 33.
3. Frederic Jameson, *Postmodernism, or the Cultural Logic of Late Capitalism* (London, 1991).
4. Curtis G. Benjamin, *A Candid Critique of Book Publishing* (London, 1977), p. 3.
5. *Independent*, 4 Oct. 1992.
6. The item was reported on an early morning Radio 4 programme – no reference data.
7. Quoted in Scott McCracken, *Pulp: Reading Popular Fiction* (Manchester, 1998), p. 3.
8. Gary Day (ed.), *Literature and Culture in Modern Britain*, vol. II (Harlow, 1997), pp. 82–4.
9. Hodder & Stoughton's marketing brand made famous in the 1930s.
10. *Bookseller*, 2 Sept. 1978.
11. See particularly the much quoted Theodor Adorno and Max Horkheimer, *Dialectic of Enlightenment* (London, 1979).
12. Clive Bloom (ed.), *Literature and Culture in Modern Britain*, vol. I (Harlow, 1993), pp. 87–8.
13. Helen Roberts, 'Propaganda and Ideology in Women's Fiction', *Sociology of Literature*, Diane Laurenson (ed.), (Keele, 1978), p. 165.
14. Nickianne Moody, 'Travels in Fictional Britain V – Cadfael Country' in the Newsletter, Association for Research in Popular Fiction, no. 7 (1999), p. 5.
15. Quoted in Liz Thomson, 'Wanting nothing but the truth: Books by Liz Thomson', *The Times* and the *Sunday Times* Compact Disc Edition (6 May 1995), pp. 1–2.
16. Clive Bloom (ed.), *Gothic Horror* (Basingstoke, 1998), p. 14.

17. Sigmund Freud, 'The Uncanny', *Complete Psychological Works*, vol. 17 (London, 1955).
18. Mary Talbot, *Fictions at Work: Language and Social Practice in Fiction* (London, 1995), p. 27.
19. McCracken, op. cit., p. 102.
20. Kate Wickens, unpublished.
21. Winfried Fluck, 'Fiction and Fictionality in Popular Culture: Some Observations on the Aesthetics of Popular Culture', *Journal of Popular Culture*, vol. 24:3 (1990), p. 49.
22. Carol M. Thurston, 'Popular Historical Romances: Agent for Social Change? An Exploration of Methodologies', *Journal of Popular Culture*, vol. 24:4 (1991), pp. 35–45.
23. Walter J. Ong, *Orality and Literacy* (London, 1982), p. 179.

Lifting the Lid: Theatre 1956–99

Michael Woolf

PROLOGUE

> It was March 1914, when I left England, and, apart from leaves every ten years or so, I didn't see much of my own country until we all came back in '47. Oh, I knew things had changed, of course. People told you all the time the way it was going – going to the dogs, as the Blimps are supposed to say. But it seemed very unreal to me, out there. The England I remembered was the one I left in 1914, and I was happy to go on remembering it that way. Beside, I had the Maharajah's army to command – that was my world, and I loved it, all of it. At the time it looked like going on forever. When I think of it now, it seems like a dream. If only it could have gone on for ever. Those long cool evenings up in the hills, everything *purple and golden*. [My emphasis][1]

John Osborne's *Look Back in Anger* (1956) signalled what appeared at the time to be a radical change in British theatre. It achieved international recognition, winning, for example, the New York Critics Circle Award as the Best Foreign Play of 1957–8. It now seems a deeply conservative play full of pain, loss and yearning for some version of an idealised past. It also offers an important context in which much of the following discussion will be located. The Colonel's speech (above) is the only sustained lyrical moment in the play and it embodies precisely a sense of dispossession and a vision of a lost Eden which explicitly or implicitly is echoed and re-echoed through the plays of this period. The loss of empire, the national search for a new global role, the failure of the futile Suez intervention, the uprising in Hungary: trends and events in 1956 signalled a sequence of lost and abandoned causes. Osborne's achievement was to articulate these post-war British dilemmas and create for them a domestic metaphor. In the enclosed world of the stage Osborne captured a historical moment for a post-imperial nation. He represents a futile retreat from the banalities of the present towards the secure comforts of a mythologised past in which everything was 'purple and golden'.

Jimmy Porter is ostensibly a polar opposite from the Colonel but he shares precisely the same yearning for an Edenic age of certainty. His pain, far from being a product of revolutionary or radical zeal, is no less than that of the Colonel – a product of dispossessed yearning. Jimmy's 'purple and golden' place is a mixture of a quasi-myth with an historical 'heroic age'. It, thus, shares with the Colonel's dreamed landscape a location that is both in and out of time:

> I suppose people of our generation aren't able to die for good causes any longer. We had all that done for us, in the thirties and the forties, when we were still kids. There aren't any good, brave causes left.[2]

The figure of 'Hugh's mother' represents some form of idealised set of values wherein Jimmy locates value. She is principally a projection of a form of working-class virtue elevated by Jimmy into an icon of lost community. Alison recognises the motivation behind the transformation of the figure in Jimmy's consciousness: 'Jimmy seems to adore her principally because she's been poor almost all her life, and she's frankly ignorant.'[3]

At the conclusion of the play Jimmy retreats with Alison into another mythic location, a fragile fantasy set against the harsh realities. This cave clearly represents another dreamed retreat and is further expression of the absence of a dynamic, radical agenda. What Jimmy seeks is not a utopian brave new world but safety; this is ultimately a futile barrier against intrusive modernity:

> We'll be together in our bear's cave, and our squirrel's drey, and we'll live on honey and nuts, – lots and lots of nuts. And we'll sing songs about ourselves – about warm trees and snug caves, and lying in the sun.[4]

In 1956, *Look Back in Anger* signalled a new departure and it would be a distortion to see the play only with the gift of hindsight. The play grew out of the English Stage Company at the Royal Court Theatre which offered an environment to a generation of innovative writers including Osborne, Arnold Wesker, N.F. Simpson and John Arden. This generation emerged from changes in British society (presaged by the Beveridge Report in 1942 which led to, among other egalitarian initiatives, the Butler Education Act of 1944). Post-war reform expanded educational opportunities and further recognised that the social structures which had sustained Britain for the first five decades of the twentieth century would not serve the nation for the next five. The play contains an assault on complacency; it seeks to move away from convention in terms of sexual behaviour and it creates its dramatic material from a class perspective rarely represented on the stage up to that point. It shares with John Wain's novel *Hurry on Down* (1953) a profound discontent with 'middle-class' material aspiration and it represents experience in non-glamorous, even sordid, locations. With all that said, the play was substantially conventional in structure. It had three acts, was located in a naturalistic environment, used mimetic speech and was shaped by what was, beneath the radical surface, a traditional 'love triangle'.

Osborne's play offers nevertheless an appropriate point of reference for what follows. This chapter will explore a number of key impulses and trends in the period but Osborne's play introduces an environment which informs explicitly or implicitly a British preoccupation with the shape of national identity in the latter half of the twentieth century. He also employed a strategy which recurs in some of the key texts of the period. Osborne developed a domestic metaphor to house these issues.[5] For a cluster of reasons, not least economic ones, much drama avoided the epic in terms of theme and production. This is, after all, a post-heroic age in which, in addition, plays were performed in many small spaces with, necessarily, small casts and low production costs.

Look Back in Anger is a key text[6] and was widely recognised as a production which presaged new directions for the period. In relation to that sense of the new, it is also crucial to see the ways in which the idea of 'theatre' itself became more fluid and elusive than it had been in previous decades.

WHAT IS 'THEATRE'?

Theatre is not a single or simple notion. An essay on the sociology of theatre would need to consider all the categories and sub-categories that are contained within the general term. It would be possible, even within London, to distinguish commercial theatre (the 'West End') from sub-sidised repertory theatre such as the National Theatre. Live plays are also delivered before audiences in spaces in pubs, restaurants and clubs, and many plays were written in the post-1959 era that were only appropriate to those forms of production.[7] Plays with small casts requiring little in the way of sets and scenery reflect economic realities as well as the prolifera-tion of non-traditional theatre venues. These 'fringe'[8] locations are able to be innovative because, for the most part, they are able to reduce costs to a point where it is possible to take risks with new work. Production costs in the West End are such that there is little 'opportunity to fail' available to new writers.[9]

A sociology of theatre would also need to consider amateur production where actor and audience frequently shift roles and where very large numbers receive their primary experience of theatre. There are also plays which, though not written especially for amateur production, have appropriate characteristics such as relatively large casts with a substantial number of 'significant' roles.

To further complicate this already quite complex picture, the development of regional theatre was a significant fact of the period. Regional consciousness is expressed partly by the creation of important theatres outside of London. The Nottingham Playhouse, the Crucible in Sheffield or the Victoria Theatre in Stoke-on-Trent are significant examples of theatres that attracted directors, playwrights and audiences with some expectation of significant innovation.[10] Regionalism is also expressed in the locations represented in plays and the use of these locations as theme and setting. The regions offer alternatives to traditional subjects, places and classes represented in conventional London theatre. This is, of course, by no means solely or even predominantly a characteristic of theatre in the period. In fact, the emergence of a regional culture is most apparent in pop music, manifest dramatically in the emergence of Merseyside as an alternative cultural centre to London. The international popularity of the Beatles offers the clearest, though by no means the only, example of cultural development independent of, and alternative to, London.

The single most important process that impacts on theatre is, paradoxically, the development of a popular medium most hospitable to dramatic writing and that is, of course, television. In addition to enhanced financial rewards, TV offered writers potentially huge audiences and access to technical mechanisms that would allow them to refine their materials and to realise the reality and/or fantasy of their vision.

A generation of writers emerged in this period who made careers substantially or solely in the medium of television. In previous decades, they might well have become significant writers of plays for the theatre. Ray Simpson and Alan Galton, and Johnny Speight are important examples. They created drama that was innovative in terms of language and in the treatment of class issues. In *Steptoe and Son* (Galton and Simpson) or *Till Death Us Do Part* (Speight), for example, they evolved characters drawn from social categories that had rarely been represented fully or sympathetically on the stage. Harold Steptoe, for example, exists by buying and selling discarded consumer goods. The pathos in the figure is represented exactly by his dignified but futile determination to rise above the status of 'rag and bone man'. In contrast, Galton and Simpson's representation of petit-bourgeois aspiration in the Tony Hancock figure in *Hancock's Half Hour* is arguably among the most poignant and skilful representation of that British dilemma of entrapment within class.

Galton and Simpson repeatedly explore class as a kind of imprisonment. Hancock's attempts to escape from a sub-class (represented by the Sid James and Bill Kerr figures) are mirrored by Steptoe's futile attempts (comic and tragic) to rise above and out of his father's world. Johnny Speight's *Till Death Us Do Part* is similarly enacted, for the most part, within the closed confines of a living room much like a prison in shape and sense. Throughout the work of Galton and Simpson, and Speight, doors slam in faces as the tyranny of class closes all options while the audience responds with pain in laughter.

Those writers work with an archetypal British theme: the persistence of the power of class. In no other national theatre is the subject so central to the evolution of the art. Repeatedly, class is represented as a form of entrapment and a defining fate. It is *the* British subject expressed by Galton and Simpson and throughout more 'serious' theatre. This is not to endorse the rather crude political assertion that class continues to dominate British life but rather to suggest that class differences offer useful dramatic devices to establish metaphors of conflict. Whether class remains a key factor in British life is a matter for the economist and sociologist to debate. What remains undeniable in this context is the persistence of class consciousness in many of the arts of this period. The issue is, therefore, not merely a concern in theatre but is a defining characteristic of British artistic production.[11]

Another factor introduced by television was the possibility that a play could last for as long as an audience could sustain interest so long as that play was segmented and delivered at intervals. Long-running series such as *Coronation Street* or *EastEnders* are examples of multi-authored plays that can, theoretically, last for ever. In another format multi-authored, thematically-linked productions, such as the *Inspector Morse* series, are limited only by the possible permutations of plot derived from original sources, or the ability to invent plots and characters that feel as if they derive from the original source. On the other hand, television also created potential for very short productions, such as thirty-minute situation comedy, that would have little hope of being presented in a theatre.

Televisual techniques have also, of course, impacted on the manner in which plays are constructed. The use of short scenes approximates the editing potential given by television. Sarah Daniel's *Neaptide* (1986), for example, is comprised of 17 short scenes giving the effect of televisual 'jump cutting'. This form of construction is widespread in recent theatre:

> The plays of Patrick Marber and of Mark Ravenhill, which have helped to take two decades off the age of the theatre-going public, have the rapidity, the ellipses and the short scenes of good television drama. They recognise that dramatists can no longer get away with talking very loudly and repetitively as if to a crowd of slow-witted foreigners.[12]

The biggest temptation for the dramatic writer that television offered, in addition to audience exposure and financial reward, was its technical potential. The medium allowed for techniques and perspectives that could only partially be created in the theatre. On television the author could, with the aid of director and cameraman, control the audience's point of view through the selective vision of the lens. This authorial power, denied the author writing for stage production, created a number of playwrights whose work was predominantly or almost entirely written for television. The pre-eminent figure among these was arguably Dennis Potter.

Potter was perhaps the first playwright to use the medium as part of his dramatic universe rather than just to transplant a potential play from theatre to television. In addition to controlling point of view, in probably his major work, *Pennies from Heaven* (1978), Potter was able to exploit the opportunities of the medium in several key ways. The repeated shift from naturalism to a mental universe inhabited by popular songs of the 1930s is achieved seamlessly because of the obvious technical capacity to edit in ways that could not be achieved in the theatre: Potter was able to direct and control the 'eyes' of the audience with the intention of imposing authorial perspective. Furthermore, the possible length permitted by the serial form enabled Potter both to segment the drama and extend it. The weekly episode afforded opportunities for more dramatic suspensions and transitions than the theatre could allow. Instead of the fifteen-minute interval (a significant space in theatre performance)[13] Potter could exploit several 'intervals' of one week. The medium also created the possibility of length which, in Potter's case, sometimes led to a lack of what might have been judicious editing.[14] Above all, perhaps, Potter's work exploited the fact of enclosure within a small screen to create a sense of a world similar but separate from that inhabited by the viewer. The boundaries of the screen both contain and frame Potter's dramatic universe, and enable it to be simultaneously real and fantastic.

Television also, of course, had a substantial impact on audiences and on their expectations. Arguably, a fear that television would reduce attendance and diminish discrimination in taste created part of the agenda for theatre in this period. Theatre had been a popular form of entertainment from Shakespeare's times through to the late Victorian era and, arguably, well into the twentieth century in the form of Music Hall and variety sketches.[15] It is apparent that one of the objectives of contemporary theatre has been to sustain the medium as a popular form.[16]

The pursuit of this objective is, in part, a characteristic of theatre in the period. It may also be expressed in the political acceptance of the notion of permanent subsidy. Inherent in the acceptance of the notion is a sense that theatre is, in some sense or another, 'necessary' and an expression of the health of society. Thus, it is in the interest of the nation, so the argument goes, to support theatre so as to maintain its accessibility to the mass even if, a cynic might argue, that mass has little or no interest in going to see plays (if they had, the theatre might not need public subsidy). It is an odd fact that even as the notion of subsidy was challenged in many areas in the 1980s of Margaret Thatcher, the theatre remained, in principle at least, sacrosanct.[17] Theatre subsidy can be seen, by the most cynical, as an expression of tax raised to support middle-class culture. The idea, for example, of a tax raised to subsidise the cost of soccer attendance was not, as far as anyone can recall, part of the political or cultural agenda of the period nor is it likely to be.[18] These issues are perhaps not central to this discussion but they help define the cultural *status* of live theatre which remained essentially unchallenged.

A significant paradox emerges from the fact that the nature of audiences combined with economic constraints leads in two seemingly contradictory directions. On the one hand, as has been suggested, for economic reasons productions become smaller in terms of cast size and setting. They are, therefore, more 'portable' and can be presented in a very wide range of locations. On the other hand, the period sees the reinvention of the lavish musical. Large-scale productions such as *Les Miserables* or *Phantom of the Opera* occupy the same theatre for years and become part of the tourist itinerary in London. Tickets are sold years ahead to tour operators and they become, like a visit to Windsor Castle, part of the necessary tourist experience in London.[19]

The musicals are, thus, transformed from production to a form of theatrical monument. Tim Rice, Andrew Lloyd Webber and Cameron Macintosh are key figures in this process. Both processes (minimalisation and monumentalism) are responses to the economic realities of theatre's new condition. They are also symptomatic of the need to reclaim audiences by redefining the product offered to them. It is also clear that these kinds of production are part of an international (at least US–UK) cultural market place. Thus, many of these productions are to be found on Broadway and in the West End at the same time and, indeed, in many of the major European capitals. Significantly, most of these productions are not located in specific national cultures or times but in a mythic location which inhabits ahistorical space.[20]

BEYOND CENSORSHIP

In an obvious sense, theatre was transformed in 1968 by the fact that theatre censorship was finally abolished, creating the potential to explore previously prohibited subjects in previously unacceptable forms.* Censorship had, of course, been challenged over many decades and in many art forms but the 1960s saw the challenge succeed in a variety of arts. Liberalisation and the testing of boundaries became characteristic of art in general. In theatre history, it would be possible to cite Noël Coward's *The Vortex* (1924) as a key play but, as has been well documented, Edward Bond's *Saved* (1965), presented at the Royal Court in a club presentation, was an immediate example of an urgent assault on conventional dramatic restraint. In any case, by 1970 the Roundhouse in North London was able to present an erotic review produced by Kenneth Tynan called *Oh Calcutta* (1968) which contained scenes of nudity that would not have been possible in the previous six decades of the twentieth century.[21] Another characteristic of theatre in this period is, therefore, an attempt to test limits and explore boundaries of 'taste' and 'sensibility'.

Such an objective is amusingly apparent in a letter from Tynan to Archbishop Lord Fisher of Lambeth who had, unwisely, tried to enlist Tynan's support for possible legislation 'to enforce the common law against the exposure of the genital organs in theatres and elsewhere.'

> . . . no, I would not support any legislation to forbid genital exposure on stage or screen. . . . If such spectacles titillate people, I see no reason to interfere with their pleasure. According to my dictionary 'titillate' means 'tickle pleasantly', which sounds to me both enjoyable and desirable. If a stage or film show causes me to have an erection, my immediate reaction is gratitude for a nice experience: to wish to ban it would seem to me churlish in the extreme.[22]

The theatre, in common with many other art forms, clearly sought to push back the limits of tolerated expression in many ways and for motives that were sometimes artistic, sometimes playful and, often, political.

This phenomenon does not, of course, exist in isolation but must be seen within the context of the tumultuous years at the end of the 1960s and the beginning of the 1970s. What emerges from the times (and throughout this period) are oppositional and contested notions of culture, history, society. The urban protests of May 1968 both expressed this and, in many forms, blurred the boundaries between theatre and protest. The streets themselves became the theatre of the young. From this source a number of groups formed and a number of playwrights emerged who saw the space between street and theatre as a logical location for a radical challenge to

---

* The 1843 Theatres Act gave the Lord Chamberlain the power to license, or otherwise, theatrical performances. The Lord Chamberlain was a Royal official without public accountability. The complete dramatic text had to be approved by this official, thus removing any potential for improvisation or development of the text while in production. Frequently, dramatists were required to make substantial textual alterations before a licence would be given.

political conservatism. One of the earliest of these groups named itself, significantly enough in this context, 'The Agitprop Street Players'. The key dramatists emerging from this milieu are probably David Edgar, Howard Brenton and David Hare. What these dramatists also shared was a commitment to the collective nature of dramatic creativity. All plays are, of course, collective enterprises. What this movement sought to do was to make strength out of this necessity (taking the example of, among others, Bertolt Brecht's Berliner Ensemble). Notable among these collectives were the Pip Simmons Theatre Group and David Hare's Portable Theatre.

Women's liberation and gay rights organisations began to make their challenges to orthodoxy by the 1970s though individual authors had treated related issues well before this time. Shelagh Delaney's *A Taste of Honey* (1958) is a much underrated example. It sympathetically presents a series of dilemmas arising from inter-racial sexual relations and offers, as a key figure, a young gay man who represents, to a substantial degree, the play's moral centre and the focus of the audience's empathy. Delaney's play is, though, individually-authored although it underwent much refinement while in preparation by Joan Littlewood's company in Stratford, East London.

Group dynamics in the politics of gender find widespread expression in theatrical performance some ten years after Delaney's play. The Joint Stock theatre collective produced many of Caryl Churchill's plays and, indeed, much radical feminist theatre has been written and produced in a collective environment. Similarly radical gay theatre moved along a related path and was oppositional in content, radical in the method of production and location. It is important, however, to make a crucial distinction between feminist and gay theatre, and plays written by women and gay writers that may well deal with themes relating to those experiences but which do not have an explicit political intention. Certainly many plays occupy a grey space between these locations.

By the end of the period, plays like Mark Ravenhill's *Shopping and Fucking* moved from 'fringe' to centre in London's West End. Ravenhill's play presents all relationships as essentially based on commercial exchange. Thus Mark pays Garry to allow him to lick his anus: 'This isn't a personal thing. It's a transaction, OK?'[23] Beneath and beyond this analysis of the commercialisation of all experience is radical pain expressed by the character of Robbie:

> I see the suffering. And the wars. And the grab, grab, grab.
> And I think: Fuck Money. Fuck it. This selling. This buying. Fuck the
> bitching world and let's be . . . beautiful. Beautiful. And happy.[24]

The violence and irony that surround this anger serve to intensify the revealed anguish and to sustain what is a fierce assault on the power of commerce in contemporary reality.

That a play with Ravenhill's radical agenda can move to the West End signals simultaneously a growth in influence and, less comfortingly from a radical perspective, a process whereby oppositional cultures are subsumed and neutralised into the safer waters of mainstream calm. The emergence of what might broadly be called feminist theatre moves in a similar direction, though there is an acute danger of categorisation and marginalisation which would locate all plays by women or overtly gay authors within a political 'genre' from which neither qualities or defects can be clearly perceived.

There is, growing out of these impulses, another tendency towards a theatre that seeks to menace and destabilise audience expectation. In one manifestation this is expressed in what is known as 'Theatre of Cruelty': a term borrowed from Antonin Artaud by Peter Brook to represent his 1962 season. While the term is inexact, it helps define a tendency for theatre to push back limits in contexts other than politics and gender. Theatre is used to assault the *consciousness* of the audience with a view, at times, to making the known world menacing. That this impulse persists through the period is made apparent in an interview with Howard Barker:

> This awful New Labour thing, with its obsession with moral messages, and its insistence on the arts having a duty to celebrate, is insidious. Theatre is not about celebration – it's about the opposite.[25]

A vivid example of this tendency is offered by David Rudkin's *Afore Night Come* (1962). The play is set in a rural location, an orchard, where an audience brought up on myths of English pastoral would expect to locate values alternative to urban disorder.[26] Instead of contrasting an urban present with a 'pastoral' view of the rural past, Rudkin exploits this place, and the associations conventionally clustered around it, to expose dark and primitive violence; simplicity equates here with a profound cruelty. Rudkin, in effect, partakes in the philosophical conflict represented by Rousseau, on the one hand, and Hobbes on the other. Rousseau's view of civilisation as a form of corruption of man's natural innocence is, effectively, abandoned in favour of Hobbes's view of society as that force which restrains mankind's natural viciousness.

If the label 'cruelty' is not especially helpful, the work it characterises serves to encompass some important trends. Firstly, this theatre signalled an alternative to the play as ritual entertainment where audiences would have a comfortable evening during which their expectations would be satisfied. The analogy is perhaps of a restaurant where the diner expects a good meal served pleasantly. In contrast, David Rudkin comes in and spills hot soup in your lap. It would be possible to cite many other examples like this which could include plays by David Hare, Ann Jellicoe's *The Sport of my Mad Mother* (1958), and Peter Brook's production of Peter Weiss's *Marat/Sade*

(1964). For these purposes and because of its dark dramatic impact, Rudkin's play will serve as representative of this trend in the theatre of the period.

Any discussion of the period needs to recognise that British theatre did not exist in a national vacuum but was influenced by, and in return influenced, world theatre, particularly that of Europe and, to some extent, that of the USA. Reference has already been made to Bertolt Brecht. At various times, the influence of European Dada and Surrealism is apparent. Brook and Rudkin, among others, were certainly responding at some level to the ideas of Antonin Artaud whose *The Theatre and Its Double* was translated into English in 1958.[27] Peter Weiss's *The Marat/Sade* had an immediate impact on the British scene after the translated production in 1964. In other contexts, the clear influence of European 'absurdist' theatre from, for example, Eugene Ionesco and, especially, Samuel Beckett[28] can be seen in many works from, among numerous others, Harold Pinter and Tom Stoppard. The purpose here is not to list a series of 'influences' but to make the point that theatre, like most other forms of cultural transmission, does not and cannot exist in national isolation. In a physical sense also actors and directors are increasingly mobile and they, thus, gain experience from a variety of national theatre cultures. An actor like Kenneth Branagh, for example, moves freely between the USA and the UK and, further, the trend for Hollywood stars to come to London to appear in limited seasons has substantially increased in recent years. Indeed, the growth of innovative theatre companies in the 1960s had much to do with three Americans who crossed the Atlantic to form influential companies: Jim Haines founded, firstly, the Traverse and then the Arts Lab; Charles Marowitz founded the Open Space, directed Joe Orton's *Loot* at the Jeanetta Cochrane Theatre, and created some radical reworking of Shakespeare; Ed Berman established Interaction. Like most forms of contemporary activity, theatre operates across geographical boundaries.

Theatre exists in contexts wider than the nation. It also clearly relates to the past as history and as myth. Further, there is a form of 'exchange' between contemporary plays and theatrical history. Edward Bond's *Lear* (1971) exemplifies some of the trends discussed here. As Bond makes clear, he shares many of the assumptions underlying the notion of 'Theatre of Cruelty' and similarly intends not to comfort his audience but to assault and disturb:

> I write about violence as naturally as Jane Austen wrote about manners. Violence shapes and obsesses our society, and if we do not stop being violent we have no future. People who do not want writers to write about violence want to stop them writing about us and our time. It would be immoral not to write about violence.[29]

That said, *Lear* illustrates two other widespread impulses. Most obviously, Bond explores and translates the dramatic literature of the past.[30] There is an obvious sense in which all art in any time reaches forward into space and time with a particular vision while, simultaneously, it reaches back to use and exploit its own historical artefacts. It is for this reason, of course, that there is no 'progress' in a linear sense in the arts. It is the nature of art, and theatre is no exception, to go simultaneously backwards and forward.

Bond's *Lear* does other important things. It offers an Apocalyptic vision in which destruction is the key process. This is, of course, a widely expressed concept in the literature of our times where disintegration rather than integration or construction is the prevailing tone. Bond also inverts moral equations and expectations in a manner that undermines conventional perceptions of 'good', 'evil', 'justice', 'order' and so on. Lear's diatribe is a tragic expression of the kind of inversion that, incidentally, informs Joe Orton's comedy:

> Whatever's trite and vulgar and hard and shallow and cruel, with no mercy or sympathy – that's what you think, and you're proud of it! You good, decent, honest, upright, lawful men who believe in order – when the last man dies, you will have killed him! I have lived with murderers and thugs, there are limits to their greed and violence, but you decent, honest men devour the earth.[31]

Bond's drama reflects a world at the edge of a precipice.

LOST EDENS: POLITICS AND NOSTALGIA

As has been argued in relation to John Osborne's *Look Back in Anger*, if there is one single reality that permeates the following discussions, it emerges out of Britain's changing role in the world. Much of what follows relates to, and locates itself in relation to, the fact of Britain's decline from a major political force to a minor international power. Britain's post-imperial reality raises over and over again the question of identity and definition both of the individual and the nation. Attitudes that are perceived as archaic are roundly ridiculed. Simultaneously, a myth of a lost age manifests itself in a myriad of forms. At one end of the spectrum, this erupts into Joe Orton's iconoclastic and satiric assault on past conventions and, at the other end, it manifests itself in a form of partly repressed nostalgia for a golden age of surety and potency: the 'purple and golden' time.

These issues are clearly expressed in plays that deal with explicit political consequences of the process of decline. Alan Bennett, for example, used the spy scandals of the 1950s as a device through which to explore the nature of allegiance in a sequence of plays. *The Old Country* (1977), *A Question of Attribution* (1988), and *An Englishman Abroad* (revised in 1988 for the theatre from the original television play) collectively explore the experiences of spies, especially Anthony Blunt and Guy Burgess, in a form where, implicitly and explicitly, the present exists in relation to a notion or myth of an 'heroic' age: in this case, the 1930s. The contrast between the mundane or defeated dramatic present and the imagined past serves to enforce a sense of decline and loss. A similar assumption of national decline is apparent in David Hare's *The Absence of War* (1993). As the title suggests, Hare presents, through a fictional dramatisation of the 1992 General Election, a post-heroic view of contemporary politics. The politicians operate in a landscape of disintegration where an incapacity to function effectively is mirrored in a loss of language. Indeed, the loss of potency in language is a theme that recurs in a number of works and operates metaphorically as another expression of decline. Silence is not the simple absence of sound but a space that reverberates with accumulated significance.

The dramatic contrast embodied within the Kahn family in Arnold Wesker's *Trilogy* (1960) draws upon some related issues. The two plays that deal with the Kahn family, *Chicken Soup with Barley* and *I'm Talking About Jerusalem* use mother–son conflicts to dramatise the distance between a past perceived as heroic and a present seen as without hope or direction. Sarah's ideology is both archaic and, in the face of her son's sense of failure, an expression of the paradoxical power of a defeated vision of something close to Eden:

> RONNIE: You wanted everybody to be happy but you wanted them to be happy your way. It was strawberries and cream for everyone – whether they liked it or not . . . the great ideal you always cherished has exploded in front of your eyes. But you won't face it. . . .
> SARAH: So I'm still a communist! Shoot me then! I'm a communist! I've always been one – since the time when all the world was a communist. You know that? When you were a baby and there was unemployment and everybody was thinking so – all the world was a communist. But it's different now. Now the people have forgotten.[32]

Wesker's play exactly captures processes discussed here: decline from some mythic projection of an ideal world drives the protagonist's sense of loss. The lost world is, for Sarah, communism but it is also characterised by Ronnie metaphorically as 'strawberries and cream'. While a more mundane image, it shares with the Colonel's 'purple and golden' the characteristic of being an attempt to make concrete in words that which is elusive: the phrases are shorthand for dreams. Further, Wesker, like Osborne, employs the combination of domestic conflict and historical moment to represent that sense of decline. While any number of other plays might be cited in these two contexts, it is appropriate to offer Sarah's simple insight as a summary of what is both theme and structure for a number of dramatic productions in the period: 'it's different now' enforces the chasm between the then and the now; all these lost Edens confront a present wherein that loss is a persistent condition of consciousness.

A HUMANIST THEATRE

Alan Bennett's oblique exploration of some lost 'heroic age' was allied to another objective. The plays, particularly *An Englishman Abroad*, seek to create audience sympathy for historical characters who, in conventional representations, are seen as traitors. In contrast to the power of a 'theatre of cruelty', there remains a significant body of plays where the objective is to create some kinds of empathy for the human condition. The persistence of what might be called 'humanist theatre' can be illustrated briefly by a discussion of Simon Gray's work.

In Gray's *Quartermaine's Terms* the central figure, St John Quartermaine, is a barely competent teacher in a school of English for foreigners. In some respects, he is a stereotypical Englishman with a limited linguistic range that is at first a comic device but is later used paradoxically to reveal emotional depth. The comic dimension of the first act is encapsulated in Quartermaine's abortive efforts to use a new slide projector for a lecture. His lecture on Oxford colleges is a failure because of his inability to handle the new technology:

> I think that's part of the problem, all those extra bits to master – anyway, one of the colleges went in upside down and wouldn't come out so I had to – to abandon technology and do it all off my own bat – you know – reminiscences of my time at the House and – anecdotes – and – you know – that sort of thing. The personal touch. But of course I ran out of steam a little, towards the end, I'm afraid.[33]

The failure is both technological and, more significantly, linguistic. Quartermaine's positive emotional universe is most frequently represented, and constrained, by the words 'smashing' and 'terrific' while 'Oh Lord' is the response to surprising experience or to dismay. The fact that he 'ran out of steam' enforces a sense of inadequacy that is, for the most part, comic. In the second half of the play Gray shifts the emotional tone (using the interval to suspend the comic momentum) and begins to reveal

Quartermaine's dependency on the community of the school and, also, the fragility of his place in that community. To some degree the situation is close to that in Harold Pinter's *The Caretaker* (1960) in that a figure is ultimately expelled from a version of community and a landscape of perceived safety.[34] The play ends with Quartermaine's sacking and Gray's achievement is to have transformed the concluding repetition of 'Oh Lord' from a measure of comic inadequacy to a revelation of pain. Quartermaine's suffering is, by that point, a curious expression of human worth beneath and beyond language.

Gray's *Life Support* (1997), in a very different context, also creates then subverts a potentially comic situation revealing the depth of feeling beneath the surface of an ostensibly unattractive figure. The comic potential is much darker in that the wife of a writer (J.G.) is in a coma after being stung by a bee. The situation contains within it a sense of a cosmic absurdity in which J.G. and the comatose Gwen are victims of some version of God's black comedy. Against this the medical staff cite the possibilities of 'miracles'. There is also the dark comedy inherent in J.G.'s continuing and busy dialogue with the silent and unmoving Gwen:

> Oh, for Christ's sake – we would agree that you're not the liveliest company at the moment, but surely they can roll you about your bed, change your sheets, mop you up, unplug and replug your tubes, change your drip, drip, drip, without needing to keep one eye on the television . . .[35]

At the end, J.G. faces the decision to unplug Gwen's life support machine in a conclusion that is profoundly undramatic in tone. Gray has, by this point, achieved, as in *Quartermaine's Terms*, a state of ambiguity (signalled in the titles) to reveal the anguish beneath the ostensible triviality of language and action. The (in)action at the play's end conceals rather than reveals the meanings that have been exposed to the audience.

This discussion intends to be a corrective to the view that all theatre in the period is marked by the kinds of assumptions underlying works previously discussed. While Gray never denies the bleak possibilities implicit in a universe marked by cosmic disorder, he also continues to affirm something persistent in the human spirit. As has also been indicated, Gray is not discussed here as some exception to a general trend but rather as exemplifying the diverse nature of theatre in this period. A similar broad perspective could have been offered by a discussion of, among others, Julien Mitchell, Arnold Wesker, Bernard Kops, Alan Bennett, some of Alan Ayckbourn's plays particularly the trilogy *The Norman Conquests* (1973 and 1974). In short, within the comedies and tragedies some elements of affirmation of the human spirit persist.

THE MUSIC HALL

It might have been possible additionally to see aspects of John Osborne's *The Entertainer* (1957) in the context of a persistent humanism but the play also offers a device that has had a curious longevity in contemporary theatre. Reference back to a music-hall tradition has offered subject matter and style in an number of significant ways. As Christopher Innes noted, Osborne used Music Hall as a context in which to explore national and cultural decline:

> The Music Hall is both a frame for the action and an image of Britain, in which the debased state of popular culture is a direct representation of social decadence.[36]

This is, though, a simplification in that reference to the music-hall tradition is a form of dialogue with the theatre's own history and, to some degree, a statement of continuity as well as, in Innes's view, discontinuity:

> Once a vital theatrical form, by the middle of the century the Music Hall was almost extinct, displaced by television sitcoms and bingo.[37]

While that is literally the case, the traditions of Music Hall offered a number of significant technical possibilities, most obviously non-realist devices, that served to draw the audience's attention towards the theatricality of the play.

In this sense, music-hall techniques such as dialogue with the audience and the resultant sense of moving fluidly in and out of 'role' supported Brechtian non-naturalistic intents. Christopher Hampton's *Tales from Hollywood* (1983) moved between quasi-music hall moments and parodies of Brechtian theatre (with Brecht represented in the play). Samuel Beckett also combined music-hall routines and language with the figure of the tramp (from Charlie Chaplin and Buster Keaton), and the dialogues of Laurel and Hardy, to create the figures in *Waiting for Godot* (1953). Music Hall, however, also offered a means of domesticating this kind of Brechtian device and rooting it in British cultural history. The 'rediscovery' of Max Wall★ in the early 1970s was part of an impulse that ought not to be dismissed as pure nostalgia. It indicates a reconnection with a significant tradition that contained within it theatrical mechanisms to penetrate and analyse the British condition.

★ Max Wall (1908–90) began in the Music Hall. His career spanned over 70 years, though his popularity waned after the Second World War. He was 'rediscovered' in the 1970s and in the last 20 years of his life played in a number of contemporary plays as well as giving television and theatre performances as a solo artist. Michael Billington's review in the *Guardian*, 4 February 1975, summarises the critical enthusiasm for Max Wall at that late stage of his career: 'The incomparable Max . . . I shall be able to tell my grandchildren that I once saw a master clown in action.'

There are elements of Music Hall in the Common Man figure in Robert Bolt's *A Man for All Seasons* (1960) but the best and clearest example of this combination of Brecht and the Music Hall is undoubtedly Joan Littlewood's production of *Oh What a Lovely War* (1963) by the Theatre Workshop in Stratford, East London. This well-documented production illustrates the significance of music-hall devices in that it presents a historical tragedy (the First World War) through a contemporaneous artistic form. The distance between the form in which the production is presented and the content juxtaposed on that form immeasurably heightens, through contrast, the impact of the facts that are flashed on to a panel above the stage. The opening of the second act, for example, juxtaposes the cast rendition of 'Oh It's A Lovely War' with statistics detailing losses at Ypres 'BRITISH LOSS 59,275 MEN', at Aubers Bridge 'BRITISH LOSS 11,619 MEN IN 15 HOURS', and at Loos 'BRITISH LOSS 8,236 MEN IN 3 HOURS'.[38]

The impact of Music Hall goes beyond the plays in that it informs theatrical production influencing, among others, Peter Brook's Shakespeare productions and, clearly, the 'hat' business in Pinter's *The Caretaker*. In terms of the trends discussed here it brings together a sense of dialogue with past forms with an attempt to combine serious content and popular presentation. At the edge of these devices is both a Brechtian impulse and an attempt to reclaim, at least metaphorically and formally, theatre as a mass entertainment. The Music Hall was, also, sometimes located at the end of the pier and that is a happy conjunction of space in which to discuss arguably the most innovative writer of the period and, certainly, the key iconoclast of the 1960s, Joe Orton.

JOE ORTON AND THE OUTRAGE OF MRS EDNA WELTHORPE

Mrs Edna Welthorpe (an ally, one suspects, of the redoubtable moralist Mary Whitehouse) was one of Joe Orton's severest critics, as her outraged response to *Entertaining Mr Sloane* (1964) indicates:

> I myself was nauseated by this endless parade of mental and physical perversion. And to be told that such a disgusting piece of filth now passes for humour.
>
> Today's young playwrights take it upon themselves to flaunt their contempt for ordinary decent people. I hope that ordinary decent people will shortly strike *back*![39]

It is, of course, entirely appropriate that Mrs Welthorpe was an invention of Orton. She is indicative of the degree to which Orton's plays spilled over into his life and, therefore, the degree to which his life spilled over into the plays.

Mrs Welthorpe's idiom is key to understanding Orton's dramatic language. Phrases like 'flaunt their contempt' and 'ordinary decent people' locate her precisely in Tony Hancock's East Cheam or in the provincial petit-bourgeois Leicester in which Orton grew up. This language is employed as some kind of fragile and illusory defence against the swirling chaos that engulfs Orton's characters. The chasm between this language of respectable restraint and the Dionysian disintegration of social order is the root of Orton's comic power. Thus, throughout *Entertaining Mr Sloane*, the term 'Mr' is consistently used as a device to sustain an illusion of conventional social order. Kath's attitude to her false teeth is, similarly, a sustained comic device both in a visual sense and as an expression of hopeless conformity to 'standards' in a world slipping towards chaos:

> My teeth, since you mentioned the subject, Mr Sloane, are in the kitchen
> in Stergene. Usually I allow a good soak overnight. But what with one
> thing and another I forgot. Otherwise I would never be in such a state.
> I hate people who are careless with their dentures.[40]

The 'one thing and another' (murder and mayhem) is the real condition of the anarchic action while the outraged 'delicacy' of 'since you mentioned the subject' signals the chasm that exists between action and language. Orton's comedy is located, precisely, in that space.

The other sources of Orton's comedy are well-documented: Orton clearly employed techniques learnt from traditional British farce, particularly that of Ben Travers, becoming in John Lahr's view, 'the master farceur of his age'.[41] Orton parts company with Travers, however, in one important respect. In *Loot* (1965), with its obvious debt to Travers's *Plunder* (1928), and *What the Butler Saw* (1969), the conditions of farce, its disjunctions and disorders, are revealed as the true nature of experience whereas in Ben Travers (and Ray Clooney, Brian Rix, etc.) the condition of farce is an aberration. At the end of those plays social order is restored whereas the last moments of Orton's major plays enforce and sustain a sense of moral chaos precisely because they take refuge in those linguistic conventions that reflect the universe defeated in the plays: 'Well it's been a pleasant morning. See you later' (*Entertaining Mr Sloane*),[42] 'We must keep up appearances' (*Loot*),[43] 'I'm glad you don't despise tradition. Let us put our clothes on and face the world' (*What the Butler Saw*).[44] Orton's theatrical world subverts notions of social order and successively reveals the corruption and sickness beneath that illusory order.

This, of course, signals Orton's profound seriousness. In a direct historical sense the figure of Police Inspector Truscott in *Loot* draws upon legal evidence given against a corrupt police officer, Detective Sergeant Harold Challenor. Orton puts into Truscott's mouth the exact words ascribed to Challenor at his trial: 'You're fucking nicked, my old beauty.'[45] The following exchange between McLeavy and Truscott send assumptions of law and order crumbling into dust:

> MCLEAVY: What am I charged with?
> TRUSCOTT: That needn't concern you for the moment. We'll fill in the details later.
> MCLEAVY: You can't do this. I've always been a law-abiding citizen. The police are for the protection of ordinary people.
> TRUSCOTT: I don't know where you pick up these slogans, sir. You must read them on hoardings.[46]

Thus, Orton destroys the notion of the police as an agency of social cohesion and justice. Notions of family, police, morality, love, religion, ethics: all the preconceived foundations of an ordered society are exposed to ridicule. The audience's laughter contains within it a profound unease at what Orton's distorting mirror reflects of our true experience.

In view of this, it is entirely appropriate that Orton's last, great play, *What the Butler Saw* should be set in a private clinic which is, in effect, reality imagined as a lunatic asylum, as is apparent in the following exchange between Drs Rance and Prentice:

> RANCE: Good morning. Are you Dr Prentice?
> PRENTICE: Yes. Have you an appointment?
> RANCE: No. I never make appointments. I'd like to be given details of your clinic. . . . You specialize in the complete breakdown and its by-products?
> PRENTICE: Yes, But it's highly confidential. My files are never open to strangers.
> RANCE: You may speak freely in front of me. I represent Her Majesty's Government. Your immediate superiors in madness.[47]

The title signals both certain sources and an intent: it directs attention to origins in Music Hall, in traditional British entertainment (farce and Victorian peepshow machines), and it demonstrates an intention to reveal and expose, from the lower-class perspective of 'the Butler', realities of British society. In this sense, Orton's work is located also within the post-war project, implicitly or explicitly, to explore the underlying nature of British society at a time when forces for change brought into question the assumptions of the past. Orton's theatrical tools are drawn also from the past in that he exploits traditional dramatic structures and outcomes (mistaken and revealed identities, concluding resolutions at the end of the play, and so on) as surgical devices, as the scalpel with which to conduct a post-mortem on the body politic, sexual, social, ethical.

There are many other influences on Orton that might be further discussed. Pinter's influence on the early plays and Oscar Wilde's impact on Orton's use of linguistic paradox,[48] moral inversion and so on have been well-documented elsewhere.[49] It would, of course, also be possible to consider the impact of Orton's homosexuality, which precedes the political manifestation of gay consciousness and is located in his persona as a sexual outlaw. Orton is, obviously as well, working within, and benefiting from, a surge of innovative creativity in the 1960s which included Harold Pinter, John Osborne, Mary Quant, the Beatles, Peter Cook and Dudley Moore, and *Beyond the Fringe*,[50] and so on. That said, the assumption here is that, despite echoes of earlier writers in his work and the fact that he is part of a discernible trend in the turbulent 1960s, his is the major original dramatic talent of the period. There is, finally, something joyfully paradoxical in Orton's perception of the world:

> I suppose I'm a believer in Original Sin. People are profoundly bad but irresistibly funny.[51]

A deep moral disquiet and consequent seriousness is expressed within the great comic structures that Orton builds and then brings tumbling down in hysterical ruins. Joe Orton owes much of this vision to Edna Welthorpe (Mrs).

THE PRESENCE OF HAROLD PINTER

The influence of Pinter on Orton's early work and Orton's pleasure at Pinter's evident approval, signal a towering presence in the theatre of this period. Pinter occupied many roles in these times as a writer, sometimes critic, director and actor.[52] In a writing career that spans 45 years his output has been prolific without, however, entirely escaping from Michael Earley's sense that 'playwrights tend to write their best plays at the beginning of their career.'[53] That is not to say that Pinter's later work is poor but rather to say that much of what he achieved as a writer was achieved by the 1970s and that, for all the power of some of the later plays, there is a tendency to rework strategies already apparent in, for example, *The Caretaker* (1960) or *The Homecoming* (1965).

A Kind of Alaska (1982) may be taken as an example. It takes its subject matter from *Awakenings* by Oliver Sachs which describes the impact of the drug L-DOPA on a number of patients who had spent many years in a state of suspended animation or sleeping sickness. Deborah awakes after many years in a comatose state and, at the end of the play, defines herself in relation to information supplied to her. She has, literally, lost all sense of her own autonomous existence:

> You say I have been asleep. You say I am now awake. You say I have
> not awoken from the dead. You say I was not dreaming then and am not
> dreaming now. You say I have always been alive and am alive now. You
> say I am a woman.[54]

As stage drama, this is a powerful evocation of the personality minimalised and unable to define self from within. In another sense, the figure has been assaulted by an external, and irrational, menace that strikes without obvious logic or reason. This is, also, crudely the experience of the tramp, Davies, in *The Caretaker*. Pinter's programme notes to the first production of that play could, broadly, apply to *A Kind of Alaska*, to *Party Time* (1991) or indeed to many other of his plays:

> The desire for verification is understandable but cannot always be satisfied.
> There are no hard distinctions between what is real and what is unreal,
> nor between what is true and what is false. The thing is not necessarily
> either true or false; it can be both true and false.[55]

This is not to minimise or discredit the work but rather to note a consistency of theme and approach throughout which does not, of course, detract from either Pinter's significance nor, indeed, the theatrical impact of any given play.

The Caretaker is, arguably, Pinter's most significant play and certainly, as Pinter recognised, it undermined traditional categories and gave shape to one form of modernity in the British theatre:

> *The Caretaker* wouldn't have been put on, and certainly wouldn't have
> run, before 1957. The old categories of comedy and tragedy and farce are
> irrelevant.[56]

Furthermore, in it Pinter captured a language that was both rooted in urban experience and transcended it, approximating at times a form of poetic abstraction. In that sense, Pinter's language is often loaded with elusive meanings while being literally comprehensible so that the audience partake of the drama and, simultaneously, are engaged with what is not said but only implied. Beckett's influence is palpable here, not least in the careful use of silence. Pinter's silence, like Beckett's, is crucial to performance and is written *as text*. These 'intervals' enforce the complex fields of meaning out of which Pinter develops a sustained vision of a world where significance and personality are unstable and shifting; where meaning is both apparent and elusive, and where fear of what lies beyond the confines of the known and the spoken is a characteristic of the human condition.

In the latter works, notably *Party Time* (1991) and *Mountain Language* (1988), Pinter has ostensibly moved towards political concerns particularly informed by what he presents as an external threat in the form of some kind of totalitarian menace. Arguably, however, this is a political version of the personal kinds of menace expressed in the earlier plays. The fact that these plays have been accompanied by real and heartfelt commitment to anti-totalitarian movements does not diminish the fact that the power of this menace in the plays is precisely the fact that it is not concrete or envisaged but implied. Any fuller discussion of Pinter's work should also note his rooted Englishness expressed in language and location and, at times, through the use of traditional comedy and music-hall routines. Michael Billington acutely focused on this comic vision in his review of *No Man's Land* (1975):

> He uses a whole battery of comic effects, including one very similar to Orton's: the combination of posh words with working-class speech rhythms. . . . It is, however, a very English joke in another sense; for it depends on the assumption that people who change their class feel obliged to change their language.[57]

This discussion of Pinter is limited by an awareness of the amount of excellent criticism that has already accumulated around his work and, therefore, by a desire to avoid redundancy. In this context, Pinter is a major presence in the evolution of theatre in this period with a significance that collectively goes beyond the single play, the single performance or the single production.

AYCKBOURN: A SINGULAR EXCEPTION

Alan Ayckbourn defies most categories and is an exception to Michael Earley's assertion that playwrights tend to produce their best work in the first years of their writing career. Ayckbourn has been a prolific dramatist for almost forty years and, while there may be no critical consensus on his work, there is very little evidence of decline. Michael Billington offers some useful perspectives:

> he is really a regional writer exploiting a traditional metropolitan form, the farcical comedy. And into this he injects a wealth of unobtrusively social detail. . . . Ayckbourn is a left-wing writer using a right-wing form.[58]

Ayckbourn has, in short, defied categorisation and, while aspects of his life and work clearly partake of the contemporary contexts discussed here, he also, self-consciously at times, occupies a unique position in the history of the theatre of these times.

In most cases the first production of an Ayckbourn play is directed by the author and opens at the Stephen Joseph Theatre in Scarborough (where he is Director of Productions and the founder).[59] The plays are, however, far from being provincial in appeal or in theme. Ayckbourn is a highly successful commercial dramatist whose plays inevitably transfer to central locations. The special status of his work is indicated by the fact that, while many of the plays transfer to the West End, a number have also gone from Scarborough to the National Theatre, notably *Bedroom Farce* (1977) and *Sisterly Feelings* (1980). In that sense, his work seamlessly crosses over from the 'fringe' to both the commercial and subsidised centre.[60]

The appeal of his work is based upon a combination of considerable wit with a consistent exploration of changing sexual and social mores. Ayckbourn occupies, in this sense, a very contemporary space but does so in ways that do not diminish a compassion for the, frequently absurd, dilemmas of his characters. Among his best work is the trilogy *The Norman Conquests* (1973 and 1974) and many of the characteristics of his writing as a whole can be demonstrated by a brief discussion of these plays.

In his introduction to the published version, Ayckbourn recognises the economic and practical realities that limit and define the nature of this work and, as has been argued, the work of many of his contemporaries:

> since we could only afford six actors, they should have that number of characters . . . ideally they should only have two stage entrances since that's the way our temporary Library Theatre set-up is arranged. . . . In these austere times most theatre managers, if not the actors, prefer small-cast plays. Owing to our scenic restrictions, they are also amenable to plays with simple sets and, in the case of the trilogy, its flexibility of presentation has naturally proved an advantage elsewhere.[61]

Collectively the three plays explore the changing shapes of sexual and social behaviour, principally as disintegration, in contexts that are ultimately comic but familiar.

In *Round and Round the Garden*, the last play in *The Norman Conquests*, the sexual comedy leads Norman towards abortive attempts at adultery: the 'conquests' are, of course, ironic. In the drunken conclusion of Act One, Norman's outburst to Reg (the husband of one of the women who resist Norman's attempts at seduction) works as simultaneously a comic moment and a revelation of quasi-romantic aspiration:

> I want us just to go. . . . And see things. And taste things. And smell things. And touch things . . . touch trees – and grass – and – and earth. Let's touch earth together, Reg.[62]

A number of elements coincide at that point. Firstly, the breakdown of language suggests that the real aspiration is beyond Norman's capacity to articulate it. The banality of language and character is thus both a comic device and a mechanism to imply a depth of emotional reality beneath the mundane surface. The names themselves are quasi-comic in their suburban ordinariness. However, Ayckbourn's achievement is to suggest that, beneath the very ordinariness of his figures, there exists some powerful potential for aspiration. The defeat of those aspirations is simultaneously comic and poignant.

This is, of course, a very popular combination of emotions for any audience and that duality runs through much of Ayckbourn's work. His writing also captures dilemmas that are common within the experience of contemporary audiences. In that sense, he manages to record effectively the preoccupations of our times in a form that is digestible, sometimes challenging, but never ultimately disturbing.

It is certainly no denigration of his writing to suggest, as others have done, that Ayckbourn is an English equivalent of Neil Simon in that he combines a profound grasp of the age with a capacity to turn this into considerable verbal wit. In this respect, he raises another significant characteristic in the theatre of the period. If, as Jimmy Porter asserts, this is a post-heroic age, it is also no longer tragic. The primary language and form of drama in this period is comedy. Tom Stoppard's *Rosencrantz and Guildenstern Are Dead* is another example of how the tragic is translated into comedy. Ayckbourn, and Stoppard and Peter Nicholls and many others demonstrate that the discontents of this civilisation are, almost inevitably, expressed in laughter.

CONCLUSION: THEATRE AND THE SEGMENTED SOCIETY

There is no single version of British culture. What exists are contested versions of British experience and culture. 'Britain' at the end of the twentieth century is a notion formed and reformed, challenged and redefined. This reality is reflected both in politics and the arts. The rise of Scottish and Welsh nationalism signals segmentation of the idea of Britain in geo-political terms but this is manifest also in gender, ethnicity and regionalism. Even in the architecture of the cities, segmentation is apparent as city centres give way to out-of-town malls, the elderly cluster in retirement communities and holidays are taken in invented landscapes of theme or vacation park. These phenomena signify fragmentation, segmentation and diversity.

While it is foolhardy to speculate too radically on the shape of the future, it is reasonable to assume that these trends will not diminish. Further development of regional institutions of cultural production might be expected, especially in view of the problematic status of some of London's major cultural centres. The crisis at the Royal Opera House is the most dramatic example of an institution under threat partially as a result of a funding crisis but also as a consequence of the sense that vital culture needs to be made outside of the 'centre' in a geographical and cultural/political sense.

It is also reasonable to assume that there will continue to be contested versions of what it is to be British. Indeed the approaching millennium encourages and intensifies the process through which culture is re-examined. At the end of the century, there is a tendency to explore the grand idea and there is no grander idea than the redefinition of self. In this sense, the emergence of writers outside of the mainstream in sexual orientation, regionalism or ethnicity is likely to gather further momentum.

In contested cultures like Britain at the end of the century it is, therefore, inevitable that some groups should take 'marginality' or ambiguities of identity as their subject matter, and that those concerns should seem of increasing importance. An example of this tendency is offered by Ayub Khan-Din's *East is East* (1996). The play examines the impact of immigration and post-colonial experience through an Anglo-Pakistani family, the Khans. In a structure that echoes and acknowledges Wesker's *Trilogy*, the Khan family exists uneasily within and outside of British identity. Wesker's Kahn family translates into the Asian Khans signalling, clearly, a similarity of cultural dilemma. Like Wesker's Jewish fathers, George Khan expresses a futile desire to retain some vestiges of traditional ethnic identity. The failure to do so is expressed in terms of generational conflict wherein the father is ultimately an emasculated and defeated figure. His values belong geographically to the home country and are rooted to the past. Thus, the clash between then and now, there and here is, in the play, also expressed in generational terms. The father's rage, ostensibly directed at this son, is in fact an expression of a divided and marginalised identity: 'Life change all a time, never know what bloody happening see's' [sic].[63] The Khan family, as George's English wife indicates, is divided by race, change and ethnic displacement:

GEORGE: I tell you Mrs, don't starting 'cause I fix you like I fix your baster kids, you all pucking trouble with me.
ELLA: They're only trouble 'cause you don't listen to them, you never have.
GEORGE: I no have to listen, I their father.
ELLA: George, you've got to understand, things aren't like they were when you were young. Kids are different today, our kids are different, they're bleeding half-caste for a start. [sic][64]

The subject of displacement is not, of course, unique to Asian-British writers. It is apparent in Wesker's work and in much Black-British writing. The hyphenated self, Black-British, Jewish-British, etc., inevitably makes the 'other place' a subject, and displacement the aura in which the drama operates. Caryl Phillips's *Where There is Darkness* (1982) is a powerful expression of this subject.

The father, Albert, on the verge of returning to the West Indies confronts his son with a version of Black-British experience that echoes the dilemma of the father expressed by Ayub Khan-Din:

> Since you old enough to switch on your ears I done been telling you black people in this country must act and feel like a tribe or they not going to survive. But what fucking use is a tribe if nobody taking any notice of the elders them? [sic][65]

Albert's disintegration, in a dramatic structure that borrows heavily from Arthur Miller's *Death of a Salesman*, is symptomatic of a dilemma of displacement:

> Don't you see that if he actually does go, the real failure that he is going to face is out there because nothing will have changed. That's the tragedy of the immigrant. They change faster than the countries they have left behind and they can never go back and be happy.[66]

The development of Black and Asian theatre faces many challenges of funding, audience, production and, in some cases, language. There are, however, indications of an increasing determination to give a voice to what has been marginalised. Organisations like Black Arts Alliance, Talawa Theatre Company, Tamasha Theatre Company, London Arts Board and so on collectively offer advice and outlet for new work albeit in a precarious economic environment.[67]

An example of the emerging importance of national and regional theatre is apparent through a brief review of some of the work of the Traverse Theatre in Edinburgh. The Traverse has nurtured important new theatrical talent, most notably that of Liz Lochhead, while sustaining the work of older writers like Ian Crichton Smith. Crichton Smith works in both English with the Traverse and in Gaelic with Tosg (Scotland's Gaelic Theatre Company). As Philip Howard, artistic director of the Traverse argues, there is a sense of mission that is simultaneously contemporary and Scottish:

> the Traverse will continue to pursue vigorously both its role as Scotland's new writing theatre, and its dedication to furthering the climate of confidence for playwrights in Scotland.[68]

As this necessarily brief discussion indicates, it is apparent that contested notions of culture and nation undermine the notion of a central, essential identity that can be designated 'British'. In the absence of such a 'centre', art is made at ethnic, gender, sexual, national margins. Paradoxically this art increasingly moves towards centrality in what we still call British culture(s).

This chapter has not attempted to impose a single model or shape on diverse cultural forms but has instead sought to find pathways through a sometimes bewildering maze. As we seek to describe this present-future it, inevitably, shifts in significance and meaning. The preceding discussion is by no means a final word nor is there a neat conclusion available. The discussion has engaged with pluralities, touched upon some discernible trends and identified continuities and schisms between past and present.

All discussions of contemporary art are, necessarily, provisional. The gift of time will bring some of these issues and judgements into other perspectives. There is, however, one clear message that emerges from this discussion and that is of the persistent energy, diversity and creativity in British theatre. At the end of this century, as at the end of the last, there is an impulse to see the death of art, be it the novel or the play, as an actual condition rather than as another notion from which, and within which, art achieves a paradoxical rebirth. This ending asserts, therefore, an instinctive belief in the vibrant future of the unborn plays and dramatists who will, as children of their creative parents, make things again new.

NOTES

1. John Osborne, *Look Back in Anger* in *Plays: One* (London, 1996), p. 66.
2. Ibid., p. 83.
3. Ibid., p. 44.
4. Ibid., p. 94. The use of this 'dreamed' place exerted, I believe, a direct influence on Edward Albee's *Who's Afraid of Virginia Woolf.*
5. It hardly needs to be said that these issues are not the sole province of theatre but, arguably, drive much of the political and social momentum of post-war Britain from political relationships with European partners to decimalisation. From the government of Harold Macmillan to that of Tony Blair there is a single thread which is, broadly, the search for a place in the world where past can be reconciled with present-future and where national identity can be retained yet compromised with changing realities.
6. I have relied, inevitably, on the written text for much of the discussion that follows although I have used my memory of particular productions (and those of others – Harold Hobson, Michael Billington, Kenneth Tynan, etc.) to inform the analyses where possible. The 'methodology' of this chapter is, therefore, pragmatic.
7. Between late 1971 and the end of 1972 three theatres opened in London that shared similar characteristics which typify this trend. The King's Head in Camden,

the Bush in Shepherd's Bush and the Orange Tree in Richmond are all located in the suburbs, are small spaces above pubs, and are known for putting on new plays.

8. The term 'fringe' was first used at the Edinburgh Festival in 1947 to describe productions that were physically located outside of the city centre.

9. From a discussion with the actress and director Anne Carroll. She also pointed out that at the Bush all the actors, regardless of role or reputation, earned (in 1997) £242 a week.

10. Alan Ayckbourn was, for example, a founder member of the Victoria Theatre.

11. Even in the 'declassed' world of pop music the theme finds expression, most notably in the Pet Shop Boys' 'East End Boys and West End Girls'. In Mike Leigh's film *Secrets and Lies* the surface issue appears to be race (a white mother is found by her lost black daughter) but that issue swiftly dissolves into a comedy of class difference. Had the theme been treated in America, it would almost certainly have been treated as a steamy race melodrama in the heated style, perhaps, of Tennessee Williams. Broadly, American culture has race as its 'default' distinction whereas, in Britain, the prevailing mode of discrimination is class.

12. Susannah Clapp, 'West End Girls (and boys)', *Observer Review*, 24 May 1998, p. 5.

13. The use of the interval wherein dramatic action is suspended is too infrequently considered. The interval(s) create some obviously significant effects including the potential to heighten tension or comic expectation, shift focus, extend the audience's space for consideration and so on. Similarly the absence of intervals signals a conscious intent not to suspend action.

14. This is, of course, a matter of opinion and contention but, arguably, *The Singing Detective* (1986) exhausts its dramatic impact before its actual end.

15. A proliferation of stand-up comedy clubs might be seen as some form of popular recreation of a form of improvisational theatre wherein the 'actor' is freed from the usual paraphernalia of stage (including set, script, cast, director, etc.) and is, therefore, able to create a 'performance' that minimalises the collaborative nature of conventional theatre. These clubs offer a form of performance in which almost all the production and performance elements are located within a single individual.

16. Figures produced by the Theatre Managers' Association indicate a significant decline in the number of tickets sold between 1991 (13 million) and 1996 (9 million).

17. That is not to suggest that theatre is well-funded by public subsidy. There appears to exist an almost permanent state of crisis with regard to subsidy although the introduction of the National Lottery has released some significant funds: £16 million was, for example, allocated for the refurbishment of the Royal Court.

18. This is despite the fact that a seat at, for example, Tottenham Hotspur Football Club is substantially more expensive than one at, for example, the Donmar Warehouse.

19. Although there are obvious seasonal variations, approximately a third of theatre audiences in the commercial theatre in London are overseas visitors (from a discussion with Nica Burns, Stoll Moss Theatres, 1997).

20. Even those musicals ostensibly 'historical' in reference, *Les Miserables* or *Miss Saigon*, use real events to generate archetypal dramatic confrontations. They are

not explorations of historical processes but use a version of history as a framing device for other concerns. This is not to suggest, incidentally, that there is anything intrinsically wrong in myth-making of this kind.

21. The revue had opened in New York prior to the abolition of the Lord Chamberlain's role as censor. The possibilities opened up by the disappearance of that role did not immediately result in a groundswell of liberal indulgence, witnessed by the fact that the vice squad attended the first night opening in London.

22. Letter to Archbishop Lord Fisher of Lambeth, 1 May 1971 in *Kenneth Tynan: Letters*, Kathleen Tynan (ed.) (London, 1994), p. 491.

23. Mark Ravenhill, *Shopping and Fucking* (London, 1996), p. 25.

24. Ibid., p. 37.

25. 'Honour Without Profit', an interview with Fiachra Gibbons, *Guardian 2*, 6 May 1998, p. 15.

26. The notion of a pastoral-rural alternative to corrupted modernity has a curious persistence and is oddly expressed in, for example, the Greenham Common protests where the women's camp (set up to protest the existence of a missile base in 1981) made a political virtue out of the necessity of a 'primitive' life-style.

27. New York, 1958.

28. In writing about British theatre Samuel Beckett always raises an issue of how to treat his work. Christopher Innes in *Modern British Drama, 1890–1990* (Cambridge, 1992) chooses to include Beckett directly as a British writer. While I have no particular quarrel with this approach, I tend to see Beckett as first an 'international' writer belonging particularly in an Irish-French milieu. This chapter will, therefore, not offer specific analyses of Beckett's work but, rather, suggest a sustained and pervasive influence. For reasons of brevity and focus, I have also chosen not to deal with the important writing of Brian Friel (and other Irish dramatists) because they deal with issues that are very specifically rooted in that national experience. The category of 'British' writing is problematic enough – Scottish, Welsh, English variables can only be inadequately treated in this context – without inviting further complexities.

29. Author's Preface to Edward Bond, *Plays Two* (London, 1989), p. 3.

30. A long and rather tedious lists of plays in this period that 'revisit' Shakespeare for a variety of motives might be offered but would stretch the reader's tolerance. It is, perhaps enough, to cite Tom Stoppard's *Rosencrantz and Guildenstern Are Dead* and Marowitz's reconstructions. The list would grow to even more intolerable length if it were to include plays that 're-examine' other significant dramatic landscapes of the past through Classical Greek theatre to Ibsen and beyond. I would like to make the general point but resist the tedium of the list.

31. In *Plays: Two*, p. 93.

32. Arnold Wesker, *Chicken Soup with Barley*, in *The Wesker Trilogy* (Harmondsworth, 1985), p. 73.

33. Simon Gray, *Quartermaine's Terms* in *The Plays of the Seventies* (London, 1986), p. 470.

34. There are arguably a number of similarities between Pinter's work and Gray's, not least in the sense that the language used is frequently meant to disguise rather than reveal meaning. Despite many other contrasts between their plays, the connection may also be indicated by the fact that Pinter has directed all of Gray's major plays.

35. Simon Gray, *Life Support* (London, 1997), p. 7.
36. Christopher Innes, *Modern British Drama: 1890–1990* (Cambridge, 1992), p. 108.
37. Ibid., p. 108.
38. *Oh What a Lovely War* (London, 1986), p. 54.
39. Cited by John Lahr in his introduction to Joe Orton, *The Complete Plays* (London, 1983), p. 17. Any discussion of Orton's work owes a great debt to Lahr's role as editor, critic and biographer. My comments on Orton are, therefore, somewhat truncated in recognition of the fact that Lahr is the preeminent and wisest of guides to Orton's work. Indeed, the contemporary understanding of Orton is formed by Lahr. I believe that it is not too fanciful to see this work in the 1990s as the product of some form of posthumous collaboration.
40. *Entertaining Mr. Sloane*, in *The Complete Plays*, ibid., p. 99.
41. John Lahr 'Introduction', ibid., p. 7.
42. *Entertaining Mr. Sloane*, ibid., p. 149.
43. *Loot*, ibid., p. 275.
44. *What the Butler Saw*, ibid., p. 448.
45. Ibid., p. 273.
46. Ibid., p. 274.
47. Ibid., p. 376.
48. This speech from *Loot* (p. 209) is an example of Orton's reworking of that Wildean technique: 'every luxury was lavished on you – atheism, breast-feeding, circumcision. I had to make my own way.'
49. See, for example, Chris Bigsby's discussion of Pinter's influence in *Joe Orton* (London and New York), 1982.
50. 'The boys were doing well, somehow putting our generation on the map. Some of those boys made *Beyond the Fringe* more than just another little Shaftesbury Avenue night of funny songs and passing sketches. It left Flanders and Swann on the other side of the planet. It had a danger to it, the feeling that as the sixties began that clever young men – *these* clever young men – could say anything, do anything, and get away with it.' Peter Preston, 'Dud's Life Beyond the Fringe', *Guardian 2*, 18 June 1998, p. 6.
51. In a letter to the *Guardian*, 19 September 1966.
52. Pinter has, in these various guises, generously encouraged other talent, Simon Gray's for example.
53. In a discussion with Michael Woolf. As drama editor of Methuen, Earley has been in a unique position to see contemporary theatre as it has evolved. He has also had a key role in making new writers available in published formats through the Methuen Drama series. This series has not only published new work but, heroically, kept it in print. It is, of course, ideal to see new plays in production but physical limitations frequently make this impossible in any inclusive fashion. The fact that we are able to sustain some broad perspectives on contemporary theatre is due, in no small part, to Michael Earley and Methuen Drama.
54. Harold Pinter, *A Kind of Alaska*, in *Harold Pinter: Plays 4* (London, 1996), p. 342.
55. Cited in Arnold Hinchcliffe, *Harold Pinter* (London, 1976).
56. Harold Pinter, 'Writing for Myself', *Twentieth Century*, February 1961, pp. 172–5.
57. Michael Billington, *One Night Stands* (London, 1993), pp. 75–6.

58. Ibid., pp. 53–4.
59. Prior to the establishment of this theatre, he produced his plays at the Library Theatre-in the-Round in Scarborough. The arguments that follow apply equally to the plays produced there.
60. It is misleading, however, to over-estimate the uniqueness of this crossover. Recent plays by Patrick Marber and Mark Ravenhill have similarly gone from fringe to the West End.
61. Alan Ayckbourn's 'Preface' to *The Norman Conquests* (Harmondsworth, 1977), pp. 10–11.
62. *Round and Round the Garden* in *The Norman Conquests*, p. 192.
63. Ayub Khan, *East is East* (London, 1996), p. 12.
64. Ibid., p. 50.
65. Caryl Phillips, *Where There is Darkness* (London, 1982), pp. 22–3.
66. Ibid., p. 47.
67. The London Arts Board has published two recent pamphlets detailing opportunities and outlets in this area: 'Black Writing' (n.d.) and 'Plan for Production, Scriptwriting: Asian Interests' (n.d.).
68. 'Introduction' to *Scotland Plays: New Scottish Drama* (London, 1998), p. xiii. The volume is in itself a testimony to the importance of the Traverse and to the vitality of drama in Scotland. It contains significant plays by Lochhead, Crichton Smith, Linda McClean, Catherine Czerkawska, Anne Marie di Mambro, David Greig and Stephen Greenhorn.

CHAPTER FIVE

British Newspapers

Nicholas Rance

The growth of British newspapers in the years from 1900 to 1929, discussed in the first volume of this series, had been dominated by a slightly earlier event, the founding by Alfred Harmsworth, the future Lord Northcliffe, of the *Daily Mail* in 1896, appealing to a readership inflated by the 1870 Education Act, and whose desiderata in relation to a newspaper were sprightliness and assorted illumination but nothing too taxing. By the 1920s, the *Daily Mail* had acquired a momentous rival in the shape of Lord Beaverbrook's *Daily Express*, intended to beat Northcliffe at his own game. Through most of the period covered by the second volume of this series, 1930–55, the *Daily Express* aptly set the pace in Fleet Street, outselling the *Daily Mail* by 1934. Another unequivocal success-story from the mid-1930s onwards, however, was that of the *Daily Mirror*, eventually to displace the *Daily Express* as market-leader: with a resort to 'strong words and compelling type', as Hugh Cudlipp recalled, the *Daily Mirror* in the 1930s ushered in 'the tabloid revolution'.[1] A preoccupation of the present essay will be to examine some of the piquant latter stages of this revolution, especially as exemplified by Rupert Murdoch's *Sun*, dominant force in the market place since the 1970s in line of succession to the *Daily Mail*, *Daily Express* and *Daily Mirror*.

The year 1956 is renowned for a cluster of portentous episodes, with more or less of a bearing on the newspaper industry. It was the year of Suez and also of *Look Back in Anger*, though with the play preceding the political crisis rather than subsuming it in the retrospect. A side-effect of the crisis was to see the *Observer*, bracingly inimical to governmental policy, overtake a torpid *Sunday Times* for the first time, with a circulation of 568,969 which did not start to level off until 1960, though typically this boost to the radical reputation of the paper was barely an incentive to advertisers (to be provided with a more alluring option by the advent in

1961 of the *Sunday Telegraph*, with a more decorous and presumably more affluent readership). Alternatively, the Suez episode set a fashion for the serialisation of war memoirs, including Churchill's in 1957 and Montgomery's in 1958, with the *Sunday Times* especially an afficionado, since patriotic readers were liable to respond to a current whiff of degeneration by wishing to hark back to the more propitious days of the Second World War. A similar impulse gave agreeable financial uplift to the literary career of Ian Fleming. The *Daily Express* had begun to serialise his novels in 1956, adding a cartoon version of James Bond and his exploits from 1957. In 1957, *From Russia With Love* epitomised the contemporary appeal of Fleming's novels, with SMERSH, in need of a fillip to morale, deciding on the British Secret Service and James Bond in particular as being alone worthy adversaries, with the Americans trailing in the field ('Good spies will not work for money alone – only bad ones, of which the Americans have several divisions').[2] The United States had offended not only by its post-war elevation to the status of twin super-power with the Soviet Union, to the exclusion of Britain, and suborning British youth with its popular culture, but recently also by castigating the Suez adventure.

1956 was also the year of a couple of landmarks with more specific relation to the development of newspapers. There was the demise of newsprint rationing which had been in force since 1940, ending an artificial trading situation in which established albeit lacklustre newspapers could thrive partly as a consequence of a sparsity of advertising outlets, and preparing the way for much more cut-throat competition in Fleet Street by the early 1960s, with the advent of colour magazines and other supplements, harbingers of the heavy-weight weekend newspapers of the 1990s. Secondly and even more significantly, 1956 was the first full year of the operation of commercial television. This was to escalate the skirmishing in Fleet Street in quest of advertising spoils, upon which 'quality' newspapers, with their circumscribed if more affluent readerships compared with those of the popular press, rely for the bulk of their income, since television now replaced newspapers as the main advertising medium.

There was a yet more radical effect on newspapers, however, in that what had been presumed to be their *raison d'être* was undermined: the twenty-four-hour cycle of a newspaper tended to lose its point as a news medium, in face of the recurring instalments of news on television. Broadsheet newspapers could try to adjust to the situation by supplying detailed background to news headlines, perhaps seasoned by an investigative twist. For the popular press, the problem might have seemed to be more intractable. The *Daily Mirror* and *Daily Sketch* began by pretending that television did not exist, despite the evidence that it was a major component in their readers' lives. An innovation of the *Sun*, as transformed under Rupert Murdoch's ownership from 1969, was to assume that it was a mistake to treat television as a rival medium: on the contrary, television, or especially its more down-home productions, would be treated in great depth. Crises in the plots of soap-operas, but also the actors' true-life romances and tribulations, were to be voraciously analysed, with characters and thespians, fact and fiction, becoming sumptuously confused. This betokened what was to become a favourite strategy in the face of the new medium, and one by no means restricted to the popular press: displaced as the primary emissary of news, newspapers would increasingly focus on providing entertainment, with fiction enjoying a doughty reputation as liable to be more entertaining than fact.

Various episodes rebounded on the *Sun* to the extent of seeming to commentators not long ago to herald a relative sunset.[3] The widow of a Falklands war hero was mythically interviewed; slanted and less than taste-ful coverage of the Hillsborough football disaster led to a boycott of the *Sun* in the Liverpool area effective enough to impinge commercially and extract an unaccustomed apology from the editor, Kelvin Mackenzie; in-voking 'rent boys' in the same breath as a rock star cost the paper £1 million in damages. The requisition of a Royal Family story for Mondays, with business traditionally slow, was accompanied by the editorial solace, 'Don't worry if it's not true' (especially since, unlike rock stars, the Royal Family did not sue; by 1992, of course, the *annus horribilis*, it was almost certainly all true, anyway).[4] The *Sun*'s debonair attitude in the face of actuality was parodied by the enticement in *Private Eye*, 'Kill an Argie and Win a Metro', but more pertinaciously by David Sullivan's *Sunday Sport* (founded in 1986, and begetter of proliferating daily *Sports*), with con-sternation about the individual so traumatised by a meeting with aliens as to turn into a fish finger and have to be sustained in the freezer, or the revelation of a statue of Elvis Presley on Mars (as in the case of the double-decker buses spotted at the South Pole, however, the astonishing disappear-ance of the phenomenon was liable to provide next week's headline). Though it has been alleged that the *Sunday Sport* is a 'cheaply produced magazine more than a newspaper', no one would thus asperse the *Daily Star*, and for a few weeks in 1987, surrealism entered the mainstream, with a sort of merger of the two organs, only for advertisers to become prim and the discovery that the public was unequal to a daily diet of absconded buses and female endowments bidding for a niche in the *Guinness Books of Records*.[5]

A sign of barefaced times was the dwindling circulation of the *News of the World*, Rupert Murdoch's first acquisition on the British market in 1968, with Robert Maxwell being pipped for ownership in the earliest of a series of such skirmishes between the two which Maxwell was 'sure to lose', Antony to Murdoch's Octavius. The parallel universe of the *News of the World*, replete with slant-eyed managers of fish-and-chip shops seducing ladies from the bacon factory, was now the workaday diet, so that British Sundays lost their special flavour of tedium being rendered more poignant by a dose of salaciousness. What is notable is not merely a slide into rampant sensationalism, by no means a prerogative of the last third of the twentieth century ('The maw of the London Minotaur is insatiable, and none that go into the secret recesses of his lair return again,' remarked W.T. Stead in his series of 1885 in the *Pall Mall Gazette*, 'The Maiden Tribute of Modern Babylon'), but into a sensationalism often deriving from unabashed fantasy (whereas the shock-horror quotient of W.T. Stead had been earned by exposing an actual phenomenon).[6]

If newspaper proprietors are assumed to be inspired at least partly by the desire to make money, they might be supposed merely to be catering to a public demand, which would transfer any burden of responsibility for a descent into an oddly vacuous kind of sensationalism compared to that pioneered by Stead on to the broad shoulders of the age. The fact that readers buy what is on sale, however, cannot be a guarantee that they would refuse something else, while there is a further rebuff to fatalism in the evidence that *Sun* readers tend to refer to their paper as a 'comic', and *News of the World* readers assume that what they are reading is all lies. John Pilger invokes, by way of contrast to a dispiriting state of affairs in the present, the heyday of the *Daily Mirror* in the 1960s, with picture-led, campaigning journalism being compatible with sales to a predominantly working-class readership of 5.25 million.[7] With Pilger initially having been cast as a pivotal figure (but he walked out some months before the launch in April 1987), the phenomenon of *News on Sunday* was a bedevilled attempt to establish the point that just because a paper was a tabloid, it was not obliged to presume that its readers were morons. Arguably, at least, the early demise of the newspaper did not comprise evidence to the contrary, since there was a failure to complement the eschewing of Newsbirds with any alternative sparkle.[8]

Superficially, Rupert Murdoch and the late Robert Maxwell may evoke earlier figures such as Northcliffe and Beaverbrook. Maxwell especially, with his exuberant physique and his cigars if not his reversed baseball-cap, might seem to have been everyone's picture of a turn-of-the-century tycoon (or if one ventures earlier, perhaps a replica of Sir Giles Overreach of the monstrous ego and of Massinger's play with the apropos title, *A New Way to Pay Old Debts*). Even apart from the momentous difference that Murdoch's newspaper empire has a much larger proportion of the market in thrall than fell to his predecessor, Lord Northcliffe, other divergences, too, between early and modern press barons, are liable to be more eloquent than the similarities. Beaverbrook was prone to avow that he ran his newspapers primarily as instruments of propaganda: there was his Empire Crusade of the 1930s, dwindling into antipathy to the idea of British entry into the Common Market in the 1950s. If Northcliffe was less opinionated, his indifference to what by 1914 had emerged as his chief money-spinner, the *Daily Illustrated Mirror*, is revealing: it was to be transferred cheaply to his brother, Harold, later Lord Rothermere, while what retained Northcliffe's interest was the more literate and stimulating *Daily Mail*. Both Northcliffe and Beaverbrook may be credited with aspirations beyond trading on the assumption that readers were bone-headed.

If the *Daily Mirror* under Maxwell's auspices at least was animated by his passion for self-promotion, a kind of 'vacuum, a moral void', as Matthew Engel has remarked,[9] seems to be a hallmark of Murdoch's operations and then to permeate his newspapers. This perhaps testifies to a cardinal distinction between Murdoch and eminent newspaper proprietors of the past: that newspapers for Murdoch are merely an element, if a crucial one, in a multinational commercial empire, which not only incorporates interests in other media (Sky television, Twentieth Century Fox), but extends to the odd airline. With profits from the *Sun* underpinning development of the Sky project, the priority was that there was money to be pumped rather than that the *Sun* should elicit such compliments as had fallen to Northcliffe's *Daily Mail*. Speaking as editor of the *Daily Telegraph*, Max Hastings suggested that two antithetical kinds of journalism were in competition: one that was 'trying to tell the truth', and another that treated 'the news as show business'.[10] So far at least as Rupert Murdoch's News International stable was concerned, this did not cash out as a distinction between broadsheet and tabloid newspapers, since a relaxed attitude in relation to the odd excess of cock-and-bull prevailed in unaccustomed areas. Murdoch's sublimely cool epitaph to the episode of high farce in which the *Sunday Times* and its expert witness, Professor Hugh Trevor-Roper, came to grief in relation to the spurious Hitler diaries, is an epitome of the perspective which to Max Hastings seemed reprehensible: 'After all, we are in the entertainment business.'[11]

The onus evidently has been on Murdoch's editors to extol the virtues of Thatcherism and the free market; any hint of heresy, such as registering the incursions and excursions of the Social Democratic Party in the early 1980s, was liable to see the proprietor at his most interventionist. There are differences, however, between the propagandist impulses of a Murdoch and a Beaverbrook, with one being how the political agenda of the Murdoch press has invited the imputation of being manifestly self-serving. One should not put too much stress on specific *quid pro quos*, since the free-market ethic would have been unfeignedly regarded as being good for a business such as the one which Murdoch was running (just as it is recorded of

Robert Maxwell that he was never more prone to revise leaders in the *Daily Mirror* than when big business was being aspersed). There was, however, a balmy intimacy between Murdoch and the Thatcher government, as *mutatis mutandis*. In the late 1990s, there has been more than a hint of Murdoch and Blair being strange bedfellows. The *Sun* endorsed Labour in the 1997 General Election, with subsequent somewhat unseemly efforts to keep it onside, such as the Prime Minister being agreeable to be deputed to elicit information concerning possible Italian media deals.

Under the Conservative government, a notably equivocal argument was sustained by John Biffen in the House of Commons for not referring Murdoch's acquisition from the Thomson organisation of *The Times* and the *Sunday Times* to the Monopolies Commission. If a newspaper was established to be loss-making, then an otherwise unacceptable deal was not subject to scrutiny. *The Times* qualified easily, but some wobbly statistics had to be brandished to suggest that the *Sunday Times* was not making a profit. On the other hand, the *Sun* had been ardent at the 1979 General Election for Mrs Thatcher, an instalment of whose gratitude had already been expressed with an accolade to the editor, Larry Lamb, mastermind of the distinctively Murdochian *Sun*, and one of a flurry of tabloid knights in the 1980s. With such scope for mutual back-scratching, it was not surprising that safeguards of the editorial prerogative accompanying the purchase of *The Times* and *Sunday Times* turned out to be not worth the paper they were written on (in an idiom resuscitated by the purchaser). Under the auspices of Harold Evans, *The Times* had demurred at least about some of the more arcane early trappings of Thatcherism, such as monetarism, a prelude to the brusque dismissal of the editor.[12]

Even apart from a whiff of pragmatism, recent propaganda efforts of the tabloid press have been prone to be somewhat unscrupulous, not to put too fine a point on it. The *Sun*'s coverage of the Hillsborough disaster epitomised the trend, adding insult to injuries and fatalities in the cause of sustaining the myth that the police were wonderful, while likely candidates for being policed (comprehending in the 1980s urban rioters and striking miners as well as football supporters) were scum. This amounts to a two-fold reversal of the once-exalted tradition of investigative journalism: apparently too barefaced to require a Sherlock Holmes, the nominated villains turn out to be not the rich and powerful, the Distillers Company of the thalidomide debacle in the 1970s or Stead's traders in youthful virginities, but merely hapless individuals who may seem to have been on the receiving end in the first place. In relation to more specifically political coverage, a newspaper tactic acquiring numbing predictability in the last twenty years or so, though of more extended lineage, is to ascribe the impetus for an ostensibly broad movement to a lone individual, who thus at least may constitute a convenient focus of attack. The movement will then be ripe to be vilified by association with a crop of alleged personal deficiencies: if so-and-so is like this or one of these, then not much space need be wasted on actually debating whatever. Mark Hollingsworth's book on the virulence of the press in the face of political dissent recounts some of the indignities suffered by demurring figures of the 1980s: Benn, Livingstone, Tatchell, Scargill.[13] Having categorised enemies within as mad or depraved or both, to apply a fine-tooth comb to the details of their arguments would be superfluous, so that a theory achieving impressive currency was that Benn's politics were merely the nemesis of drinking too many mugs of tea. The peculiar concerted ferocity of such attacks in recent times seems rooted in a familiar state of affairs: that with the solitary exception of the *Guardian*, national newspapers are merely segments of much more extensive commercial empires, with a corresponding querulousness in the face of any imputed red menace.

A couple of issues in relation to the development of newspapers over the period should be brought into focus: the connotations of the exodus from Fleet Street from 1985, led by the transit of Rupert Murdoch's titles to Wapping, but also the state of the British press prior to the Murdoch explosion (with a harvest of chagrin to be reaped, the International Publishing Corporation, owners of the *Daily Mirror*, had been induced to sell the original broadsheet *Sun*, a Liberal-tinged paper neither fish nor flesh, cheaply to Murdoch in 1969). John Pilger's assault on the consequences of Murdoch stresses the merits of the *Daily Mirror* in particular in the 1960s: celebrations of transformations in pop culture with the emergence of the Beatles were compatible with a series on the plight of the elderly in Liverpool, while the paper had the distinction of being alone in Fleet Street in denouncing the American invasion of Vietnam, with the Labour government as fawning cheer-leaders. A more jaundiced view of the situation which was an article of faith to initiators of the *Sun* was that the *Daily Mirror* had given their own fledgling intruder an opening by having become too earnest and solemn for its readers: copies of the informative supplement, *Mirrorscope*, cited by Pilger as a mark of distinction, allegedly were to be seen littering London buses and tubes, manifestly discarded as unread. From the perspective of the late 1990s, the *Daily Mirror* would seem evidently to have committed hara-kiri by a misconceived attempt to compete with the *Sun*, involving in the 1980s spasms of nipples and more sustained Bingo competitions (and as almost might seem to be honourably conceded by a switch to the more sparse title, the *Mirror*). There is a further argument, however, that the press as a whole has caught a dose of Murdoch's levity or crassness or both, with broadsheets not his own being liable to combine a servility to the powers-that-be with a penchant for tittle-tattle, and a more aspiring curiosity in the ill-odour once registered by Matthew Arnold in remarking on the word as having no sense in England 'but a rather bad and disparaging one'.[14]

The *Daily Mirror* of the 1960s was by no means averse to exploiting the odd frolic. The divorce case of the Duchess of Argyll was one of the sensations of 1963, an *hors-d'oeuvre* to the Profumo affair, with speculation especially fomented by 'AN UNKNOWN MAN – who appeared nude – without his face showing – in photographs with the Duchess'.[15] If one looks again, however, at the paper's coverage of the Profumo scandal, there are reasons to be impressed: the *modus operandi* of the *News of the World*, bequeathed in a less endearing version to the *Sun*, of prurience subsiding into a moral, is not much in evidence. A more robust approach was betokened in the wake of Profumo's resignation speech, admitting that he had lied to the House of Commons in denying an affair with Christine Keeler:

> God knows, he was never a good Minister; it seems now that he is not a very impressive man. But there is guilt in many a heart, and skeletons in many cupboards.
> The question is: *What the hell is going on in this country?*[16]

So capacious a view gave the newspaper a ready reply to the *Guardian*, accusing the *Daily Mirror* of gutter-journalism in buying Keeler's memoirs, while the subsequent involvement in the case of the flagrant slum landlord, Peter Rachman, 'protector' of the eighteen-year-old Mandy Rice-Davies, was a further chance to confute the charge of an obsession with merely sexual shenanigans: 'Profumo's own delinquency is pettifogging when set beside the repulsive assault on society organised by Peter Rachman.'[17] Neither making a fetish of Profumo's misdemeanours nor in a mood to underrate the import of the specific case, the *Daily Mirror* steered a reputable path between the myopic pragmatism of the *Daily Telegraph*, mustering a Murdochian defence in advance of Murdoch for relishing a scandal (it was 'on the popular taste of the nation in 1963, and not on that section which serves it through the Press', that reproach should ultimately fall),[18] and the sentimental though doubtless canny moralising of Lord Hailsham, cheered on by the *Daily Express* and *The Times*, alleging that the affair was not a party issue, but 'a national moral issue': as if, remarked the *Daily Mirror*, 'the entire British public had been caught in bed with Miss Keeler'.[19]

On the other hand, the *Daily Mirror* was less in command by 1967 in the face of a scandal of a riper 'permissiveness', when the emancipationist and reactionary fevers stirred by the 'Summer of Love' came to a head with drugs charges against the principal members of the Rolling Stones, to serve precisely as scapegoats for a premonition of national moral decay, with a touch of old-fashioned sadism in response to the verdict: 'The dreamlike world of pop music came down to earth yesterday when Rolling Stones

Mick Jagger and Keith Richard swapped their millionaire homes for prison cells.'[20] Like nearly all of the press, with the *Guardian* as a predictable albeit honourable exception, the *Daily Mirror* might have taken apt admonishment from William Rees-Mogg's editorial in *The Times*, 'Who Breaks a Butterfly up on a Wheel?', with its plea to traditionalists to 'be sure that the sound traditional values include those of tolerance and equity'.[21] There is liable now to seem a fustiness about newspaper coverage generally of the cultural exuberances of the period; more to the point, however, one may be able to recall that this is not merely the effect of long retrospect. To such an extent, it is the less surprising that the brashness and uncouthness of the born-again *Sun* were to find a market among more youthful readers, admittedly with a seamier version of the 1960s 'sexual revolution' (which, however, lent the smut a spurious respectability), but then, after the 1960s, the public was less easily shocked. Despite the famous leader, *The Times* was reduced to an habitual dependence on inverted commas, terminally embarrassed by 'happenings' and 'hippies'. The popular press, however, was also prone to flounder. 'And with the temperature in the 80s, the Hippies rounded it off with a dip in the Serpentine. Real cool', was a sprightly caption in the *Daily Mirror*.[22] As the voice of youth, the paper had not much progressed since its forlorn compulsion of the 1950s to hold rock 'n' roll parties, observing the degenerates at close quarters and being grateful if they didn't bite.

Confirming Murdoch's status as a devil-figure for the left was the removal in 1985 of his newspapers to Wapping, and so to their production as expedited by the 'new technology', with 'direct input' by journalists from their keyboards to the pages rendering superfluous National Graphical Association typesetters with their ancient Linotype machines. This is an episode to which books have been devoted, not least as signalling 'the end of the Street', with journalists on national newspapers bidding farewell to the camaraderie of Fleet Street and the heroic excesses of El Vino's, to move east to a curiously cocooned environment, at a remove from events and contacts as from supporting watering holes.[23] Alternatively, Murdoch's exodus is liable to be reviled for dirty tricks during ostensible negotiations with the printing unions, lured into a strike the more economically to be rid of them. For more than a year, journalists were conducted to Fortress Wapping, with its German razor-wire, in armoured buses, with unionists and their allies ensuring that the progress would be turbulent. It is not only those on the political right, however, who have difficulty in feeling sorry for the printing unions, in the wake of decades of importunate 'old Spanish customs', with Mickey Mouses collecting £1100 for a sixteen-hour week doing invisible and unnecessary work. In his television documentary of 1997, John Pilger is less than successful in trying to soften the impact of the verdict of a champion from the golden age of the *Daily Mirror*, the late Hugh Cudlipp, by putting the accent on Murdoch's Machiavellianism (which almost certainly was included in what Cudlipp could forgive): 'It should be remembered that Murdoch's great contribution . . . was not the *Sun*, or the *News of the World*, but defeating unions who were making it impossible to produce newspapers of any sort. I forgive him a lot for that.'[24]

Cudlipp's tribute, however, must be tinged with unconscious irony, since the flurry of fresh newspapers anticipated in the aftermath to Wapping and sensationally diminished costs of production has failed to materialise, or at any rate to survive. Of the four national newspapers launched in the 1980s, the only survivor is the *Independent* (the casualties being *News on Sunday*, the *Sunday Correspondent* and *Today*), and ultimately the effect of Wapping has been to produce less diversity rather than more. Despite what his newspapers preach for the enhancement of others, it has never been a tenet of Murdoch in relation to his own commercial affairs that competition is good for the soul, and he has prophesied with a degree of fortitude that in the medium to long term only three daily papers will survive – his own *The Times* and the *Sun*, and the *Daily Mail* to cater for a middle market (though in recent years, formerly austere broadsheets have been supersensitive to the success of the *Daily Mail*, reincarnated as a 'compact', and bent on themselves democratically subsiding to embrace a middle market). The aim of declaring the current price war is to hasten fulfilment of the prophecy, with the immediate target being the *Independent*, while also locking horns with Conrad Black's Hollinger group which owns the *Daily Telegraph*. Murdoch's ability to sustain such a war derives precisely from what optimists saw as the liberating move to Wapping, yielding huge profits which could be pumped into satellite television and so in turn generate even huger profits (to be eked out by the common knack of multinational companies of paying the barest minimum of tax; whatever may be the current nationality of a newspaper tycoon, it will not be at the expense of a partiality for the Netherland Antilles). There is then the supplementary irony that while Conservative MPs argue for the necessity of measures to control the expansion of the empire, Rupert Murdoch's new friends in New Labour regard such measures as primitive and superfluous.

One may posit in relation to a press saturated by wider commercial pressures a more salubrious state of affairs in the past; to a large extent, however, features inherent in the medium will produce an affinity between how newspapers and the brazen popular fictions of which Lord Northcliffe had been an assiduous if sometimes perplexed student will be apt to gloss actuality. In relation to the case-study which follows of coverage of the pursuit and trial of the Yorkshire Ripper, for instance, there were exigent reasons why the speculations of psychiatrists would be anathema at least to tabloid newspapers. The format of the popular press is too sprightly and effervescent for even relatively enlightened editors to appreciate the merits of learned disquisitions on schizophrenia: sentences and paragraphs of minimal duration will be more prone to disseminate a brisk and punchy 'common sense'. If the latter tends to predominate generally in our perception of crime, however, since abhorrence of the deed is not conducive to abstruse reflection about causality, one may ascribe to journalists a specialised and active role in contributing to the 'stability and survival' of such a perspective.[25] Functioning in harmony with a perhaps prevalent reluctance to delve beneath the surface are the so-called 'professional imperatives of journalism'.[26] Such imperatives as 'personalisation', 'immediacy', 'dramatisation', convey a similar message. If the crucial question is what qualifies as news, the answer will be either personalities or precisely defined happenings or events, so that an ideological dimension is already incorporated in what counts as newsworthy. An obsession with personalities will suggest that specific persons rather than social structures are candidates to be at fault; while a palpable event potentially qualifies as news, underlying causes or processes which may have persisted for years are for the birds. Especially liable to be forfeited, then, to the 'professional imperatives of journalism', will be the antecedent dimensions to news stories, whose sacrifice will help to ratify the drift of such bluff analysis of ostensibly discrete events as is to be found in the leader-columns of the popular press.

'A DREADFUL, LONG-RUNNING DETECTIVE STORY': REPORTING THE CASE OF THE YORKSHIRE RIPPER

Bob Roshier has remarked of the principles governing newspaper reporting that 'The dangers of our experiencing crime through the "fantasy world" of crime fiction are almost certainly no more important than the dangers of our experiencing it through the selective reporting of actual events.'[27] 'If any literary work is too long to be read at one sitting', wrote Edgar Allan Poe in his essay, 'The Philosophy of Composition', 'we must be content to dispense with the immensely important effect derivable from unity of impression.' Presumably it was to some extent in deference to this principle as well as to the demands of the American magazine market that not only Poe's poems (the focus of his essay is on the composition of 'The Raven'), but also his detective stories, were usually contrived to be brief. The significant relative exception, however, is 'The Mystery of Marie Roget', in which Poe's detective, Dupin, presumes to solve an actual and current mystery, that of the ostensible murder of Mary Rogers in New York State, with events being transposed in the story to France: it is more than twice as long as 'The Murders in the Rue Morgue' or 'The Purloined Letter' (and after all, Poe and his detective come to grief in confounding a botched abortion with a murder). If the appeal of detective fiction has relied on conveying the genial impression that the criminal's lot is in more or less sprightly fashion to be identified as such and apprehended, the real-life hunt for the Yorkshire Ripper spanned more than five years at a cost of four million pounds, so that Poe's perplexities in relation to 'The Mystery of Marie Roget' seem to resonate in the characterisation by the *Sunday Telegraph* of the hunt as 'a dreadful, long-running detective story'; perhaps especially dreadful in being long-running.[28]

The sundry blunders committed by the police are notorious: thus they were misled by the teasing and, as would transpire, bogus tapes into virtually eliminating any potential suspect without a Geordie accent, while the discovery of the blood-stained handbag of one of the victims did not lead them to notice the adjacent corpse. Effectively skirted in newspapers, however, is an acknowledgement of what at least at the time was the essentially baffling nature of the conundrum posed to the police. As Victorian newspapers sometimes had the grace to concede in the case of Jack the Ripper – 'Not a trace is left of the murderer, and there is no purpose in the crime to afford the slightest clue, such as would be afforded in other crimes almost without exception,' wrote *The Times*[29] – so there was the odd concession a century later, as the *Daily Mail* reckoned the dilemmas associated with tracking down a similarly enigmatic killer: 'He chose his own ground and his own haphazard timing – sometimes with long gaps between killings. He struck at random. There was no apparent motive.'[30] Nevertheless, in contemporary newspaper coverage, the stress on police blunders comes to constitute a way of turning a blind eye to the measure of the problem, and the popular press insisted that a panacea was available through calling in Scotland Yard, just as, in Conan Doyle's fiction, Scotland Yard was constantly under pressure to call in Sherlock Holmes.

The Times had rounded off its lament about the elusiveness of Jack the Ripper with the sentiment, 'All that the police can hope is that some accidental circumstance will lead to a trace which may be followed to a successful conclusion.'[31] In January 1981, the arrest of Sutcliffe prompted a release of accumulated nervous tension: after the long wait, newspapers, like the police, were notably unconcerned that he had yet to be tried let alone convicted. The situation was potentially the more charged since the manner of his arrest – he was routinely interrogated after being found in a red-light area with a prostitute in a car displaying false number plates – was the epitome of 'accidental circumstance': a resolution of a sort, but not one to suffuse the apprehension of the criminal with an aura of ineluctability. As even fictional representatives of the FBI in pursuit of a serial killer have been reduced to ruminate: 'Scary how it works. Bundy gets pulled because a taillight's out. Son of Sam gets nailed because of a parking ticket.'[32]

Himself a reader of the *Daily Mail*, Sutcliffe was asked his opinion during the trial about 'what sort of man newspapers made the Ripper out to be', and fastidiously replied, 'a monster'.[33] The resort to Gothic metaphor would isolate as aberrations not only the savagery of the crimes but also any special difficulties presented by the chase, rather than the latter being accountable, say, to a peculiarly perplexing line in crime. There may then be the ancillary thought, however, that the world would be yet further enhanced minus the occasional monster. In one report in the *Daily Mail*, the ostensible monster simply vanishes. 'Sutcliffe . . . was the ultimate invisible man. Four paces in any direction from his place in the dock . . . and he would have melted into any crowd of three.'[34] The swerve to insist on the serial killer as merely ordinary has its own hazards: in Patricia Cornwell's fiction, a penchant for the concept of the monstrous serves by way of counterbalance to a political correctness on the alert to spot disconcerting affinities between the attitudes to women of the average male chauvinist such as Kay Scarpetta's colleague, Lieutenant Marino, and those evinced by the serial killer. On the other hand, if the branch may bear our weight for the short time that we step on it, then a farewell to monsters has its charms.

Meeting in advance of the case being heard, counsels for defence and prosecution had settled between them that a plea of guilty of manslaughter rather than murder, on the grounds of diminished responsibility, would not be contested. This pact was overturned, however, by the judge, who insisted that the 'mad or bad' issue should be argued before the jury. The latter took six hours to decide by a majority of ten to two that Sutcliffe was bad rather than mad, though within three years he had been moved from an ordinary prison to Broadmoor Hospital, having been agreed by doctors to be clinically insane, a paranoid schizophrenic. In relation both to the legal outcome and to press coverage, Agatha Christie's wistful comment about the period of her first ventures into detective fiction is apropos: 'We had not then begun to wallow in psychology.'[35] Having been efficiently apprehended, the villain should then plausibly embody the root of all evil in the particular case: hints of childhood traumas implying that the trail of guilt recedes or that he is less than fully responsible for his actions will be an irritant. In recent crime fiction, the psychiatric virtuoso may be besmirched by being doubled with the figure of the serial killer, as with Hannibal Lecter in Thomas Harris's *The Silence of the Lambs*, or by blabbing about the strategies of the chase to a social circle transpiring to include the serial killer. A psychiatrist at the trial had responded under interrogation: 'Any doctor can be wrong. Of course I could be wrong. But I don't think I am.' As translated into tabloidese, however, this acquired a sensationalist boost in the headline in the *Sun*: 'Perhaps I've been duped by Sutcliffe.'[36] Condemning the vetoed pact between defence and prosecution, the *Sun* had cryptically remarked: 'There is a great deal of public anxiety already about the Ripper and the failure of the police to arrest him earlier.'[37] To have accepted that Sutcliffe was mad would have been as though he had been enabled once more to escape the net.

As the *Daily Telegraph* remarked with affordable sophistication, 'the explanation of madness' might have the defect of allowing 'society to put its evil outside itself, instead of facing its ever-present reality'. To ascribe to Sutcliffe a monopoly of responsibility for his crimes, however, was equally calculated to let society off the hook, and such was the newspaper's stress in applauding the verdict, which ought to help to fortify faith in a creed to which sensible people already subscribed, even if apparently not so fervently that reinforcement was redundant. The axiom to be reaffirmed was 'that people who do the most revolting and pointless things may yet be respons- ible for their actions. That belief is essential for the strength and sanity of society.' The shrill proposition is thus advanced that social sanity is in need of underpinning by the presumption of the Ripper's sanity, but then with the nonchalant modification that merely such an *ex cathedra* gloss on events as the *Daily Telegraph* is currently proffering will suffice to save the day as the requisite social super-glue: if 'someone is *said* [my emphasis] to be responsible for his actions, even if they are utterly horrible and quite unlike those of most people, then the reality of his deeds confronts everyone. He is not an animal, or a robot gone wrong, but a fellow citizen who chose to do what he did.'[38] *The Times* adopted the quizzical tone of the Victorian political commentator, Walter Bagehot, celebrating the utility of the institution of royalty, despite the lacklustre quality of the individuals currently embodying it, as supplying salutarily misleading fodder for the popular imagination. The issue of truth or falsehood was dismissed as irrelevant: the person of Sutcliffe was no less dwarfed by symbolic baggage than were those of Bagehot's puppet queen and her lumpish son. Conceding that 'from a common sense point of view, it is pure nonsense even to ask whether Sutcliffe was sane', the leader avowed: 'There is more at stake in a trial of this exceptional character than the fate of the prisoner. It is a public catharsis, an exorcism.'[39]

In an interview published in 1983, P.D. James remarked of detective novels and what may have been their enhanced allure at the particular moment (by the early 1980s, the flowering of Thatcherism had helped to banish doom and gloom with the hint that the ethic of detective fiction was the merest sturdy realism) that they 'provide a puzzle . . . which is solved by human ingenuity and by logical deduction, in other words, by the human brain. I am sure that this is part of their appeal in a world in which we are increasingly coming to believe that so many of our social problems are literally beyond our capacity to solve and that we are at the mercy of vast impersonal forces, social and economic, against which we are absolutely powerless.'[40]. *Pace* Bob Roshier's suggestion of a kinship between the phantasms of popular fiction and those of the press, one may see how an insistence on a human capacity to shape rather than being the creature of circumstances informs reporting of the Yorkshire Ripper case no less than the run of detective fiction. A compensatory element dominates press coverage of the trial and verdict: if the phenomenon of the serial killer elicited problems which reduced the police to impotence, there would be all the more emphasis on the defendant's own ability to override what at any rate professional bleeding-hearts might deem to be 'overwhelming circumstances'. The popular and quality press are only at odds in that the latter are equivocal or brazenly pragmatic in eventually applauding the verdict. As for editors at the other end of the market, the political ethos of the early 1980s, so allergic to a whiff of abstraction, merely dovetailed with the 'professional imperatives of journalism', so that in a sense their knighthoods fell to them like ripe pears.

CONCLUSION

By way of coda, it is worth glancing at a few books preoccupied with the state of newspapers over the period. S.J. Taylor's commentaries on the modern press are notably breezy and enthusiastic, even or perhaps especially when she is chronicling the profane deportment of the tabloids: in *Shock! Horror! The Tabloids in Action*, with its empathic title, the surplus of cynicism of the popular press seems to be found positively exhilarating.[41] Her latest book is on Esmond Rothermere, a relatively respectable theme, as is implicit in the preference for the term 'compact', rather than 'tabloid', to express the format of the *Daily Mail* since the 1970s. Here Taylor is evinced as a serial hero-worshipper, paying tribute to successive news legends. Among those celebrated is the reporter, Vincent Mulchrone, afflicted by 'a great sadness. . . . He had wanted to be a poet, a writer of lyrical prose, and he had never made it,' a lament ostensibly a refugee from 'Pseud's Corner' rather than the 'Street of Shame'.[42] Unabashed, however, Taylor's narrative is as straight-faced and starry-eyed as Philip Gibbs's sterling novel of 1909, *The Street of Adventure*, the phrase which *Private Eye* would feel constrained to modify.

Other recent perspectives on the press have made for more enervating reading. Gordon Burn's novel, *Fullalove*, ponders on 'a post-Wapping world where everything runs faster, does more, has a longer battery life and costs less'; a premonition of the journalist-protagonist is that he may be 'an actual carrier, a cross-pollinator of misery and annihilating despair and doorstep human anguish, and not merely its privileged witness.'[43] Burn is himself the author of a distinguished study of the Yorkshire Ripper case, and a character in the novel reflects in disconcerting postmodernist fashion on the possibility of a vicious affinity between 'the journalist and the murderer' (to borrow the title of Janet Malcolm's book with a less esoteric slant on a similar anxiety). 'The individual is overwhelmed by an incomprehensible flood of signs, surfaces and space. . . . We live in an inebriated state of consciousness. Which is why we need the murderers. Murder, rape, natural disaster, atrocity stories on a daily basis.'[44]

Burn is writing a 'devastating' indictment, as a review cited on the cover of the paperback edition of the novel would proclaim, whereas the author of a different kind of book, Richard Siklos's biography of Conrad Black, proprietor of the *Daily Telegraph*, is temperately admiring of his subject, but the overall effect similarly verges on the bleak. Black's avowal that maximising annual cash flow is essentially why he is in business need not occasion too much shock or horror, but it is a running theme in the book that Black is so little enamoured of freedom of the printed word as concerning the exploits of the rich and powerful ('If the small guy's guardian is the media, then the small guy is in bigger trouble than I thought'), that he rivals the late Robert Maxwell for litigiousness.[45] His complementary but, considering his avocation, necessarily somewhat paradoxical opinion of investigative journalists is that they are 'swarming, grunting masses of jackals'.[46]

Ian Fleming's James Bond cropped up earlier in this essay; to reinvoke spy fiction, Taylor's sustained high spirits in relation to the modern press resemble a John Buchan contriving to flourish in the rebarbative world of John Le Carré: 'It was a foul, foul operation. But it's paid off, and that's the only rule.'[47]

NOTES

1. Hugh Cudlipp, *Walking on the Water* (London, 1976), pp. 96, 233.
2. Ian Fleming, *From Russia with Love* (London, 1977), p. 39.
3. Note the subtitle of Peter Chippindale and Chris Horrie, *Stick It Up Your Punter!: The Rise and Fall of The Sun* (London, 1992); originally published in 1990.

4. Ibid., p. 106.
5. Colin Seymour-Ure, *The British Press and Broadcasting since 1945* (Oxford, 1991), p. 26.
6. W.T. Stead (anonymously), *The Maiden Tribute of Modern Babylon* (London, 1885), p. 2.
7. John Pilger, *Hidden Agendas* (London, 1998), pp. 371–441. There was a preview of the argument in a Carlton television documentary, *Breaking the Mirror* (18 February 1997).
8. See Peter Chippindale and Chris Horrie, *Disaster! The Rise and Fall of News on Sunday* (London, 1988).
9. Matthew Engel, *Tickle the Public: One Hundred Years of the Popular Press* (London, 1996), p. 279.
10. Raymond Snoddy, *The Good, the Bad and the Unacceptable: The Hard News about the British Press* (London, 1993), p. 140.
11. Robert Harris, *Selling Hitler* (first published in 1986), in *The Media Trilogy* (London, 1994), p. 567.
12. For a first-hand and suitably jaundiced account, see Harold Evans, *Good Times, Bad Times* (London, 1983).
13. Mark Hollingsworth, *The Press and Political Dissent: A Question of Censorship* (London, 1986).
14. 'The Function of Criticism at the Present Time' in P.J. Keating (ed.), *Matthew Arnold: Selected Prose* (Harmondsworth, 1970), p. 141.
15. *Daily Mirror*, 9 May 1963.
16. *Daily Mirror*, 6 June 1963.
17. *Daily Mirror*, 15 July 1963.
18. *Daily Telegraph*, 27 September 1963.
19. *Daily Mirror*, 17 June 1963.
20. *Daily Mirror*, 30 June 1967.
21. *The Times*, 1 July 1967.
22. *Daily Mirror*, 17 July 1967.
23. Linda Melvern, *The End of the Street* (London, 1986).
24. *Breaking the Mirror*, Carlton television, 18 February 1997.
25. Steve Chibnall, *Law-and-Order News: An Analysis of Crime Reporting in the British Press* (London, 1977), p. 22.
26. Ibid., p. 12.
27. Bob Roshier, 'The Selection of Crime News by the Press', in S. Cohen and J. Young (eds), *The Manufacture of News: Deviance, Social Problems and the Mass Media* (London, 1973), pp. 28–39.
28. *Sunday Telegraph*, 10 May 1981.
29. *The Times*, 10 November 1888. Quoted in Philip Sugden, *The Complete History of Jack the Ripper* (London, 1995), p. 324.
30. *Daily Mail*, 23 May 1981.
31. Sugden, op. cit.
32. Patricia D. Cornwell, *All that Remains* (London, 1993), p. 435.
33. *Daily Mirror*, 13 May 1981.
34. *Daily Mail*, 30 April 1981.
35. Agatha Christie, *An Autobiography* (London, 1978), p. 452.
36. *Sun*, 13 May 1981.
37. *Sun*, 25 May 1981.
38. *Daily Telegraph*, 23 May 1981.

39. *The Times*, 23 May 1981.
40. Diana Cooper-Clark, *Designs of Darkness: Interviews with Detective Novelists* (Bowling Green, 1983), p. 19.
41. S.J. Taylor, *Shock! Horror! The Tabloids in Action* (London, 1991).
42. S.J. Taylor, *The Reluctant Press Lord: Esmond Rothermere and the Daily Mail* (London, 1998), p. 167.
43. Gordon Burn, *Fullalove* (London, 1996), pp. 25, 1.
44. Ibid., pp. 195–6.
45. Richard Siklos, *Shades of Black: Conrad Black and the World's Fastest Growing Press Empire* (London, 1996), p. 399.
46. Ibid., p. 340.
47. John Le Carré, *The Spy Who Came in from the Cold* (London, 1990), p. 209.

CHAPTER SIX

British Cinema:
A Struggle for Identity

Lez Cooke

The year 1956 marked the beginning of a new era in British cinema, just as it did in politics, literature, theatre and popular music. Yet the dawning of this new age may not have been readily apparent at the time, the significance of the new developments only becoming evident some years later. British cinema in the mid-1950s was characterised by the same sense of complacency that pervaded the country as a whole and which was about to be wiped away by the anger of a new generation. From 1954 through to 1958 the most successful British films at the box office were *Doctor in the House* (1954), *The Dam Busters* (1955), *Reach for the Sky* (1956), *Doctor at Large* (1957) and *The Bridge on the River Kwai* (1958), films which either mythologised Britain's wartime exploits or reflected the comfortable well-being of a nation enjoying the benefits of affluence and full employment. It was not until towards the end of the decade that an undercurrent of dissatisfaction began to surface in British cinema, a sense of unease which manifested itself in several ways.

First, and closely linked to the 'Angry Young Man' movement in literature and the theatre, came the 'new wave' of film-makers, led by Lindsay Anderson, Karel Reisz and Tony Richardson, who were part of the 'Free Cinema' movement which surfaced in February 1956 with a screening of some short, mainly documentary, films at the National Film Theatre. This first programme of films, which included Anderson's *O Dreamland* (1953) and the Reisz/Richardson *Momma Don't Allow* (1956), was a small but important step on the road towards introducing a new realism into British cinema, not the heroic, class-bound realism which had helped to make British cinema's wartime reputation, but a new social realism reflecting the 'lived culture' of the working classes and the emerging mid-1950s youth culture. This, arguably, was the first sign of a break with the past which was to be matched by other developments in the arts in 1956 but which

143

would not come to fruition in the mainstream cinema until 1959 with the release of *Room at the Top*, Jack Clayton's film of the John Braine novel, and Tony Richardson's film version of *Look Back in Anger*.

While this 'new wave' in British cinema is clearly linked to contemporary developments in literature and theatre, and was to provide the most celebrated expression of a reaction against the prevailing social conformity, there were other developments in the cinema of the time which provided evidence of a growing unrest in mid-to-late 1950s Britain.

Alongside the 'new wave' the late 1950s and early 1960s also saw an increase in the number of 'social problem' films being produced. This loosely-connected group of films pre-dates the 'kitchen sink' genre and, in relation to youth, can be traced back to the early 1950s, or even the late 1940s, with films like *The Blue Lamp* (1950) and *Cosh Boy* (1952). The late 1950s and early 1960s saw a new cycle of films reflecting moral panics around youth, with such evocative titles as *Violent Playground* (1958), *Beat Girl* (1960) and *The Wild and the Willing* (1962), and these were supplemented by films dealing with other 'social problems', such as race, in *Sapphire* (1959) and *Flame In The Streets* (1961), and homosexuality, in *Victim* (1961). The 'problems' here had different causes and consequences but represent in general a questioning of, and a challenge to, the prevailing social consensus.

Another break with tradition, and a development of a rather different order, came in the supernatural form of the horror films produced by Hammer in the late 1950s. In the mid-1950s Hammer cashed in on the low-budget science fiction boom that had emerged in America in the early 1950s with a film version of *The Quatermass Experiment* (1955), based on the 1953 BBC television series. The film proved to be very successful at the box office and was followed by further low-budget films exploiting contemporary concerns about radiation and the Bomb. These films helped to pave the way for the even more successful cycle of gothic horror films which Hammer produced over the next ten years, beginning with *The Curse of Frankenstein* (produced in 1956, released in 1957).

Although apparently unrelated, there is a link here with the other late 1950s developments in British cinema. While the Hammer horror films are far removed in form and content from the 'kitchen sink' and 'social problem' films of the time the common factor they all share is an awareness of a changing constituency as far as the cinema audience is concerned.

Cinema attendance declined considerably in the second half of the 1950s, dropping from 1,182 million in 1955 to 501 million in 1960. A number of factors were responsible, of which the rise of television as a new form of mass entertainment is perhaps the most obvious. But what is more significant in terms of the break with tradition in British cinema in the late 1950s is the changing composition of the audience. Television represented part of a shift towards home-based leisure in the 1950s, a shift reinforced by an increased ability to buy houses and domestic goods as a consequence of the economic boom. In this situation it was the older cinema-going audience that stopped attending, bringing a decline in the habitual family audience and leaving the younger generation, and teenagers in particular, to form the bulk of the audience. In this new social situation it is easy to see why the film industry recognised the need to break with tradition. There was an audience emerging which wanted a new product, something different to the old, safe and predominantly middle-class cinema and something that wasn't available on television. Films about youth, music, sex, the fantastic and the supernatural provided an escape for this younger audience from the increasingly comfortable home-life of their parents and from a Britain that was becoming increasingly conformist and complacent as the 1950s wore on. These new developments constituted a triple-headed attack upon the status quo in British cinema in the late 1950s, marking a transition to a new cultural climate. Youth, and working-class youth in particular, was spearheading the assault on middle-class, conservative values and would move centre stage in the 1960s.

The extent of the change could even be seen in the mainstream cinema of the late 1950s. 1958 saw the release of the first of the *Carry On* films and in 1959, the year in which *Look Back in Anger* and *Room at the Top* were released, *Carry On Nurse* was the most successful British film at the box office. At first glance the *Carry Ons* seem like no more than an updating of the successful *Doctor* films for a new generation and a new social and cultural climate. To some extent this is true, and in box office terms this clearly proved successful, but on another level the *Carry On* films represented a challenge to prevailing standards of decency and social acceptability. What the *Carry On* films introduced, along with their negative stereotyping and reactionary elements, was a subversive attitude towards forms of authority and an anarchic disruption of state institutions, contained within a popular comedy format. While the other new tendencies in British cinema exerted pressure from more subordinate, marginal positions, the *Carry On* films were busy subverting from *within* the dominant culture. In this respect even the *Carry Ons*, in other ways clearly part of mainstream culture, can be seen as part of the challenge to conformity and consensus in Britain in the late 1950s and on into the 1960s.

The history of British cinema in the three decades following this break with tradition is one of buoyancy and optimism in the 1960s, followed by decline in the 1970s after the withdrawal of American funding at the end of the 1960s, and the emergence of a more radical independent film culture in the 1970s. This in turn fed into the establishment of Channel 4 as an 'alternative' television channel in the early 1980s and it was Channel 4 in particular, with its commissioning of low–medium budget films, which was largely responsible for a revival in British cinema in the 1980s as film-makers, both mainstream and independent, responded in different ways to the Thatcherite assault upon the social and cultural advances made since the 1950s. As the century drew towards its close, and the long Conservative hegemony was finally ended by the election of New Labour in 1997, the fortunes of British cinema seemed, once again, to be on the rise as a new generation of film-makers and actors emerged.

THE BRITISH 'NEW WAVE'

So how 'new' was the 'new wave' of the late 1950s and in what ways did it represent a break with tradition in British cinema?

The most obvious departure was in the focus upon working-class char-acters located in the industrial landscape of the Midlands and North of England. The 1930s and 1940s working-class comedies of Gracie Fields, George Formby, Frank Randle and others had often been set in the North, which was where the majority audience for these films was to be found. When Fields and Formby became national stars it was as a result of broaden-ing their appeal and moving away from exclusively provincial settings. But the appeal of the 'new wave' films of the late 1950s extended beyond their industrial milieu, suggesting a breaking down of the North–South divide and a commonality of interest which went beyond regional differences.

The dominant aesthetic in British cinema in the post-war period was a comfortable middle-class one. Whether it appeared in the literary/theatrical tradition of Rank, the comedies of Ealing, or the expressionist cinema of Powell and Pressburger, the prevailing tradition was undeniably bourgeois and the authentic voice of the working class was little in evidence. So when the new voice of the 'Angry Young Man' burst onto the scene in the mid-1950s, and subsequently onto the cinema screen, it really did seem like a breath of fresh air which would blow away the cobwebs of the old cinema.

That this new voice was male was undeniable. The authors on whose books and plays the 'new wave' films were based were predominantly male. The directors of the films were male (and predominantly middle-class) and the films were based around male central characters who were played by a new generation of actors led by Albert Finney, Alan Bates and Tom Courtenay. It is here that the problems begin in assessing the extent to which these films represent a 'breakthrough' in British cinema, for where are the women? And when they do appear how much of a change is there in their representation? On the evidence of *Look Back in Anger*, which had started the revolution in the theatre, there is little to be said for a breakthrough in the portrayal of women. The anger of Jimmy Porter, the archetypal angry young man, is expressed at the expense of his subservient middle-class wife whose role is stereotypically domestic. As the daughter of a retired colonel Alison is seen by Jimmy as a representative of the old social order and becomes the butt of his endless tirades of abuse, to such an extent that the film, even more so than the play, seems unremittingly misogynistic. Jimmy Porter's rage against complacency and conformity is directed not so much at the establishment as at the women who are on the receiving end of his abuse.

Look Back in Anger is not an isolated example. In *Room at the Top* Alice is a victim of Joe Lampton's selfishness in his quest for upward mobility. In *Saturday Night and Sunday Morning* (1960) Brenda is a victim of Arthur's self-interested philosophy of 'having a good time' when she gets pregnant and is forced to endure a horrific and unsuccessful backstreet abortion in an attempt to conceal her adultery from her husband. In *This Sporting Life* (1963) Mrs Hammond, in some ways a strong, independent character, is ultimately a victim of Frank Machin's rugged and traditional masculine values. In numerous films the women's potential for independence is cut off when they become pregnant, usually because, like Arthur in *Saturday Night and Sunday Morning*, the men fail to take any precautions in their pursuit of 'a good time'. Women are degraded and belittled in other ways too, not least through being shown as submissive and conformist in relation to the rebelliousness of their male counterparts. John Hill has noted how this often manifests itself in terms of a difference in cultural values, where women are associated with what is invariably seen as 'the new trivial and facile mass culture' of the period, while the men are associated with more 'authentic' cultural activities such as 'the old traditional working-class culture of the brass band' which signifies the cultural and class difference between Vic and his mother-in-law in *A Kind of Loving* (1962):

> this juxtaposition of values is effected in terms of a contrast between men and women. While the brass band is all-male, the superficial values of the new 'affluence' are linked inextricably with women, whose obsession with house, television, clothes and physical appearance is persistently emphasized throughout the film.[1]

This opposition can be seen again and again in the 'new wave' films, from Alison's domesticity in *Look Back in Anger* to Doreen's concern with her appearance and desire to own one of the new homes on the housing estate, towards which Arthur rebelliously throws a stone at the end of *Saturday Night and Sunday Morning*.

147

To argue, as Robert Murphy does in his critique of Hill's assessment of the role of women, that 'these incandescently intense women have a seriousness, an emotional weight, altogether lacking in the pathetically trivial roles women had to play in most 1950s British films' is to overlook the extent to which women are victimised and rendered subordinate to the central male characters in the 'new wave' films.[2] There is no real possibility of comparison here with the strong women in *film noir* who we remember despite their 'punishment' (often by death) at the end of the films, for in the *films noirs* the male characters were relatively weak in relation to the women, whereas in the British 'new wave' films it is the opposite. While the 'new wave' films may have offered more serious roles for women than previous 1950s films, women are ultimately defined in relation to the leading male characters, upon whom our narrative attention is focused.

The other way in which the reputation of the 'new wave' films as a 'breakthrough' might be questioned is in terms of their form. While it is reasonable to argue that the films introduced a new element of social realism into British cinema by foregrounding working-class characters, industrial settings, working-class homes and working-class culture, it is also reasonable to question the efficacy of these representations. As John Hill argues in his excellent book on the British 'new wave', the conventions of narrative employed in the films are in line with the conventions of classic narrative cinema in placing the focus of attention upon individuals (the angry young man) rather than groups and requiring problems to be resolved on the personal level, rather than on the social level.[3] By developing the stories as dramas of the individual, a typical strategy in mainstream narrative cinema, the onus is then placed upon that individual to achieve a personal resolution of the narrative problem, which is usually the desire of the individual to break free from the constraints of his social conditions of existence.[4] But as the problem is a social one the only real possibility of breaking free would require a change in society, a solution which cannot be achieved on the personal level within which the films operate. Hence the conformist resolutions of many of the films where the central male character 'settles down' or, like Arthur in *Saturday Night and Sunday Morning*, lamely throws a stone at the symbol of conformity (the housing estate), lacking any other means of expressing resistance.

The conventions of realism employed, while breaking with tradition in the extent to which they foreground the social reality of working-class life, can also be seen to contribute to the same problematic. For by favouring what John Hill describes as 'an epistemology of the visible' the films are unable to delve beneath the surface of visible reality and examine how fundamental social change might be achieved.[5] Just like Arthur and his fellow angry young men we, literally, can see no possibility of change, because the conventions of realism employed cannot accommodate it.

Having expressed these reservations about the efficacy of the 'new wave' films there are grounds for concluding on a more positive note. To borrow an argument put forward by John Caughie in a different context, there are circumstances within which it is possible to see representations as progressive in spite of their limitations and apparent inability to suggest the possibility of change:

> Under certain conditions . . . it may be politically progressive to confirm an identity (of sexuality or class), to recover repressed experience or history, to contest the dominant image with an alternative identity.[6]

The 'new wave' films can be considered progressive in the extent to which they 'confirmed an identity' for working-class audiences in the late 1950s and in so doing contested the dominant middle-class image which was prevalent in British cinema at the time.

THE SOCIAL PROBLEM FILM

The 'social problem' films of the period present a slightly different case, although similar reservations could be raised about their ability to initiate social change.

Two main types of social problem film can be identified, although the boundaries between the two are often blurred. On the one hand there are the 'serious' social problem films made from a middle-class, white, liberal perspective and attempting to address one of the three main social problems of the period (youth, race, sexuality). On the other hand there are those films which seem less concerned to address the problem seriously than to exploit the issue for public consumption. John Hill locates *Beat Girl* (1960) and *That Kind of Girl* (1963) in the latter category where sensationalism rather than seriousness seems the objective. In each film the 'problem' revolves around the threat of sexuality, especially female sexuality, to 'normal' family life (and, by implication, to the established social order). As in all good moral panics sexual promiscuity is seen as the first step in an escalating spiral leading, in the case of *That Kind of Girl*, to venereal disease and criminality! It is not just female sexuality, however, that is identified as a 'problem' but 'youth culture' generally:

> As with *Beat Girl*, diverse social phenomena are pulled together into one composite image of deviance, embracing beatniks, strip clubs, students and CND, all linked as one by the threat of sexual excess.[7]

The ideological function of the films is to denigrate permissiveness and endorse the moral superiority of family life, but the way in which the films realise this makes them available for alternative readings. Family life, on the whole, is presented as far less exciting and attractive than the coffee bars and clubs frequented by the wayward youth in the films, and while the moral message may be clear the argument is far from persuasive. Like all 'exploitation' films both *Beat Girl* and *That Kind of Girl* dose the moral pill with plenty of salacious sugar.

The liberal discourse of the 'serious' social problem films, on the other hand, usually avoids such crude moralising, although the attempts to take a more positive attitude towards the problem often results in a degree of ambivalence in the moral message. This is noticeably the case in the films dealing with the 'problem' of race.

The 'race riots' in several British cities in 1958, as Britain reaped the consequences of immigration policies designed to encourage cheap labour onto the job market, resulted in several films addressing themselves to this new social problem. *Flame in the Streets*, adapted for the screen by Ted Willis from his play *Hot Summer Night*, was an attempt by Rank to cash in on (and thus exploit) the problem by casting John Mills as a liberal trade union official who is forced to confront his own racial prejudice and, perhaps more significantly, the far more hysterical prejudice of his wife when his daughter announces her intention of marrying a young black teacher. The evocative title suggests an exploitation scenario with the problem spiralling out of control to replicate the real-life 'race riots' of three years earlier. To some extent the narrative does develop along these lines, but the street confrontation towards the end of the film, stirred up by a group of Teddy Boys, never develops into a full-scale riot and it fails to match the hysterical outburst of the mother when confronted with the thought of her daughter sharing a bed with a black man: 'I'm ashamed of you. When I think of you and that man sharing the same bed. It's filthy . . . disgusting. . . . It makes my stomach turn over. . . . I want to be sick.' The 'problem' is relocated as a problem within the white family, a problem of personal prejudice, rather than a political problem. Indeed on the political level of the workplace, Jacko Palmer (John Mills) forcefully argues the case for the promotion of a black worker, convincing the initially hostile white workforce to vote in favour of their black colleague. At this level the problem is seen as one that can be resolved, whereas on the personal level the resolution of the problem is not so easy.

Sapphire also locates the problem of race as a problem of personal prejudice, for the white police inspector, Learoyd, for the lower middle-class family into whom the murdered black woman, Sapphire, was due to marry, and, in a token suggestion that racial prejudice can work both ways, in the admission of the wealthy black barrister Slade that his father would not have allowed him to marry Sapphire because she was 'part white'.

The narrative trajectory of the film revolves around this degree of racial ambivalence. Sapphire is of mixed race and has severed her connections with the black community when she discovered that she could 'pass for white'. This enables considerable mileage to be gained from references to the 'innate nature' of blacks, with Inspector Learoyd, in particular, acting as the mouthpiece for bigoted racial attitudes which are then exposed as ignorant and foolish. While the intention of the film-makers is to present a range of attitudes, opinions and prejudices in the representation of race, there is nevertheless a tendency to over-compensate in the direction of positive representation, leading to an idealised and somewhat unrealistic view of a black community where there are no really 'bad' characters. For example, Sapphire's visibly black brother, Dr Robbins, is presented as a totally unblemished, highly sympathetic character – middle-class, educated, and amiably tolerant of all the prejudice with which he is confronted, including the hysterical outburst (note the similarity to *Flame in the Streets*) of Mildred, the married sister of Sapphire's fiancé, when she confesses to killing Sapphire at the end of the film. Dr Robbins then delivers the 'reformist' message in a speech illustrating his unique ability to overlook the prejudice which he encounters every day in his doctor's practice and which others have displayed throughout the film.

Even the black underworld characters that Inspector Learoyd visits in the run-down tenement building are portrayed as harmless, jovial characters and completely deferential to the solitary white police detective who enters their territory, a somewhat unlikely scenario given the racial tensions of the time and the degree of oppression blacks were experiencing. While its heart is in the right place *Sapphire* suffers ultimately from the liberal attitudes of its white producers whose efforts at 'social engineering' through positive representation is somewhat at odds with the 'realist' aesthetic which the film adopts.[8]

HAMMER HORROR: THE RETURN OF THE REPRESSED

The 'new wave' and 'social problem' films of the late 1950s and early 1960s broke with tradition by introducing a new social content into the dominant aesthetic form of British cinema, that of realism. The other major development in the cinema of the time represented an even more radical departure. Not only did the cycle of gothic horror films initiated by the release of *The Curse of Frankenstein* in 1957 represent a break with tradition in terms of their supernatural subject matter, they also represented a decisive departure from the aesthetic of realism which had dominated British cinema since the 1930s.

The valuing of 'realist' films over other forms of cinematic expression had, to a great extent, been a consequence of the cultural values of the middle-class critics who were (and still are) largely responsible for determining what is valued and what is denigrated within the institution of the cinema. Anyone who doubts the power of the critics need look no further than the critical response to Michael Powell's *Peeping Tom* on its release in 1960 when it was subjected to such an overwhelmingly hostile reception that it effectively ended Powell's film-making career, the hostility expressing a sense of betrayal that a leading exponent of British cinema should venture into such 'downmarket' territory. Powell, in his collaborations with Emeric Pressburger, had never really been an exponent of the 'realist' school but had always been concerned with definitions of Britishness and aspects of British culture. *Peeping Tom*, however, was a venture into an area considered dubious and sordid by the critical establishment and his reward was to be ostracised.

That the critics are not always in tune with popular opinion, however, is evident from the box-office success of films like the Gainsborough costume melodramas in the 1940s which were critically reviled but proved to be hugely popular with cinema-goers. Such was the case with the low-budget films produced by Hammer in the 1950s, films which were targeted at the new youth audience which was emerging as the main market for films, as television and home-based leisure took away the traditional family audience. The critics, in their role as guardians and definers of cultural taste, reacted with distaste to these manifestations of 'low culture' which were not only lurid and lascivious in their subject matter but flouted any allegiance to realism in their expressionist style.

While the rejection of any adherence to the tradition of British realism in these films was enough for the establishment critics to dismiss them, this may have been the very reason why the new youth audience lapped them up. In their espousal of any concern with contemporary social reality films like *The Curse of Frankenstein*, *Dracula* (1958), *The Mummy* (1959), *The Hound of the Baskervilles* (1959), *The Curse of the Werewolf* (1960), *The Gorgon* (1964) and numerous others offered an imaginary escape from the complacency and conformity of British society at the end of the 1950s and on into the 1960s. Exploiting the opportunities created by a relaxation in censorship (the 'X' certificate had been introduced in 1951 and was an important part of the marketing of many youth-oriented films in the mid–late 1950s), coupled with a demand for new forms of entertainment, more exciting and daring than television could provide, Hammer, as an independent company operating on the margins of the mainstream film industry, saw the opportunity and the need for a new product: new subjects for a new audience. Its 'Cold War' trilogy, *The Quatermass Experiment* (1955), *X – The Unknown* (1956) and *Quatermass II* (1957), had already begun this process of targeting a new audience, exploiting contemporary anxieties about the atomic bomb. The move into gothic territory was simply an extension of this, recognising that the threat of 'the monster' resulting from atomic radiation was an important part of the appeal of the science fiction films. In this respect Hammer was not foolhardily going against the social realist grain in offering a supernatural and fantastic escape from reality with its venture into gothic horror, it was capitalising on the real fears and concerns of young people, as well as exploiting (and contributing to) a growing permissiveness in representations of sex and violence.

Another reason for the critical rejection of, or indifference to, the Hammer horror films and others which departed from the realist aesthetic is that it is much less easy to see them as a 'reflection' of British society. This again points to the limited critical framework of those critics whose approach to British cinema has been primarily 'sociological' and whose concern to see films in terms of their relationship to society has led them towards valuing films that are 'truthful' in their depiction of social reality. This approach inevitably values verisimilitude over allegory and metaphor – hence the favouring and critical elevation of realist films over fantasy and other forms of cinema which do not lend themselves to this particular critical approach.

While one should be wary of any attempt to see films as simply 'reflecting' society, this need not prevent us from considering the relationship between Hammer's gothic horror films and British society in the late 1950s and seeing the films as highly stylised mediations of contemporary social concerns and developments. Peter Hutchings has discussed two ways in which the films can be seen to articulate with British society:

> In the case of Hammer in the 1950s, its work can be seen to have involved seizing upon aspects of a contemporaneous social reality that were not naturally connected – in particular, shifts in gender definition and changing notions of professionalism – and weaving these into an aesthetic unity in the interests of making horror relevant to a British market.[9]

Shifting definitions of gender, especially for men, are evident in all kinds of film in the period: from the rugged and repressed male heroes of the war films, to the more domesticated 'new men' of the *Doctor* films, to the troubled male characters in the 'new wave' and 'social problem' films; traditional notions of masculinity were changing as British society became more home-orientated and sons grew up in households where the father was often absent, having not returned from the war. Peter Hutchings identifies a similar 'problematisation of masculinity in the post-Empire, consumerist British society of the late 1950s' in films such as *The Mummy*, *The Hound of the Baskervilles*, *The Gorgon* and other Hammer films of the period:

> The stress laid in these films on troubled father–son relationships is symptomatic of a view they all share that the transmission of patriarchal power from one generation to the next has become blocked. In order to represent this situation, each film mobilises distinctly oedipal elements, with a succession of male characters shown as inadequate in the face of demands emanating from a usually absent father and as troubled by a forbidden desire for a woman.[10]

Similarly, Hutchings finds evidence of 'professionalism' in the films which could be seen to articulate with contemporary concerns. The need for a more 'professional' approach to managing society was increasingly felt towards the end of the 1950s in order to counter a perceived 'amateurishness' in British politics that was seen as responsible for a decline in Britain's standing as a world power. Hutchings discusses how this more professional approach was embodied in the very operational structure of Hammer as a film company and, despite the fact that they are operating in different historical circumstances, is also represented in the films themselves in the shape of leading Hammer characters like Baron Frankenstein, Van Helsing, and Sherlock Holmes who, with their rational, scientific methodology, might be seen as representative of the 'professionalism' that was required for Britain to confront the problems of a new, modern era:

> It does seem from this that Hammer's privileging of the professional at this moment in social history enabled it, in an almost prescient fashion, to tap into a widespread feeling that British society was in transition. In this way Hammer offered itself to its audience as a particularly 'modern' intervention into British culture (in opposition to the traditional virtues extolled by many Ealing films from the 1950s). It is possible that the outrage of a handful of film critics over Hammer horror arose in part as a reaction against the relatively new ideas of British national identity proposed by the films.[11]

In their own way the Hammer horror films were as much involved in the struggle to redefine national identity in the late 1950s and 1960s as were the 'new wave' and 'social problem' films of the period.

CARRY ON AND THE 'CARNIVALESQUE'

> The carnival, according to Bakhtin, was characterized by laughter, by
> excessiveness (particularly of the body and the bodily functions), by bad
> taste and offensiveness, and by degradation. The Rabelaisian moment and
> style were caused by a collision of two languages – the high, validated
> language of classical learning enshrined in political and religious power,
> and the low, vernacular language of the folk. The carnivalesque is the
> result of this collision and is a testament to the power of the 'low' to insist
> upon its rights to a place in the culture.[12]

Given their negative stereotyping of women, gays and ethnic groups and
their relentlessly puerile obsession with bodily functions it is difficult today
to see the *Carry On* films as constituting part of the 'break with tradition'
represented by the 'new wave' and Hammer horror films of the late 1950s.
Yet, as with the 'new wave' films, which also seem reactionary in some
respects today, it is possible to argue for the *Carry On* films as mildly
subversive within the more conservative social context in which they were
first seen.

To a large extent they were continuing an established comic tradition
that can be traced back through Norman Wisdom, the Crazy Gang and
George Formby to music-hall variety acts. As such they can be firmly
located within a tradition of popular culture which is both mainstream,
because of its popularity, yet which embodies qualities of subversion and
resistance to dominant (high) culture because of its 'low' cultural attributes.

The three main comic strategies employed within the variety tradition
are those of slapstick, farce and innuendo – all of which are evident in the
Carry On films. Where the *Carry Ons* depart from their predecessors,
however, is in the degree to which they stretch the rules of social acceptability. Undoubtedly they profited from, and were a response to, the
relaxation in moral codes at the end of the 1950s, and their popularity can
be seen in part as a legitimisation of the new sexual codes. They were thus
able to go further in terms of sexual innuendo and situations than previous
comedies and in doing so represented a break with the moral constraints of
the previous generation.

This may not seem like such a radical departure when compared to the
'permissiveness' of the 'new wave' and 'social problem' films and the X-
certicate sex and violence of the Hammer horror films, but the significance
of the *Carry Ons* has to be seen in the context of their position as a central
part of the popular culture of the period. On one level it may be the case
that what the *Carry On* films were doing was simply diverting audience
anxieties into laughter, rather than forcing audiences to confront the anxieties

and problems of the time as in the 'new wave' and 'social problem' films, and it is easy to see how this might have suited the mainstream film industry, enabling it to offer the older, traditional cinema-going audience a new product, one more likely to entice them back to the cinema than the more youth-oriented 'new wave' and Hammer horror films. On the other hand, when compared to equally popular mainstream films of the time such as the *Doctor* series (*Doctor in Love* followed *Carry On Nurse* as the top box office film in 1960), the *Carry On* films presented an unprecedented display of vulgarity and 'bad taste' and an anarchic challenge to accepted standards of decency and permissiveness. As such they can be seen as 'carnivalesque' in their celebration of the vulgar and the grotesque, a deliberate affront to accepted cultural standards, and it is in this respect that they represent a radical response to the conformity of late-1950s British society.

While there is no denying the extent to which the *Carry On* films now seem reactionary and anachronistic, their significance as part of popular culture in the late 1950s and 1960s should not be underestimated. As Marion Jordan has written in one of the few serious considerations of the films:

> In their day, and despite their denying any place to women in their pantheon – portraying them, indeed, as gaolers, sexual objects, or unnatural predators – they nonetheless asserted by their themes, and by the gusto with which they were presented, a lower-class, masculine resistance to 'refinement'; an insistence on sexuality, physicality, fun; on the need for drink in a kill-joy world, for shiftiness in an impossibly demanding industrial society, for cowardice amid the imposed heroism.[13]

THE EMPIRE STRIKES BACK?

The developments in British cinema described above represented not only, in their different ways, a break with the prevailing 'stiff upper lip' tradition of 1950s British cinema, they also marked the beginnings of a revival in the British film industry, despite the continuing decline in audiences. It was a revival which did not go unnoticed in Hollywood. In the 1960s, as Britain became the focus, and London the centre, of a cultural revolution in the arts, all of the major Hollywood film studios set up London offices in an effort to cash in on the new developments. United Artists was first and foremost in this American invasion. Developing a link with Woodfall, the production company responsible for many of the 'new wave' films, United Artists financed *Tom Jones* (1963), a bawdy costume drama adapted by John Osborne from the Henry Fielding novel, after Woodfall had failed to find a British backer for it. The film proved to be a big commercial and critical success, winning four Oscars at the 1964 Academy Awards (the first time since 1948 that a British film had won the award for Best Picture). For Osborne, director Tony Richardson, star Albert Finney and British cinema generally this was a turning point, marking the end of social realism and the beginning of a new era.

Prior to this, however, United Artists had struck it rich with another British picture, the first of a series which would prove its popularity and profitability at the box office over the next three decades. In the context of the other late 1950s and early 1960s developments in British cinema *Dr No* (1962), *From Russia with Love* (1963), *Goldfinger* (1964) and the other James Bond films which followed, seemed curiously out of place, a return to the conservative values of an imperial Britain where there were no uncertainties about gender roles or class relations:

> Bond was a dream figure in a traditional mode, not a social rebel like the screen figures at war with the reality of society around them. Unlike them, he was not aggressively youthful: at the age of thirty, Connery could scarcely be that. He was not anti-authority: obedience to the father-figure of M and a worshipful distance from the surrogate sister-figure of Miss Moneypenny were carefully preserved in each film. Bond served his country at a time when that country's confidence in its old imperial potency had been shaken by Suez and the retreat of the old certainties; so in that sense he was both a salve for the wound and a sentimental, nostalgic bandage.[14]

Playing down the Cold War scenarios of the Fleming novels and pitching Bond against SPECTRE (Special Executive for Counterintelligence, Terrorism, Revenge and Extortion), instead of the Russian Intelligence Service SMERSH, the Bond films set about redefining and reinstating a sense of patriotic national identity at a time when that identity was in the process of being eroded by social, political and cultural developments. With a cool, playboy hero representing a conservative British establishment, *Dr No*, and the hugely popular films which followed provided the exotic and expensive other side of the coin to the relatively low-budget indigenous British films of the time, such as *A Kind of Loving* (1962), *The Loneliness of the Long Distance Runner* (1962), *Nothing but the Best* (1963), *A Hard Day's Night* (1964) and *The Knack* (1965).

However the success of the Bond films cannot be explained simply by their resurrecting the glory days of imperial Britain, but more by the way in which they reworked old ideologies for a new age and a new audience. The casting of Sean Connery as James Bond was important here, not only because he epitomised the traditional cool-but-rugged masculine hero, but because he represented a new classlessness, an important part of his appeal to male audiences in the 1960s. With his suave demeanour and authoritative masculine control he did not alienate working-class audiences in the way that the middle-class heroes of 1950s films had. Furthermore, in the transition from the novel to the screen the character of Bond had undergone a significant change which matched the new 'professional' ethos of the 1960s, rather than the gentlemanly 'amateurism' of the 1950s:

> he was now made to point in the opposite direction – towards the future rather than the past. Functioning as a figure of modernisation, he became the very model of the tough abrasive professionalism that was allegedly destined to lead Britain into the modern, no illusions, no holds-barred post-imperialist age, a hero of rupture rather than one of tradition.[15]

The emphasis upon spectacle and new technology was also part of this process of modernisation. With the wartime spectacle of 1950s films like *The Dam Busters* and *The Bridge on the River Kwai* now out of date, the huge futuristic sets, exotic locations and spectacular explosions in the Bond films were simply an updating of the old spectacle for new times. Similarly, developments in new technology and the role it would play in the modernisation of Britain was very much on the agenda when the first Bond films appeared. In 1963 Harold Wilson had called for a new Britain 'forged in the white heat of a technological revolution' in a rallying cry that was destined to sweep away the old Conservative government which, after twelve years in office, seemed as archaic and outdated as the war films of the 1950s.[16] Hence the significance of the new technology and gadgetry in the Bond films which, like the professionalism embodied in the figure of Bond, helped to define the films as looking forward to a new Britain, while at the same time casting sentimental and nostalgic glances back to Britain's recent imperial past.

The Bond films, therefore, were by no means entirely reactionary, although with the emphasis on a womanising playboy as the modern hero of the films they were far from progressive in their sexual politics. Their success revolved around and depended upon this combination of the traditional and the modern, providing an illustration of patriarchal and nationalistic ideologies being redefined and reproduced for a new, more liberal era.

'SWINGING LONDON'

The years from 1962 to 1964 mark an important period of transition in British cinema. During this time a cultural shift occurred: a shift from realism to fantasy, from North to South, from the masculine narratives of the 'kitchen sink' films to the more female-oriented narratives of films like

Darling, *Georgy Girl* and *Up the Junction* and from the working-class culture of the 'new wave' films to the new 'classless' pop culture. The success of *Dr No* provided an early indication that the public was growing weary of the grim realism of the 'kitchen sink' films and was ready to sample other pleasures. While 'kitchen sink' films were still being produced in 1962, by 1964 social realism had been displaced by the energy and exuberance of the new pop culture. Apart from the Bond films, which were more international in their style and iconography, three films produced in the period symbolise the cultural shift that was taking place in British society.

Billy Liar! (1963) was a key transitional film, marking the end of the 'new wave/kitchen sink' cinema but not yet able to break free from its influence. Directed by John Schlesinger, and based on the play by Keith Waterhouse and Willis Hall (which was itself based upon Keith Waterhouse's 1959 novel), the film had one foot in the social realism camp and one foot in the world of fantasy, the latter represented in the film by the daydreams which enable Billy Fisher (Tom Courtenay) to escape from the drab reality of life as a clerk in a provincial Northern town. Utilising the potential of the larger cinemascope screen – one immediately noticeable departure from the confined frames of 'kitchen sink' realism – to give vision to Billy's surreal and often grandiose daydreams, the film moves fluently between realism and fantasy, highlighting its pivotal role on the cusp of a new era. And in the character of Liz (Julie Christie) the film introduced a liberated, modern heroine, someone who, unlike Billy, has broken the chains of a constricting life in a Northern town and travelled south to London, to the city that represents modernity and the future and that was emerging as the hub of the new youth culture. When Billy chickens out of taking the night train to London with Liz at the end of the film it represents more than his personal inability to break free, being symptomatic of the failure of the late 1950s/early 1960s 'kitchen sink' generation to find a solution to the existential problem portrayed again and again in the 'new wave' films.

The other key film of 1963, *Tom Jones*, has already been identified as a new departure for Woodfall Films, marking the company's move away from Northern social realism towards a subject which, based upon Henry Fielding's eighteenth-century novel, was far removed from life in the provinces in late-1950s Britain, being closer in mood and style to the carnivalesque celebration of the *Carry Ons*. The film's director, Tony Richardson, adopted a more flamboyant cinematic style which eschewed the monochrome realism of the 'new wave' films in favour of a more colourful, stylised approach which anticipated the stylistic experiments and looser narratives of the 'swinging London' films that were to follow. Jeffrey Richards has commented on the significant change of direction taken by Richardson, Osborne and Finney in the film:

The style they adopted was far from the reverent naturalism of previous classic novel adaptations. It was jokey and knowing, and it employed slapstick comedy, speeded-up action, captions, asides to camera and an urbane narration. This irreverent eclecticism, inspired by the techniques and ethos of pop art, set the tone and style for the rest of the decade.[17]

The third key film of the period was *A Hard Day's Night* (1964) which marks the feature-film debut of the Beatles, probably the leading signifiers of modernity and the new pop culture. Richard Lester, the film's director, recognised the importance of the cultural breakthrough that the Beatles represented and was determined to capture on celluloid the significance of the moment.

> I was aware when we were filming it that they were producing an effect on the entire population of Britain, for better or worse, which badly needed to be documented. I think they were the first to give a confidence to the youth of the country which led to the disappearance of the Angry Young Men with a defensive mien. The Beatles sent the class thing sky high: they laughed it out of existence and, I think, introduced a tone of equality more successfully than any other single factor that I know.[18]

A Hard Day's Night begins where *Billy Liar!* ends, only in this case the lads take that train to London, immediately signalling their distance from, and difference to, the trapped 'kitchen sink' protagonists and symbolically marking the cultural shift from the North to the South. Over the next few years London would become the central location for film production in the UK as not only British but also American companies flocked to cash in on the capital's new cultural status. *A Hard Day's Night* also saw a shift in film style. Richard Lester, who had previously worked on television commercials, took the stylistic approach adopted by Tony Richardson in *Tom Jones* much further, utilising accelerated action, freeze frames and other non-naturalistic techniques to disrupt the conventional narrative flow and heighten the fantasy of the new pop culture for which the Beatles were ambassadors. The film was produced very quickly, a factor which was important in capturing the mood of the moment before it passed, and the sense of life being lived very fast and to the full is perfectly matched by the Beatles quick-fire dialogue and Lester's frenetic visual style.

If these three films were transitional, Lester's next film, *The Knack* (1965), marked a complete break from social realism and the arrival of a new genre of 'swinging London' cinema. That 'swinging London' is a more appropriate epithet than the less geographically specific 'swinging sixties' is emphasised by Alexander Walker:

> *The Knack* was the first of the 'London' films. It contains the alfresco experience of the capital in the summer of 1964, at which time all who lived there had become vividly aware of a great sense of unleashing – that

young people had taken it over, or were about to stage a *coup de jeunesse*. The Beatles had of course enormously assisted this feeling: by the very over-reporting of them, the mass media had given shape to the crowd's expectancy, and though their natures were pre-eminently provincial, localised in Merseyside, it was to the capital that they had transferred their work-base and all the hysteria that was attached to it.[19]

The Knack marks its difference from social realism not only through its visual style – which is almost avant-garde in its use of accelerated motion, jump cuts, bleached images, 'Brechtian' captions and other anti-realist techniques – but also in centring its narrative around a young woman (Rita Tushingham) who, like the Julie Christie character in John Schlesinger's *Darling* (1965), travels from the provinces to the metropolis in search of excitement and adventure, emphasising London's new status as a cultural mecca. While the film's proto-feminism may seem naive today the subject matter was almost incidental. It is the modernist style which is the real content of the film and it is this which still seems fresh and imaginative.

The peak years for 'swinging London' films were 1965–6 and it was appropriate and significant that the emergence of a new cinema, liberated in style and subject matter, should coincide with the arrival of the new Labour government, elected to office by a slim margin in 1964, after thirteen years of Conservative rule, and given a vote of confidence in March 1966 when re-elected with a much-increased majority. The 'winds of change' which swept the country in the mid-1960s were more significant than those of which Harold Macmillan had spoken in 1960, at least as far as British cinema was concerned. The social, political and economic changes ushered in by the new Labour government were reflected in the cultural sphere through a revolution in the arts. That the explosion of cultural creativity affected mainstream cinema as well as the more marginal independent film culture (the London Film-Makers' Co-op was set up in 1966 as a production, distribution and exhibition base for experimental film-makers) was an indication of how profound the revolution was.

The stylistic experiment and innovation of these films was more than mere effect, however. It represented a challenge to the conventional ways of seeing and understanding the world, a questioning of accepted norms, a threat to the status quo. The old nineteenth-century realist/bourgeois mode of representation which the dominant cinema had adopted was no longer adequate or appropriate in a world of widening horizons and expanding consciousness. Deconstruction was the name of the game:

> Fantasy sequences (in which everything becomes possible), slapstick (in which the world collapses into chaos), outrageous visual jokes, distancing devices such as the use of a narrator, inter-titles or direct address to camera spread across films as different as *The Bliss of Mrs Blossom* and *Poor Cow, Here We Go Round The Mulberry Bush* and *If. . . .*[20]

But by 1968, when Lindsay Anderson's *If...* was released, the carefree, hedonistic atmosphere of the pop culture had given way to a new climate, fuelled by demonstrations against the war in Vietnam and moral panics over drugs, in which the cultural revolution of the mid-1960s took on a more political dimension as a new counter-culture emerged to threaten the hegemony of the state.

If... (1968) was one of several films which reflected the change in mood. Only five years separate it from Anderson's previous film, *This Sporting Life* (1963), but the two films are a world apart and illustrate just how far-reaching the cultural revolution of the mid-1960s had been. *If...* mixes fantasy, satire and revolution in its story of rebellion at an English public school and signals a move away from the apolitical hedonism of the 'swinging London' films towards a more overtly political content. While its resolution of armed insurrection at the school is symbolic rather than a call to arms, its anti-authoritarianism undoubtedly caught the revolutionary mood of the times, and in the film's revolutionary hero, Mick Travers (Malcolm McDowell), *If...* presented a character to give voice to the growing discontent of the counter-culture, a Jimmy Porter for the late 1960s.

Where *If...* is symptomatic of a move away from the hedonistic pop culture, *Performance* (filmed in 1968, released in 1970) was the final nail in the coffin of the 'swinging London' genre. While not as self-consciously 'political' as Anderson's film, *Performance* does mark a shift away from the frivolity of the pop culture towards an exploration of the darker side of the British psyche in the 1960s. The film revolves around a culture clash arising out of the confrontation between James Fox's renegade East End gangster and Mick Jagger's reclusive pop star and this collision of cultures is accompanied by a fragmentation of the narrative, vividly expressed through Nic Roeg's disorientating visual style, as the gangster loses his sense of identity under the influence of drugs and the liberated lifestyle of the counter-culture. *Performance* is a metaphor for a changing Britain where the old certainties and values have been discarded but where there is no certainty about what is to replace them. It marks the end of an era in which there had been an explosive upheaval in social, sexual, moral and cultural attitudes, the shock waves from which were to echo through the next two decades.

THE 1970S: MAINSTREAM DECLINE AND THE RISE OF INDEPENDENT CINEMA

The pop bubble had burst well before the release of *Performance* in 1970 and the American companies which had flocked to Britain in 1963–4 had begun to withdraw before the decade was out. It is largely for this reason that mainstream British cinema in the 1970s has been seen as uninspired and uninspiring, caught, as Andrew Higson puts it, 'between two more significant moments': the creative optimism of the 1960s and the creative renaissance of the 1980s.[21]

Cinema-going continued to decline in the 1970s, but where in the 1960s the decline had been offset by a revival in film production, British cinema in the 1970s was fighting a rearguard action all the way. The withdrawal of American finance was followed by an exodus of British cinematic talent as directors and actors went to work in Hollywood, while those that did not, like Ken Loach, who had made his first cinema films in the late 1960s, tended to work more in television.

With the financial support of the American companies removed, cinema was once more subject to the eroding influence of the small screen, especially since television had now moved over to colour transmission, thus compensating for what it had lacked in the battle against the more colourful 'swinging sixties' films.

Cinema attempted to counter the threat of television in several ways, firstly by continuing to produce big screen spectaculars like the Bond films which, although American-financed and hardly indigenous in their subject matter, continued to prove their popularity at the box office with five top box-office hits during the decade. Secondly, cinema continued to target the youth market, now the bulk of its audience, and at the same time cash in on the popular music boom of the 1950s and 1960s, with a series of youth-oriented music films, such as *That'll Be the Day* (1973), *Stardust* (1974), *Tommy* (1975), *The Rocky Horror Picture Show* (1975) and *Quadrophenia* (1979). Thirdly, cinema attempted to feed off television by scavenging its successful programmes, especially situation comedies, and remaking them as cinema films. Among the sitcom spin-offs were *Dad's Army* (1971), *On the Buses* (1971), *Steptoe and Son* (1972), *Please Sir!* (1972), and *The Likely Lads* (1976), while, among the popular drama spin-offs, two feature films were made to cash in on the small-screen success of the police drama series *The Sweeney*. The Monty Python team also turned to the cinema, making four feature films during the 1970s following the success of their ground-breaking TV series. While some of these TV spin-offs were very successful at the box office, especially in the early 1970s (*On the Buses* making a tenfold profit on its £90,000 budget to become the top box-office film of 1971), on the whole this parasitical activity was a sign of how impoverished British cinema had become after the heady days of the 1960s.

With the withdrawal of American money, and no help coming from the new Conservative government which was elected in 1970, British cinema went into a familiar decline. When a Labour government was returned to power in 1974, and began developing plans for a British Film Authority, hopes were raised. But with the economy in trouble, rising unemployment and increasing industrial unrest, Labour had other concerns and its plans for the British film industry died with its election defeat in 1979.

Where the British film industry in the 1960s had reaped the full benefits of the fruits of post-war affluence and reflected that sense of well-being in its films, the late 1960s and 1970s saw a collapse in the post-war consensus. To an extent, the increasing polarisation and radicalisation in social and political life was mirrored in the cinema. While the mainstream British cinema went into decline, an energetic and radical independent cinema emerged to give expression to voices of opposition and dissent during the decade.

Two kinds of 'independent' cinema might be identified in Britain in the 1970s. On the one hand there is the 'independent' cinema advocated by the Association of Independent Producers (AIP) which wished to see an indigenous British cinema emerge to challenge the hegemony of Hollywood. The AIP lobbied for government funding and protection for a national cinema, without much success in the 1970s, but its efforts did reap some reward in the 1980s, partly as a result of the support of Channel 4 for British film production and partly because of the heritage-style film renaissance inspired by the success of *Chariots of Fire*.

The other kind of independent cinema that emerged in the 1970s was more radical in its form and politics, an 'oppositional' cinema, rather than the mainstream 'alternative' proposed by the AIP. Although the Independent Film-Makers' Association was formed in 1974 to co-ordinate its activities and act as a mouthpiece for the sector, this more radical independent cinema was diverse in its forms and practices, embracing experimental and avant-garde film-makers as well as more political agit-prop and feminist groups. The experimental/avant-garde film-makers were largely based around the London Film-Makers' Co-op, which had been set up in 1966, but the more political/agit-prop groups (Cinema Action, the Berwick Street Collective, Amber Films, the London Women's Film Group, and others) emerged following the political events of 1968 and shared many of the concerns of their counterparts of the 1930s: the workers' film groups which emerged in opposition to the dominant capitalist cinema of the time. Like this earlier model of oppositional cinema, the independent cinema of the 1970s was concerned to work outside of the mainstream practices and structures and develop alternative forms of production, distribution and exhibition, attracting funding where and when it could. The significance of this oppositional cinema resides not just in the films it produced but in the role it played as part of an alternative film culture in the 1970s, informed by the hugely influential development of film theory during the decade and supported by film magazines and journals like *Afterimage*, *Framework* and *Screen*:

The film groups were both products and producers of a climate that laid increasing stress upon the importance of culture and ideology for the development of any serious strategy for social change, and their practical activities contributed to the shaping of a new theory and practice of cinema. In contradistinction to the mainstream industry, with its commitment to profitable entertainment, the search for a mass audience and a primarily 'box office', or market, orientation towards that audience this other sector developed in partial, contradictory and hesitating ways the 'conditions of possibility' for a more socially responsible recasting of the institutions of cinema.[22]

Where many mainstream 1960s films had incorporated non-naturalistic techniques into their narratives this had, on the whole, been more for aesthetic effect than to radically disorientate the viewer and foreground social contradictions in the Brechtian sense. But this was precisely the intention of the more radical film-makers of the 1970s, whose ideological objectives were not just cultural but social and political change, an object-ive that was becoming more urgent as the crisis in international capitalism deepened. The problem for the movement was how best to achieve this while working very much on the margins of the dominant culture. While its social impact was limited the achievement of the independent cinema of the 1970s was in developing an oppositional film culture which was more vital, and whose influence has been greater, than the impoverished main-stream film culture of the decade.

BRITISH CINEMA AND THATCHERISM

Reflecting upon how, despite its 'invigorating and exciting' influence, the late 1950s/early 1960s British 'new wave' had failed to sustain a renaissance in British cinema, Leonard Quart writes, in his contribution to a collection of essays on 'British Cinema and Thatcherism':

> It wasn't until the Thatcher era, 1979–90, that genuine signs of an English film resurgence could again be seen. Margaret Thatcher took power during a time of profound economic trouble, government impotence, and declining national prestige. In dealing with these problems, she helped construct a much different social and political world than the one promoted in the fifties by the centrist consensual politics of Prime Minister Harold Macmillan. The accompanying film renaissance stands as one of the more positive by-products of the Thatcher ethos, though in an almost totally oppositional and critical manner.[23]

It is one of the ironies of the 'Thatcher ethos' that a political regime which did nothing to help the film industry, and everything to try to eradicate both socialism and the progressive social changes made since the 1950s, should have been responsible for encouraging a renaissance in British cinema in the 1980s. The extent to which this cinema was 'oppositional and critical' is open to question but there can be no doubt that Thatcherism did, perhaps unwittingly, revitalise British film-making, not so much in the quantity but in the quality of films produced, lending support to the argument that repressive political climates can motivate and mobilise creative energies rather than suppress them.

The standard-bearer for the mainstream renaissance was *Chariots of Fire* (1981) which did much to initiate a new genre of 'heritage' cinema in the 1980s with its nostalgic remembrance of a victorious moment in British history when the British athletics team was successful at the 1924 Olympic Games. The film was the first of a series which looked back to an earlier period of British history when the nation was still 'Great', possessing an empire and with more rigid and hierarchical divisions between the classes and the sexes. With its release coinciding with the Falklands War, which occurred shortly after the film had received four Oscars at the 1982 Academy Awards, including the award for Best Picture, *Chariots of Fire* inevitably became caught up in the jingoism of the time, which Thatcher and the Tory press did much to encourage. Consequently the film acquired a reputation as a flag-waving Thatcherite film, despite the fact that it was completed before the outbreak of the Falklands War, despite the fact that the original version of the script was written before the Thatcher government even came to power, and despite the fact that the political leanings of the film's producer, writer and director were to the left of the political spectrum.

The film certainly received no help from the Thatcher government in getting made, the bulk of its finance coming from American and Egyptian sources, and in its story of 'two main characters fighting against various kinds of bigotry', cultural, racial and religious, it ostensibly champions the underdog and the outsider against the establishment.[24]

But the Thatcherite project held no great love for the kind of establishment and tradition which the film ostensibly criticises and in its advocacy of individual achievement and self-enterprise the film ironically found itself in accord with the new Conservative ideology:

> *Chariots of Fire* remains overtly critical of an England built on rigid class demarcations and aristocratic hauteur, but in its stead it implicitly endorses the Thatcherite ethos of a nation based on a meritocracy of the ambitious, the diligent and the gifted. In the film's vision, the Establishment's values begin to shift, becoming more tolerant of individual difference and comprehending that the future no longer rests solely within their control.

But the film's idea of a more dynamic, diverse nation, one where a man like Abrahams has the chance to succeed, is depicted with as much uncritical sentimentality as the Cambridge masters treat their own hierarchical and racist vision of Britain. It's a fitting message for a Thatcher-ruled England where the traditional class lines give way to individual achievement, usually defined in terms of wealth and status.[25]

The problem which *Chariots of Fire* creates for itself resides in the contradiction of wanting to present a social critique of a bigoted and hierarchical establishment while employing a visual aesthetic which celebrates the very ethos which it wishes to condemn. The sumptuous *mise en scène* of this and other heritage films of the 1980s, like *Another Country* (1984), *A Passage to India* (1985), and *A Room with a View* (1986), ultimately detracts from any attempt at social criticism, glossing over any contradictions and inequities which the films may be seeking to expose and subordinating them to a visual aesthetic which romanticises the past, 'inviting a nostalgic gaze that resists the ironies and social critiques so often suggested narratively by these films'.[26] Several of these 'heritage' films have been adaptations of the novels of E.M. Forster (*A Passage to India. A Room with a View, Maurice, Where Angels Fear to Tread, Howard's End*) but, as Andrew Higson notes, the seductive visual style of the films has tended to take precedence over the social criticism of the novels:

> The novels explore what lies beneath the surface of things, satirizing the pretentious and the superficial, and especially those who are overly concerned with keeping up appearances rather than acting according to the passions of the heart. The films, however, construct such a delightfully glossy visual surface that the ironic perspective and the narrative of social criticism diminish in their appeal for the spectator.[27]

Only 24 British feature films were produced in 1981, including *Chariots of Fire*. In 1982, however, the number had increased to 40, and by 1987 it had risen to 55. The introduction of a fourth television channel in 1982 had much to do with the increase, probably far more than any renaissance which may have been inspired by the success of *Chariots of Fire*.

Channel 4 was set up with the remit of providing an alternative to the existing provision on British television and the commissioning of low-budget indigenous British films was from the beginning an important part of its policy. Acting as a 'publishing house' rather than as a producer of its own programmes the new channel commissioned films from independent production companies, putting up part (sometimes all) of the budget (in most cases less than £500,000) and thus giving important impetus to an impoverished film production sector in the early 1980s. Some of these films received a limited (but important from the point of view of publicity) cinema release before their television screening, while others were premiered on Channel 4, in the channel's 'Film on Four' slot, and not seen in cinemas at all. Thus a blurring of the distinction between cinema and television drama, which had become more pronounced during the 1970s with single plays on television increasingly taking on the appearance of low-budget British films, was reinforced during the 1980s as Channel 4, and subsequently the BBC and the other ITV companies, involved themselves more and more in the commissioning of feature films.

Of the many films financed by Channel 4 in its early years *The Plough-man's Lunch* (1983) provides a good contrast to a more prestigious cinema release of the time like *Chariots of Fire*. Unlike *Chariots*, *The Ploughman's Lunch* took a contemporary look at Britain, focusing on a journalist who works for the BBC and who is writing a book on Suez 'revising its humiliating history so that it can be viewed as a predecessor worthy of the imperial Falklands victory'. [28] The journalist, James Penfield (Jonathan Pryce), is ambitious, selfish and self-seeking, an embodiment of the Thatcherite philosophy of individualism and self-enterprise. However, the journalist is by no means a figure for audience identification. His ruthless ambition and deceitfulness are displayed and exposed in a detached manner and the world that he inhabits is similarly portrayed in a cold, distanced way, thus avoiding the seductiveness of *Chariots'* more lavish visual style.

The Ploughman's Lunch is just one of many British films financed by Channel 4 in the 1980s, providing evidence of a genuine renaissance in British cinema after the doldrums of the 1970s. While not all of these films have been as overtly political or contemporary in subject matter (part of *The Ploughman's Lunch* was actually filmed at the 1982 Conservative Party conference), it is a good example of a 1980s film which is unambiguously critical of the Thatcher ethos, unlike the more celebrated and equivocal *Chariots of Fire*.

Another Channel 4 film which was oppositional to and critical of the Thatcher ethos was *My Beautiful Laundrette* (1985). Contemporary in subject matter and eschewing the seductive visual style of the heritage films, *My Beautiful Laundrette* offers a multicultural perspective on Thatcher's Britain. Written by Hanif Kureishi, a young British Asian, and directed by Stephen Frears, a leading exponent of indigenous British film-making in the 1980s, *My Beautiful Laundrette* offered an 'ironic salutation to the entrepreneurial spirit in the eighties that Margaret Thatcher championed'.[29] Ironic because the entrepreneurs here are an extended Pakistani family who have taken the Thatcherite ideology to heart and turned the tables on the old colonial order. Thus Omar, a young ambitious member of the family, persuades his uncle to let him run a launderette as a part of the family business, employing his white, male lover Johnny to work for him, while Johnny's unemployed, racist peers hang around outside: the new disenfranchised underclass of

Thatcher's two-tier Britain. The film was ironic also in portraying a gay relationship at a time when the Tories were introducing legislation designed to prevent Labour-controlled local authorities from pursuing policies which might be seen to be supportive of gay and lesbian relationships. The unexpected success of *My Beautiful Laundrette* on its cinema release seemed to prove that a substantial number of people disagreed with this particular attempt by Thatcher to turn the clock back to a pre-permissive, more homophobic era.

The film ends with the entrepreneurial ambitions of the family in ruins, relationships (apart from that between Omar and Johnny) broken up, and violent conflict between the white and Asian communities, with Johnny reluctantly taking the side of the Asian family against his old mates. There is no way, therefore, in which the film can be seen to be endorsing Thatcherism. On the contrary, *My Beautiful Laundrette* provides a damning critique of the socially divisive policies which the Thatcher government was pursuing.

Another multicultural perspective on Thatcher's Britain was offered in *Handsworth Songs* (1986), a documentary produced by the Black Audio Film Collective, one of several black film-making workshops set up in the early 1980s. As previously noted, the development of an independent film workshop sector was one of the positive aspects of British film culture in the 1970s and Channel 4 gave renewed impetus to the sector as part of its commitment to innovative and radical alternatives to the mainstream, being one of the initiators of a Workshop Declaration which was designed to legitimise and encourage the production of those more experimental and oppositional forms of cinema which, during the 1970s, had been funded by organisations like the British Film Institute and Regional Arts Associations.

Where *My Beautiful Laundrette* was made on a budget of £650,000 and screened in the 'Film on Four' slot, *Handsworth Songs* was made for just £11,000 and screened in the late night 'Eleventh Hour' slot set aside for more 'minority interest' films. Even so, a late-night screening on Channel 4 could enable a film like *Handsworth Songs* to reach a far larger audience that it could from screenings in film workshops and the few independent cinemas that might show it. With its mixture of different forms and modes of address, *Handsworth Songs* departs significantly from the more conventional narrative strategy of a film like *My Beautiful Laundrette*:

> Variously described as a 'documentary' and a 'film essay' on race and civil disorder in Britain today, *Handsworth Songs*, as its title suggests, in fact owes more to poetic structures than to didactic exposition. Familiar TV and newspaper reportage is juxtaposed with opaque, elusive imagery, newsreel and archive material is reworked, and sound is pitted against image to release a multitude of unanswered questions about the underlying causes of 'racial unrest'. The result is a powerful combination of anger and analysis, of lyricism and political strategy, elegy and excavation.[30]

In combining different forms, materials and modes of address the film constructs a lament for what Britain had, in the past, offered its immigrant communities and contrasts this with the reality of life for ethnic communities in Britain in the 1980s, a reality which is seen in the aftermath of riots in Brixton, Birmingham and Toxteth. This reality is highlighted in the footage of Margaret Thatcher speaking on television about the 'fear of being swamped' by ethnic minorities, juxtaposed with slow-motion footage of a young black man being literally 'swamped' by police who overpower him as he runs down a street trying to evade them. The fear of 'the Other' given voice by Thatcher is contrasted with the reality of life on the street for the disenfranchised black underclass in Thatcher's Britain.

These four films – *Chariots of Fire*, *The Ploughman's Lunch*, *My Beautiful Laundrette* and *Handsworth Songs* – provide a cross-section of British film-making in the 1980s, by no means entirely representative but giving an illustration of the diversity of film practice in a decade when the conditions for producing films as variously lavish, engaging, provocative and challenging as these were far from conducive. As Thomas Elsaesser has written of this period of creative renewal in British cinema:

> the Thatcher years implicitly and explicitly asked what it meant to be British – or English, Scottish, Irish, or Welsh, or to be from the North, the Midlands or the South. The decade also questioned what it meant to be a British filmmaker. The polarizations along lines of class, of race, of religion, of nationality and language recalled similar breakups elsewhere in Europe. They make the 1980s a period of momentous social shifts well beyond Thatcherism and support the view that violent social tensions are often the best soil for the flowering of resilient, contesting, and confrontational arts, obliging artists to rediscover themselves as social counterforces and moral consciences.[31]

THE BRITISH FILM RENAISSANCE OF THE 1990S

Despite the fluctuations in British film production in the post-war period cinema admissions were in continual decline from the high point of 1946 until 1984, when cinema attendance bottomed out at 54 million. Thereafter each year (except 1995 when there was a slight drop) saw a rise in the number of people attending cinemas, from 78 million in 1987 to 139 million in 1997, and an increase in the number of cinemas from 648 (1,215 screens) in 1987 to 747 (2,383 screens) in 1997.[32]

However, this revival in the exhibition sector did not especially serve the interest of British films, as the increase in the number of cinema screens was largely as a result of the building of multiplex cinemas by American-owned companies, for the purpose of screening more of what the distributors and exhibitors believed the British public wanted: Hollywood films. While some multiplex cinemas are more adventurous than others in their programming, there is usually little space or incentive for them to programme more than the occasional non-Hollywood film, and with the growth of multiplexes, not to mention the proliferation of satellite and cable TV movie channels, the number of independent and arthouse cinemas declined in the corresponding period.

With the policy of the Conservative government, under its new leader John Major, being no more supportive of the British film industry than it was during the 1980s, and with the American hegemony over film exhibition continuing, British cinema continued to struggle in the 1990s. Yet, despite all the odds being stacked against it, British films of quality continued to get made, often reaping rewards and acclaim at film festivals around the world.

Two of the biggest box-office successes in the first half of the decade were *The Crying Game* (1992) and *Four Weddings and a Funeral* (1994). Given its unlikely combination of transvestism and Irish Republican politics, the huge success of *The Crying Game* in America, where it took over $60 million at the box office, was unprecedented. Not at all bad for a film that cost only a little over £2 million to make, but its success came too late to save Palace Pictures, the production company responsible for it, whose fortunes had been declining since the successes of the mid-1980s.

Four Weddings and a Funeral was also a low-budget production, costing less than £3 million, yet it was an even bigger box-office success, taking more money at the UK box office in 1994 than any Hollywood film (£27 million) and performing exceptionally well in America, where it took over $50 million. The success of *Four Weddings*, however, was perhaps more predictable, being a contemporary 'heritage' film, made with one eye very much on the American market, and featuring a new British star, Hugh Grant. Its success proved the continuing popularity of the heritage genre, at home and abroad, and not just with middle-class audiences on the art cinema circuit (where the 1991 Merchant-Ivory production of Forster's *Howard's End* went down very well) but in the multiplexes, where *Four Weddings* took most of its money.

In the second half of the decade a new kind of heritage cinema emerged in the shape of films like *Brassed Off* (1966) and *The Full Monty* (1997). While retaining iconographic links with the late 1950s/early 1960s 'new wave', these films marked a significant departure from the more middle-class 1980s heritage film in that they focused on Britain's industrial heritage and the social and cultural effect on the labouring classes of the decline in mining and steel communities in the postwar period, especially the devastation brought to those communities by the Thatcherite policies of the 1980s. They marked a departure also because these were films that appealed to both arthouse and multiplex audiences. They were crossover films which were both critically and commercially successful, combining an iconography of British realism with elements of comedy and melodrama in a winning mixture. So successful was *The Full Monty* in this respect that it grossed over £50 million worldwide to become the most successful British film ever at the box office. It was undoubtedly helped by being partly financed (though at £3.5 million the budget was still small) and distributed by Fox Searchlight, an American company, whereas *Brassed Off* was essentially a TV production, partly financed by Channel 4. *Brassed Off* was perhaps closer to the social realist tradition of British cinema with its focus on a mining community in decline and the attempt of the community (and particularly the men in that community) to win some respect through the traditional working-class pursuit of the brass band. *The Full Monty*, in contrast, combined social realism with comedy in its story of unemployed steelworkers who form a group of male strippers in order to earn some money. The film was seen as a 'feelgood' movie and marketed as a comedy, but there is a darker side to it – it is after all about male unemployment in a depressed industrial city – which makes it a postmodern hybrid combining realism and fantasy, a serious social issue disguised as light entertainment and played for laughs. The phenomenal commercial success of the film tended to obscure the social message, but who can calculate how effective the film was ideologically, in describing the desperation of an industrial community in decline? As *The Full Monty*'s screenwriter, Simon Beaufoy, has noted:

> The marketing, of course, focused on the fact that it's a rip-roaring comedy about a bunch of strippers, when in fact there are only three minutes of stripping in the entire film. I get particularly pleased when people comment on the sadness at the heart of the film. For me, they've got it. It seems that political messages have to be so hidden in films these days that they are almost invisible.[33]

Another 1990s film which could be described as a crossover film, breaking down the old division between arthouse and mainstream, was *Trainspotting* (1996), based on the novel by Irvine Welsh. *Trainspotting* was another Channel 4 production, made on a budget of £1.7 million, but, like many of the films from the new 1990s film-making generation, it was conceived with the large cinema screen, and not the small television screen, in mind. *Trainspotting* was bolder in its rejection of social realism, incorporating surrealistic fantasy sequences within its fast-moving narrative, and adopting a more 1990s attitude in its use of a 'Britpop' soundtrack and its focus on youth and drug culture. It was also significant for presenting a quite different take on 'Scottishness' at a time when Hollywood films like *Braveheart* (1995) and *Rob Roy* (1995) were appropriating and mythologising Scottish history.

Scottish film-makers and stars have been at the forefront of the renaissance in British cinema in the 1990s. In foregrounding 'Scottishness', as distinct from 'Englishness', contemporary films like *Trainspotting* have contributed to a debate about national identity and what it means to be 'British' in the 1990s. Along with Welsh films like *House of America* (1996), Irish films like *The Boxer* (1997), multicultural films like *Bhaji on the Beach* (1993), and regional English films like *Brassed Off* and *The Full Monty*, the notion of a unified national identity, and a distinctively British cultural identity, was shown to be no longer tenable in the more fragmented and multicultural Britain of the 1990s.

Trainspotting was the most successful British film at the box office in 1996, taking over £12 million in the year. It helped to give impetus to a renaissance in British cinema in the mid-1990s and, despite its far from glamorous subject matter, contributed to the rebranding of Britain as 'cool Britannia', a term which became ubiquitous following the landslide election victory of the 'new' Labour Party under Tony Blair's leadership in 1997.

> *Trainspotting's* box office performance in the UK and around the world was great news for the UK industry. It appeared for a while as if our film industry was able to address a young audience in the way British musicians have done so successfully since the 1960s. The success of *Trainspotting's* cutting edge soundtrack album, not to mention the presence of several Britpop stars at the *Trainspotting* party in Cannes, suggested a rare creative energy, a moment at which British cinema became hip again. This was also reflected in the film's distinctive marketing campaign which not only heralded the arrival of the film but also spawned a series of parody advertisements and gave graphic designers the opportunity to use orange wherever possible – an affirmation of what was 'cool'.[34]

Claire Monk has argued that *The Full Monty*, a far greater international success than *Trainspotting* and therefore potentially more influential, also contributed to the re-branding of Britain under New Labour by offering an imaginary resolution, especially for working-class men, to real and intractable problems:

> *The Full Monty* fantasises a post-industrial Britain in which a flexible former manual workforce can remould themselves, with only temporary pain, into new careers in the creative and entertainment industries currently so heavily favoured by the nation's image-makers – or, to describe the activity of stripping more cynically, a career which replaces the sale of labour with the commodification of the body.[35]

What is most distinctive about British cinema in the 1990s is its diversity. *The Crying Game, Four Weddings and a Funeral, Brassed Off, Trainspotting* and *The Full Monty* – among the most commercially successful films of the decade – already give some indication of the cultural diversity of 1990s British cinema. Add to that list some of the films made by established film-makers in the 1990s: Terence Davies with *The Long Day Closes* (1992), Peter Greenaway with *Prospero's Books* (1991), *The Baby of Macon* (1993) and *The Pillow Book* (1995), Mike Leigh with *Life is Sweet* (1990), *Naked* (1993), *Secrets and Lies* (1995) and *Career Girls* (1997), Ken Loach (who enjoyed his own renaissance in the 1990s) with *Riff-Raff* (1991), *Raining Stones* (1993), *Ladybird, Ladybird* (1994), *Land and Freedom* (1995), *Carla's Song* (1996) and *My Name is Joe* (1998), Sally Potter with *Orlando* (1993) and *The Tango Lesson* (1997), plus a few films from the new generation that emerged during the decade: Carine Adler's *Under the Skin* (1997), Kevin Allen's *Twin Town* (1997), Gurinder Chada's *Bhaji on the Beach* (1993), Shane Meadows's *Smalltime* (1997) and *TwentyFourSeven* (1998), Michael Winterbottom's *Butterfly Kiss* (1994), *Jude* (1996), *Welcome to Sarajevo* (1997) and *I Want You* (1998), and the cultural and aesthetic diversity of British cinema in the 1990s becomes apparent.

Many more films could be mentioned, but what the above list illustrates is that British cinema in the 1990s is a pluralistic cinema. No longer is it a cinema dominated by an ideology and aesthetics of realism but a cinema which embraces a variety of forms, representations and ideologies. This is partly a consequence of responding to an increasingly multicultural and multiracial society, fragmented by regional, ethnic, class and political differences, but it is also a response to the pervasiveness of Hollywood, which continues to dominate British cinema screens with ever more spectacular and expensive blockbusters.

British cinema has usually been at its most interesting when it has gone its own way, not concerning itself unduly with the creation of a national cinema which might compete with Hollywood. Like the late 1950s 'new wave', the horror films of Hammer, the 'social problem' films of the 1950s and 1960s, the films of 'swinging London', the independent cinema of the 1970s, and the challenges to Thatcherism in the 1980s, British cinema in the 1990s has usually been most interesting when it has taken risks and been innovative and adventurous, exploring the regional, racial, sexual and cultural diversity of Britain, rather than producing films that present a romanticised and archaic image of Britain and its national heritage, even if these are the kind of films which are most marketable abroad, especially in America.

With the number of British films increasing from 30 in 1989 to 128 in 1996, there was certainly a renaissance in British film production during the decade. There was also a cultural shift, from the production of heritage films like *Howard's End* (1991), *The Remains of the Day* (1993) and *Four Weddings and a Funeral* (1994), to a new post-industrial British cinema in the second half of the decade with films like *Trainspotting*, *Brassed Off* and *The Full Monty*. This cultural shift was given impetus by the political transition from Conservatism to New Labour in 1997, and the tax concessions and Lottery funding which followed the election of the Labour government gave rise to the hope that a real renaissance in British cinema might be possible. However, with the continuing American hegemony over distribution and exhibition, the story of British cinema at the end of the century continued to be that of a sporadically vibrant yet precarious cinema, struggling to define and establish its own identity against the cultural imperialism of Hollywood.

NOTES

1. John Hill, 'Working-class Realism and Sexual Reaction: Some Theses on the British "New Wave"', in James Curran and Vincent Porter (eds), *British Cinema History* (London, 1983), p. 308.
2. Robert Murphy, *Sixties British Cinema* (London, 1992), p. 33.
3. John Hill, *Sex, Class and Realism: British Cinema 1956–1963* (London, 1986), chapter 3.
4. The only 'new wave' films where the central character is not male are *A Taste of Honey* (1961), based on the play by Shelagh Delaney, and *The L-Shaped Room* (1962), based on the novel by Lynne Reid Banks. While each of the central female characters in these films show degrees of independence, they could hardly be described as being in control of their own destinies and are just as 'trapped' as their male counterparts, even more so in that they both become single mothers and are forced to return to the shelter of the families from which they had tried to escape.
5. Ibid., p. 61.
6. John Caughie, 'Progressive Television and Documentary Drama', *Screen*, vol. 21, no. 3, 1980, pp. 33–4.
7. John Hill, op. cit., p. 119.
8. The argument about 'social engineering' forms part of Kobena Mercer's introduction to a collection of essays on black images in British television, *The Colour Black*, edited by Therese Daniels and Jane Gerson (London, 1989), p. 5.
9. Peter Hutchings, *Hammer and Beyond: The British Horror Film* (London, 1993), p. 21.
10. Ibid., p. 70.
11. Ibid., p. 65.
12. John Fiske, *Understanding Popular Culture* (London, 1989), pp. 81–2.
13. Marion Jordan, 'Carry On . . . Follow That Stereotype' in James Curran and Vincent Porter (eds), *British Cinema History* (London, 1983), p. 327.

14. Alexander Walker, *Hollywood, England: The British Film Industry in the Sixties* (London, 1986), p. 191. (First published 1974.)
15. Tony Bennett and Janet Woollacott, *Bond and Beyond* (London, 1987), pp. 238–9.
16. Francis Wheen, *The Sixties* (London, 1982), p. 61.
17. Jeffrey Richards, 'New Waves and Old Myths: British Cinema in the 1960s' in Bart Moore-Gilbert and John Seed (eds), *Cultural Revolution? The Challenge of the Arts in the 1960s* (London, 1992), p. 227.
18. Quoted in Alexander Walker, op. cit., p. 236.
19. Ibid., p. 264.
20. Robert Murphy, op. cit., p. 3.
21. Andrew Higson, 'A Diversity of Film Practices: Renewing British Cinema in the 1970s' in Bart Moore-Glibert (ed.), *The Arts in the 1970s: Cultural Closure?* (London, 1994), p. 217.
22. Simon Blanchard and Sylvia Harvey, 'The Post-War Independent Cinema – Structure and Organization' in *British Cinema History*, op. cit., p. 232.
23. Leonard Quart, 'The Religion of the Market' in Lester Friedman (ed.), *British Cinema and Thatcherism* (London, 1993), pp. 16–17.
24. Hugh Hudson, quoted in 'Charioteers and Ploughmen' by Sheila Johnston in Martyn Auty and Nick Roddick (eds), *British Cinema Now* (London, 1985), p. 100.
25. Leonard Quart, op. cit., pp. 25–7.
26. Andrew Higson, 'Representing the National Past: Nostalgia and Pastiche in the Heritage Film' in *British Cinema and Thatcherism*, op. cit., p. 109.
27. Ibid., p. 120.
28. Leonard Quart in *British Cinema and Thatcherism*, op. cit., p. 28.
29. Susan Torrey Barbara, 'Insurmountable Difficulties and Monents of Ecstasy: Crossing Class, Ethnic, and Sexual Barriers in the Films of Stephen Frears' in *British Cinema and Thatcherism*, op. cit., p. 221.
30. Pam Cook, Review of 'Handsworth Songs' in *Monthly Film Bulletin*, 54 (638), 1987, pp. 77–8.
31. Thomas Elsaesser, 'Images For Sale: The "New" British Cinema' in *British Cinema and Thatcherism*, op. cit., p. 54.
32. Source of statistics, *BFI Film and Television Handbook 1999* (London, 1998), p. 29–30.
33. Simon Beaufoy, 'Hidden Agendas' in *Sight & Sound*, vol. 8, no. 3, March 1998, p. 61.
34. Nick Thomas, 'UK Film, Television and Video: Overview' in Eddie Dyja (ed.) *BFI Film and Television Handbook 1998* (London, 1997), p. 33.
35. Claire Monk, 'Underbelly UK: The Underclass Film and the 1990s British Cinema Revival', Conference Paper for 'Cinema, Identity, History – An International Conference on British Cinema' at the University of East Anglia, July 1998.

CHAPTER SEVEN

Television

Lez Cooke

The year 1956 saw the dawning of a new era for British television. Until September 1955 the BBC had enjoyed a monopoly of the airwaves, firstly with radio and then, from 1936, with a fledgling television service which was abruptly closed down on the outbreak of war in September 1939, recommencing transmissions in June 1946.

In the ten years after the war, before the arrival of commercial television in the mid-1950s, the new medium was an expensive luxury, enjoyed in the immediate post-war period by a small middle-class elite of less than 25,000 households, in the London region only, until 1949, when the service became available in the Midlands and from 1951 in the North of England. By 1953 transmissions could reach 85 per cent of the population, but by March of that year only 2 million households owned television sets.

The televising of the Coronation of Queen Elizabeth in June 1953 was an important landmark for British television, with an estimated 20 million people watching the event on sets owned by neighbours and friends and on large screens erected in public venues for the occasion. The event proved to be an excellent marketing exercise for the new medium, stimulating sales and seeing the number of licences double to 4.5 million by 1955.

But the real explosion in television ownership, corresponding to the decline in cinema-going in the 1950s, followed the arrival of commercial television in 1955. The Conservative government, on its return to office in 1951, was sympathetic to proposals for a commercial television service but it took another three years of heated debate before a Bill was passed authorising the setting up of the Independent Television Authority to oversee the introduction of commercial television in Britain. While many people, including some Conservative politicians, feared that commercial TV would bring a decline in the high moral and cultural standards that had been set by the BBC, a significant number, including a large majority of

Tories (some of whom had business interests in the advertising industry), saw the potential for profit in a commercial television system. Needless to say, the case for commercial TV was made on the basis of the greater freedom and choice which competition would bring for the viewer, rather than the profits that might ensue for both the advertising industry and the television companies. The main concern of those opposed to the introduction of commercial television in Britain, and also of some of those in favour of it, was the possibility that the introduction of advertising might lead British television down the slippery slope towards the more overt commercialism of American TV, which involved sponsorship and the advertising of products *within* programmes. Great care was taken therefore to introduce controls on the nature and amount of advertising that would appear on the new commercial channel and, above all, to ensure that advertising was separated from the programmes, being contained within clearly defined 'commercial breaks'. Independent Television (ITV) began transmitting in the London region on 22 September 1955, but it took up to four years for the new service to become available to the rest of the British Isles, and even then it could only be received if an existing set had been converted to receive the new channel or a new set purchased. In February 1956 ITV became available in the Midlands and from May 1956 in the North of England. Other regions had to wait a little longer: Scotland – August 1957; South Wales and the West of England – January 1958; the South of England – August 1958; the North-East of England – January 1959; the East of England and Northern Ireland – October 1959.

By 1960 72 per cent of the population had access to both ITV and the BBC and 10.5 million licences had been sold: more than a tenfold increase in a period of just ten years. In the corresponding period cinema-going more than halved, falling from 1,396 million admissions in 1950 to 501 million ten years later.

THE IMPACT OF ITV ON THE BBC

For the first year ITV struggled financially as it tried to increase audiences in order to attract enough advertising revenue to survive. The limited availability of the service was a problem but as this was gradually overcome the policy of populist programming designed to maximise audiences proved a winning formula and by 1958 the ITV companies were beginning to show a profit. By 1959 Independent Television had become, in the famous phrase of Roy Thomson, chairman of Scottish Television, 'a licence to print money'.

The BBC had anticipated a drop in audience share to 40 per cent, but by 1958 ITV's more popular programming had succeeded in capturing 79 per cent of the audience among viewers who had access to both channels. To some extent the BBC was a victim of its own complacency, the same complacency which characterised British society generally in the mid-1950s. Under its first Director General, John Reith, the BBC saw itself as not simply responsible for providing a public service but as having a responsibility for the 'cultural enlightenment' of the listening and viewing public. Its public service remit was to provide education, information and entertainment in its programming. The emphasis, however, was clearly placed upon 'educating and informing' and the 'entertainment' had distinctly 'high' cultural values, Reith's mission being to encourage the mass of the people to learn to appreciate 'higher' things. This paternalistic attitude had been stated by Reith as early as 1924:

> It is occasionally represented to us that we are apparently setting out to give the public what we think they need, and not what they want, but few know what they want, and very few what they need.[1]

This philosophy was carried over into television and continued to form the cultural policy of the BBC long after the departure of Reith in 1938. While some concessions were made to the popular audience with the expansion of television in the early 1950s the overall profile was still predominantly middle-class and 'culturally enriching'. Even the more popular programming of *The Grove Family* (1954–7) and *Dixon of Dock Green* (1955–76) seemed unadventurous and conservative alongside the unashamed populism of ITV which scheduled down-market, audience-grabbing programmes like *The Adventures of Robin Hood* (1955–9), *Sunday Night at the London Palladium* (1955–67), *Double Your Money* (1955–68) and its stablemate *Take Your Pick* (1955–68) alongside popular American imports like *I Love Lucy* (1955–57), *Gunsmoke* (1956–61) and *Rawhide* (1959–63).

The ITV companies, in other words, initiated a shift in programming away from the BBC's 'giving the public what they *need*' to 'giving the public what they *want*' and in terms of ratings this soon proved to be a successful policy. One advantage that ITV had over the BBC was that it was regionalised, whereas the BBC was more centralised and metropolitan in its structure and outlook. Where the BBC addressed a national audience from a middle-class, Home Counties perspective, ITV offered a range of programming targeted at audiences differentiated by class, region and generation. Programmes like *Cool for Cats* (1956–61) and *Oh Boy!* (1958–9) were clearly aimed at the teenage audience and designed to capitalise on the new rock and roll youth culture of the 1950s, while *Coronation Street* (1960–) was primarily aimed at a northern working-class audience, in sharp contrast to the BBC's earlier attempt at a television soap opera, *The Grove Family*, which focused on a lower middle-class family in a southern, suburban locale.

It seems significant, in retrospect, that *The Grove Family* only lasted three years. *Coronation Street*, while not specifically intended for a younger audience, was more in tune with the social realism that was proving popular at the cinema box office in films like *Room at the Top* (1959) and *Saturday Night and Sunday Morning* (1960). Where the cinema had lost a large share of its family audience, however, the 'kitchen sink' drama of *Coronation Street* flourished and it soon became one of the most popular programmes on television, with audiences exceeding 20 million by mid-1961.

If *Coronation Street* represented the popular end of ITV's drama schedule, *Armchair Theatre* represented the serious end, with its prestigious Sunday evening slot and single plays written by television playwrights (as opposed to *Coronation Street*'s more anonymous and less well paid scriptwriters) and featuring adaptations of the work of well-known authors like F. Scott Fitzgerald, Oscar Wilde and John Wyndham. *Armchair Theatre* had begun in 1956, but it was after the appointment in 1958 of Sydney Newman, who had made his name as a producer of ground-breaking TV drama in Canada, that *Armchair Theatre* really began to make its mark, especially once Newman had shifted the emphasis towards the commissioning of original work from playwrights like Ted Willis, Harold Pinter and Alun Owen, who received the award of 'TV Playwright of 1959–60' for his three plays: *No Trams to Lime Street* (tx. October 1959), *After The Funeral* (tx. April 1960) and *Lena, O My Lena* (tx. September 1960). With these and other indigenous plays, *Armchair Theatre* made its own contribution to the genre of Northern working-class realism that was sweeping all before it in the theatre, literature and the cinema. Innovative in terms of its style as well as its subject matter, *Armchair Theatre* proved popular too, frequently featuring among the top ten programmes between 1958 and 1962 and often attracting audiences in excess of 10 million. But above all it enabled ITV to go some way towards fulfilling its public service commitment, which was in danger of being abandoned in the relentless pursuit of ratings and advertising revenue.

However, for the Pilkington Committee, which had been set up by the government in 1960 to consider the development of broadcasting in Britain, ITV had gone too down-market in its pursuit of ratings. When it reported in 1962 the committee was scathingly critical of the low standards of ITV, deeming that the channel had not done enough to maintain standards of quality in its programming and too often descended to the levels of 'triviality'.

There was a Reithian slant to the committee's findings which the BBC did much to exploit, a hint of cultural snobbishness which valued that which was seen as 'culturally enriching' while despising the more populist programming which it saw as 'mindless entertainment for the masses'. This superior attitude was given dubious support in the late 1950s by the behavioural school of mass communications research, which saw the media, and television in particular, as responsible for brainwashing the 'less discerning' viewers (i.e. the working classes). In this respect the Pilkington Committee was a product of its time. The mechanistic argument that television addresses a 'passive' viewer has been strongly challenged by subsequent mass media research, which has become considerably more sophisticated since the late 1950s, placing more emphasis upon the variety of ways in which viewers actively produce their own readings of television programmes and the extent to which individual readings of programmes vary considerably according to the age, gender, ethnicity, social class, religious and political beliefs of the viewer.

By 1960, the peak year of profitability for the ITV companies and the year in which Pilkington began investigating, the commercial channel had grown somewhat complacent. The BBC meanwhile, stung by the inroads which ITV had made into its audience, and recognising that the committee was inclined against the populism of ITV, actively courted Pilkington and was rewarded with the third television channel, which the committee recommended should be awarded to the BBC. The government endorsed this recommendation and BBC2 began transmitting in April 1964 on the new, technically superior, 625-line UHF frequency.

THE 'GOLDEN AGE' OF BRITISH TELEVISION

The 1960s occupies a distinctive place in the short and tightly compressed history of British television. Sandwiched between the confident assurances of the postwar years, dominated still by the Reithian paternalism of the BBC, and the harsher, more pragmatic and largely economic imperatives of the 1970s, lies an era characterized by experiment, innovation and a particular sort of cultural iconoclasm.[2]

During the course of the Pilkington Committee's investigation, and while the ITV companies were busy fighting among themselves over advertising revenue and ignoring Pilkington, the BBC began developing new programmes under its newly-appointed Director General, Hugh Carleton-Greene, who presided over what many consider to be the BBC's 'golden age' in the 1960s. In 1962, the year in which Pilkington reported, the BBC introduced a raft of new programmes designed to regain the initiative from ITV. These included *Compact*, a twice-weekly soap-opera that ran for three years, *Dr Finlay's Casebook*, a weekly medical drama that ran until 1971, *Steptoe and Son*, a hugely popular situation comedy written by Ray Galton and Alan Simpson which regularly attracted audiences of over 20 million, *That Was The Week That Was*, a satirical programme that was both popular and political, and *Z Cars*, a gritty police drama in the social realist tradition which revolutionised fictional representations of the police and ran for 16 years. In addition the BBC lured Sydney Newman away from ITV and installed him as Head of Drama at the beginning of 1963, an appointment which seemed symptomatic of the extent to which the BBC had regained the initiative by marrying popular and 'quality' programming. No longer mainly an elitist organisation, the BBC was now developing quality programmes for a mass audience and, with the ITV companies galvanised by the criticisms of the Pilkington Report and the awarding of the third channel to the BBC, British television embarked on a new period of creativity, experiment and innovation.

Of the new programmes, *Z Cars* provides a good illustration of how the BBC was attempting to revitalise its programming for the new decade. Not only was the series set in the North-West, featuring characters who were identifiable by their regional accents as well as their working-class attitudes and mannerisms, the programme took account of social and demographic changes, such as the decline of the old working-class communities and the development of new towns, and the replacing of the friendly neighbourhood bobby on the beat with policemen in patrol cars – the 'Z cars' of the programme title – more removed from the public they were supposed to serve.

Z Cars was hailed as a breakthrough for its increased realism, moving away from the studio confines of naturalistic drama like *Dixon of Dock Green* and *Armchair Theatre* to include more location filming and embracing a faster narrative style. The series was also more realistic in its content and proved immediately controversial when, in the first episode, the public image of the police as beyond reproach was challenged by the portrayal of individual police officers as wife-beaters and gamblers.

Like *Coronation Street*, *Z Cars* was influenced by the social realism of the 'kitchen sink' films and novels and was progressive in relation to what had gone before, especially with regard to police drama. But *Z Cars* went further than *Coronation Street* in trying to fulfil the public service remit of education, information and entertainment, all within the same programme. The 'education' took the form of a focus upon social issues and problems which were rarely resolved but highlighted in an attempt to raise public awareness. The 'information' came in the representation of new modes of policing and the utilisation and display of new technology, and the presentation of this within the popular entertainment format of the police series enabled the programme to reach a large audience of 9 million initially, growing rapidly to 14 million before the end of the first series. This popularity persuaded the BBC to extend the original 13-part series to 31 episodes and to commission a second series. By early 1963 *Z Cars* was attracting 16 million viewers and had become the most popular drama series on BBC television – although some way behind *Steptoe and Son* which had an audience of over 20 million viewers by this time.

These figures give an indication of the extent to which, by 1963, the BBC had recovered in its battle with ITV for viewers. While ITV programmes still dominated the ratings, *Z Cars, Steptoe and Son, Dr Finlay's Casebook*, and subsequent popular BBC programmes like *Till Death Us Do Part* (1966–75) and *Dad's Army* (1968–77), together with the small but significant inroads which BBC2 made into the total audience share with its more specialised and eclectic programming, enabled the BBC to co-exist on a more equal footing with ITV during the 1960s and on into the 1970s. After the late-1950s ITV assault on the BBC monopoly, British television settled down to a comfortable, complementary duopoly.

Two other drama series will serve to illustrate the BBC's creative response to ITV in the 1960s. *Doctor Who* (1963–89) was one of Sydney Newman's initiatives in popular drama programming on his arrival at the BBC. Originally targeted at 9–14-year-olds, the programme quickly attracted an adult audience with its dual focus on fantasy and a contemporary interest in space travel and new technology. The 1960s Doctors were also to some extent anti-establishment figures, outsiders who had an 'alternative' appeal as the mid-1960s pop culture transformed into the late-1960s counter-culture.

Doctor Who was an attempt to break with the rather conservative tradition of previous BBC children's television and was in the liberal-populist tradition of BBC programming in the 1960s, reflecting a move towards liberalism in society which became more pronounced after Harold Wilson's Labour government ended thirteen years of Tory rule in 1964. The series was also firmly in the public service tradition of the revitalised BBC, which was now geared towards providing quality programmes for a 'popular' audience, rather than quality programmes for a 'quality' audience as it had before ITV.

Sydney Newman had been appointed by Hugh Carleton-Greene with the intention of injecting new life into the BBC's drama output and Newman was instrumental in developing popular, quality drama which did not lose sight of the BBC's public service remit. Verity Lambert, producer on the first *Doctor Who* series, has identified the way in which Newman wanted not only to modernise children's television drama but to combine the educational and the informational in a manner that was not 'teacherly' or patronising:

> He was trying to find something which took into account the new things that fascinated kids, like space and other planets, and certainly he felt that he wanted a programme which, while not necessarily educational as such, was one which children could look at and learn something from. In the futuristic stories they could learn something about science and in the past stories they could learn something about history in an entertainment format.[3]

Another drama series that Newman was responsible for at the BBC was *The Wednesday Play* (1964–70), one of the most important and influential vehicles for radical and innovative television in the 1960s. Continuing and extending the ground-breaking work of ITV's *Armchair Theatre*, *The Wednesday Play* provided a forum for challenging, socially-conscious drama, presented in the form of single plays with a distinctly left-of-centre slant. Plays like *Up the Junction* (1965) and *Cathy Come Home* (1966) have since been acknowledged as ground-breaking dramas for the manner in which they combine naturalistic acting, true-to-life characterisation and situations, with an observational camera style and narrational voiceover which gave a quality of documentary realism to the drama.

Up to the early 1960s most television drama had been transmitted 'live', with occasional film or (after 1958) video inserts of scenes shot on location. Even *Z Cars*, despite an increased use of film and video inserts, was still being transmitted 'live' well into 1963. Thereafter, as the amount of pre-recorded material being inserted into programmes increased, there was a move to pre-recording programmes for later transmission, thus avoiding the technical problems which occasionally afflicted 'live' productions. The increasing use of new lightweight 16mm film cameras for location work further removed *The Wednesday Play* from its historical connection to theatrical drama, enabling a greater verisimilitude and, in many cases, sharpening the political edge of the drama.

Some of the most radical and innovative work produced for *The Wednesday Play* series came in the mid-1960s with plays like Dennis Potter's *Stand Up, Nigel Barton* and *Vote, Vote, Vote for Nigel Barton* (both 1965), David Mercer's *And Did Those Feet?* (1965) and *In Two Minds* (1967), Nell Dunn's *Up the Junction* (1965), Jeremy Sandford's *Cathy Come Home* (1966) and Jim Allen's *The Lump* (1967), all politically-challenging, socially-conscious work, much of which proved controversial, irking the conservative sensibilities of self-appointed guardians of public morality like Mary Whitehouse, who had started her campaign to 'clean up TV' in 1963.

Despite the shift away from theatre, *The Wednesday Play* was still primarily a writer's medium, but in the hands of directors like Ken Loach, who directed several *Wednesday Plays*, there were signs that the single play on television was becoming more of a director's medium, a development which the shift towards using film, and the subsequent utilisation of a more cinematic style and visual grammar, only served to reinforce.

With the introduction of these and other ground-breaking programmes like *Late Night Line-Up* (BBC2, 1964–72), *Man Alive* (BBC2, 1965–82), *Tomorrow's World* (BBC1, 1965–), *The Frost Report* (BBC1, 1966–7), *Omnibus* (BBC1, 1967–) and, at the end of the decade, *Monty Python's Flying Circus* (BBC1, 1969–74), the BBC opened up something of a 'culture gap' between themselves and ITV in the 1960s. While ITV programmes like *Coronation Street*, *Double Your Money*, *Take Your Pick*, *Sunday Night at the London Palladium* and *Opportunity Knocks* (1964–78) topped the ratings, and the youth-oriented 'pop' series like *The Avengers* (1961–9), *The Saint* (1962–9), *The Prisoner* (1967–8), *Department 'S'* (1969–70), and *The Champions* (1969–71) provided the escapist fantasy to contrast with the BBC's more earnestly realist aesthetic, only ITV programmes like *University Challenge* (1962–87), the investigative current affairs programme *World in Action* (1963–), and the *Monty Python* forerunners *At Last the 1948 Show* (1967) and *Do Not Adjust Your Set* (1967–8), came anywhere near to challenging the cultural hegemony that the BBC maintained in terms of stimulating, innovative and socially-conscious programming in the 1960s.

BRITISH TELEVISION IN THE 1970S: A MIRROR TO SOCIETY?

What is most noticeable about British television in the 1970s, given the growing instability in the social, economic and political sphere resulting from a breakdown in the post-war political consensus, is the degree of stability enjoyed by both broadcasting institutions throughout the decade, With unemployment and the cost of living rising, the 'affluence' that had characterised British society in the 1950s and 1960s evaporated. The 1970s, in contrast, was marked by an escalation in industrial disputes and growing social unrest. This impacted upon television when, with the introduction of a three-day working week in 1973 as a result of an industrial dispute involving the coal miners, the government ordered the closing down of the evening television service at 10.30 p.m., ostensibly to save electricity.

Despite the turmoil in the wider society the cosy duopoly of the BBC and ITV continued, with the audience share continuing to be split fairly equally throughout the decade. Three new ITV companies had come into existence in 1968 when the franchises had come up for renewal, and colour television had also been introduced in the late 1960s (although because of the cost of sets it did not become widespread until the mid-1970s), but there were to be no more structural changes or developments in British television until the 1980s. ITV did lobby for a second channel early on in the 1970s but it was 1982 before the fourth channel finally arrived, and then not as an ITV2.

After conceding the cultural high ground to the BBC in the 1960s ITV fought back in the 1970s with an increase in 'serious' programmes to complement its popular diet of situation comedies, soap-operas and light entertainment. Another broadcasting committee, under the chairmanship of Lord Annan, had been set up by the new Labour government in 1974 and when the committee issued its report in 1977 it noted a marked improvement in the quality of ITV programming. Meanwhile the BBC, suffering more from the harsher economic climate than ITV, continued with its strand of radical and innovative drama in the new *Play for Today* series, which replaced *The Wednesday Play* in 1970. A variety of high-quality work was produced for *Play for Today*, including political dramas like *Rank and File* (1971), written by Jim Allen and directed by Ken Loach, social-conscience dramas like *Edna the Inebriate Woman* (1971), written by Jeremy Sandford, who had written *Cathy Come Home* in the mid-1960s, John McGrath's *The Cheviot, the Stag and the Black, Black Oil* (1974), a radical reading of Scottish history featuring the 7:84 theatre company, Mike Leigh's biting satires on social class, *Nuts in May* (1976) and *Abigail's Party* (1977), Dennis Potter's controversial *Brimstone and Treacle* (1976, but banned and not shown until 1987) and his lament for the lost innocence of childhood, *Blue Remembered Hills* (1979), and Caryl Churchill's *The Legion Hall Bombing* (1978), another controversial play, this time about Northern Ireland.

The single plays of *Play for Today* were complemented by several landmark drama series and serials in the 1970s, including Dennis Potter's *Pennies from Heaven* (1978), G.F. Newman's *Law and Order* (1978) and the Ken Loach/Jim Allen/Tony Garnett four-part series *Days of Hope* (1975). The latter described the lives and changing political experiences of three working-class characters between the years 1916 and 1926, each episode focusing on one significant historical moment in that period: the Great War, the miners' strike of 1921, the first Labour government in 1924, and the General Strike of 1926. The concentration on crucial moments of labour history and the emphasis on the miners in two episodes was of particular significance given the miners' strikes of 1972 and 1973–4.

Employing a naturalistic style, and clearly favouring a revolutionary analysis of the political events of the period, the series provoked considerable controversy and brought forth accusations of political bias against the BBC. It was also the subject of significant academic debate in the pages of the theoretical journal of film and television, *Screen*.[4]

The public debate highlighted the drama-documentary form of the series as contentious because of the way in which a naturalistic style was used to present the events depicted as authentic, and therefore 'true', hence the accusations of distortion and left-wing bias. What clearly worried the right-wing critics and Conservative politicians who made the accusations was that a forthright socialist perspective on the events could be presented on the main BBC channel at peak time. The accusation that the drama-documentary style distorted the truth was just a smokescreen, however. What was really at issue was the radical political content that this naturalistic style so effectively communicated.

That *Days of Hope* came so soon after the 1973–4 miners' strike, which had led to the downfall of Ted Heath's Conservative government, was clearly a significant factor, helping to explain the vehemence of the right-wing attacks upon the series. It served to emphasise the ideological role that radical TV drama could play at a time when the political consensus was breaking down and industrial and class conflict were once more back on the social agenda after a period of relative harmony. It also reaffirmed the effectivity of television, and BBC TV drama in particular, as a forum for political debate and oppositional voices, providing one instance in a growing number of political controversies involving television programmes in the 1970s.

The academic debate around *Days of Hope* was of a more rarefied nature, being concerned with the relationship between dramatic form and politics and the ability of popular television dramas, in particular, to have a significant political effect upon the viewer. The debate hinged upon the question of realism and the particular naturalistic style that *Days of Hope* had adopted. Essentially, the case for *Days of Hope* as radical TV drama was put by Colin McArthur when he argued against the dominant *Screen* position of the mid-1970s, which was critical of forms of representation (including films and TV dramas) which utilised the 'bourgeois' form of the classic realist text, even if the 'content' was oppositional. McArthur argued that the style adopted by the makers of *Days of Hope* was effective and appropriate for communicating its socialist argument and that the retention of certain 'classical features' rendered the series accessible to a popular television audience in a way that the kind of Brechtian anti-realist text that *Screen* was advocating in the mid-1970s would not have been. Colin MacCabe responded by arguing that the problem with *Days of Hope* was not just that it adopted the 'bourgeois' form of the BBC costume drama but that, in doing so, it adopted the 'closed' form of the classic realist text. Because of this MacCabe questioned the limited nature of the knowledge which the viewer acquires about the events depicted, arguing that by apportioning the blame for the defeat suffered by the working class in the General Strike to the Labour leadership the series offered no vision of social change which could be acted upon by contemporary viewers. An anti-realist strategy (such as that adopted by John McGrath in *The Cheviot, the Stag and the Black, Black Oil*) might have interrupted the naturalistic drama to remind viewers of the recent confrontation between miners and government, thus drawing direct political parallels and suggesting ways in which lessons might be learned from past experience.

An important footnote to this academic debate was added by John Caughie in a 1980 *Screen* article on 'Progressive Television and Documentary Drama'. Moving on from the argument about the relative merits of different formal strategies, Caughie argued for the necessity of taking the conditions of production and reception of programmes into consideration, not just the political context in which the drama is produced but also the institutional context within which the programme is made and screened:

> Unlike films or plays, television programmes are seen all at once (and reacted to all at once) by a national audience. Because of this, it becomes difficult, and unrewarding, to establish the final conditions for the progressiveness of television. The conjuncture in which programmes are screened has to be critically identified; and because the programmes are made within basically conservative institutions which are both highly determined and highly determining, their place within the politics of the institutions has also to be brought into consideration.[5]

Caughie's contribution was to argue for the possibility that television pro-grammes might have political effects upon the viewer that cannot be measured by focusing on the formal operations of the text alone. In doing so he signalled a shift of emphasis in the academic study of television towards the 'determining' role of the television institutions and the political and economic context of production, as well as giving greater emphasis to the social and political context of reception and the ability of the viewer to make 'pro-gressive' readings of television programmes, aspects which were to become increasingly important in the academic study of television in the 1980s.

Given the way in which the controversy surrounding television dramas like *Days of Hope*, *The Legion Hall Bombing*, *Law and Order*, and *Death of a Princess* (1980), became public, the significance of these academic debates about realism and the drama–documentary form was not limited to the academic journals within which they were conducted. Questions of the impartiality of the broadcasters now became a legitimate part of the debate as the old certainties and beliefs crumbled along with the political consensus.

The extensive research that the Glasgow University Media Group carried out into the role of television news in reporting industrial disputes in the 1970s also met with a hostile reception, this time mainly from the television companies who found their reputation for being impartial and independent reporters of the facts being called into question, to the extent of being accused of being biased in favour of management and the state in industrial, economic and political reporting.

This question of impartiality and the role of broadcasting in helping to define public understanding of a wide range of political events, from the escalating troubles in Northern Ireland, to industrial disputes at home and an increasing concern over law and order, put the neutrality of television onto the agenda to an extent that had not previously been experienced by the BBC and ITV. In a decade in which consensus was breaking down and being replaced by conflict and increasing political polarisation, television found itself under scrutiny and often under fire from the left and the right. The BBC in particular, following its liberal–populist slant of the 1960s, found itself increasingly under attack from the right for its 'oppositional' drama in the 1970s and *Days of Hope* was just one example of how the BBC managed to attract the wrath of the establishment.

With law and order becoming a central political issue in the 1970s, the role of the state became more coercive, leading to the strikes, conflicts and confrontations which characterise British society during the decade. In such an atmosphere it was inevitable that television would attempt to engage with these social and political developments. Where the analysis of these developments in news, current affairs and documentaries drew attention from Left and Right concerning questions of bias, television's fictional output, as we have seen with *Days of Hope*, was also under scrutiny, and not only in prestigious series and single plays.

The increased emphasis upon the coercive role of the state in maintaining law and order saw the emergence of a new kind of police drama on television in the mid-1970s. The long-running, but now hopelessly anachronistic, *Dixon of Dock Green* was finally laid to rest in 1976, but a year earlier ITV had introduced a new breed of policeman in the shape of the aggressive, rule-breaking Regan in *The Sweeney* (1975–8). Taking its series title from cockney rhyming slang (Sweeney Todd/Flying Squad) the focus in *The Sweeney* was on the new kind of policing which was more prevalent in the new social circumstances of increasingly violent crime in the 1970s. While the series was careful not to condone Regan's correspondingly violent tactics without qualification, it was clear that in the exceptional climate in which a breakdown in law and order threatened to undermine social order the violent means employed by members of the flying squad justified the ends when it came to exercising the rule of law.

The Sweeney proved to be massively popular with the viewing public and, by all accounts, with the police themselves, marking a sea change in the representation of the police on television. Thereafter, television crime series became more diverse in their representations of the police and less wary of showing them as vulnerable to corruption than in the days when society had required them to be either paternalistic and parochial, like Dixon, or glorified social workers, like the police in *Z Cars*.

Television never mirrors society in a direct or simplistic manner, its representations are always one step removed from their real-life referents. Yet British television in the 1970s did reflect and engage with the social and political developments of the decade in a variety of programmes, of which the dramas discussed here provide just a few examples. By the end of the decade the political fragmentation and industrial turmoil which the country had been experiencing since the election of Heath's Conservative government in 1970 culminated in the election of a new and more radical Conservative government under Margaret Thatcher's leadership, and television suddenly found itself subject to a new political agenda which would bring an end to the old BBC/ITV duopoly and threaten the future of public service broadcasting in Britain.

THE 1980S: CHANNEL 4, COMPETITION AND DEREGULATION

There was no question that, by 1980, television was the principal form of mass entertainment in Britain, having long since surpassed cinema in that respect. By 1970 cinema admissions were down to 193 million per year, less than half of the 1960 figure. The decline continued throughout the 1970s and, by 1980, the figure had halved again, to 96 million. During the 1970s the number of television licences issued had risen from 15 to 18 million and by 1980 the average household was watching over 5 hours of television per day.

Following the election of the Thatcher government television became increasingly subject to market forces in the 1980s. The concept of public service broadcasting, where the television companies had a duty to provide a mixed diet of education, information and entertainment for a diverse viewing public, came increasingly under threat in the new economic climate as the government introduced policies designed to deregulate broadcasting and introduce a more competitive ethos. But this new brand of Toryism did not have things entirely its own way and there was considerable resistance in broadcasting, as there was in society in general, to the Thatcherite agenda.

The 1980 Broadcasting Act, which gave birth to the fourth television channel, was marked by a struggle between two ideologies. On the one hand there was the old paternalistic Conservatism which valued the notion of public service and which took up the recommendation of the Annan Committee that the fourth channel should cater for a variety of different audiences by providing diversity in its programming. On the other hand there was the new enterprise philosophy of the right wing of the Conservative party which favoured competition and the freedom of the market. The demands of the new Conservatism were met by the stipulation in the Broadcasting Act that Channel 4 would not produce its own programmes, as the BBC and ITV did, but would commission programmes from a variety of independent production companies who would compete for contracts, thus conforming to the competitive ethos favoured by Thatcher and the free marketeers.

From the moment of the announcement in the Queen's Speech in 1979 that the new Conservative government was to go ahead with the fourth channel, various organisations on the left lobbied hard to ensure that the new channel would not be an ITV2 and that the ITV companies would not be among the 'independents' who would contribute programmes to it. The Independent Film-Makers' Association, an organisation representing experimental and radical film-makers, was among the groups lobbying for representation on the new channel. Thus the activities of the independent film-making sector, informed by the oppositional politics and aesthetic theory which had been developed in relation to radical film and television drama in the 1970s, came to have an input into the formation of Channel 4, ensuring not only that the new channel had the 'distinctive character' that the legislation required of it, but that many of the programmes supplied by the independent producers had a radical edge to them, thus subverting and exploiting the competitive ethos which had been written into the constitution of the channel. Among the clauses of the 1980 Act pertaining to the fourth channel it was stipulated that programmes should 'contain a suitable proportion of material calculated to appeal to tastes and interests not generally catered for by ITV' and that the channel should 'encourage innovation and experiment in the form and content of programmes'. A large number of the recommendations of the Annan Committee did therefore find their way into the legislation that gave birth to Channel 4 and the decision to finance the channel by a subscription from the ITV companies, who were allowed to keep the advertising revenue that they sold on the new channel in their own region, meant that Channel 4 was not in competition with the ITV companies for advertising and for audiences. This gave the channel the freedom to develop a distinctive cultural alternative to the existing ITV companies, and to the BBC as well.

Among the wide variety of programmes that were aired by Channel 4 in its early years were *Brookside*, an 'alternative' soap-opera which soon proved to be Channel 4's most popular programme, *The Comic Strip Presents . . .* , a series of comedy-dramas presented by some of the new generation of alternative comedians, many of whom went on to feature in their own programmes on other channels, *The Tube*, a music programme designed to provide an alternative to the staid format and chart music of the BBC's *Top of the Pops*, programmes like *Black On Black*, *No Problem!*, and *Tandoori Nights* which were targeted at black and Asian audiences and designed to cater for those minority audiences which were not being addressed by the other channels, and *The Friday Alternative*, a current affairs programme which deliberately set out to provide a different perspective on news and current affairs to the perspectives offered by the other channels. In doing so *The Friday Alternative* soon ran into trouble with its programmes, like one edition on the Falklands War, which questioned the British Task Force decision to sink the Argentine troop ship, the *Belgrano*, with huge loss of life. Like other programmes which Channel 4 scheduled, this edition of *The Friday Alternative* offered a space for the dissenting voices of those opposed to the war.

The case of *The Friday Alternative*, which was axed for 'consistent left-wing bias' after less than a year, raised an interesting question about 'impartiality' on the new channel. Supporters of *The Friday Alternative* argued that the programme was providing an alternative to existing current affairs programmes which attempted to be impartial in their reporting and, in so doing, ended up reinforcing the status quo. *The Friday Alternative*, they argued, was simply addressing this imbalance in news reporting by giving space to dissenting voices and alternative viewpoints. While it was accepted that Channel 4 programmes were not required to be balanced *within* programmes, they were expected to provide a balance of viewpoints over a series of programmes. *The Friday Alternative* was deemed not to have done this and was axed, to be replaced by *Diverse Reports* which balanced a left-wing viewpoint one week with a right-wing viewpoint the next.

Other Channel 4 programmes also proved controversial, especially those that dealt with gay and lesbian issues, offending the sensibilities of the puritanical and outraging the hypocritical tabloid press. But these and other programmes were, as Sylvia Harvey notes, important in widening the bounds of acceptability on British television:

> the Channel's willingness to engage with its audience's interests in sexual matters, whether in *Out on Tuesday* (1988) or *Sex Talk* (1990), was to expand the horizons of what was possible in television in general. Without

its new, often forthright, witty and imaginative approach it would be difficult to imagine the appearance of Carlton's *The Good Sex Guide* on mainstream ITV at the beginning of 1993. In this sense Channel 4 affected the whole ecology of British broadcasting, extending the range of subjects that might be dealt with by television.[6]

The radical nature of many Channel 4 programmes is all the more surprising given the reactionary political climate in which it emerged. It did, arguably, take some of the pressure off the BBC, enabling the latter to continue producing radical TV drama alongside its more mainstream programming. One such drama was *Boys from the Blackstuff* (1982), a five-part series written by Alan Bleasdale and developed from his own single play, *The Black Stuff* (1980). The series of plays, transmitted just prior to the debut of Channel 4, was in the tradition of the social-issue drama pioneered by the BBC in the 1960s and 1970s. Its development coincided with a huge rise in unemployment as a consequence of the policies of the first Thatcher government and its story of the effects of unemployment on a group of tarmac workers in Liverpool caught the mood of the moment as unemployment topped 3 million for the first time since the 1930s.

First shown on BBC2, in the Sunday evening 'arts' slot, the series was not obviously targeting a mass audience, being conceived more in the 'serious' drama tradition of *Play for Today*, but, attracting a positive critical response and with audiences in the region of 3–5 million, *Boys from the Blackstuff* proved enough of a success to merit a quick repeat on BBC1 at the beginning of 1983, when its audience increased, peaking at nearly 8 million for the final episode. Using black humour as an important means of audience identification, and being filmed mainly on video rather than film, *Boys from the Blackstuff* revived debates in academic circles about the relative merits of realism, naturalism and non–naturalism in TV drama, debates which had been played out several times before, not least in relation to *Days of Hope*, in whose radical footsteps the series was seen to be treading.

In the more reactionary conjuncture of the early 1980s the case that John Caughie had made, in 1980, for a more limited definition of progress-ive TV drama, one which takes into consideration the political context within which television programmes are made and seen, seemed particularly appropriate to the Bleasdale series. The following passage might well have been written with *Boys from the Blackstuff* in mind:

> Under certain conditions, of which the present may be one, I want to be able to say that, *for television*, in its specific conditions, it may be politically progressive to confirm an identity (of sexuality or class), to recover repressed experience or history, to contest the dominant image with an alternative identity. Documentary drama seems to me to have occupied a progressive role within television insofar as it has introduced into the discourses of television a repressed political, social discourse which

may contribute to an audience's political formation, and may increase its scepticism of the other representations which television offers.[7]

In contrast to the heritage drama serials and films of the early 1980s – *Brideshead Revisited* (1981), *Chariots of Fire* (1981), *The Jewel in the Crown* (1984), to name but three – *Boys from the Blackstuff* did indeed seem to introduce 'a repressed political, social discourse', and a contemporary social realism, into British television, at a time when the national mood was being mobilised by the right in support of an outdated image of empire which saw its ultimate, ludicrous manifestation in the 1982 Falklands exploit.

To what extent *Boys from the Blackstuff* contributed to the audience's political formation or increased its scepticism of these other representations is a matter for conjecture, but judging by the way in which the character of Yosser Hughes was embraced as something of a national folk hero, with his 'gissa job' catchphrase being chanted from the terraces at Anfield, the home of Liverpool Football Club, the series had clearly struck a chord. On an ideological level it formed part of the widespread opposition to Thatcherism in the early 1980s that had manifested itself more forcefully in the riots which took place in London, Manchester and Liverpool a year before the series was broadcast.

Other BBC dramas, like *Threads* (1984), a drama–documentary depicting the consequences of a nuclear attack upon Sheffield, *Edge of Darkness* (1985), a complex six-part thriller which skilfully used the serial form to take the audience on a journey which begins like a detective *film noir* and gradually opens out to expose the role of the state in the manufacture of weapons–grade plutonium at a nuclear waste reprocessing plant deep in a disused British coal mine, *The Monocled Mutineer* (1986), also scripted by Alan Bleasdale from a true story about a First World War mutiny in the British army, and Dennis Potter's convoluted musical thriller *The Singing Detective* (1986), all reinforced the reputation of the BBC for producing quality drama and for not bowing to political pressure when the dramatic voice was radical and opposed to the dominant ideology.

Also, in 1985, the BBC introduced a new soap-opera designed to rival ITV's ratings-topping *Coronation Street*. *EastEnders*, however, was from the beginning intended to be more up-to-date than *Coronation Street* in its subject matter and portrayal of an ethnically-mixed community in the East End of London. Like *Brookside*, *EastEnders* engaged with social issues, from unemployment, racial and sexual prejudice, the emergence of HIV and Aids as a lethal new disease, to mugging, rape and murder. While based around family units, *EastEnders* did acknowledge other life-styles and it also gave more emphasis to men and youth than other TV soaps. *EastEnders* quickly emerged as the most popular programme on the BBC, with audiences topping 20 million within a year, exceeding the audience for *Coronation Street* by more than 5 million in 1986–7.

While its drama output was not quite as impressive as the BBC's, or inclined to prove as controversial or deal with social issues to the extent that BBC drama did, ITV proved itself more than capable of producing quality programmes in the 1980s, not only with its heritage serials, but also with popular series like *Minder* (1979–94), *Widows* (1983) and *Inspector Morse* (1987–97). The latter emerged as hugely popular in the late 1980s, suggesting that television drama did not have to focus on working-class mores to attract a mass audience. Part of the appeal of *Inspector Morse* was no doubt its heritage iconography: lovingly photographed images of the dreaming spires and college lawns of Oxford, coupled with the perennial appeal of investigative detective drama. But its huge popularity may also have been a reflection of how popular tastes were changing in late-1980s Britain, under the influence of nearly ten years of Tory ideology and incentives for the working class and lower middle-classes to redefine themselves as upwardly mobile and aspirational.

'Quality' was to become an important issue in television in the late 1980s, especially after the government published a White Paper in 1988 entitled 'Broadcasting in the 90s: Competition, Choice and Quality' which placed the issue of 'quality' in broadcasting firmly on the political agenda (although it was thought by many commentators to be an indication of the government's priorities that 'competition' preceded it in the title). One of the most controversial clauses in the White Paper was the proposal that, when the ITV franchises came up for renewal, they should be awarded to the highest bidder, a policy that was clearly in line with the competitive doctrine of the Conservative government.

The proposal sparked off a major debate about the threat to public service broadcasting posed by the proposals in the White Paper. While the immediate threat to the BBC was deferred until 1996 when the BBC's Charter came up for renewal, the proposal that the ITV companies should bid for their licences in a multi-million-pound 'auction' raised the spectre of new companies gaining licences purely on the grounds of their financial muscle, with no guarantees that they would fulfil a public service commitment to inform, educate and entertain, as the existing ITV companies had done. With the government favouring competition and letting market forces rule it was feared that there would be nothing to stop future ITV companies going completely down-market in their programming, jettisoning the public service commitment to supply less popular programmes to minority audiences, in the pursuit of the large audiences they would need to attract sufficient advertising revenue to finance their franchise bids.

However, perhaps anticipating the opposition that this proposal would generate, a 'quality threshold' was outlined in the White Paper which was intended to ensure that some element of a public service commitment would have to be guaranteed by the successful bidders:

> The 'threshold' consisted of three key requirements for the Channel 3 licensees: to provide regional programmes; to show 'high quality news and current affairs . . . in main viewing periods', and 'to provide a diverse programme service calculated to appeal to a variety of tastes and interests'.[8]

Between the publication of the White Paper and the eventual passage of the 1990 Broadcasting Act through parliament intense lobbying took place, led by organisations like the Campaign for Quality Television, to ensure that this quality threshold was raised to include a wider range of programmes and also to ensure that an 'exceptional circumstances' clause was added to the Bill that would enable the Independent Television Commission, which would oversee the issuing of the new licences, to veto a higher bid if it was not satisfied that the quality threshold could be fulfilled.

In these circumstances the existing ITV companies were concerned to demonstrate the quality of their programming and it was significant that lavish and expensive drama serials like *Brideshead Revisited* and *Jewel in the Crown* were cited as the kind of programme that would be under threat as a result of the government's proposals. These prestigious serials were seen by critics to epitomise 'quality' in ITV programming. They were also programmes which, because of their focus on particular aspects of British heritage, were very lucrative in terms of overseas sales, and their success may explain the production of numerous other ITV period dramas in the late 1980s, like *Paradise Postponed* (1986), *The Charmer* (1987), *Hannay* (1988–9), *Agatha Christie's Poirot* (1989–), as well as the 'contemporary' heritage drama of *Inspector Morse*.

In a 1990 article examining the idea of 'quality' in television, Charlotte Brunsdon identified four 'quality components' which characterise this kind of heritage television drama: *literary source* – lending literary prestige to the more 'vulgar' medium of television; *the best of British acting* – prestigious actors with a theatrical background who lend 'class' to television drama; *money* – enabling high production values; *heritage export* – the representation of 'a certain image of England and Englishness (with little reference to the rest of Britain), in which national identity is expressed through class and imperial identity'.[9] In other words, 'quality' in TV drama may be defined as a combination of high production values and 'high culture' values. Given the popularity of these programmes, however, and their ability to attract overseas sales, it seems less likely that they would have been at risk in the ITV franchise auction than would more radical dramas and investigative documentaries and current affairs programmes, which generally attract smaller audiences and are far less likely to be sold overseas. It has been argued that one such programme, Thames Television's *Death on the Rock* (1988), a documentary which had investigated the killing of three IRA paramilitaries by the British army in Gibralter, had so angered the government that it had been a catalyst in the decision to put the ITV contracts up for tender, with the ulterior motive being that the ensuing auction would diminish the likelihood of such programmes being produced in future by the ITV companies. The subsequent loss of Thames's franchise in the 1991 auction confirmed, for many, the political motivation behind the new legislation.

In the course of these arguments many looked to the appearance of satellite TV on the British television landscape as a harbinger of things to come in the more deregulated broadcasting world favoured by the Tories. Rupert Murdoch's Sky TV had begun transmitting in February 1989, financed by a mixture of sponsorship, subscription and advertising and heavily subsidised by its parent company, Murdoch's News Corporation. Criticised by many for its cheap, down-market programming, Sky raised the same fears that had been voiced about ITV when it was first introduced in the mid-1950s: that, as a commercial TV channel, it would sacrifice quality in pursuit of profits. These fears were exacerbated with Sky because it was not subject to the same regulations as the existing terrestrial broadcasters. By the end of the year Sky had attracted over a million subscribers in Britain.

In April 1990 Sky was joined by British Satellite Broadcasting (BSB). Using more sophisticated technology, BSB had a more up-market profile than Sky, but coming on air a year later, and having spent huge amounts of money publicising its launch, BSB was always fighting a losing battle in the satellite TV war. In November 1990, a day before the new Broadcasting Act became law, BSB, losing £8 million a month, was forced into a merger with Sky, itself losing £2 million a month, and the new company became BSkyB.

BRITISH TELEVISION IN THE 1990S

The introduction and growth of satellite television in Britain, which had gained more than four million subscribers by 1997, together with the slower development of cable TV, with just over two million subscribers in 1997, was symptomatic of the fragmentation of television in Britain in the 1990s. By 1997 satellite and cable had captured nearly 12 per cent of the audience and with the introduction of digital television in 1998 promising an explosion of hundreds of new channels, the shift towards a more competitive broadcasting environment, which had been initiated by Thatcher's Conservative government, was well under way.

In the midst of all this deregulated activity a fifth terrestrial channel appeared on the scene in 1997. While not available to the entire country, and with reception problems plaguing its introduction, Channel 5 was slow to make an impact, but with its low-budget mixture of imported drama and TV movies, late-night erotica, and its own chat shows and soap-opera (*Family Affairs*), Channel 5's share of the market had grown to 5 per cent by 1998. The growth of cable and satellite, and the introduction of Channel 5, had an inevitable impact on the existing channels. Interestingly it was ITV which suffered most, with its share of the total audience dropping throughout the decade from over 40 per cent to less than 33 per cent in 1997. In contrast, BBC1's share of the audience, which had been less than ITV's for some time, fell less sharply, although it did drop below 30 per cent for the first time in its history in 1998. However, the combined BBC1 and 2 share remained at over 40 per cent, with BBC2's share increasing to compensate somewhat for BBC1's slight fall. With Channel 4, the main public service contender to the BBC, holding on to a 10 per cent share of the audience, it seemed that there was a substantial and loyal audience for the diverse programming of the public service channels and that it was the commercial network of the ITV companies which was going to be most affected by the new cable and satellite channels and the commercial Channel 5. With the concept of public service broadcasting under threat in the more competitive, deregulated environment of the 1990s, a rearguard action was mounted in order to defend it, even to the extent of erstwhile critics of Reithian paternalism being forced into defending the old BBC notion of public service broadcasting in the face of those who would like to see market forces dictate the kind of service that was available to the public.

This new competitive environment, Anthony Smith argued in 1993, would:

> only tend to underline the need for a television company which can
> still offer a comprehensive range of programmes, constantly working to
> increase the viewers' range of tastes rather than solely to seek maximum
> consumer satisfaction. That may conjure up in the democratic mind of the
> 90s a somewhat paternalist image, but large numbers of people do indeed
> want to be given that which they do not yet realise they need.[10]

The drift in the market-oriented 1990s was towards a market research-led model of broadcasting, especially in ITV, whose programmes, whether drama, comedy, light entertainment or documentary, became increasingly ratings-led, tending either towards the formulaic or the sensational, or sometimes both. The hugely popular Yorkshire Television production *Heartbeat* (1991–) was a prime example of this. Extensive market research was done on *Heartbeat* in an attempt to maximise its audience appeal. Some ingredients were rejected, others emphasised, while others were added in order to construct a drama which would appeal to as broad a section of the audience as possible. The resulting product, while reaching a mass audience to make it one of the top rating programmes of the decade, was a drama which was light entertainment at its most bland, making for undemanding Sunday evening viewing. Robin Nelson has described *Heartbeat* as a popular postmodern drama, in which there is a *bricolage* of elements designed to appeal to a more fragmented television audience. The approach, he argues, marked a significant departure in television drama production in the 1990s:

> *Heartbeat* serves as an example of the development of a drama series in part through the application of the methods of market research undertaken by Audience Planning at the ITV Network Centre. The approach clearly marks a shift from the writer- and producer-led, supply-side aesthetics in drama production of the past.[11]

Or, to put it another way, it marked a shift from the old public service ethos of 'giving the public what they need' to 'giving the public what they want'.

The problem, of course, with this market research-led approach to television production, is that if you ask people what they want they are inclined to refer to programmes that have gone before which they have enjoyed. They are not inclined to ask for new forms and new kinds of programme with which they are unfamiliar. The approach does not allow for the fact that there may well be 'large numbers of people [who] do indeed want to be given that which they do not yet realise they need', as Anthony Smith put it.

Not that all television was as bland as *Heartbeat* in the 1990s. Quality drama series like Granada TV's *Prime Suspect* (1991–), *Cracker* (1993–) and *Band Of Gold* (1995–6), Central TV's *Kavanagh QC* (1995–), and Yorkshire TV's *A Touch of Frost* (1992–), to name but five, demonstrated that drama on the commercial network could be popular without being bland and formulaic. And despite the increasing pressure on ITV to go down-market in order to retain its audience, the ITV companies continued to produce some serious factual, investigative programmes, alongside the more obvious audience pullers like London Weekend Television's *Blind Date* (1985–) and Granada's *You've been Framed* (1990–).

The BBC meanwhile, under Director General John Birt, had a troubled time in the 1990s. Birt was recruited from ITV in the late 1980s, quite clearly to bring a more commercial, competitive edge to the BBC in the new broadcasting environment. His streamlining of the organisation and introduction of an internal market system, known as 'Producer Choice', was extremely controversial and won him few friends. But with the backing of the BBC's governors he spent much of the 1990s pushing his cost-cutting policies through. The enterprise alienated many of the creative personnel at the BBC, many of whom left to work independently. Writers and directors of a more radical persuasion found it increasingly difficult to get their work accepted, let alone produced, and BBC1, in particular, was criticised for too often pandering to the mass audience, being more concerned about competing in the market place and losing its audience to the new commercial broadcasters.

It became increasingly evident that BBC1 was no longer prepared to take risks with cutting-edge programmes of the kind which had built its reputation in the 1960s and 1970s. Instead the channel offered a mixed diet of popular drama and situation comedies like *EastEnders*, *Keeping up Appearances* (1990–), and *One Foot in the Grave* (1990–), light entertainment programmes like *Noel's House Party* (1991–) and the revived 1970s game show *The Generation Game* (1990–), with Bruce Forsyth once again hosting, alongside the ever-popular period costume dramas like *Middlemarch* (1994) and *Pride and Prejudice* (1996), which successfully tapped into the hugely popular heritage industry of the 1990s.

Not that BBC1 completely abandoned more challenging programmes. The police series, *Between the Lines* (1992–4), about the Complaints Investigation Bureau of the Metropolitan Police, was a more glossy version of the controversial drama–documentaries of the 1970s, such as G.F. Newman's *Law and Order* which was also about corruption in the police force. But as the 1990s wore on BBC1 became increasingly less confident about transmitting this kind of drama. Instead it was left to BBC2 to take risks with the more contentious, anti-establishment drama, and with other potentially controversial programmes. Significantly several of the more radical dramas broadcast on BBC2 were from Tony Garnett's World Productions company. Garnett had been a prime mover in the 1960s behind some of the more controversial *Wednesday Plays*, such as *Up the Junction* and *Cathy Come Home*, and in the 1970s with *Days of Hope* and *Law and Order*. After spending most of the 1980s in America, Garnett returned to find TV drama demoralised and unadventurous. Recognising that the single play had been all but replaced by the TV film, Garnett saw the potential for popular series drama to take up the banner which the more radical single plays had once carried.

> Series are enormously difficult to keep fresh. It's easy to be repetitive and formulaic and it's easy to turn them into a branch of manufacturing, but if you fight hard against those things there are enormous benefits. The long-running series is the natural form of television, the equivalent of the nineteenth century episodic novel. If you can get an audience wanting to

share a particular milieu with the same characters week after week, then
you can explore a world and a set of ideas and individuals at length,
through time, which is a great opportunity.[12]

This Garnett did with *Between the Lines, Cardiac Arrest* (1995–6) and with one
of the cult programmes of the nineties, *This Life* (1996–7), which ran for
two series and was one of BBC2's big successes. Based around the personal
and professional lives of a group of young, middle-class characters, *This Life*
clearly struck a chord with its 1990s audience and there was great dis-
appointment when a third series was not commissioned, Garnett no doubt
being wary of the tendency for series drama to become 'repetitive and
formulaic'. Not only was *This Life* radical in showing the social and sexual
habits of its central characters in explicit detail, with accompanying 'realistic'
language, it also adopted a fresh visual style, with restless camerawork and
fast cutting complementing the frenetic life-styles of its characters.

After the success of *This Life* on BBC2, and the even bigger success of
World's popular BBC1 drama series *Ballykissangel* (1996–), Garnett could
really do no wrong as far as the BBC was concerned. In 1998 he offered
BBC2 an eight-part series called *The Cops*, another documentary-drama
portrayal of the police reminiscent of some of the more controversial police
dramas from the BBC's 'golden age' of radical drama, not least the early
Z Cars, in which Garnett had himself appeared as an actor.

With these and other programmes like the nine-part drama serial *Our
Friends in the North* (1996), the award-winning comedy *Absolutely Fabulous*
(1992–5) and the realist sitcom *The Royle Family* (1998), BBC2 emerged to
challenge Channel 4 as the natural home for radical, alternative, innovative
television in the 1990s. Although Channel 4 continued to produce some
controversial, cutting-edge programmes, such as Chris Morris's irreverent
current affairs spoof *Brass Eye* (1997), the channel was increasingly subject
to commercial pressures in the 1990s, following the stipulation in the 1990
Broadcasting Act that it should sell its own advertising, which came into
effect in 1993. With the threat of privatisation also hanging over Channel
4, especially while the Conservative government was in power, BBC2 was
able to regain some of the ground that it had conceded to Channel 4 in the
1980s. The increase in BBC2's ratings during the decade, and the acclaim
the channel received for dramas like *Our Friends in the North, This Life* and
The Cops, suggested that there was still a sizeable audience for BBC2's
stylish and adventurous brand of public service broadcasting.

In the fragmenting market place of British television in the 1990s the
traditional concept of public service broadcasting was gradually redefined.
No longer was television a medium where one or two broadcasters could
monopolise the airwaves with a mixed diet of education, information and
entertainment for a mass audience. Increasingly *niche* television was becoming

the name of the game, with a growing number of broadcasters targeting a select audience, with channels dedicated to sport, news, films, music, or re-runs of old TV programmes – such as UK Gold, a joint BBC and Thames Television enterprise dedicated to showing archive material from the libraries of the two companies.

In these changed circumstances the competition for audiences became much more intense as an ever-increasing number of channels competed for a diminishing share of the market, a situation exacerbated by the prospect of yet another mode of transmission, digital TV. One consequence of this was that the old notion of a widely shared viewing experience was becoming less common. While 15 million people or more might still tune in religiously to ITV or BBC1 for *Coronation Street* or *EastEnders* the days of such massive audiences for single programmes seem numbered as channels multiply and the audience fragments into dozens, perhaps hundreds, of smaller interest groups. The national television 'event', like the funeral of Princess Diana, which attracted an audience of nearly 20 million to BBC1 on 6 September 1997, despite also being covered by ITV, is now very rare. Yet in the 1960s and 1970s such audience figures were commonplace.

With television fragmenting, and the electronic media converging with the emergence of the Internet as a serious competitor for TV, British television, after barely more than fifty years, was in a state of flux as the century drew to a close. But with many quality programmes still being produced in the more straitened circumstances of the late 1990s, the scenario, feared by many people, of a completely 'dumbed-down' broad-casting system still seemed a long way off.

NOTES

1. Quoted in Asa Briggs, *The History of Broadcasting in the United Kingdom, Volume 1: The Birth of Broadcasting* (London, 1961), p. 238.
2. Jeremy Ridgman, 'Inside the Liberal Heartland: Television and the Popular Imagination in the 1960s' in Bart Moore-Gilbert and John Seed (eds), *Cultural Revolution? The Challenge of the Arts in the 1960s* (London, 1992), p. 139.
3. Quoted in John Tulloch and Manuel Alvarado, *Doctor Who: The Unfolding Text* (London, 1983), p. 39.
4. Extracts from this debate have been republished in an Open University reader edited by Tony Bennett, Susan Boyd-Bowman, Colin Mercer and Janet Woollacott, *Popular Television and Film* (London, 1981), Pt IV.
5. John Caughie, 'Progressive Television and Documentary Drama' in *Screen*, vol. 21, no. 3, 1980, reprinted in Bennett et al., ibid., p. 349.

6. Sylvia Harvey, 'Channel 4 Television: From Annan To Grade' in Stuart Hood (ed.), *Behind the Screens: The Structure of British Television in the Nineties* (London, 1994), p. 118.

7. John Caughie, op. cit., p. 350.

8. John Corner, Sylvia Harvey and Karen Lury, 'Culture, Quality and Choice: The Re-Regulation of TV 1989–91' in Stuart Hood, op. cit., p. 7.

9. Charlotte Brunsdon, 'Problems With Quality' in *Screen* 31:1, Spring 1990.

10. Anthony Smith, 'The Future of Public Service in Broadcasting' in Wilf Stevenson (ed.), *All Our Futures* (London, 1993), p. 9.

11. Robin Nelson, *TV Drama in Transition* (Basingstoke, 1997), p. 75.

12. Tony Garnett, quoted in Patricia Holland, *The Television Handbook* (London, 1997), p. 133.

CHAPTER EIGHT
British Art

David Masters

THE AVANT-GARDE MOVES HOME: PARIS TO NEW YORK

In 1948 the American art critic Clement Greenberg claimed that 'the main premises of Western art have at last migrated to the United States, along with the center of gravity of industrial production and political power.'[1] This voice spoke for a confident nation, one that had emerged from the Second World War powerful in every quarter: militarily, politically, economically and culturally. For many artists in Europe, Greenberg's words represented the unpalatable but not altogether surprising realisation that Paris was no longer the avant-garde centre of modern art. In Britain, from the 1950s onwards, young artists aspiring to be modern could no longer afford to ignore what the Americans were doing.

The British abstract artist Robyn Denny (b. 1930) was a student at the Royal College of Art in 1957 when he and some friends had a confrontation with their tutor John Minton. Denny had started to produce large boards on which paint and bitumen had been dropped, dribbled, smeared and finally set alight. When shown at the college's 'Sketch Club' Minton had satirised and ridiculed the work. To him it was meaningless and irrelevant: 'Why,' he said, 'you could call it anything.'[2] Denny and fellow student Dick Smith sent him an open letter:

> To your generation the thirties meant the Spanish Civil War; to us it means Astaire and Rogers. For you 'today' suggests angry young men, rebels without causes; we believe in the dynamism of the times, where painting being inseparable from the whole is an exciting problem linked now more than ever with the whole world problem of communication and makes its essential contribution to the total which is knowledge.[3]

This set the priorities. While young British artists were not in thrall to American culture they recognised its relevance to modern life and modern art practice. Minton, on the other hand, belonged to an older generation of English neo-Romantics that included Michael Ayrton and John Craxton. Reputations had been established during the war years when their work was seen to resonate with an English poetic sensibility, but Minton's suicide in 1957 symbolised the end of this era. The English art critic Lawrence Alloway, who throughout the 1950s and 1960s proved himself to be an astute observer and supporter of modern British art, commented several years later that artists such as Denny had 'escaped from Samuel Palmer on-the-rocks without becoming the 51st state'.[4]

'THE SITUATION IN LONDON NOW'

By the late 1950s and early 1960s London had become 'Swinging London', as shops took on a more lively appearance and sold a range of new products packaged by a new generation of artists and graphic designers. In 1959 Denny was commissioned to undertake a mural for the men's outfitters Austin Reed. He recalled that, 'They wanted a picture which would show a new London of fashionability.'[5] His painting consisted of words such as 'London', 'biggest', 'wide' and 'great' in a collage of typographical styles using primary colours. In 1963, the Beatles were photographed in front of it, in what now reads as a fitting emblem of a time when London was perceived as a vibrant cultural metropolis and source of innovation. It is not surprising that many young artists, designers, architects, photographers (and the writer Lawrence Alloway) took up residence in London, mostly around Ladbroke Grove and Holland Park.

This confidence and optimism found in the younger artists, as seen above in the 'Sketch Club' row, also found expression in the exhibition *Situation*. This was a show of abstract painting held in London in 1960 which, according to William Turnbull, who was a participating artist, got its name from the phrase 'the situation in London now'. Alloway was there once again championing the work of the eighteen artists who took part. These included Gillian Ayres (b. 1930), Bernard Cohen (b. 1933), Robyn Denny and John Hoyland (b. 1934). Throughout the show there was an emphasis on 'largeness', with all but one painting being over thirty square feet. The paintings were made to be imposing and aimed to dominate the viewer's vision. Yet there was little stylistic unity here. Works ranged from the gestural, more informal abstracts of Ayres to those by Cohen and Denny where the canvas was divided into just a few areas or fields and colour was frequently vibrant and hard-edged. These latter works tended to disturb the viewer's usual expectation of subject and background in a picture. Instead shapes and colours appeared unstable and unsettled. This interest in an 'op art' – one that created a sense of 'perceptual instability', as Coleman put it, had become the preoccupation of Bridget Riley (b. 1931). Her paintings are frequently composed of narrow bands or repetitive shapes, sometimes in monochrome, at other times using the dynamic effects of simultaneous contrast. This careful tuning of contrast, colour and shape produces works which aggressively attack and engage the viewer's vision.

Coleman, like Alloway, acknowledged the debt these artists owed to post-war American art:

> while some of the artists here are still in the process of assimilating what they have discovered through the Americans, the character of all the work is becoming recognisably individual. (Not recognisably 'British', however, the desire to be British by attempting to isolate British [sic] usually results, when it arises, in a full stop.)[6]

ABSTRACTION – A NEW REALISM?

Coleman's comment revealed, just as it did in Alloway's earlier quote, that these artists were anxious to produce innovative work that was marked out as both progressive and individual. It meant avoiding any slavish copying of American avant-garde practice on the one hand, and a resolute determination to escape the stifling constraints of much conservative British art on the other. Such tension often provided a stimulus for artists throughout the period covered in this essay. This was true for the abstract painter Patrick Heron (1920–99). He bought a house in St Ives in 1955 and his work shares with other artists based around this town a characteristic concern for the landscape. His paintings of the early 1950s often consisted of recognisable subject matter and these were greatly influenced by the linear quality of George Braque's work. Later in the decade, however, he started to produce 'stripe' paintings that were experiments in 'pure' shape and colour. *Horizontal Stripe Painting: November 1957–January 1958*, for example, consists of bands of soft-edged reds, with some in white, yellow and magenta. The saturated and sensuous use of colour testifies to his belief that its primary role was not to depict people, scenes, etc. but a formal one: 'to push or bring forward the required section of the design.'[7]

Heron's shifting artistic interests seemed to be rooted in his growing awareness that there were new issues for painting to address. In 1956 he had seen *Modern Art in the United States* at the Tate Gallery. His enthusiasm for the work of the American abstract painters Pollock, de Kooning, Rothko, Still and Kline was considerable. He wrote of America that 'your new school comes as the most vigorous movement we have had since the war. . . . We shall now watch New York as eagerly as Paris.'[8] What struck him was the 'size, energy, originality, economy and inventive daring' of the works. But Heron's enthusiasm was not unreserved. Their work may be ground-breaking in its exploration of art's formal elements, he thought, but where was it leading to? It lacked the 'worked-up paint quality such as one never misses in the French'.[9]

Heron's articles on art for the *New Statesman* in Britain and *Arts* in America during the 1950s reveal him to be a perceptive and articulate writer. He maintained a critical distance from the American artists by asserting what he felt to be the strengths of the European tradition, but he was also careful to distance himself from what he regarded as a strain of conservative modern art at home. To him this was epitomised by the social realism of the 'Kitchen Sink' artists such as John Bratby (1928–92), Jack Smith (b. 1928) and Edward Middleditch (1923–87). They were so called because their work was often of mundane domestic subjects or bleak industrial landscapes. Their champion was the Marxist writer and artist John Berger who was to become well known in the early 1970s for his influential and polemical Marxist critique of art and society called *Ways of Seeing*. For Berger such social realist work was political in the sense that it was a truthful representation of the detail, hardship and dignity of working-class life. Its familiar subject matter and apparent empathy with the minutiae of daily life was accessible to 'ordinary people'. It was not art for art's sake and 'elitist' like much modern art.

Heron took issue with this in an article written in 1955 called 'Art is Autonomous'. He wrote: 'John Berger's art criticism is always full of exhortations: the painter should do this and must do that in order "to communicate" (as he always put it) with the widest possible audience.'[10] Heron continued: 'This is the hierarchy: politics comes first, criticism second and art last. I put these in exactly the opposite order. . . . Art for me is not a servant but a master. . . . The work of art is in some profound sense an independent, live entity. It has its own life.'[11] Heron's argument here for the autonomy, or self-sufficiency, of art practice expresses succinctly the cleft that had opened up between the interests of Modernism on one hand and Realism on the other.

But Modernists such as Heron who were pursuing abstract painting never stopped arguing that their work was realist. Their practice, they asserted, was a process of discovery; of seeking and finding a new response to modern experience. Moreover, contrary to their critics, they maintained that there was also a moral aspect present in the work: the receptive and perceptive viewer could not fail to be moved and challenged by good abstract art.

. . . AND THE SITUATION IN ST IVES

Despite the social realist claims for modern art it seemed that the pulse of modern developments were felt more strongly from America than anywhere else during the 1950s and early 1960s. Those who were developing abstract painting with an interest in American practice were not only based in London. Cornwall, and St Ives in particular, still remained a focal point. The sculptor Barbara Hepworth (1903–75) and the painter Ben Nicholson (1894–1982) had been central figures in establishing this small coastal town as a flourishing avant-garde art community in the 1930s. Hepworth was to remain in St Ives for the rest of her life, while Nicholson left in 1958 and gave his studio to Patrick Heron. One of the legacies of this older generation of avant-gardists was a continuing interest shown by younger artists in the pursuit of an abstract art that never completely excluded associative references to the landscape. This can be seen in the work of Terry Frost (b. 1915) and Peter Lanyon (1918–64). Lanyon's paintings of the early 1950s, such as *St Just*, 1953, show clear topographic references to the location despite a loose and expressive handling of paint. His later work, however, provides more of a sense of moving through and experiencing the landscape rather than any recognisable depiction of it. He had made his mark by staging a one-man show in New York in 1957 and had got to know the Americans Gottlieb, Kline, Motherwell and Rothko. Unfortunately his enthusiasm to know the landscape better led to his early death from a gliding accident.

Two other artists associated with St Ives might be singled out for their particular contributions to the development of abstract art. Roger Hilton (1911–75) settled in the town in 1965. His paintings from the mid-1950s onwards often consist of a sensuous use of line and colour and frequently maintain a figurative element that evokes both the female nude and the landscape or, at times, a combination of both. Alan Davie (b. 1920) was a regular visitor to St Ives. More than Hilton, though, he had been greatly influenced by American art, particularly by the work of Jackson Pollock. He held his first show in New York in 1956 and met Pollock in 1957.

Davie's paintings seem to suggest, as did many of Pollock's earlier works, a subterranean world of myths and folklore. Both artists painted in a richly textured way and often made use of drips and smears. What became more uniquely Davie's own, though, was his continual pursuit of decorative images, often inspired by other cultures, which were for him an expression of what was both primordial and mystical. Hepworth had often made reference in her sculptures to the mystery of the landscape around her and to ancient menhirs. It might be suggested that Davie too found a similar source of inspiration in St Ives and in the Celtic legends associated with Cornwall.

The above discussion suggests that during the 1950s and 1960s there was a rich vein of abstract art developing in Britain, though not all of it was clearly related to the work of the American painters. Those artists known as the constructivists included Anthony Hill (b. 1930), Kenneth Martin (1905–84), Mary Martin (1907–69) and Victor Pasmore (b. 1908). Their work generally consisted of shallow, geometric reliefs which, unlike the expressionism of much of the abstract painting, was often cool and understated. Pasmore had made the first reliefs in 1951 based on theories and ideas which pursued the idea of 'essential' structures unrelated to the appearance of the external world. There was also a belief that such work, in relation to architecture had the ability to change and transform social life. In this sense they also owe something to the legacy of *Circle* in the 1930s whose idealism had united artists such as Ben Nicholson, Barbara Hepworth and Naum Gabo.

IG, TIT AND POP

The constructivists were shown in an exhibition called *This is Tomorrow* (TIT) which opened at the Whitechapel Gallery, London on 9 August 1956. The show was divided into twelve groups and featured, among other things, construction and sculpture based on both architectural concerns and microscopic investigations. It also contained a varied response to the images generated by popular culture. The common theme in all of this was the ambition to show the collaborative efforts of art and architecture, and to demonstrate how the modern artist needed to engage with the products of mass communication. In the words of Richard Hamilton (b. 1922), a member of the organising 'Independent Group' (IG) it was about 'the development of our perceptive potentialities to accept and utilise the continual enrichment of visual material'.[12] One of Hamilton's contributions to 'Group two' of the TIT show, which was also used as a poster, was his now iconic montage of magazine imagery: *Just what is it that makes today's homes so different, so appealing?*, 1956. In this work cut-outs of a muscle man and a nude girl occupy a modern-equipped interior with a glimpse of an advertisement for an Al Jolson movie through a window. Hamilton's use of images that were 'transient, expendable, inexpensive, mass produced, youth-oriented, witty, sexy, gimmicky, glamorous and "big business"' featured in his work.[13] Yet, as with other works such as the painting *Hommage à Chrysler Corps*, 1957 where there is pictorial ambiguity between a Chrysler car and a voluptuous woman wearing an 'Exquisite form bra', they remained satirical, often drawing attention to the way that mass advertising represented gender types.

One of Hamilton's colleagues in IG, and also contributing to TIT, was Eduardo Paolozzi (b. 1924). He too explored the wealth of popular images through montages and this preoccupation conditioned the sculpture for which he is probably better known. In his view: 'All human experience is really just one big collage.'[14] *Head*, 1957 is a bronze cast with fragments of nails, bolts, wood and found objects to provide the 'collage' appearance present in much of Paolozzi's work. His mural which currently decorates Tottenham Court Road tube station also has this collage-like effect.

Hamilton and Paolozzi are representative of the earlier 'pop' artists in this country. Their interest in American culture lay in mining a rich source of mass imagery: the products of a 'culture of plenty' which was also rapidly developing in this country. All of this was clearly at odds with the 'high culture' of much abstract art previously discussed. Indeed, Alloway had challenged Greenberg's dismissal of mass culture as mere 'Kitsch' by suggesting that 'pop' art might be seen as a new realism in the form of a genuine engagement with modern experience:

> Sensitiveness to the variables of our life and economy enable the mass arts to accompany the changes in our life far more closely than the fine arts. . . . Therefore it is no longer sufficient to define culture solely as something that a minority guards for the few and the future (though such art is uniquely valuable and as precious as ever).[15]

LATER POP

Other artists associated with 'pop art' emerged in Britain during the 1960s. Many of them were students at the Royal College of Art in the late 1950s and early 1960s and all of them showed an interest in figurative art, in contrast to the abstract artists already discussed. Although, like the IG, many of these artists looked to America as a rich resource of popular imagery, their art practice was distinct from American pop artists such as Andy Warhol, Jasper Johns and Robert Rauschenberg. Peter Blake (b. 1932) received a first-class diploma from the Royal College in 1956. His work of the 1960s evoked a nostalgia for childhood memories and favourite television and film stars including wrestlers, film stars and rock and roll musicians. The painting *Self Portrait*, 1961, is typical in several respects. He stands dressed in denim jacket, jeans and baseball boots which for the time were ahead of the fashion. His lapels and jacket are covered in badges of rock and roll stars and other memorabilia. In his hand he holds an Elvis magazine. Blake renders his figure and background with the 'flatness' associated with flashlight photography. His *Toy Shop*, 1962, reflects the same interest in childhood memories but breaks away from painting. It is a wall-mounted relief which reconstructs the front of a small village shop, including a real door and window. The window is stuffed with the small and cheap toys that children would have bought in the 1950s. Blake will probably remain in the minds of those who were teenagers in the 1960s for his album cover design for the Beatles' *Sergeant Pepper's Lonely Hearts Club Band* in 1967.

The 'Young Contemporaries' exhibition of 1961 included the work of four artists who were at the Royal College together: R.B. Kitaj (b. 1932), Patrick Caulfield (b. 1936), Allen Jones (b. 1937) and David Hockney (b. 1937). In their different ways they contributed to the variety of pop art practice in this country. Kitaj's paintings seem to hit a more intense and subdued note than the others. His *An Early Europe*, 1964, shares with his contemporaries the use of flat, bright colours and a montage-like effect of images, but he also explores an interest in left-wing politics and his understanding of national identities. Jones's *Bus 11*, 1962, uses many of the same colours as Kitaj but they are employed in a more affirmative, celebratory way. The painting is an irregular shape and represents the movement of a bus where the viewer catches glimpses of the passengers who are wearing bright 1960s clothes. Caulfield again uses flat, bright colours but his subjects, often of everyday modern interiors and still lifes, are often reduced to just a few coloured areas outlined in black. *After Lunch*, 1975, is of a man in a room painted in shades of blue apart from a fish tank on a table and a view of a castle, lake and mountains behind it. These are rendered with a great attention to realistic detail and contrast ironically and playfully with those other parts of the work painted in a bland, textureless way.

David Hockney is the artist from this quartet who has probably maintained the highest public profile since the 1960s. His work has passed through many stages and changes in style and he has involved himself in a range of practices apart from painting including book illustration, set design, photography, poster design and etching. His early work from Royal College days, *We Two Boys Together Clinging*, 1961, which alludes to his 'coming out' as a homosexual, employs a rough, graffiti-like approach which is still indebted to European exemplars such as the French painter Jean Dubuffet. In the 1960s he travelled to America and painted his 'swimming pool' series where he openly celebrated the male nude. These works are developed from his own photographs, often Polaroids, and they are usually composed of just a few, elegantly placed elements painted in bright colours. The painting technique itself is not expressive but maintains the cool detachment of a photograph. In the late 1960s and 1970s he used the same approach for a series of double portraits, for example, *Mr and Mrs Clark and Percy*, 1970–1, ('Mr Clark' is the fashion designer Ossie Clark and 'Percy' is the cat). These portraits – another was of his parents – have an uneasy quality about them. Although of two people there seems to be no implied relation-ship between these couples: they seem isolated, alone, uncommunicative.

Hockney's painting and drawing throughout his career have demonstrated an admiration for Picasso's protean creativity and for the highly tuned sensitivity that Matisse showed towards colour and the decorative qualities of painting. Hockney's popularity as an artist seems to be, in some part, because of his ability to produce work that has instant appeal. This echoes Matisse's famous aphorism that painting should appeal to the weary viewer in the same way that a comfortable armchair does.

CHALLENGING MODERNISM: ARTISTS WITH ATTITUDE

The development of pop art during the late 1950s and 1960s seemed to endorse Alloway's assertion that it represented a new form of realism. Other work emerging at that time contributed to a growing sense that Modernism as a critical paradigm for understanding modern art had reached something of a crisis. For some, including Heron, the arrogance of American critics such as Greenberg had led to a kind of 'Cultural Imperialism'.[16] The influential criticism of Greenberg and the younger American Michael Fried (b. 1939) insisted on art's autonomy. The primary concerns of art, accord-ing to these men, were artistic ones. In Greenberg's view the artist was involved in a rigorous self-examination of art's formal elements (e.g., shape, colour, texture, form) thus using 'the characteristic methods of a discipline to criticise the discipline itself'.[17] What made a work of art good was, to use Clive Bell's term, the artist's ability to create 'significant form'. For Greenberg and Fried in the 1960s this imperative for formal innovation seemed to lead inexorably to abstract art. Any explicit concern by the artist for 'subject matter' or political commitment was seen at best as irrelevant and at worst deleterious to a work's 'quality'. Such 'quality' resided in a work that stirred our 'aesthetic emotions'. Or, as Roger Fry put it at the start of the century, it produces 'an existence more real and more important than any that we know of in mortal life'.[18] Greenberg said that he knew when he was in the presence of great art because: 'It makes me feel like I'm dancing six feet off the ground.'[19]

These were large claims indeed, yet such 'quality' was considered by both Greenberg and Fried to reside in the work of two sculptors during the mid-1960s. The first was the American David Smith (1906–65) and the other was the English sculptor Anthony Caro (b. 1924). Caro had been Henry Moore's assistant in the early 1950s and his work at this stage was figurative, often depicting the female nude. Unlike Moore's approach to sculpture based on carving, however Caro developed an interest in con-struction. By the mid-1960s he was producing abstract sculptures made from steel elements, not unlike a three-dimensional cubist collage. Once constructed they were often painted in a single colour to unify the separate elements. Fried described the artist's practice like this:

> A characteristic sculpture by Caro consists . . . in the mutual and naked
> juxtaposition of the I-beams, girders, cylinders, lengths of piping, sheet
> metal, and grill that it comprises rather than in the compound object that
> they compose.[20]

Fried believed that Caro's sculpture had 'presentness', a concept not unlike Clive Bell's 'significant form'. For him this was achieved through the artist's ordering and balancing of the internal relationships of the sculpture. Furthermore, as Fried had put it, 'presentness is grace'. In other words the viewer would be rewarded with an aesthetic experience (similar to the one described by Fry above) which would lift him or her out of the humdrum experiences of everyday life, 'grace' literally being 'time off' from such mundane and superficial concerns.

The essay by Fried from which the above quotation is taken was a strategic one. On the one hand it represented a succinct statement of the Modernist position regarding the 'quality' of good art, but it was also an attack aimed at a group of young American artists often referred to as Minimalists, or by Fried as Literalists, who were emerging at that time and challenging the tenets of Modernism. Although, as we have seen above, there were artists and critics in Europe who were clearly feeling marginalised by the Modernist art being promoted by critics such as Greenberg and Fried, the clearest signs of some growing opposition were beginning to take root in America itself. A characteristic work by the American 'Minimalists' Carl Andre (b. 1935), Robert Morris (b. 1931) or Donald Judd (1928–94) would often consist of the repetition of simple units. Andre's *Equivalent VIII*, 1966, or 'the bricks' as it is usually referred to, is often only remembered for the occasion when an enraged visitor threw paint over it at the Tate Gallery, London. For Modernists such as Greenberg and Fried, in stark contrast to a Smith or a Caro, such work failed because it had no formal interest whatsoever. For Andre this was just the point: 'I don't want the detail of a structure to be interesting, you know, beautiful effects and so forth. This doesn't interest me at all. I want the material in its clearest form.'[21]

Andre's reaction against the 'art object' was symptomatic of a broader disillusionment that was setting in amongst younger artists both in America and Europe. Modernism as a critical paradigm was perceived by them as having become institutionalised and moribund. The British artist Victor Burgin (b. 1941) assessed the situation: 'Late Modernism stood for *order* . . . everything in its proper place, doing its duty fulfilling its preordained role in patriarchal culture.'[22] The London-based Pakistani artist Rasheed Araeen (b. 1935) has added a distinctive contribution to the debate about Modernism since he moved here in 1964. His practice as an artist, writer, activist and curator has concentrated on disturbing and unsettling the institutionalised claims on modernism and the marginalisation of Afro-Caribbean and Asian artists. In 1989 he curated an exhibition at the Hayward Gallery, London, called *The Other Story* which featured over 200 works from 24 modern artists who were Afro-Caribbean or Asian. He saw this exhibition as a necessary polemic which challenged the modernist paradigm of the artist as 'white, male, individual [and] heroic'. He felt that there was a need to 'interrogate the nature of its narrative; to reveal the underlying myth which disguises those contradictions inherent in its claim of objective superiority, both historical and epistemological.'[23]

During the 1960s there was growing evidence that some of the younger generation were being spurred on by their newly developed confidence. Rather than slipping into despair and passivity over social and political issues such as the Cold War or the Vietnam War, they challenged what they perceived to be the cant of established cultural and political practices and institutions. Much of the oppositional character of the 1960s and 1970s in Britain owed a lot to the critical work started by intellectuals on the left, such as Stuart Hall, E.P. Thompson and Raymond Williams, in the late 1950s. As Thompson has observed, the founding of the New Left in Britain was part of an international movement, with similar critical positions being taken up in America and other European countries. This movement had no real basis for cohesive political action, and indeed by the late

1970s had fragmented considerably. Yet one of its principal unifying characteristics was a re-examination of, and challenge to orthodox power structures in politics and culture. The civil rights movement and radical feminism were just two of its products. For many, the student rebellions of the late 1960s – in Europe and America – were something of a watershed.

But if the 'art object' epitomised those aesthetic values which were being challenged by the younger artists, what was to replace it? The response to this was a diversity of practices which tend to fall under the umbrella of 'Conceptual Art'. It had become clear that although post-war British artists had drawn considerable strength from the example of transatlantic Modernism during the 1960s some of the avant-garde initiative was clearly returning to Europe. The British-based, American artist associated with conceptualism at the time was Michael Craig-Martin (b. 1941). He commented in retrospect that, 'Whereas I think of Minimalism as essentially a New York art, Conceptualism from the very beginning seemed international.'[24] A focus for the international development of Conceptual art was the exhibition *When Attitudes Become Form* held in 1969, firstly in Berne, Switzerland, then at the ICA, London, and subsequently at Krefeld, Germany. This included the British artists Barry Flanagan (b. 1941), Bruce McLean (b. 1944), Richard Long (b. 1945) and Victor Burgin (b. 1941).

WHEN CONCEPT REPLACED THE UNIQUE ART OBJECT

Barry Flanagan's earlier work of the 1960s examined the premises of conventional sculpture. *Pdreeoo*, 1965, for example used plaster inside a retaining skin which, as it dried, found its own shape. In this way the nature of the medium itself, rather than the traditional skills of a sculptor, became the determining factor in the creation of this work. Richard Long was another artist interested in exploring the idea of sculpture which was not dependent on a conventional notion of artistic skill. His art works were often ephemeral and open to the vagaries of time where the weather or another person might change what he had created. His *A Line in Ireland*, 1974, is just that. It consists of a low-lying row of rocks pulled together from the bleak and craggy surroundings to form a line. The landscape asserts its own sense of order into which Long has subtly intervened.

One of the responses by artists to the problem of the 'unique art object' was to contemplate disposing of it altogether. In some cases it was replaced with a written record, sometimes taking the form of a description or instructions which would enable viewers to imaginatively re-create the work for themselves. This might be considered a democratic gesture where the work of art, instead of being possessed by a wealthy purchaser, could be 'owned' by anyone prepared to engage with it. Long's *A Hundred Mile Walk*, 1971–2, consists of a map of Dartmoor with a circle circumscribing the terrain covered. Alongside this is a photograph of the area and a terse phrase to evoke each day spent walking: '*Day 1 Winter skyline, a north wind . . . Day 3 Suck icicles from the grass stems . . . Day 7 Flop down on my back with tiredness. Stare up at the sky and watch it recede.*' It was as though the 'art work' in this case was the accumulated sensory experiences of the seven days. To become imaginatively involved the active viewer could pursue the visual and written clues and consider the relationship between real experiences and representations of them.

Similar concerns seemed to underlie the practice of artists working in a variety of other media all of which challenged the traditional hierarchy where painting and sculpture were dominant Keith Arnatt (b. 1930), John Hilliard (b. 1945) and Victor Burgin all worked with photographs. Arnatt's *Invisible hole revealed by the shadow of the artist*, 1969, and Hilliard's, *Camera recording its own condition*, 1971, explored the way that the medium conceals or distorts reality. Burgin created *Photopath* in 1968/9 which is a long photograph rolled out in a strip across the gallery floor. The photograph is of the area of floor it is covering. This seems to invoke layers of response in the viewer. Firstly, despite its 'flatness' it still commands space (as Andre's low horizontal sculptures do). It also invites the viewer to enquire into the nature of artifice and reality.

This philosophical questioning of the premises of art and constructions of reality were at the basis of much Conceptual art practice. It was important to Art and Language, a group of artists and art historians formed in England in 1968. They were unusual in that their art was a collective process, made after a series of conversations between the members. *Index 01*, 1972, consisted of eight filing cabinets containing texts from their journal *Art-Language* and other writings by members of the group. In this piece the viewer was invited to become a critical participant, reading the texts and cross-referencing them with each other.

Perhaps the most notorious of these early Conceptual artists were Gilbert and George (b. 1943 and 1942). Ambiguity, paradox and satire seem to be common elements in their work. Dressed in the suits and ties that have become their hallmark they performed as 'living sculptures'. In *Singing Sculpture*, for example, they appeared in the gallery repeatedly singing snatches of Flanagan and Allen's *Underneath the Arches*. In these early pieces, along with other works which documented their ordinary, mundane lives they seemed to raise issues about the boundaries between life and art.

The above examples of British Conceptual art are far from comprehensive but they do provide a flavour of the varied opposition to 'the establishment' mounted by younger artists in the 1960s and 1970s. It is also important to remember that their work represented a strategic intervention in the discourses of art criticism and practice. Such an intervention could not be maintained by repeating the same strategies. Many of the artists discussed above have gone on to respond to fresh demands. Art and Language, for example, have returned to painting, Flanagan started to carve in stone again in the early 1970s, Burgin developed work which combined a use of text and photographs, and Gilbert and George have produced many large photographic works using a grid format, although still using themselves as the subject.

A CRISIS OF MODERNITY? THE EMERGENCE OF POSTMODERNISM AND ANTI-MODERNISM

The connection between developments in art and those that take place in the wider context of society are complex. We have seen how during the 1960s in particular there was a challenge from younger artists towards institutions in the cultural and political spheres. It is now generally conceded, though, that Western societies underwent some epochal shifts during the 1970s and 1980s which challenged fundamental ideas about culture and society. The British historian Eric Hobsbawm has assessed the period:

> The history of the twenty years after 1973 is that of a world which lost its bearings and slid into instability and crisis. And yet, until the 1980s it was not clear how irretrievably the foundations of the Golden Age had crumbled.[25]

1973 was the year of the OPEC crisis and the quadrupling of oil prices. But this was a symptom rather than a cause of some significant changes that many believed were taking place. In short this was seen as an indication that the West was slipping into economic stagnation, if not decline and that 'progress' remained elusive.

The French philosopher Jean-François Lyotard was one of the key theorists of postmodernism. He wrote:

> Simplifying to the extreme, I define postmodern as incredulity toward metanarratives. This incredulity is undoubtedly a product of progress in the sciences.[26]

217

For Lyotard the 'Golden Age' was indeed past. The 'metanarratives' he speaks of were the 'grand themes' of the Enlightenment, such as freedom, justice, truth, beauty, and the idea of the artist as prophet and seer. The postmodern, he asserted, was to be characterised by pluralism, fragmentation and a suspicion of ultimate 'truth'. Art, if it was to be any good, would have to demonstrate 'incredulity', giving no certain answers and little comfort.

One further theoretical twist to the idea of the postmodern might help to illuminate the developing situation in British art and society. If what Lyotard is describing is the function of vanguard art in a postmodern period, other theorists and critics have described another form of postmodernism or, more accurately, an *anti*-modernism. For the art critic Hal Foster it is a 'postmodernism of reaction' or a repudiation of modernism.[27] This was a principal feature of neo-conservatism during the 1980s and of the Thatcher government here in Britain. It was articulated by the Conservative MP David Willetts, who during the 1980s was a member of the Prime Minister's Downing Street Policy Unit. For him the decline of modern British society started with the intellectual and cultural milieu of Bloomsbury and Fabianism which encouraged an attitude of irresponsible defiance towards social mores and a lack of respect for authority.[28] The implication here is that the development of cultural modernism had seriously undermined the stable structures of society through an overemphasis on change, individuality and freedom. Unlike Lyotard, who encouraged artists to 'wage a war on totality', neo-conservatives looked for ideologies which would once again galvanise and unify society. In Britain, as elsewhere, such anti-modernism manifested itself in a reactionary articulation of 'national identity'.

'NOSTALGIA FOR THE UNATTAINABLE'

So what did conservative art in Britain look like in this postmodern period? A response to this seems inevitably to involve a paradox of some kind because one of the main advocates of such art was the ostensibly 'left wing' critic Peter Fuller. His main mouthpiece was the journal *Modern Painters*, first published in Spring 1988, named after John Ruskin's nineteenth-century publication. Fuller took on a rival glossy art publication, *Artscribe*, edited at the time by Matthew Collings. In Fuller's first issue he staked out his ground:

> As an editor, Collings proved himself devoted to the pursuit of those things
> – represented by the Turner Prize, the Saatchi Collection, and Art and
> Language – which *Modern Painters* would like to see transformed or eradicated.

Fuller felt that the historical moment was ripe for those in authority to lead others out of the chaos generated by modernism. The art that was needed, claimed Fuller in his first editorial, was that which could 'minister to the human spirit even in these troubled times'. The first issue of *Modern Painters* had features about artists of an older generation such as Lucian Freud, David Bomberg, Graham Sutherland and Francis Bacon, but also included an article about the younger painter Therese Oulton (b. 1953). Fuller's preferences were not merely idiosyncratic but seemed to gain approval from a broad constituency. The common feature uniting these different artists was that, for him, their work engaged with the nature of the 'human condition' and offered the possibility of redemption from the turmoil and rootlessness of modern life (except, as Fuller noted, in the case of Bacon, whose work ultimately dealt with 'meaningless despair'). Fuller aimed to restore a canon of great British art largely by identifying those artists who he believed had maintained or returned to the national tradition of figurative and landscape painting. Above all it was the 'British' attributes of individualism, eccentricity and dilettantism which enabled these artists to resist the destructive effects of modernism and internationalism. The contributors to *Modern Painters* and the range of artists critically accepted by the journal seem too disparate to establish any common ground and politically they cover the entire spectrum. One possible common denominator is that those supporters of Fuller's position seemed to be galvanised by a form of *cultural* as opposed to political conservatism evident through a persistent pessimism about modernism's achievements.

SOME WENT MAD . . . SOME RAN AWAY

The aspirations and anxieties of Fuller and his constituency might be seen in Lyotard's terms as symptomatic of those who search for images of consolation, 'wholeness' and a 'nostalgia for the unattainable' in a postmodern age that in reality only seems to offer fragmentation, consumerism and superficiality.[29] So what other art emerged from the 1980s and 1990s? The Royal Academy of Arts in London held an exhibition in 1987 called *British Art in the Twentieth Century – The Modern Movement*. This retrospective of a century of British art showing the work of seventy artists was inevitably selective and consequently much criticised. Although abstract art was celebrated, with Howard Hodgkin chosen as one of the artists for the gallery 'Three Painters of This Time', the dominant theme was of a national tradition 'naturally' inclined towards the figurative and concerned with an exploration of the 'human condition'. The show confirmed the reputations of 'giants' such as the sculptor Henry Moore, who had a room to himself, and the painters Francis Bacon (1909–92) and Lucian Freud (b. 1922). Bacon's reputation had been built on paintings that were seen by many as penetrating studies of the anguish and tragedy of modern life. In 1988 he achieved a further accolade by being chosen as the first British painter to be exhibited in Russia during the period of *Glasnost*.

The Royal Academy exhibition and *A Paradise Lost*, another show of 1987 held at the Barbican Art Gallery, London, which re-appraised British neo-Romantic art between 1935 and 1955, both took a backward look at the century and retrospectively asserted a canon of 'great modern British art'. If these two shows represented a trend during the 1980s which tended to slip into nostalgic reverie of a 'golden age' there were other, younger artists who set their sights on addressing the present and what it was like to respond to the demands of a changing and uncertain modern world. Their practices might fit Hal Foster's definition of a 'postmodernism of resistance': 'a counter-practice not only to the official culture of modernism but also to the "false normativity" of a reactionary modernism.'[30]

A group of sculptors emerged in the 1980s that included Tony Cragg (b. 1948), Richard Deacon (b. 1949), Anish Kapoor (b. 1954), Julian Opie (b. 1958), and Bill Woodrow (b. 1948). Although their artistic interests and practices were diverse they were all shown at the Lisson Gallery, London. The first three have also won the Tate Gallery's Turner Prize for innovative modern art. Cragg's work often invites us to think afresh about materials we take for granted. In *Untitled*, 1993, for example, there are items of furniture arranged together which are transformed and given a textural unity by having hundreds of hooks screwed into them. Kapoor's work is more meditative and often plays with ideas of illusion and reality, drawing from his preoccupation with Asian culture. *Mother as a Void*, 1988, is a large half-egg shape made from fibreglass, coated in a matt blue pigment, as many of his sculptures are. This pigment has a depthlessness about it which draws the viewer in to investigate the sometimes elusive placement of solid planes and surfaces. Woodrow's sculptures show humorously and explicitly how materials can be transformed. In *Twin-tub with a Guitar*, 1981, he has cut out the panels from a washing machine and folded the metal into the shape of an electric guitar, thus transforming the obsolete washing machine into the raw material for something new. Both are still joined together with the cut-outs in the washing machine matching exactly the material used for the guitar.

Some of those younger artists who have made the greatest impact over the last decade were born in the 1960s, attended Goldsmiths' Art College, London, and were tutored by Michael Craig-Martin. *Freeze* was an exhibition held in London in 1988 and curated by the 23-year-old Damien Hirst. This show is often seen as an early indication that there was a new optimism, energy and fashionablity about young British artists which had not been in evidence since the 1960s. In 1994 Hirst curated another show, *Some Went Mad . . . Some Ran Away*, at the Serpentine Gallery, London, where he ambitiously brought together fifteen artists from Britain, Europe, Japan and the United States. It was here that his lamb preserved in a glass case of formaldehyde called *Away from the Flock*, 1994, was vandalised. Such was the passion that some of this work provoked.

Many of the British artists introduced through these exhibitions became more publicly known through the controversial Royal Academy show *Sensation* in 1997 featuring work from the Saatchi collection. There was no stylistic unity here and the range of media is equally diverse and varied. Hirst was represented by eight works which together seemed to explore a range of conflicting themes including death, horror, order and beauty. There was also sculpture from Rachel Whiteread (b. 1963), Sarah Lucas (b. 1962) and Mona Hartoum (b. 1952). Whiteread takes casts in plaster of the inside of objects which have varied in scale from a complete house to a bathroom sink. She says: 'I am making objects that are . . . very much like tombs . . . how you know there is something inside but you never actually see what it is.'[31] Lucas, reworking the Surrealist technique of the 'found object', addresses questions of sexuality. Hartoum works with video, often showing the inside of the body, and Gillian Wearing (b. 1963), the Turner Prize winner of 1997, again uses video to explore the often disturbing, sometimes humorous aspects of human behaviour.

Painting also remained in evidence at this show. Fiona Rae's abstracts self-consciously reject the idea of producing a 'pure' or 'universal' art but search instead for an 'ambiguous standpoint' in paintings that 'have that unsettling quality of something about to fall apart'.[32] Gary Hume, another Turner Prize winner (in 1996), uses gloss paint to produce paintings which he describes as 'beautiful but blunt',[33] while Chris Ofili (b. 1968) combines a return to 1960s psychedelia with ironic social comment. Marcus Harvey (b. 1963) joined the ranks of the infamous when his portrait painting of Myra Hindley met a hostile reception. It was based on the familiar media image of Hindley but the face, instead of being constructed from the usual half-tone dots found in newspapers, was made from children's hand-prints. Many saw Harvey's reworking of this image as a grotesque celebration of a woman convicted of child murder, although it might also be argued that the work was effective in questioning the way this iconic image of Hindley has become the personification of everything evil in our society. Like the Andre and Hirst works on other separate occasions, this painting too was finally vandalised during the exhibition.

The French theorist Jean Baudrillard has suggested that there is no longer any simple 'reality' to experience in modern life but only a 'hyperreality' constituted from a world of shifting representations, codes, styles and signs which pervade our lives. If this is so it might be said that some of the recent work we have just considered by younger artists engages with such experience by frequently employing irony, pastiche and parody in their art. Although these devices have always been employed by avant-garde artists in the past, it would seem that in postmodern art these are often used more extensively and self-consciously.

If we survey the British art that is covered in this essay it would seem that although good art will never be measured merely by its ability to shock, 'modern' rather than simply 'contemporary' art must always provoke and disturb our conventional way of experiencing and understanding the world. At the end of the twentieth century there are signs of both continuity and change in the work of younger British artists. Some, such as Damien Hirst and Julian Opie, find that the conceptual art of the 1960s and 1970s still provides fertile ground to plough and, despite the expanding range of media available to use and incorporate into art work, it is also apparent that the 'traditional' media of painting and sculpture still offer a productive way forward for some artists. Although Clement Greenberg's critical perspective on modern art is now generally regarded as anachronistic, his maxim that good art should 'keep culture moving' still holds true. The best British art of the period has done just that and has earned itself an international reputation.

NOTES

1. C. Harrison and P. Wood (eds) *Art in Theory, 1900–1990* (London, 1992), p. 572.
2. Quoted in the exhibition catalogue, *The Sixties Art Scene in London*, Barbican Centre, London, March–June, 1993, pp. 87–8.
3. Ibid., p. 28.
4. Ibid., p. 91.
5. Ibid., p. 47.
6. Ibid., p. 90.
7. From the essay by Heron, 'Space in Colour', 1953, from *Painter as Critic, Patrick Heron: Selected Writings*, Mel Gooding (ed.) (London, 1998).
8. 'The Americans at the Tate Gallery', March 1956, ibid., p. 104.
9. Ibid., p. 102.
10. 'Art is Autonomous', September 1955, ibid., p. 93.

11. Ibid., p. 94.
12. From Hamilton's statement for 'Group two' in the catalogue of TIT.
13. Letter to Peter and Alison Smithson, 16 January 1957, In *Collected Works, 1953–1982* (London, 1982), p. 28.
14. Quoted in 'Paolozzi: Barbarian and Mandarin', Timothy Hyman, *Artscribe*, 8, September 1977, p. 34.
15. Lawrence Alloway, 'The Arts and the Mass Media', 1958, reprinted in *Art in Theory*, op. cit., p. 701.
16. Patrick Heron, 'A Kind of Cultural Imperialism?', *Studio International*, February 1968, reprinted in *Painter as Critic*, op. cit., pp. 162–9.
17. Clement Greenberg, 'Modernist Painting', 1965, from an edited version in *Art in Theory*, op. cit., p. 755.
18. From Fry's 'An Essay in Aesthetics', 1901, reproduced in *Art in Theory*, op. cit., pp. 78–86.
19. Quoted in Florence Rubenfeld, *Clement Greenberg – A Life*, (New York, 1997), p. 258.
20. Michael Fried, 'Art and Objecthood', 1967, from an edited version in *Art in Theory*, op. cit., p. 829.
21. Carl Andre quoted in the catalogue for his exhibition of sculpture at the Whitechapel Art Gallery, London, 1978.
22. Victor Burgin, 'The Absence of Presence', written in 1984 and reprinted in his book, *The End of Art Theory – Criticism and Postmodernity* (London, 1986), p. 47.
23. Rasheed Araeen 'Introduction: when chickens come home to roost', from the exhibition catalogue, *The Other Story*, Hayward Gallery, 1989, p. 9.
24. Michael Craig-Martin, 'Reflections on the 1960s and early "70s"', *Art Monthly*, no. 114, March 1988, pp. 3–5, p. 4.
25. Eric Hobsbawm, *Age of Extremes – The Short History of the Twentieth Century, 1914–1991* (London, 1994).
26. Jean-François Lyotard, 'The Postmodern Condition', 1979. An edited version of this appears in *Art in Theory*, op. cit., pp. 998–1000.
27. For a discussion of this see Hal Foster, *Postmodern Culture* (London, 1985).
28. See David Willetts, *Modern Conservatism* (London, 1992); see chapter 2, 'The Advance of Socialism: 1900–1950', pp. 18–31.
29. A phrase used by Lyotard in 'What is Postmodernism?', from an edited version in *Art in Theory*, op. cit., p. 1015.
30. *Postmodern Culture*, op. cit., p. xii.
31. The artist, from the exhibition catalogue *The British Art Show 1990*, Hayward Gallery, London.
32. The artist, ibid., p. 92.
33. The artist, ibid., p. 66.

CHAPTER NINE

Popular Music since the 1950s

Andrew Blake

The story of British pop is too well known. There is a clear linear narrative of successive youth musics and styles – a story this chapter will retell. However, much is lost if we assume simply that popular music since the 1950s is an Anglo-American product for and by young people. 'I have not . . . mentioned the quite remarkable popularity of Billy Cotton, whose music . . . was the very antithesis of that of Frankie Lane or Elvis Presley . . . the manifestation of the interests of an older generation,' announced Edward Lee, writing just after Cotton's death.[1] Danceband leader Cotton had a forty-year career on radio and television which ended only with his death in 1969; his shows were typical of British popular music outside pop, mixing dance music with the humour of the music-hall tradition. To keep in mind some of the music which is hidden by pop's assumptions, I will trace several different traditions, making connections across time and space. Emerging alongside the usual story of pop will be a richer and more complex history of popular music since the war.[2]

POPULAR MUSIC BEFORE POP

British popular music from the nineteenth century onwards operated within a wide repertoire, including religious and classical music, operetta, and song and dance musics from both folk and urban traditions. Amateur and semi-professional musicians played and sang in brass bands, orchestras and choirs. Despite the development of recording and broadcasting, and the subsequent triumph of machine-made, disembodied sound, local participatory music-making remains widespread. Amateur performances of Handel's *Messiah*, or the Gilbert and Sullivan operettas are still routine occurrences, as are semi-professional folk and rock gigs.[3] There has always been a great deal of popular music outside mainstream recording and broadcasting, including many of pop's innovative moments – such as the home-made instruments of 'skiffle' groups in the 1950s, punk in the 1970s, and small-label dance music in the 1990s.

Seeing British popular music as an adjunct of American music necessarily sweeps much of this mixed repertoire, and the scale of democratic participation in performance and composition, under the table. But there are also neglected forms of professional music-making which are important to our story. Music Hall's tradition of songwriting and performing, for instance, can be traced through bands like the Beatles, the Small Faces and the Kinks in the 1960s, the pantomimic camp of Roxy Music and David Bowie in the 1970s, the witty stories of Squeeze and lovable cockneys Chas 'n' Dave in the early 1980s, to their inheritors like Pulp and Blur in the 1990s.[4]

By the end of the nineteenth century there were music halls in most large towns and cities, and their shows had audiences across the class spectrum – a point confirmed by the presence since 1912 of the annual Royal Variety Command Performance, in which light entertainers perform before members of the royal family. Music hall artists were important in the early history of the recording and broadcasting industries in Britain; indeed, entertainers such as Morecambe and Wise (whose television career spanned the 1960s and 1970s) stretched aspects of the format into the second half of the twentieth century. This was the performance world entered by late 1950s and early 1960s pop bands, all of which performed on variety bills alongside older-style entertainers (a distinctive youth concert circuit, based on colleges, emerged in the later 1960s).

Another British source of popular music is the 'musical comedy' – which Andrew Lloyd Webber has used to become one of the most successful of post-war musicians. This is not a copy of the American musical – indeed it was established as an antidote. One of the earliest, Noël Coward's *Bittersweet* (1929), was a response, he said, to 'the endless succession of slick American Vo-do-deo-do musical farces in which the speed was fast, the invention complicated, and the sentimental value negligible'.[5] His suspicion of Americanism was widely shared. Many regarded American music – from ragtime and jazz through rock 'n' roll – as both morally perfidious and commercially dangerous; anxious isolationism was common among British musicians in a market threatened by American imports. Well into the 1950s the Songwriters' Guild of Great Britain was pressing the BBC to play a part in 'the creation of a specifically British culture in the realm of the song'.[6] In fact commercial song remained an Anglo-American hybrid. However, anti-American sentiments, implicitly important in the Britpop of the 1990s, are also present in the variety tradition, movements such as the Songwriters' Guild campaign, and through the protection organised by the British Musicians' Union.

In 1930 the dance band section of the Musicians' Union was set up to police the membership of dance bands, and to exclude Americans. A 'needletime' agreement, negotiated with BBC radio, restricted the amount of recorded material it could broadcast (much of which was American), so guaranteeing employment for British musicians. Visiting American artists were licensed. These protective measures were matched on the other side of the Atlantic, though until the Merseybeat boom of the 1960s the only loss appeared to be to British audiences. Elvis Presley's only visit to Britain was to touch down at a remote Scottish airbase as a brief journey breaker, though Bill Haley, Little Richard and Jerry Lee Lewis did tour in the UK. British pop would not have happened without this protection.

ASPECTS OF AMATEURISM: FOLK ROOTS AND R 'N' B

Amateur participation in folk song remains strong. But the collection, preservation and performance of songs and dances was dominated in the first third of the twentieth century by middle-class cliques. There was an important change in the post-war period. Communists A.L. Lloyd and Ewan MacColl, seeing folk song as a source for radical politics, promoted the songs of the industrial working class of the North of England, Scotland and Wales; to these were added songs of American radicals such as Pete Seeger, and the folk-blues of the American deep South. Some blues enthusiasts rechristened this country blues as 'authentic': visiting blues musicians from the USA were criticised if they used electric guitars, to their confusion.[7] Nevertheless, many blues fans were also fans of its electric, urban derivative rhythm 'n' blues. The Rolling Stones and many other bands owe their origins to these enthusiasms.

The influence of folk itself spread widely beyond the club circuit. In the early 1960s its participatory nature made it part of CND's protests against military power; this lineage continues. Ecological protest and the anti-roads movement, with roots in an imagined Celtic or pagan past, are often accompanied by non-technological music-making (though there are also important connections between New Ageism, paganism and the high-technology music associated with illegal raves). Folk melody became widely available through various currents in rock music, from the relaxed folkishness of Pentangle, the more fundamentalist Albion Band, and the rockier Strawbs in the 1960s, to more politically tinged Celticism – for instance the London-Irish Pogues in the late 1970s, and in the 1990s Scottish bands like Runrig, Capercaillie and Coelbeg, who have used their 'national' musics to promote ideas of cultural and political independence.

PROFESSIONALISM AND POP

These enthusiasms are a long way from the professional world of post-war light music. By the 1950s, whatever the aspirations of the Songwriters' Guild, the commercial popular song was dominated by the restricted range of topics and structures associated with the (American) Tin Pan Alley model: the AABA format, 'moon in June' romantic lyrics, and the predominance of ballads or medium-paced over uptempo songs. Professional dance bands, meanwhile, played polite versions of American musics such as swing and Latin. This limited range was subverted in the late 1950s by the new American rock 'n' roll and rockabilly, and by the do-it-yourself simplicities of skiffle.

But although rock 'n' roll made its presence felt in the late 1950s, before the Merseybeat boom of the 1960s 'pop' did not exist as a standalone phenomenon. Take a glance at British popular music in 1960, through some of the top twenty best selling singles, the 'chart', of that year. There is rock 'n' rollish material clearly aimed at 'teenagers' (e.g. 'Poor Me' by Adam Faith and 'Please Don't Tease', by Cliff Richard), alongside songs targeted at older people (Perry Como's 'Delaware', or Ken Dodd's 'Love is like a Violin'), and a large number of novelty/humour items such as Rolf Harris's 'Tie me Kangaroo Down, Sport', Lonnie Donegan's 'My Old Man's a Dustman', and Brian Hyland's 'Itsy Bitsy Teeny Weeny Yellow Polka Dot Bikini'. The comedy elements are part of the music-hall line; the older-audience material is medium-tempo or slow Tin Pan Alley popular song; the more energetic teenage songs are either American or a pastiche of the new youth musics from the USA. (The most successful American artists on this year's chart were not Elvis or Pat Boone but the Everly Brothers, who had four number ones.) American popular music is already global at this point, whereas British (both light and pop) is local.

The arrival of Merseybeat interrupted a cosy national music business. Built on the various lineages identified above, in the early 1950s there was a national music industry based on radio performance (on the BBC Light Programme) and the sale of sheet music. This system had clear advantages for songwriters, and in a more limited way for performers, and it survived the early years of rock 'n' roll relatively unscathed. The music business acknowledged the new youth market, and catered for it, but it saw popular music as a wider field and tried to address that field as a whole. The first generation of British 'teen idols' sang songs by other people, and, with an eye to long careers, became general light music entertainers, with, for example, Tommy Steele's career on stage and in film very much a contemporary continuation of music hall: Cliff Richard, after a lifetime as a pop singer for the family, received a knighthood in 1995.

THE 1960S AND AFTER

This insular system was interrupted by the success of the Beatles (whose first three number one singles were in 1963), and principally by the establishing of John Lennon and Paul McCartney as songwriters as well as performers. Professional non-performing songwriters no longer dominated earnings. Other bands which formed around songwriters (such as the Rolling Stones and the Mick Jagger–Keith Richards partnership; the Who and Pete Townsend; the Kinks and Ray Davies) became similarly successful. Because of this redirection of earnings, the writer/performer was a more independent figure than the Tommy Steele-type teen idol. The basis of light music production was fractured (though not broken, as the 1980s success of Stock, Aitken and Waterman as writers and producers, with their stable of name-and-face performers, and their 1990s equivalents the Spice Girls, indicates). Thanks to the continuing international success of British pop, musicians who wrote their own songs, and performed and recorded them with more than modest success, could now expect to become millionaires, and to have some control over the shape of their careers – moving away from dependency on managers, agents and record companies.

So this interruption in the mode of musical production caused a distinct shift in the *social* (as well as the economic) position of the popular music performer. This was obvious even in the early years of the British pop revolution. One of the clichés of Britain in the early 1960s is that it was becoming a 'classless society'.[8] The London arts and media world of the early 1960s seemed to confirm the notion that youth and talent had transcended the remaining social barriers of class. The aristocratic photographer

Anthony Armstrong-Jones, soon to marry Princess Margaret and become Lord Snowdon, negotiated London's mean streets at the wheel of a Mini; cockney Michael Caine displayed his accent with pride, and displaced the middle-class actors of Ealing comedy (in such films as *Alfie* and *The Ipcress File*), while sometime milkman Sean Connery brought his Scottish brogue to the film role of James Bond. Models Twiggy and Jean Shrimpton brought new accents as well as new shapes to the world of haute couture. All these suggested that talent was more important than birth, and would be rewarded.

Youth was portrayed as a homogeneous entity driving Britain forward. 'I hope I die before I get old', wrote Pete Townsend in the 1965 Who song 'My Generation'. Class was no longer the motor of history – youth took the wheel instead, with the willing agreement of a Labour government whose vision of modernisation had moved sharply away from the politics of the previous, 1945–51, Labour administration. Leading exporters, the Beatles were not nationalised, but awarded a collective MBE medal in 1965. At a time of economic difficulty (with the car industry, for example, on the cusp of its decline to foreign-owned, kit-assembly status) British music was exported worldwide for the first time, and record companies and music publishers, recording studios and session musicians based in London became leaders of the world music market for a decade: a global industry matched the American.

The wealth, the export sales, the press attention, all changed the social position of pop stars. The new subjectivity which they experienced was one reason for the musical change towards the end of the 1960s, when under the influence of the politics and poetics of the American hippy movement, and the drug LSD, pop attempted to transcend the limits of chart-based monthly obsolescence and produce lasting work. The Underground scene which launched the careers of Pink Floyd and Jethro Tull among others was soon tagged 'progressive music'. As bands hired orchestras for tours, and made albums rather than singles the focus of their recording work it was claimed that the musical form was indeed 'progressing' beyond the limits of pop. The Who, for instance, stopped producing singles and turned to the quasi-operatic 'concept album', *Tommy* (1969).

Not everyone wanted to go beyond pop in this way. The result was divergence; by the early 1970s pop had fragmented into many different genres. Some (e.g. Yes, ELP) copied classical values of form, or sought the middle-class respectability which jazz had already obtained, while others (such as the Sweet and other Glam rockers, and teenybop bands like the Bay City Rollers) remained obstinately committed to the instant attractions of pure pop. Acts like Roxy Music and David Bowie meanwhile used the whole panoply of dress and makeup, album cover art work and choreographed stage performance to make a new kind of musical performance art. Art school graduate Malcolm McLaren watched with interest, before helping to create another integrated symbolic package, punk, through his partnerships with designer Vivienne Westwood and band the Sex Pistols.

THE AMBIVALENCE OF BROADCASTING

But punk was not mainstream pop (if there is, or remembering those 1960 charts, if there ever was, such a thing), partly because it was marginalised by the national broadcasting service. The BBC was set up as a monopoly in 1926. Though prevented by its Charter from advertising, it has in fact been complicit with the commercial practices of the record industry (potential chart material is still at the time of writing 'playlisted' by radio producers on a weekly basis). Though rivalled by commercial television since the 1950s, BBC radio enjoyed a monopoly over the national broadcasting of pop music which only the actions of the Conservative government of Mrs Thatcher finally challenged, setting up privately-owned national radio stations from the late 1980s.

The dedicated BBC pop network Radio 1 was established as late as 1966, and then only under severe pressure from commercial 'pirate' radio stations and their backers in the City of London.[9] Before this point pop on radio had been a small part of the Light Programme's output. The absence had led to 'pirates' such as Radio Caroline broadcasting from ships anchored outside territorial waters, and which broadcast pop records with chat from DJs, on the model of American radio stations. Radio 1 was at first confined to the AM waveband, with consequent poor sound quality (singles are still mixed as 'radio edit' versions, their sound compressed to cope with AM's limited frequency output). The needletime problem meant that it could not be an all-day record station. Though this restriction has since been negotiated away, Radio 1 has always been conservative, responding late to changes in its audience's tastes and preferences. Since the later 1960s there has been constant innovation in popular music forms, and the BBC has usually been one or two steps behind in granting them airtime. Progressive music and its antithesis, punk, were treated with suspicion, and heavy metal, ambient house, ragga, bhangra and other forms, however 'popular' in terms of sales, were not usually played on daytime Radio 1.[10] In the mid-1990s, competition from new stations and inner-city pirates prompted an attempt to capture a younger audience, with a claimed emphasis on the tastes of the under-24s, though this meant Britpoppy guitar rock rather than dance music. Radio 2 by this time, which had inherited the Light Programme mantle when Radio 1 was established, was broadcasting 'classic' pop, catering for the over-30s by reproducing the music of their youth.

Pop on television, meanwhile, has always been a problem. When television was established in the 1950s its soundtrack scores and theme tunes were dominated by light music; music-based shows, such as the *Billy Cotton Band Show* or the *Black and White Minstrel Show*, reproduced the music-hall/variety agenda which led the radio Light Programme. Until the advent of the MTV video music channel (available on cable and satellite since the late 1980s) pop was confined to a few weekly slots,[11] though the BBC did institute one show which became a national institution: *Top of the Pops*, a half-hour chart rundown based on studio performance. By the 1980s, pop video television had mainfested itself through MTV and its derivatives, programming sequences of material provided for them by the record companies. This had a spin-off back into terrestrial television, with more video material in pop and youth programming; but the impression remains that neither the BBC nor the commercial channels could work out the place of popular music on television, the most important national institution of the post-war half-century. Late-night shows imply that pop is for young people only, and that it would alienate the mainstream audience to carry say a Madonna gig as opposed to a football match involving Maradona, on prime time. When the National Lottery was launched in 1994, and the BBC won the contract to broadcast the draw, the accompanying theme was light music of the type which had launched variety television in the 1950s: Billy-Cottonish big-band arrangements.

YOUTH AND MUSIC

How, then, have musical cultures changed in the face of the conservatism of the dominant broadcasting media – a conservatism usually shared by the bigger music companies? The sociology of youth is vital to our understanding of the shifts which occurred here. However important bands and musicians were, the base for this transformed superstructure – the teenage and young people who bought the records and dressed in copycat outfits – has been a focus of attention since the invention of the 'teenager' in the 1950s. Nevertheless, pop sociology typically tells a partial story. The consumer of pop has consistently been theorised in particular and rather restricted ways.

While the emergence of the teenager as folk devil, consumer category and sociological subject, was derived from American ideas and marketing strategies, British sociological research qualified the American picture. American teenagers were products of their parents' prosperity. They spent their parents' money, drove their parents' cars, went to college and so on. The young British people labelled as 'teenagers' (and seen as a problem) came from working or lower middle-class families. They spent money they had earned themselves in dead-end jobs they entered at 15 or 16; their ability to spend in this way ended with marriage, usually in their early 20s. Commodities such as pop singles, portable record players, and portable transistor radios were aimed at these young consumers. But these were all cheap items, for people who were neither affluent nor socially mobile. The minority of young people who stayed at school and went to university were culturally different – their musical tastes more likely to be for classical, jazz or underground music than chart pop. There were no unicultural/classless teenagers.

As Stan Cohen claimed, groups of teenagers with shared tastes in dress and music, such as mods, were labelled deviant 'folk devils' by police and the media.[12] Through these 'moral panics' repressive policing was introduced. This routine of youth demonisation and consequent legislation has continued to operate, especially around events such as pop festivals; rave music and its parties were quickly demonised by the tabloid press in the late 1980s, and repressive legislation was enacted in 1994 to control them.

Sympathetic academic studies such as Cohen's identified groups of young people as 'subcultures', with fiercely owned collective tastes and identities. Through their fashion, music, sport, drug use and other practices, subcultures rejected the dominant or preferred codes of taste and behaviour agreed by the rest of society. By interpreting the cultural products of mass society in their own ways, and by using available items of dress to form symbolic uniforms of their own, young people could 'resist through rituals'.[13] A key text is *Subculture: The Meaning of Style* (1979), Dick Hebdige's catalogue of youth subcultures from teds to punks. In Hebdige's view British subcultures are engaged in a long imaginary 'phantom dialogue' with black American and Caribbean culture, focused around dress and music, and embracing their marginality against mainstream white culture. Subcultural studies have gone on to deal with the club cultures of the 1990s, and has added more sophisticated ways of considering ethnic relations and especially gender[14] ('youth' does not just mean young men, as it had done in some of the sociology of the 1960s).

This remains an important way of seeing the consumption of popular culture; but here too there is a tendency to hide certain areas of experience from history – not just music for older people, but for those whose rituals do not seem, on the face of it, to resist very much. However important punk was, for instance, we should not ignore the concurrent weekend alternative culture, the disco boom. It was *Saturday Night Fever* and the hits of ABBA, not *Never Mind the Bollocks it's the Sex Pistols*, which dominated the British charts in 1978. And there *was* a disco subculture, built on the smaller Northern Soul movement and the adoption by gay men's clubs of the Europdisco of the 1970s and its subsequent developments (hi-nrg, and later house and techno). The soul/disco 'subculture' of the late 1970s on, catering for virtually anyone aged from the teens to the early thirties, was based around dance musics which were largely absent from BBC airplay. Record stores imported 'rare grooves' from America, while a new wave of inner city pirate radio stations broadcast these musics – reggae, soul, funk, jazz-funk, rap, and from the late 1980s the many forms of dance music. Despite opposition from both the record companies and the Home Office to stations which paid neither licence fees nor royalties (opposition which included police raids, the confiscation of equipment, and the arrest, fines and even imprisonment of the pirate DJs), pressure to provide airtime for these musics eventually led to the granting of licences to several new stations including the Kiss FM chain.

While the soul weekenders offered no resistance to consumer capitalism in general, as conflicting centres of power and pleasure – involving illegal entrepreneurship around drugs and broadcasting, and thereby oppositional to the state and its official economy – they were at least as subversive as the punks.[15] Rave (to use the most convenient phrase), perhaps the last subculture, started from this subculture of music and parties: again the derivation of the phenomenon comes from Northern Soul, Chicago gay clubs, Ibiza's nightlife, and the chemically-aided ethnic and musical mix of the big cities.[16]

THE URBAN SOUNDSCAPE

So while the British-American dialogue continues, and has remained important in the emergence of British hip-hop, house and techno musics among other forms, there are more voices in play: since the 1950s a mixture of musics intersecting in the various urban centres have produced among other things new local forms of Caribbean-derived music such as reggae and the 'new ska' of two-tone, and Asian musics reworked through the use of technology and the influence of Western pop to produce bhangra. British cities have been the site of these cultural developments for two related reasons.

233

Firstly, the success of the early 1960s pop groups made London into a world musical centre. It was to that 'swinging' London, mythologised as the place of classless social mobility where young talent could find its true reward, that Jimi Hendrix came in 1966, to escape from the stereotyped role of the black r 'n' b guitarist, and to forge a new expressive language of guitar playing. Hendrix developed this from r 'n' b, the solo guitar voices of American urban blues players like B.B. King and Buddy Guy, and the more obsessive English blues guitarists like Peter Green and Eric Clapton. Working outside the cultural, ethnic, political and legal constraints which had made the blues and r 'n' b in the USA, but inside the constraints defining musical value in Britain, guitarists performing in British blues bands like the Graham Bond Organisation, John Mayall's Bluesbreakers and the Yardbirds abstracted the virtuosity of the musician.[17] Hendrix, in London, could more easily become the inspired solo voice. And he did. Singer Marsha Hunt followed the same path in order to realise her ambition: 'The American music scene was still severely segregated. They wanted me to be a soul singer, but I wasn't into bubble haircuts and short dresses, I wore leather and I had a large Afro. I said, I wanna sing rock. They said, black women don't sing rock. So I had to come to London to do it.'[18]

Both Hendrix and Hunt were important in the early story of the underground as it experimented with music of a power and scale beyond the three-minute single (and mind-altering drugs to match). The melting-pot of this relatively unsegregated city led to innovations in other directions. Jamaican jazz saxophonist Joe Harriott was among the first wave of Caribbean immigrants to Britain, arriving in 1951. He attempted in the middle 1960s to create a specifically post-colonial music, with Indian as well as Caribbean and white musicians and styles: the result he called Indo-Jazz Fusions. Indian music in Britain, meanwhile, gained exposure on the Beatles' *Sergeant Pepper* (as with the *Indo-Jazz Fusions* album, released in 1967). Again, it was through London that this post-colonial interaction took place: it continued to do so in the 1990s, with the Caribbean/Asian group Shiva Nova, for example, reworking the rhythms of through-composed, jazz and South Asian musics in similar ways, while Nitin Sawney and Najma Akhtar moved between North Indian forms and jazz, Sheila Chandra created a hybrid musical spirituality, Talvin Singh made music for the dance/club world, and young white band Kula Shaker propagated a neo-hippy Hinduism, complete with sitar and tabla atmos behind the guitars.

Another post-colonial transformation occurred in the early 1970s. Reggae had been based on the economics of an impoverished island, in which cheap recordings were made and played in public by DJs, with a small number of professional musicians working in the studios and hardly any live bands. Entrepreneur Chris Blackwell, owner of the Island label, imbued reggae with the more ostentatious values of the global music economy. For a while, thanks to Bob Marley's success, reggae became part of stadium rock: expensive studio recordings, and world tours by groups of musicians, became routine, while the album rather than the single became the most important form of production. Since Marley's success, reggae rhythms have become part of the orthodoxy of popular music all over the world. Reggae and the musics derived from it, meanwhile, have in some ways returned to their roots. Developments, from dancehall to ragga and their own subsequent derivatives, are based on the MC- or DJ-based 'versioning' performance mode which was the norm before Island Records' intervention. Meanwhile another derivative based on studio techniques, dub (which was pioneered in Jamaica by King Tubby in the early 1970s and has been developed in Britain by, for example, Adrian Sherwood working with bands such as African Headcharge), has been crucial in the development of high-technology dance musics including jungle/drum 'n' bass.

The second reason for the importance of Britain as site for the transformation of pop musics is the nature and extent of post-war, post-colonial immigration. Since 1945, millions of people from the Caribbean and from India and Pakistan have settled in the bigger British cities. This has produced markets for musical forms developed by and for specific ethnic groups, and provided the site for their interaction with existing forms: for example the infusion of reggae in the Rock Against Racism movement of the later 1970s.

Since then, the success in Britain of the many house-derived musics since 1988 is due in part to a reggae aesthetic which makes bass and drums the most important part of the mix. A typical early house 'band' name, Bomb the Bass, and the typical acid house track title 'Bass: how low can you go?' emphasise this aesthetic, which has been underlined in later house-related dance music by bass lines well below the normal capabilities of the bass guitar. These are often made using old analogue synthesisers, such as the Roland TB303, or more recent and technologically modern clone machines capable of similar sounds. The commercialisation of the speedy dub/techno form which was first known as jungle underlines the continuing importance of this Caribbean-influenced, bass-end aesthetic: a music which, even if called 'intelligent drum 'n' bass', is perforce of the body as much as of the mind.

LET'S MIX AGAIN

So musical innovation has continued partly because of the urban presence of new populations.[19] There is a long line of 'mixed race' bands: from

Coventry two-tone bands like the Special AKA and Selecter, and from Birmingham, UB40, through Culture Club and the Thompson Twins in early 1980s pop, to 1990s bands such as Massive Attack, who use soul, jazz-funk and reggae samples as the bases for tracks which explore their places in the urban melting pot.[20]

Both musical style and ethnic identity are in this mix, which configures the city as a culturally-interactive space which has involved people and their musics from all over the world. Apache Indian, raised in the Handsworth suburb of Birmingham, uses English, Punjabi and Jamaican patois inter-changeably, rapping across language and dialect on the back of rhythm tracks which owe more to dancehall reggae than to Indi-pop, for all their use of dhol and tabla drums. Meanwhile Britain has seen the evolution of 'bhangra', developed originally from a North Indian folk music but driven as well by the technologies of European dance music. Partly because of its continuing use of lyrics in Punjabi, bhangra has a whole political economy, as well as a whole subculture, of records, videos and live concerts.[21] Having been successfully reverse-colonised by the music of the Caribbean, Britain has also become partly Asian, a promise confirmed when in late 1996 'Dil Cheez', a Bally Sagoo track sung in Hindi, entered the mainstream pop chart, while a little further underground the politicised rap of Asian Dub Foundation and Fun'da'mental asserted the confidence of the South Asian presence in British life.

While Asians used African-American forms and drum 'n' bass developed dub, it was all too easy to see another phenomenon of the 1990s, Britpop, as dangerous nostalgia. Playing around with the music of the past – the 1960s in particular – bands like Blur and Oasis were, it seemed, recreating a triumphant moment of a predominantly white society. And yet this reading *is* too easy; Massive Attack and Sheila Chandra are just as concerned with using the music of the past – and the music of the Beatles is not in any simple sense 'white'. It is partly black-derived, and because of its success it is part of the virtually universal heritage that is pop, through which we all live, as we have done for forty years. No doubt their pastiche of the 1960s accounts for the mass appeal of the very deliberately Beatles-like Oasis: their albums are bought by those in their 40s as well as in their 20s. By the 1990s, it was no longer possible to see pop as the music of the young; it had become not pop but popular music. Oasis are the inheritors of Billy Cotton as well as their acknowledged masters, the Beatles.

Oasis have also acknowledged the importance of their home city, Man-chester, which has produced waves of musical innovation in club/dance culture and in guitar rock alike. The city maintains its capacity to transform what it contains, producing new forms and new ways of consuming those forms. Through these points of contact, mutation and development, music's living history continues. The city and the communication technologies of the global village offer the spaces and soundscapes in which people actively create forms, signs, meanings and the mode of production in which they are situated. Drum 'n' bass is not an act of interpretation but of creation. Through these connections and relationships 'the popular' is redefined, and – because of the continued, relatively powerful position of the British music business – the resultant musics are propagated worldwide, to form new modes of connection in their turn, in other urban spaces. There is, in other words, no conclusion to this chapter. . . .

NOTES

1. Edward Lee, *Music of the People* (London, 1970), p. 148.
2. The argument in this chapter is based on the second chapter of A. Blake, *The Land Without Music. Music, Culture and Society in Twentieth Century Britain* (Manchester, 1997).
3. Compare e.g. R. Finnegan, *The Hidden Musicians. Music Making in an English Town* (Cambridge, 1989); N. Mackinnon, *The British Folk Scene* (Buckingham, 1993); S. Cohen, *Rock Culture in Liverpool. Popular Music in the Making* (Oxford, 1991).
4. Aspects of this connection are discussed in J.J. Beadle, *Will Pop Eat Itself? Pop Music in the Soundbite Era* (London, 1993), p. 39; M. Sinker, 'Music as Film', in J. Romney and A. Wootton (eds), *The Celluloid Jukebox* (London, 1995), pp. 107–8; A. Blake, 'The Echoing Corridor: Music in the Postmodern East End', in T. Butler and M. Rustin (eds), *Rising in the East. The Regeneration of East London* (London, 1996), pp. 197–214.
5. Lee, op. cit., p. 139.
6. A. Briggs, *A History of Broadcasting in the United Kingdom*, vol. 4 (Oxford, 1995), p. 692.
7. G. Boyes, *The Imagined Village. Culture, Ideology and the English Folk Revival* (Manchester, 1993), p. 213.
8. This section is compressed from A. Blake, 'Britische Jugend: Gibt es noch/ British Youth: does it still exist?', in N. Bailer and R. Horak (eds), *Jugendkultur Annäheurungen* (Vienna, 1995), pp. 206–38.
9. This is the view of J. Hind and S. Mosco, *Rebel Radio* (Pluto 1985); but note the qualification offered in S. Barnard, *On the Radio* (Milton Keynes, 1989), pp. 40–1.
10. A useful account of the evolution of Radio 1 in relation to its less conventional programming is K. Garner, *In Session Tonight. The Complete Radio 1 Recordings* (London, 1993).
11. Attempts to find the right youth music TV format are discussed in Briggs, op. cit., vol. 5, pp. 200–6.
12. S. Cohen, *Folk Devils and Moral Panics. The Creation of the Mods and Rockers* (London, 1972).

13. See S. Hall and T. Jefferson (eds), *Resistance Through Rituals* (London, 1976).
14. See M. Nava, *Changing Cultures. Feminism, Youth and Consumerism* (London, 1992); A. McRobbie, 'Settling Accounts with Subcultures', reprinted in S. Frith and A. Goodwin (eds), *On Record* (London, 1990), pp. 66–80.
15. See I. Chambers, *Urban Rhythms. Pop Music and Popular Culture* (London, 1985), pp. 187–9.
16. See A. Melechi, 'The Ecstasy of Disappearance', in S. Redhead (ed.), *Rave Off* (Aldershot, 1993), p. 37.
17. An interesting account of the British blues scene, and its development towards rock, is D. Heckstall-Smith, *The Safest Place to Be* (London, 1988).
18. L. O'Brien, *She Bop. The Definitive History of Women in Rock, Pop and Soul* (London, 1995), p. 294.
19. S. Jones, *Black Culture, White Youth* (London, 1987).
20. E.g. Massive Attack's version of 'Home of the Whale', by Owen Hand, *Massive Attack ep*, Wild Bunch Records, WBRDG 4. Compare the explicit multi-culturalism of British rap band the Brotherhood: 'One Mixed Race, one Black, one Yid' on *Elementalz*, on Virgin Bitem, CDBHOOD1 7243 8 41324 2 2. For a genealogy of the urban mutations which helped to produce Massive Attack's particular mix, see P. Johnson, *Straight Outa Bristol. Massive Attack, Portishead, Tricky and the Roots of Trip-Hop* (London, 1996).
21. Bhangra has yet to find its historian; one early approach is S. Bannerjee and G. Baumann, 'Bhangra 1984–8: Fusion and Professionalisation in a Genre of South Asian Dance Music', in P. Oliver (ed.), *Black Music in Britain*. A general exploration is G. and A. Sharma and J. Hutnyk (eds), *Dis-Orienting Rhythms. The Politics of the New Asian Dance Music* (London, 1996).

CHAPTER TEN

Technology 1956–99

John Morris

WHAT IS TECHNOLOGY AND WHERE IS IT TAKING US?

'The future is not what it was'

Anon

Two previous essays in this series concern the development of technology: 1900–29 and 1930–55. What seems quite extraordinary when we consider the period of 1956 to the end of the century is the acceleration of change during the last forty-five years in comparison with the previous periods. Although the first half of the century showed remarkable developments in engineering, electronics, aviation, communications, computer science, polymers and indeed the application of nuclear energy (all these developments being themselves accelerated by each of the World Wars) the *nature* of applied science and technology seemed and still seems in retrospect, however alarming the changes were potentially, of a kind: one which humankind could try to use and adapt for their benefit.

The reality was no doubt different: people were *not* controlling the new technology even then, but the point is that it looked as if they could: that the benefits outweighed the problems, especially in areas like medicine and agriculture, entertainment and travel. Now we are down to the final months of this century, for many observers it would seem preposterous to pretend – as most governments still do – that humans are in control of the spiralling rate of change and that high tech. developments are largely or universally a benefit to humankind. Yet major writers on technology and its impact on society reach differing conclusions both about its value and its very nature.

The dictionary definition of 'technology' is two-fold:

(a) the theory and practice of applied science;
(b) the means and knowledge used to provide objects necessary for human sustenance and comfort.[1]

We should keep these two points in mind when we ask the question: What is technology becoming as we reach the twenty-first century? Lewis Wolpert's, *The Unnatural Nature of Science* (1992), provides us with a good approach to the question even though it will also leave many disagreeing with his conclusions. Wolpert makes a clear distinction between technology – which he sees as being about making things which help people to live more easily and comfortably: the wheel, the bed, tools for agriculture, etc. – and science, which is about ideas that are 'unnatural', 'alien' and non-human. 'Not until the nineteenth century', claims Wolpert, 'did science have an impact on technology.' Moreover the laws that govern science are contrary to common sense: they 'cannot be inferred from normal day-to-day experience'. 'Science often explains the familiar in terms of the unfamiliar': 'There are more molecules in a glass of water than there are glasses of water in the sea. There are . . . more cells in one finger than there are people in the world.'[2] He might have added that splitting one tiny atom can kill 100,000 people.

Thus in the last two hundred years technology has changed from being a force, a system, that could be harnessed on behalf of humankind and their lives on this planet into being something non-human and indeed often inhumane. Yet with a 'logic', which shocks as much as it baffles, Professor Wolpert writes in his conclusion: 'Science is bound to play a central role in our lives. It is to science and technology that we shall have to look for help to get us out of future problems in which we now all find ourselves – future problems that involve both environmental pollution and overpopulation.'[3]

Another example of the general continuing uncertainty about the nature and impact of high technology is revealed if we look at the question of the acceleration of change in the last thirty-five years. To many, the ever-increasing acceleration is self-evident. For example, Nathan Myhvold of Microsoft says that all his products are obsolete after eighteen to twenty-four months. Yet to others it is only apparent.[4] In his book *Media Technology and Society* (1998) Brian Winston repeatedly argues that the 'Information Revolution' is nothing of the sort, that in fact it is 'largely an illusion, a rhetorical gambit and an expression of technological ignorance'.[5] Winston's argument is fascinating and powerfully argued. It owes something perhaps to ideas expressed in Daniel Boorstin's *The Republic of Technology* (1978) to the effect that no technologies ever die out completely, but leave bits of themselves lying around. Thus 'the pile of debris' that 'grows skyward' indicates a continued continuity with the past going back to the earliest days of the Industrial Revolution or even before. Indeed Winston argues further:

The term 'revolution' is therefore quite the wrong word to apply to the current situation. Indeed, it is possible to see in the historical record not just a slower pace of change than is usually suggested but also such regularities in the pattern of innovation and diffusion as to suggest a model for all such changes. Repetitions can be seen across this diverse range of technologies and across the two centuries of their development and diffusion.[6]

However, to base your argument for social continuity solely on the nature of technology seems to me naive, especially if you claim as Winston does that 'there is nothing in the histories of electrical and electronic communication systems to indicate that significant major changes have not been accommodated by pre-existing social formations.'[7] For clearly it is not enough to look at the technologies involved: their impact on humanity and society has also to be observed and assessed. And, moreover, the question arises: how assessed? Is there not a danger if your assessment depends on the very techniques that have been created by advances in information technology? The very fact that the capability of computers doubles every twelve to eighteen months begs questions that cannot be faced, let alone answered, by just looking at the history of technological development. Perhaps it is for reasons such as these that Imperial College, London, created a chair devoted to the public understanding of science and technology. Awareness of the disparity between the rapidity of technological change and people's ability to cope with it is increasingly appearing in the popular press.

Here are some recent examples:

> Technology, operating in a free market, increases wealth rapidly and spreads affluence. It not only deepens and makes permanent the chasm separating the poor from the rest and builds up huge fortunes. . . .
>
> The outstanding example is Microsoft which did not exist 23 years ago. It has passed General Electric as the world's biggest company and its market capital, at £163 billion, is more than the wealth of scores of countries. It has transformed thousands of investors into millionaires. . . .
>
> Modern super-wealth is based on intellect and education, and the way in which a combination of both, exploiting the resources of new technology, can produce wealth at astonishing speed.
>
> Charles Murray . . . in his epochal book *The Bell Curve* . . . shows that the chasm between rich and poor deepens because technology eliminates unskilled labour while increasing rewards for those who become expert in its use.[8]

A further example is the recent newspaper report that some London streets have been dug up as many as sixty times in one year in order to accommodate developments in communications: cable, wiring, etc., to say nothing of the needs of privatised water companies, new traffic systems and so on.[9] Yet another example is the steady demise of old-fashioned personal banking services during the last few years with tens of thousands of jobs disappearing. Technology is and always has been a power, a force, that is 'about itself' but in its earlier simpler forms, that is until the nineteenth century, technology could be seen as largely beneficial to people – indeed as their increasingly powerful servant. Its transformation in this century into an extraordinary, unprecedented, power – or, if you prefer, a series of linked co-operating powers – increasingly corrosive of socialised humankind is, largely due to technology's greater and greater involvement with science, which is – to quote Lewis Wolpert – 'unnatural'.[10] Furthermore, there is growing evidence that the new scientific technologies of the late twentieth century impose themselves on people and society, that we cannot do without them and that they are effectively 'narcotic'.[11]

There is not the space in this essay to do full justice to the discussion in the sense of dealing with the *minutiae* of technologies and their development during the last thirty-five years. But it seems that there are two areas of extraordinary development which require particular attention. One is the explosion in the transmission of information – its digitalisation, its globalisation. The other is the area of genetic engineering. Both areas of development bring with them grave ethical questions. Moreover, it appears that the two areas – the electronic and the genetic – are actually part of the same phenomenon, as their ability to share the word 'engineering' would suggest.

THE INFORMATION EXPLOSION

> Those images that yet
> Fresh images beget. . . .

> W.B. Yeats

If we cast our minds back to 1960 – assuming we are old enough to do so – we will remember that the computer so far as it existed at all in our consciousness would for the vast majority of people have been so remote as to be something which, whether or not we knew it impinged on our lives, was the concern of large companies or state-run industries. The computer was their business: we were just interested in whether we received our gas or electricity or whether trains ran on time or planes landed safely. Now, forty years later, the power – and problems – of computerisation impinge on almost every significant decision we have to make: witness the recent alarms, warnings and reassurances concerning the 'millennium bug', in relation to which IBM, no less, informed us that 'Time is running out. This is a survival issue.'[12] Yet, the computer (the PC, together with keyboard and printer), having effectively mutated with the discovery of even more diverse printed circuits, has spread to the home as in a previous generation had the vacuum cleaner and the television set – the luxury becoming inevitably a necessity – as it reduced in size, increased in efficiency and, through its accelerating power of influence, infiltrated almost every aspect of life. Admiring Babbage's insight and understanding of future developments in computerisation – as early as 1864 – Donald Cardwell has commented:

> the rise of the computer, while it cannot replace [trains, ships, machine tools, etc.] is an instance of the rise of a radically new technology: the engineering of intelligence. . . . Just how far it will go cannot possibly be predicted: . . . it is . . . likely that we are on or are approaching the steepest part of the ascent and that the limits of electronic technology are not in sight.[13]

Let us take another example of the information explosion: television, a phenomenon this writer first witnessed as a 14-year-old schoolboy in 1951. I had cycled some three miles to a friend's house and watched intrigued the black and white moving images. The programme was *Café Continental* hosted by Hélène Cordet and the whole experience seemed to me then as quaint and cosy: looking at a little box of tricks you might see at a fairground side-show. Yet as years passed one channel grew to two (with the advent of commercial TV) and then to three. Colour television arrived and the number of channels rose ultimately to five. More than enough choice, one would have thought. But satellite and cable brought more and more channels for subscribers who were prepared to pay for specialist programmes or repeats or indeed for sports coverage that had been hived away from the accessibility of terrestrial television. And in 1998 we learnt that digital television will offer not just dozens but hundreds of channels; for example, one company, Ondigital, plans to provide thirty channels and Skydigital no fewer than one hundred and forty channels! And of course the BBC and ITV will correspondingly expand while cable will seek to emulate the expansion of satellite transmissions.[14]

When the telephone was invented by Alexander Graham Bell in 1873 someone remarked that now a housemaid in London would be able to talk directly to a housemaid in Glasgow about the kind of things housemaids talk about. I wonder what that snobbish person would have made of the Internet, of the 'multi-media super-highway'? Or of the types of distance learning or conferencing performed by organisations such as the Oracle Corporation? These are powerful technologies performing extraordinary functions, but they are not of themselves neutral. I am not only saying that the value of the information they store or communicate is not necessarily as impressive as the technology that stores and communicates it. I am also saying that the way information is transmitted affects both the content (*à la*

Marshall McLuhan's 'the medium is the message') and the reception of the information. We, the human race, are increasingly, it seems to me, locked into a process, a kind of closed circuit, that has become global. McLuhan, of course, also spoke of 'the global village', yet even he, I suspect, would not have expected the size of the media reaction – some would say over-reaction – to the death of Princess Diana or the instantaneous worldwide transmission, lasting several hours of lurid details, concerning the alleged sexual activities of the President of the United States of America.

The remarkable spread in the use of mobile telephones is a further indication of how we are becoming caught up in a process that is biological as well as technological. We increasingly carry with us gadgets that are effectively extensions to our body organs: phones, alarms, pace-makers, hearing-aids, etc. As we shall see later we are potentially, in the view of major thinkers, on a threshold that could take us in the direction of a kind of benevolent 'robotisation' of the human race.[15] Indeed the miniaturisation and fusion of systems are clearly key elements in the future development of the information explosion. It also seems only a matter of time before we will be able to buy a – perhaps portable – machine that is radio, TV, telephone, fax, computer and word-processor all rolled into one. I note that the coming 'Web TV' will link television to the Internet.

The Internet itself certainly possesses enormous power and a potential whose social effects are far from clear. When we hear that 'traditional' booksellers of Cambridge are selling books 'on line' and that Richard Noble raised £320,000 via the Internet to help finance his attempt on the world land-speed record we recognise the significance of this phenomenon to business and commerce – something which Bill Gates and Microsoft were strangely slow to realise. It was after Tim Berners-Lee had created the World Wide Web in 1992 that Microsoft started belatedly – in the mid-1990s – to break into the world of the Internet, causing some absurd objections from those who saw 'Cyberspace' as a pure element not to be sullied by ungainly manoeuvrings of multi-billion dollar media giants trying to gain the upper hand. Needless to say, what was occurring was the chief players in this market place using the new technology to minimise any threat to their business rather than developing radically the awesome power of the Internet.[16]

Nevertheless the very power unleashed by the 'multi-media super-highway' has necessitated actions and reactions from operators and customers alike. I am referring not only to the explosion in the number of cyber-cafés (one, at least, I understand is in Katmandu) or to the extraordinary rush at all levels of education to embrace and afford the use of the Internet in the teaching of traditional subjects – and this only a few years after the claims that conventional computers in every class-room would 'do the trick'.

What I am at pains to stress is that the Internet has brought its own problems of overload. In the last four or five years techniques have been developed to try to control and rationalise the growth in Internet use, hardly surprising since three customers join every second and it takes only a minute and a half to register. Browsers who wish to 'surf the net' will be able to use METADATA (labels on information or data about data) so that the user can find and identify the information required. Stanford University has developed a Web Directory – the equivalent of Yellow Pages for our telephone system – called YAHOO INC: the first word being an acronym for 'Yet Another . . . Oracle'.[17]

Yet the dangers are obvious – or should be. We could well become too dependent on a system close to overload and one entered via computers that face breakdown from the 'millennium bug', computer virus or some other gremlin. (The closest we have come to world war during the last fifteen years was when on two occasions computer error occurred.) Then there is also the mis-use of the Internet. We have all read of terrorists, paedophiles, pornographers and other fanatics offering and receiving help, information and images through the Internet. Enthusiasts for this technology speak sententiously of 'Protocols' providing operational rules. Yet the system seems impossible to police and, as with genetic engineering, any code of behaviour is likely to exist only insofar as it is voluntarily adhered to.

While there are concerns about these developments and the pace of change that demands an ever more rapid response from humankind, it should be recorded also that there is admiration and amazement at the extraordinary power and sophistication of the latest stages of evolution of 'high tech.' in the field of electronics, digital information systems, pattern recognition and robotics. Moreover, like the readers of this essay, I use the products of technology and in general enjoy using them. Yet having said the above and accepted the benefits and comforts that go with the most recent developments, I am also of course drawing attention to our inevitable and inescapable reliance on these products. Furthermore, experts in the field, those at the cutting edge of electronics and robotics warn increasingly of the dangers faced by humankind if we do not find the means and the social-political will constantly to stand-back, monitor and indeed try harder to control future developments rather than allow them to control us.[18]

One last general caution: demonstrably we have not been good at making predictions about the future effects of technology and we do not easily grasp the reality. In the 1970s there was a lot of convincing talk about the technology of the near future making life easier and doing away with the need for work. For those with a job the reverse has been the case: 'high tech.' has produced stress, strain and illness such as 'sick building syndrome'

(SBS) caused by using photocopiers and laser printers or eye-inflammation and headaches caused by long gazing at visual display units. More particularly 'high tech.' in the work place (e.g. e-mail and the fax machine) is peremptory and demanding, requiring acceleration rather than ease. '[If] you are trying to do the kind of work with long hours and tight deadlines that is expected from office workers nowadays, then you will need a quality environment which supports you physically,' said a recent newspaper article, with the suggestion that such an environment is increasingly difficult to provide *because of* the inevitable presence of high tech. machinery in the office.[19] Other areas of the information explosion are even more difficult to judge. Credit cards, bank cards, reward cards, etc. are increasingly easy to use: the outlets that accept them are ever more accessible. It seems only a matter of time before plastic will replace conventional money. Yet these cards are in reality tiny programmed machines outside the control of those who use them and capable of containing secret or incorrect or incriminating information. So perhaps the greatest single danger that faces us as the information explosion continues to expand is that we collectively lose a clear sense of reality or rather that the reality we accept is in fact unreal, that we are creating a simulation of culture, that we are moving ever closer to the world of 'virtual reality' first portrayed in William Gibson's *Neuromancer* (1984). Already, for many, 'cyberspace' is a reality into which they enter daily and have their being: a realm engendered by 'the global communications and computing infrastructure'. As Howard Rheingold remarks, 'this is not fiction' because the required technology is available:

> The head-mounted displays (HMDs) and three dimensional computer graphics, input/output devices, computer models that constitute a VR system make it possible, today, to immerse yourself in an artificial world and to reach in and reshape it.[20]

Indeed, It may be said that high tech. society has continued to put in place the rudiments of an incipient, global, VR laboratory which we encounter in our daily lives and that an increasing lobby is growing in order to press for reform and control.

GENETIC ENGINEERING

> The event on which this fiction is founded has been supposed, by Dr Darwin, . . . as not of impossible occurrence.
>
> Mary Shelley, Preface to *Frankenstein*[21]

The two parts of this essay, 'The Information Explosion' and 'Genetic Engineering' seem to be separate. Yet it is increasingly clear that what links developments is more significant than what might be thought to separate them. For example, what is happening in genetics can be said to be full of future implications, and indeed applications, that will involve electronics, computers, digital systems, etc. Whatever scientists like Steve Jones may say to the contrary, invoking Mary Shelley's *Frankenstein* to deride lay observers,[22] it is undeniable from the evidence of history that, despite the setting up of groups in Britain such as the Human Genetics Advisory Committee, ethical considerations will in the long term take second place to financial and technological ones on a world scale.

During the last four or five years of the twentieth century developments in genetics and genetic engineering have taken on an absurd yet nightmarish quality, like an Alice in Wonderland world gone out of control. The Human Genome Project – the laborious mapping and classifying of the entire human gene bank – has been gently mocked by Steve Jones ('a matter of perspiration rather than inspiration' he called it)[23] but behind it there has been serious endeavour to track down the origins of major inherited disorders such as cystic fibrosis and Huntingdon's chorea through the examination of DNA sequences and chromosome mutations and deficiencies. Yet the world we are moving into, where genes can and will be chosen or eliminated or even patented, is clearly fraught with profound dangers and ethical dilemmas, as we shall be seeing in this essay. Is it 'human' as we now understand the word to be able to decide in advance not only perhaps the height and the hair colour of an individual but whether he or she lives or is eliminated according to whether the genetic make-up will or will not allow the possibilities of some inherited disease? Insurance companies are already 'taking on board' these chilling considerations.

There are recent developments in agriculture. The genetic modification of food crops has entailed a whole gamut of revelation and speculation undoubtedly intensified by the information explosion I have previously discussed. Are the activities of Monsanto, the giant company in the forefront of research and development of genetically modified food products, *inevitably* dangerous? Do they represent an attack on bio–diversity? Does their ability to use herbicides, pesticides and insecticides more powerfully represent an ever-greater threat to wildlife and 'the balance of nature'? Will their crops, especially when grown next to organic farms, lead to 'genetic pollution'? What safeguards are there? And will not money be drained away from conventional research because more profit attaches to genetic engineering?

Undoubtedly all these relate in the public mind to a sheep called Dolly. It seems that some kind of psychological border was crossed in July 1996 as far as the public acceptance of genetic engineering is concerned. A recent informed description of Dolly's creation has more than a hint of the activities of Dr Frankenstein:

> [Ian Wilmut's] colleague Keith Campbell sucked the nucleus out of an egg from a ewe, creating an egg that had no genes at all, an egg that would soon die if it did not get a new nucleus. Then he began the process of adding the nucleus of an udder cell to the bereft egg.
>
> Campbell slipped an udder cell under the outer membrane of the egg. Next he jolted the egg for a few microseconds with a burst of electricity. This opened the pores of the egg and the udder cell so that the contents of the udder cell, including its chromosomes, oozed into the egg and took up residence there. Now the egg had a nucleus – the nucleus of the udder cell. In addition, the electric current tricked the egg into behaving as if it were newly fertilized, jump-starting it into action. After 277 attempts to clone an udder cell, Wilmut's group succeeded and Dolly was created.[24]

If such experiments were legitimate they were brought under suspicion with the sudden suspension of Dr Arpad Pusztai from another research institute – the Rowett – after he had claimed that transgenic potatoes he had created stunted the growth of 'guinea-pig' rats and were effectively toxic. Dr Colin Merritt of Monsanto was reported to be 'delighted' yet within six months Pusztai's findings were vindicated by a panel of scientists. Moreover financial connections were revealed between the Rowett Research Institute and Monsanto and indeed as the press dredged for evidence it became clear that such financial links involving research into the genetic modification of food both vegetable and animal involved the British and American governments as well as, it was alleged, public figures like Lord Sainsbury and Lord Hollick – both Labour peers, the former a Science Minister and supermarket proprietor.[25]

Other newspaper stories of frightening absurdity had been appearing, as if the *Daily Sport* had transferred its headlines to *The Times* and *Telegraph*: a gene from a brazil nut implanted in soya had caused allergy and asthma; new 'springy' bread had been made from genetically modified wheat; there were new multi-coloured 'rainbow' lettuces and there were tomatoes for supermarkets engineered to optimum size, shape and shelf life; a mouse had been given a human ear and mice were also cloned, as was a dog.[26] It is in the nature of applied science and technology that it would only be a matter of time before the formerly unthinkable became not only thinkable but apparently inevitable. With the Dolly experiment repeated in Wisconsin early in 1998, only this time using a loan egg from a cow, minus its genetic material, in which to insert a sheep's DNA, there appeared such startling possibilities of creating transgenic mammals that H.G. Wells's *The Island of Dr Moreau* began to appear science faction rather than fiction.[27] And of course talk of the cloning of man became serious talk. A Dr Richard Seed of Illinois working in Chicago claimed he was ready to begin within three months if he had sufficient funding, while Professor Lee Silver of Greenburg University, also in the United States, said that geneticists were prepared to clone human beings, in part because it would provide a new hope for childless couples for whom *in vitro* fertilisation had failed.[28] Subsequently, while ruling out the legality of human cloning in Britain, the Human Genetics Advisory Committee with what is perhaps typically British compromise has accepted the recommendations that, in theory anyway, every foetus could have its own cloned 'twin': preserved frozen genetic material for the 'harvesting' of spare-part organs. It could also provide replacement tissue in emergencies: muscle cells to patch up hearts; bone marrow to help victims of leukaemia; brain cells to avert Parkinson's disease. Such technology is not far in the future and indeed may be with us by the time this book is published. It has been developed by Dr Austin Smith of Edinburgh University working in association with Roslin Institute (of Dolly fame) and the University of Wisconsin who claim they have found a way to grow unlimited supplies of embryonic tissue which can be turned into specialised cells.[29] Of this planned procedure Peter Garrett of *Life* has said: 'The idea that you can store genetic copies of yourselves and then one day convert them into particular types of tissue is a violation of all kinds of philosophical and ethical traditions.'[30]

We may claim that we can ignore such ethical questions or even that such questions are not really ethical at all but practical. Yet such dilemmas – as to whether genetic scanning could or should be used to eradicate prior to birth, perhaps even prior to conception, diseases such as leukaemia or Huntingdon's chorea – raise questions that are more than 'practical' for even the most thick-skinned hard-headed operatives of future societies. For such questions are more than just a headache for insurance firms. If you can eradicate disease by genetic manipulation you can also decide, as already mentioned above, hair colour, skin texture, perhaps even the sexual orientation of children. If you can do these things you are fundamentally changing the idea of what it means to be human.

The present situation, with its Frankenstein overtones, is for many so nightmarish. It is due to an approach which sees human beings, indeed life, as commodities to be used and manipulated and which employs scientific technology to achieve it. It is an approach which reached its greatest inhumanity in Soviet Russia and Nazi Germany but which has never been abandoned since its early development in Britain during the Industrial Revolution. It is an approach which, as we shall see, links the two parts of this essay: the electronic and the genetic.

In 1994 there appeared in a special edition of *Scientific American* an article which could be described, almost literally, as 'mind-boggling'. In it Marvin Minsky asks the question: 'Will Robots Inherit the Earth?'[31] Any doubts that what I have called 'the information explosion' and the remarkable developments in genetic engineering in recent years are fundamentally linked would be removed by examining Minsky's approach. It is the approach of a Professor of Media Arts and Sciences at the Massachusetts Institute of Technology, co-founder of the Artificial Intelligence Laboratory, who designed and built the first neural network learning machine. In the article Minsky effectively criticises the way our genetic system operates in that it was 'not designed for very long term maintenance'. There is not a direct relationship between genes and cells or a blue-print to guide genes in rebuilding worn cells. For that the body would need its own computer capable of routinely checking the integrity of its systems. As yet no animal has evolved such a scheme but making new genes and installing them is of course increasingly feasible. And, in any case, adds Minsky, there is another approach to combating bodily wear and tear: replacing each organ that threatens to fail with a biological or artificial substitute. For, after all, our bodies are just machines – or, rather, a collection of machines:

> Hearts are merely clever pumps. Muscles and bones are motors and beams. Digestive systems are chemical reactors. Eventually we will find ways to transplant or replace all these parts.[32]

Conceding that a brain-transplant will not work because you cannot simply exchange your brain for another and remain the same person, he nevertheless continues

> we might be able to replace certain worn-out parts of brains by transplanting tissue-cultured foetal cells. This procedure would not restore lost knowledge, but that might not matter as much as it seems.[33]

The trouble with the human being as at present constituted is that he/she (it?) wears out too quickly and does not have time to develop the required potential. But, claims Minsky, this fault could be eliminated by further advances and our lives transformed since 'no part of the brain will be out-of-bounds for attaching new accessories. In the end, we will find ways to replace every part of the body and brain and thus repair all the defects and injuries that make our lives so brief.'[34]

While admitting that we will thus become machines, Minsky urges us to think of these machines as our own 'mind-children' created by techniques like nanotechnology, placing each atom and molecule precisely where it is wanted and leading to body parts that are in effect replaceable microscopic computers, of unparalleled speed and efficiency, produced on an assembly line:

> Once we know what we need to do, our nanotechnologies should enable us to construct replacement bodies and brains that will not be constrained to work at the crawling pace of 'real time'. The events in our computer

chips already happen millions of times faster than those in brain cells. Hence, we could design our 'mind-children' to think a million times faster than we do. To such a being, half a minute might seem as long as one of our years and each hour as long as an entire human life-time.[35]

Now such writing is not, or thinks it is not, the stuff of a latter-day H.G. Wells. When Marvin Minsky argues that some day individuals will not be made by chance but 'composed' in accord with 'considered desires and designs' he is totally serious while, perhaps unknowingly, echoing the eugenicist philosophy of Wells's *A Modern Utopia* (1905). Such proto-fascism would, it seems, be inevitable in the kind of future systems envisaged by Minsky. And when he asks for the final time, 'Will robots inherit the earth?' he answers: 'Yes, but they will be our children.'[36]

As is always the case with late twentieth-century (early twenty-first-century) 'scientific technology' the blessings are inseparable from the nightmares inherent in its very nature. As early as 1987 it had been shown that the most significant developments in genetic engineering could allow genes to be 'manipulated, altered and transferred from organism to organism, even to transform DNA itself', thus allowing the rapid reproduction of organisms such as bacteria to be used as 'chemical factories' producing useful, sometimes life-saving, substances such as insulin, hormones, antibiotics, interferon and vitamins. Because a number of human diseases are the result of individuals being unable to produce for themselves chemicals which have a metabolic role, it follows that there are great advantages in producing large quantities of 'pure' chemicals from non-human sources. Methods have been devised for isolating the human DNA responsible for producing insulin, say, or thyroxine, and combining it with bacterial DNA so as continually to provide the required substance. This DNA, which is the result of a combination of two different organisms, is called 'recombinant DNA'. A collection of genetic information can thus be built up into a 'genome library', while these techniques can be used in the process of gene cloning in which multiple copies of a specific gene can be produced and then used to manufacture large quantities of valuable products that can treat a whole range of diseases and disorders. Moreover the scope of recombinant DNA technology is not restricted to medicine: it is possible to transfer genes which produce toxins with insecticidal properties from bacteria to higher plants such as potatoes and cotton so that they have built-in resistance to pests. The possibilities seem endless: for example, the development of oil-digesting bacteria to clear up oil-spillages.

Yet the very power of such technology brings with it, of course, profound ethical problems and indeed dangers. For example, whatever we may hear to the contrary from vested interests, it is impossible to predict with any accuracy the ecological consequences of releasing into the environment genetically engineered organisms. The delicate 'balance of nature' in an environment could be upset. Escaped organisms designed ('manufactured') for one environment could be lethal in another. Viruses which can transfer genes from one organism to another could take 'advantageous' genes from plants and animals and transfer them to their competitors, making the latter infinitely more harmful. Indeed the escape of a single pathogenic bacterium into a susceptible population could result in considerable damage to an entire species. Even more sinister perhaps, bearing in mind Professor Minsky's essay and the latest developments in cloning, is the possibility – even probability in the long term – that the ability to manufacture genes could allow human characteristics or behaviour to be altered. What could result if such a process 'fell into the wrong hands', whether of individuals, groups or governments, can hardly bear thinking about.[37] We are, after all, already in a world where scientists speak confidently of cloning human beings or even fusing human and animal tissue for new medical practices.

OUTCOMES OF THE HIGH TECH. PROCESS

The danger of the past was that man became slaves. The danger of the future is that men may become robots.

Erich Fromm

We live in a world in which people are increasingly processed, in which each succeeding generation is becoming less able to defend itself. It is clear that humans have been and are continuing to be 'guinea-pigs' in the vast process we call 'high technology'. We have decaying nuclear power stations and a growing mountain of nuclear waste.[38] In the old Soviet Union there is the legacy of Chernobyl and a rotting fleet of ships powered by nuclear fuel that cannot be decommissioned. The hole in the ozone layer grows bigger each year. These facts are relevant and important because they gave us evidence of how we should regard developments in electronics and genetics. Almost suddenly it seems the quasi-Sci-Fi ideas of Marvin Minsky's 1994 article, 'Will Robots Inherit the Earth?'[39] have become in five short years distinctly and disturbingly possible. And when we read of computer chips in the brain allowing thought to control computers and of a Cambridge company called Cyberlife Technology creating 'live creatures' that inhabit computers[40] it is clear that what is occurring is not only of course unprecedented and patently uncontrolled in any meaningful sense, it is an absolute threat to the survival of the human race.

It should be no surprise, therefore, that one characteristic which has emerged powerfully in the last few years is that the 'New Technology', so arguably benign earlier in the century despite the World Wars, the destruction of the environment, etc., now terrifies. So much so that it commands scary articles in the tabloid press – even, at times, in the broadsheets. Paul Johnson has written of 'My Fears for Our Future', anticipating a world with no human values, in which technology has outstripped morality, a world to be inherited by future generations of 'designer babies': a world in which 'Man plays God.'[41] Dr Jacqueline Laing has written of the 'Dawn of the Frankenstein Age' in the countdown to the first human clone and warns: 'We are now entering unknown territory. The miracle of life is being coldly reduced to a disposable commodity.'[42] Professor Lee Silver – the geneticist referred to above and author of *Remaking Eden: Cloning and Beyond* – warns against 'brave new worlds' and 'Breeding Supergods'.[43] And in a moving and profound article Bryan Appleyard, author of *Brave New Worlds: Genetics and the Human Experience*, writes of his feelings on the death of his niece Fiona, crippled from birth with muscular dystrophy and surviving against all odds until the age of thirty. The tragic dilemma he highlights is this: the Fionas of the future will not exist if genetic technology continues unabated. She would never be allowed a birth: a person of unique intelligence, personality and courage would be screened out because the muscular dystrophy gene has now been discovered and it would be detected and eliminated. The foetus would be aborted to avoid stress to parents and family. But what about Fiona? As Appleyard puts it:

> it should be obvious that those we classify as handicapped are more human than the rest of us. The failures of their bodies are enhanced versions of our own deficiencies. When this is combined – as it was in Fiona – with a formidable intellect and imagination, the effect is overpowering. This, truly, is what we all are, an infinite mind tied to an all-too-finite and crippled body.

Appleyard concludes by warning of the coming world 'devoid of any ethical concept of what constitutes the human self', in which 'the dominant force . . . is the medical-industrial complex . . . selling eugenics as a privatised industry', adding:

> The concept of the self being sold by this force is essentially consumerist. The self can be improved, altered or aborted when it is found to be deficient. It is not a moral absolute, it is merely a chance product of its genes. Such a view represents such a fundamental change in our interpretation of the human world that, once it is fully accepted, nothing will remain unchanged. We shall have become shrunken, more spiritually impoverished entities, but . . . too stupid to be aware of the fact.[44]

Such ideas had been remarkably anticipated over fifty years ago by the historian G.M. Trevelyan when writing about industrial and commercial effects on the population during the late Victorian period: that is just before the advent of twentieth-century technology. He said that 'the stage is set for the gradual standardisation of human personality.'[45] I would indeed argue that there has been a continued and relentless move throughout this century towards the standardisation and exploitation of both mind and body and that the works of the great utopian and anti-utopian writers – Wells, Zamiatin, Huxley and Orwell – are still pertinent in their anticipations. The impact upon mankind, especially in the last forty years of this century, and particularly in 'the advanced world' of applied science and technology and emanating primarily through the information explosion and genetic engineering, has been a kind of processing into which we all increasingly have to fit.

Symbolic of this process and of the fact that even now many are unaware of it – including, officially, all the governments of the world – is the worthy German citizen who obeyed orders without question by following instructions beamed to his BMW's satellite-guided dashboard navigation system even though this meant ignoring the clear visual evidence that he and his wife would end up in the river Havel. Indeed the event led one commentator to write:

> could the story be a warning metaphor for the rest of us? Day by day, we connive to make ourselves more helpless by heaping ever more trust and responsibility upon the technology with which we surround ourselves. . . . We are rapidly losing the ability to see for ourselves, and I fear that before very long we will be joining the German man and his wife in the river.[46]

When we read such observations we are reminded of the ideas of Marshall McLuhan to the effect that the modern technologies are extensions or adaptations of our bodily systems and that as these technologies ever more rapidly advance in power and sophistication there is a grave danger, even an inevitability, that they take over completely. To use a more homely image: the tail will wag the dog. Certainly we are caught (trapped?) in the middle of something which I have called a 'process' and at the moment we show no sign of being able to escape from it – indeed, as I have said, there is no official awareness that there is anything to escape from. Therefore, by and large, we serve the process – are in a real sense its servants. We not only do not 'pull out the plug': we cannot afford to. George Orwell in one of his rants at technology asked: why do I not walk to London? And his answer was: because a Green Line bus stops outside my house.[47] But significant and valid though that observation still is, we need to take account of the extraordinary, explosive, development of technology since Orwell made those remarks in the 1930s. In his last book, having witnessed the use of science and technology during the Second World War and in particular the creation of the atomic bomb, H.G. Wells the former champion of science said that man was a doomed species and deserved to be because he could not handle the new technology.[48]

It is remarkable how often creative writers have anticipated the future of science and technology, so it should come as no surprise that terms like 'robotics', 'Frankenstein foods' and 'cyberspace' derive from literature. Writers are, as Ezra Pound said, 'the antennae of the Race'.[49]

FINAL THOUGHTS

> Present fears
> Are less than horrible imaginings.
>
> Shakespeare

We are it seems just at the beginning. The ever-accelerating thrust forward in technology at the end of the century is breath-taking and alarming: moreover its ability to amaze and surprise and for it to adapt and co-operate with its various branches on all levels makes it act as if it were some kind of organism. Technology is 'about' replication and it is as if it were creating a kind of 'mock-up' of man or, as John Monk puts it, a 'digital effigy'.[50] The appearance in recent years of terms like 'wired flesh' and 'digital flesh' suggest the awareness (of those at the cutting edge of research that sees the greatest co-operation between 'the information explosion' and genetic engineering) that rather than technology being an extension of the body, it is becoming the opposite: the body is becoming an extension of the technology. In the world we are fast approaching – even already entered – we will have to 'meet the machines on their own terms'. Work done at the MIT Media Lab by Thad Starmer and others in producing 'nomadic radio' and at the University of Toronto by Steve Mann whose body has been 'permanently adapted' for ultra-sensory communication, and indeed in Britain where Kevin Warwick of Reading University has had an implant linking him to a computer, takes the world into areas such that the word 'technology' would need redefining if you wanted it also to refer to, say, bridge-building or playing a record. This newest of new technology is ever more clearly concerned with itself. Technology always has been, of course, but such is its development as I write in March 1999 that clearly humankind's control of events is becoming progressively more fragile and less predictable. It is for this reason that the performance artist STELARC, who transforms into a machine, and other protesters such as Arthur and Marilouise Croker have a growing impact that divides those who have an interest in the latest technological developments into pros and cons.[51] Perhaps the greatest irony of the late twentieth century is that those who protest – sing, write, perform or even just demur – have to use the high tech. media to get their message over. It is indeed richly ironic that programmes which warn of the dangers of the new technology urge viewers and listeners to contact their web-sites for further information. Yes, 'communication is power', but who will have this power in the future? Man or machine? Or will they be indistinguishable?

NOTES

1. *Longman Dictionary of the English Language* (Harlow, 1984), p. 1541.
2. Lewis Wolpert, *The Unnatural Nature of Science* (London, 1992), pp. 3–25.
3. Ibid., p. 178.
4. In 'Cyberbrain': a BBC Radio 4 *In Business* interview with financial correspondent Peter Day, 11 January 1999.
5. Brian Winston, *Media Technology and Society – A History: From the Telegraph to the Internet* (London, 1998) p. 2.
6. Ibid., pp. 1–2. Winston also quotes from Walter Benjamin's 'Theses on the Philosophy of History', *Illuminations* (New York, 1969).
7. Ibid., p. 2.
8. Paul Johnson writing in the *Daily Mail*, 17 September 1998.
9. *Daily Mail*, 18 September 1998.
10. Wolpert, op. cit.
11. And also addictive. It is an argument established memorably in William Sargant's *Battle for the Mind* (London, 1957). It has more recently been reinforced in a series of programmes called *Digital Planet* made by the Open University and broadcast on BBC 2 in January, 1999. In his book called *Virtual Reality: Exploring the Brave New Technologies of Artificial Experience and Interactive World from Cyberspace to Teledildonics* (London, 1991) Howard Rheingold has written: 'We can't stop VR, even if that is what we discover is the best thing to do' and adds it could create 'electronic LSD', that is 'simulations so powerfully addictive that they replace reality' (p. 19).
12. See Simon Reeve and Colin McGhee, *The Millennium Bomb: Countdown to a £400 billion Catastrophe* (London, 1996), pp. 163–4 and *passim*.
13. Donald Cardwell, *The Fontana History of Technology* (London, 1994), pp. 483–4.
14. Professor Charles Handy of the London Business School in 'Thought for the Day' on the *Today* programme, BBC Radio 4.
15. See Kevin Warwick, *The March of the Machines: Why the New Race of Robots will Rule the World* (London, 1997).

16. Winston, op. cit., pp. 333–4.
17. *The Web Story*, an Open University programme broadcast on BBC 2, 19 October 1998.
18. Warwick, op. cit.
19. *Daily Mail*, 1 October 1998, p. 25.
20. Rheingold, op. cit., p. 16.
21. The Darwin referred to here is of course Erasmus Darwin, grandfather and precursor of Charles, who published *The Loves of the Plants* (1789) and *Zoonomia, or the Laws of Organic Life* (1794–6).
22. Steve Jones, *The Language of the Genes* (London, 1994), Chapter 15, called 'Fear of Frankenstein'.
23. Ibid., p. 75.
24. Gina Kolata, *Clone: The Road to Dolly and the Path Ahead* (Harmondsworth, 1998), p. 25.
25. *Daily Mail*, 6, 17 and 22 February 1999. See also *Mail on Sunday* and *Observer* of 21 February 1999.
26. Such stories abounded during 1998. See the *Daily Mail*, 20 January, 9 and 10 June and 25 August. An article by Prince Charles in the *Telegraph* of 8 June attacking the makers of genetically modified food and speaking of their 'playing God' attracted a lot of interest and took on a 'keynote' significance for 'the man (and more particularly woman) in the street'.
27. *Daily Mail*, 20 January 1998. On 24 August a radio report stated that 'Clonapet' services were being offered on the Internet.
28. The report concerning Dr Seed was made on radio and television 7 January 1998, and Professor Lee Silver on 24 August and subsequently.
29. *Daily Mail*, 14 January 1999.
30. Ibid.
31. Marvin Minsky, 'Will Robots Inherit the Earth?', *Scientific American*, October 1994, vol. 271, no. 4, 86–91.
32. Ibid., 88.
33. Ibid.
34. Ibid., 89.
35. Ibid., 90.
36. Ibid., 91.
37. See the excellent discussion in Glenn and Susan Toole, 'Genetic Engineering', *Understanding Biology for Advanced Level* (Cheltenham, 1991), pp. 158–61.
38. See Ray Kemp, *The Politics of Radioactive Waste Disposal* (Manchester, 1992) especially Chapters 3 and 4.
39. Minsky, op. cit.
40. Reported on BBC Radio 4 on 16 October and 14 December 1998, respectively.
41. *Daily Mail*, 2 January 1999.
42. *Daily Mail*, 9 December 1998.
43. *Daily Mail*, 29 January 1998. Cf. also Geoffrey Lean, 'Big Brother is waiting at the Checkout', *Evening Standard*, 26 January 1999.
44. *Sunday Times*, 3 January 1999.
45. G.M. Trevelyan, *English Social History: A Survey of Six Centuries, Chaucer to Queen Victoria* (London, 1948), p. 585.
46. Pete Clark writing in the *Daily Mail*, 13 December 1998.
47. George Orwell, *The Road to Wigan Pier* (1937; Harmondsworth, 1962), p. 175.

48. H.G. Wells, *Mind at the End of its Tether* (London, 1945), especially pp. 17–19 and 30.

49. 'Henry James' in T.S. Eliot (ed.), *The Literary Essays of Ezra Pound* (London, 1954), p. 297. It is difficult to think of a major scientific or technological development of the last two hundred years that has not been anticipated in literature: Tennyson's 'In Memoriam' and 'Maud' anticipated Darwin's theory of evolution, Stevenson's *Dr. Jekyll and Mr. Hyde* Freud's ideas concerning 'dissociation' and H.G. Wells's *The Time Machine* Einstein's 'Special Theory of Relativity'. It is indeed true, as Percy Wyndham Lewis put it, that writers are 'the first men of a Future that has not materialised' (in *Blasting and Bombardiering*, 1927).

50. John Monk of the Open University took part in the *Digital Planet* series. (See Note 11, above.) The programmes also had valuable commentary from Kevin Warwick of Reading University.

51. Ibid.

CHAPTER ELEVEN

Epilogue and Overture

Clive Bloom

As the twentieth century slowly moved through the last years of its final decade a new sense of hope and purpose pervaded anticipations of the millennium. *Sensation*, an appropriately named showcase for Britain's leading younger artists, opened at the Royal Academy during the autumn of 1997. The exhibition attracted widespread publicity and scandal, being at once greeted as a revival of 1960s energy and as 1990s decadence. The long queues, media interest and artistic collective talent suggested a new beginning, with Britain as the 'hip' heart of culture just as it had been thirty years before when new artists had led the way. In the same year, Tony Blair, Britain's youngest Prime Minister since Pitt and leader of a revived Labour Party, won a huge victory over an exhausted and 'corrupt' Tory party. By the river Thames, a giant dome would house an exhibition looking to the next century – youthful and technological. Princess Diana had become the most famous and most glamorous person in the world: half-way between film star, glamour model and saint. And Britpop heralded Labour's new millennial 'cool Britannia'.

But things were not as they seemed. *Sensation*, on closer inspection, housed little that was new or truly innovative, little that suggested an artistic revolution. The very exhibition itself had been put together from the Saatchi collection whose owner, Charles Saatchi, had risen to fame and prominence under Margaret Thatcher. His wealth was derived from advertising, one of his chief clients being the Conservative Party. The exhibition itself, glowered over by a retro-image of child-killer Myra Hindley, included work by Britain's most famous artist of the late twentieth century, Damien Hirst. Hirst's, *The Physical Impossibility of Death in the Mind of Someone Living*, a giant fish tank filled by a tiger shark floating in formaldehyde solution, suggested less a brave new future than dead yuppiedom. The shark itself, dumb, moronic, tatty in its decay, suggested no brave tomorrow, whilst

259

Hirst's other work appeared little more than an unpleasant side-show freak display of animal carcasses – a type of ecofascism.

As for Tony Blair, a patent admirer of Mrs Thatcher and her reforms of welfare, it would not be long before he too would be tough-talking the welfare state into line, leading a Labour Party no longer so financially nor ideologically tied to its union base nor tied to traditional socialism. The Millennium Dome, like a circus tent, rose without sense of purpose or knowledge of what might fill it. The Dome would have to succeed despite almost total national disapproval of its vast cost. Like the century to come, there seemed little sense of purpose to the whole thing. And under all, the knowledge that the millennium had relevance only to Christians suggested not only the exclusion of a large percentage of Britain's population (all of its Asian and Jewish citizens) but also that it made no sense as a secular event.

On 31 August 1998 Princess Diana, returning home with her lover Dodi Fayed from a night at the Paris Ritz, was fatally injured in a car crash. In 1998 the two most popular films in Britain were *The Full Monty*, about a group of unemployed steel workers who fight their economic impotence by flaunting their sexual potency during a one-night striptease in front of wives and friends, and *Titanic*, the story of doomed romantic love aboard the most famous doomed ship of all, taking the hopes of early twentieth-century progress to the bottom of a watery grave.

The plain fact remained that the end of the twentieth century could offer little more than a requiem to itself rather than a fanfare for the future. Millennialism seemed, by a curious twist of fate, to have peaked in the 1960s, and it is no coincidence that this was the very period (in art, attitudes, popular music, fashion, etc.) that the 1990s chose to appropriate as a fitting symbol of itself. Yet what the 1960s had at best the 1990s had not at all: progress, modernisation, enlightenment, liberalism, purpose had all lost lustre and been discredited; space travel still had not opened up the cosmos to ordinary tourists; technology had created no new leisure culture in which humans could enjoy greater creativity, and if atomic warfare had not wiped out the planet ecological and terroristic activists threatened to do so. The actual hopes and dreams of 1960s radicalism became the empty rhetorics of 1990s management culture.

What ironically vanished in the 1990s was a rhetoric of progress – a language properly aimed toward and attempting to encapsulate the *idea* of a future. Of course, this is not to argue that time has stood still, but that since the fall of the Berlin Wall in 1989 the philosophy behind ideas about historical change and significant events has been dramatically challenged, specifically the theory and practice of Marxism, counterweight to capitalism.

Out of the struggle between these two ideologies came the Cold War, but with the end of the Soviet Bloc (Ronald Reagan's 'evil empire') and a new era of détente it appeared that Western liberal democracy was the only historically significant process, temporarily interrupted by a counter-force based on essentially false promises. Russia began economic reforms on Western lines. Nationalism re-emerged alongside democracy in the former Soviet Empire. The idea of a late- or post-capitalism out of which Europe, America and Japan were emerging now seemed a hollow dream. Instead, capitalism seems to be going through an even more vital phase, despite (or even because of) the vicissitudes of Far Eastern national economies. The end of Marxist 'history' marked the end of history as ideologically motivated and determined. The triumph of liberalism and therefore of individualism over collectivism seemed complete. It cannot be doubted that the future will be determined by a tension between a growing capitalist anarchism and larger, authoritarian governments (exemplified by a widening gap between the enfranchised and the marginalised). Moreover, new world power blocs will create strange alliances and geopolitical antagonisms.

In Britain, by a curiosity of fate, Thatcherism's assault on the legacy of the 1960s, an attack from within and *against* her own party, had the effect not only of creating a less tolerant and open society but also of demolishing the party political differences within which democratic values must be asserted in a parliamentary system. The rise of the big party has effectively cancelled parliamentary democracy for almost thirty years (1979 to 2008) whilst strengthening the power of governmental control and its subsidiary agencies. The rise of the 'eco-warrior' has done nothing to challenge this, nor will it.

Even the leading British music groups seemed to be affected by management culture, despite their reinvigoration of pop music. The refreshing nature of Blur, Pulp, Oasis, Supergrass or Suede was that they appeared to attempt to rethink and reconstitute pop music as a genre, one sufficiently old to have gained a venerable tradition. Yet this reawakening was itself less anti-establishment than anti-modernity. It was no coincidence that Blur's art-school-educated Damon Albarn (a friend of Damien Hirst), chose actor Phil Daniels to do the voice-over on 'Park Life', at once a song nostalgic not only for the 1970s and Daniels's own retro film *Quadrophenia* (the *Who's* own nostalgic reappraisal of the mid-1960s) but also for the working-class community Daniels's voice conjured up. Oasis (authentically working-class) directly borrowed from the Beatles and singer Liam Gallagher metamorphosed into a Lennon lookalike as the 1990s progressed. The revival of the 1960s and 1970s was repeated in the videos of both groups. Yet also underlying these artistic and fashion trends was another side: aggressive, cynical and (curiously for pop musicians) anti-American, from Damien Hirst's Blur video *Country House* which satirised American artist Jeff Koons to Jarvis Cocker of Pulp attempting to attack Michael Jackson at an awards ceremony or Oasis insulting American audiences and spitting on stage. This bad boy image was not the anti-establishment attitude prevalent in pop during the 1960s or even 1970s but rather the entrepreneurial bragging and cultural nostalgia of one form of patriotic Thatcherism, a form caught in embryo in the 1979 thriller film *The Long Good Friday* (itself an anticipation of the 'yuppie' revolution of self-made men). The knowingly post-modern pastiche evident in *both* music and videos made a music that, whilst singable and popular, lacked the necessary commitment to youth's anarchy and the refusal to conform found in authentic rock.

British pop had become by the late 1990s a form of retrogressive and reformist flag-waving exemplified by the hugely popular use of a union flag worn as a mini dress by 'Geri' of the Spice Girls. When Jarvis Cocker of Pulp asked 'where shall we be in the Year 2000?' he already knew – somewhere in the mid-1970s, a future already caught in the net of a past too wonderful to leave.

THE ROLE OF THE UNIVERSITY

The British university system has greatly changed over the last hundred years. At the beginning of the century only a tiny (and wealthy) proportion of the population enjoyed higher education. This meant, on the whole, the exclusion of middle- and working-class men, almost all women (from whatever class) and the possible ostracism of minority groups (such as Jews or Indians) who did get to university. Oxford and Cambridge still retained iron links to the Church of England. The attitudinal changes that followed the First World War provided only limited access to excluded groups and this continued with the redbrick university-building of the 1950s and 1960s, which coincided with the new educational opportunities provided by the welfare state. The organisation of lesser training and art colleges into polytechnics in the 1970s led to a great broadening of education via local public control and by the late 1980s such polytechnics, with their commitment to non-standard students, older returners or to those unable to attend traditional universities, were themselves renamed as 'new' universities catering both for the usual needs of higher education and the local needs of less advantaged communities. Although higher educational intake greatly increased in the 1980s and 1990s less than 15 per cent of the population actually enjoy higher education by the late 1990s. Whilst the new universities are dedicated to 'open' access this is not the case with the traditional establishments. With the ending of the binary divide between universities and polytechnics a new formula was soon found to continue the division between universities (whose title rendered them indistinguishable to outsiders). Older universities, with large government grants and endowments, renamed themselves (for official consumption) *research* institutes, suggesting that the 'newer' universities were merely training establishments.

Changes made in 1997 in government policy towards student grants are likely to 'trap' many at local universities, and whilst access may be increased changes will probably not impact on traditional or older universities at all. Indeed, access to higher education (in the name of democratic participation and egalitarianism) shows no signs of widening access to traditional knowledge rather than to reskilling *through* that knowledge. The widening of access has spawned a whole new vocabulary and a change of definition as to the purpose of education in 'life-long learning' processes. The older universities have almost entirely resisted or ignored this rhetoric so that educational division between the haves and have nots may even grow because of wider university access. Not what you know being important but where you went.

CRITICISM AT THE END OF THE CENTURY

The complexity of twentieth-century culture was matched by a correspondingly diverse and complex series of attempts to map it. The sheer weight of intellectual debate would have startled a Victorian, even more so because much of the consequences of Victorian social and cultural questioning form the basis of debates in the last hundred years. Beginning around the First World War and becoming institutionalised in the academies during the 1920s and 1930s a whole world of rarefied specialisms began to appear in order to tackle the questions, what is the meaning of culture? What is the status of literature? What is the nature of the human condition? Such questions were driven by problems that had arisen from the last third of the previous century, and the solutions – Marxism, Freudianism, liberalism and feminism – formed the framework for the ideological positions which animated academic thought. All of the debates which surrounded cultural problems were attempts to provide *sufficient* explanations for a century which appeared to move without meaning, morality or consequence. The problem of defining personal value, and consequently providing societal stability in a century of war, migration, civil disobedience, revolution and individual alienation, generated a war of words over the nature of cultural activity and the relationship such activity had to the central values of civilisation.

263

The emergence of literary studies as an academic discipline is an index of many of the arguments about value and cultural validation. The emergence of English Literature as the core of the modern humanities curriculum (thus replacing philosophy or classics) was based on a model which was both dynamic and conservative. Such a model required both professional attention to the technical details of modernity and the basic (and contrary) impulse toward a pre-modern and traditionalist organism. There is a clear continuity between T.S. Eliot in the early 1920s and I.A. Richards and F.R. Leavis later, both in terms of formal practical analysis and attention to the details of the tradition of English Literature. Leavis rejected Richards's pre-emptive theorising but retained his belief in practical and empirical reading and the essential value of literature to the community as a measure of 'health' and as a measure of moral cohesion. This adherence to the organic community (and its death) and a socialistic 'programme' of cultural analysis informs the later work of Richard Hoggart, Raymond Williams, George Steiner and the historian E.P. Thompson, all of whom show or openly acknowledge the influence of Leavisite humanism. The theoretical incursions of French critical thought from the late 1920s onwards, peaking and retreating in the middle 1980s, allowed a wide interpretation of humanist and Marxist practice without replacing them with continental anti-humanism. The rise of cultural studies, feminist linguistics and discourse analysis, post-colonial and media studies, born out of the fragmentation of the previous disciplines of English, History and Philosophy have not usurped the central place of English studies in most universities. Moreover the analytic practices in these new areas rarely supersede the older empiricist, humanist approaches they claim as redundant.

At the end of the twentieth century critical theory and practice have diversified, lost cohesion and a sense of purpose, perhaps, but hardly changed their underlying approaches. The assured continuance of new analytic practice, namely in cultural and media studies (electronically produced 'texts') does not suggest that English is under threat. English Literature will still retain a certain cachet and outlive fashionable changes, although it cannot be forgotten that only 100 years ago the study of contemporary English Literature was seen as a dangerous new fashion which threatened a classical education!

NEW AND FUTURE APPROACHES

The traditional books of the English literary tradition still retain a hold over the reading public and the academic specialists employed to analyse their significance: D.H. Lawrence and Jane Austen have not been replaced by the 'textuality' of cyberspace and Shakespeare is still, and will remain, a *required* component of all secondary educational and most higher educational establishments. What has changed is not the popularity of the 'classics' but the way academics read them. Older formal and practical exercises in 'correct' reading have been replaced by a greater contextualisation and approaches governed by non-literary concerns: feminism, gender studies, semiosis and post-colonial ethnicity. The rise of popular literary studies has placed great attention on the formal properties of genre but has done this in a way that takes up a *moral* position antithetical to the older studies of the canon. The integration of gender-based or ethnic approaches is now a regular feature of almost all literary courses and in some universities is a requirement. These approaches have had their greatest impact in cultural and media studies and have filtered back into literary circles. It may very well be that these approaches will diminish in years to come with a return to more formal practices and greater emphasis on the traditional body of English Literature.

These newer approaches have proved they provide only a limited revision of traditional perspectives and they have not revolutionised English as a subject. Indeed the easy assimilation of these approaches into the management-speak of university chancellors suggests that they contain reactionary, revisionist and deeply conservative elements antithetical to their original literary programme. Political correctness is the new authoritarianism of the late twentieth century. As we move into the twenty-first century it is clear that there is no one orthodoxy to which critics adhere, instead there is a competitive and heterodoxical group of approaches which are often mixed and matched eclectically. The tentative appearances of new human approaches (based on some Leavisite principles), new literary historical studies and eco-criticism have still to make a mark on mainstream literary debate. What is assured is the continuing rise in attention given to non-literary cultural artefacts even if the approaches remain relatively static. The postmodern theoretical landscape has not yet replaced the modernist paradigm, rather incorporating it into a melange of possibilities.

BRITISH CULTURE AT THE MILLENNIUM

The Millennium Dome tempts us with its carnival of the future, but the new techno-world may hide more prosaic realities and yet more intractable problems. After 100 years of economic growth and social change and despite the much-heralded end of working-class impoverishment in the glow of late capitalist consumerism, little has changed to alter the actual social fabric of Britain. The ownership of land and exercise of power remain essentially with the very same type of people who had it at the start of the century; corporations and multinationals control most wealth and remain in the hands of those financial institutions (and families) that ran Britain before the First World War; a very large proportion of the British population still live in poverty; family structures continue to disintegrate; union power has ceased to exist; criminality has not been stamped out despite increasing use of surveillance; the class system is more entrenched than ever; racism is a fact of inner city life; redundancy has become a matter of expectation for those unable to meet the exhortation to reskill. Thatcherite policies are now the bedrock of reinvented Labour under prime minister Tony Blair; *plus ça change, plus cést la même chose.*

It is undoubtedly true that Britain became a more fair and equal society between 1948 and 1979, but it is equally true that the grains of social welfare and liberalised attitudes were soon slowly being removed, and it can be claimed that although far from halcyon the great period of social reform and cultural vitality was a mere experiment from which rights and expectations were soon slowly withdrawn. Britain in the late 1990s is undoubtedly a less liberal and equitable society than in, for example, the late 1950s, a decade usually considered repressive and conformist.

It remains to be seen whether Scottish and Welsh devolution, the reform of the House of Lords and emerging social welfare policies will radically alter Britain into being a more compassionate place whose individual citizens feel a greater participatory urge than hitherto. It is unlikely that such a change will come about. Scottish and Welsh 'independence' may produce harder and cruder nationalisms, the reform of parliament just allow for stronger and less challengeable government, social policy changes create a more managed and compliant populace.

The reconstitution of power relations which Labour policy will determine until at least 2004 will probably continue under a Tory party which may gain victory after Labour has had two terms in office. Labour's reform of power will almost certainly benefit Conservatism as both parties effectively abandon their old twentieth-century *raisons d'être*. Instead political consensus may allow the rise of large fringe parties or sudden eruptions of single-issue groups, especially in Wales and Scotland and around ecological issues (cloning, GM food issues, management of water policy, etc.). As nationalism and regionalism grow forms of extremist politics may also emerge where local disenfranchised groups of the poor or elderly feel threatened. It may well be that such stirrings occur in the countryside, rather than the inner city, where those that farm or live off the land begin to find their way of life threatened, as actually occurred in 1997. *The questions of the twenty-first century may well be the nature and freedom (the rights) of the citizen, where responsibility and duty are used as governmental catch phrases to diminish choice, access and freedom of action. Could the first British refusnik appear by mid-century?

The possibility of an ethnically diverse, regionally vibrant, economically booming country playing its full part in the European Union on the strength of the Euro and fully engaged in the process of technological innovation may well be attractive and greatly to be desired. The Millennium Dome heralds such an age. And such an age is predicated on ethnic and regional diversity and tolerance underpinned by a fully digitalised information network embracing every aspect of economic and cultural life.

The question of what forms culture may take or what genres may arise requires us to look back into the twentieth century and forward into the next. It is quite clear that literature (the printed word) will not simply vanish as so-called 'dumbing down' continues. Instead, the novel, for instance, will become further enmeshed within a complex web of other media possibilities both televisual and filmic. Even the traditional serious narrative novel (central to the English tradition) is in no fear of extermination given a new lease of life via prize promotions and sales hype. The remarkable recovery of the film industry and the emergence of the multiple cinema in Britain suggest a rise in film-going in the next century as cinemas become leisure centres catering for pre- and post-film entertainment. The book and film are unlikely to fade away: both offer total, embracing experiences and both offer the consumer the simplest and cheapest means of retrieval for what are highly complex and sophisticated forms of cultural artefact.

What will change will be the multiplicity of means of retrieval, especially through digitalisation and computing. Neither books nor films will be able to exist as just themselves, as cyberculture offers a multiplicity of options for experiencing them: linear retrieval will become fully holistic as cyberspace becomes able to reproduce photographic realism via digitalisation. This is a prediction we can safely make based upon current technological knowledge. What remains beyond the next fifty years is another matter.

Index

A Taste of Honey, 102
Absence of War, The, 106
Absolute Beginners, 61
Absolutely Fabulous, 201
abstraction, 206–8
Ackroyd, Peter, 66
Adler, Carine, 174
advertising, newspaper, 126
aesthetics of popular fiction, 89–92
Afore Night Come, 103–4
African Headcharge, 235
Akhtar, Nijma, 234
Albert Angelo, 63
Albion Band, 227
Alexandria Quartet, 55–6, 60
Allen, Jim, 184, 186
Allen, Kevin, 174
Alloway, Lawrence, 205, 212
Althusser, Louis, 17, 19
Alvarez, Alfred, 42, 59
amateur music making, 224–5
amateur theatre, 97
Ambler, Eric, 80
Amis, Kingsley, 12, 53, 54
Amis, Martin, 60, 70–1
Anderson, Lindsay, 143, 162
Andre, Carl, 214
Ang, Ien, 87
Angry Young Men, 53, 143, 146

Annan Committee (on broadcasting), 186, 191
Another Country (film), 167
anti-modernism, 53, 217–18
Apache Indian, 236
Appleyard, Brian, 253
Araeen, Rashid, 214
Archer, Jeffrey, 64, 78
Armchair Theatre (series), 180, 182
Armitage, Simon, 45
Arnatt, Keith, 216
art, 204–22, 259–60
Art and Language (group), 216
Artaud, Antonin, 103, 104
Arts Lab, 104
Artscribe, 218
Asian Dub Foundation, 236
Asian–British theatre, 118–19
Asian-derived music, 233–5
Association for Research in Popular fiction, 76
Association of Independent Producers, 164
Attitudes Become Form (exhibition), 215
Auden, W.H., 29
audience shares, TV, 198
autobiography in poetry, 37–44
Ayckbourn, Alan, 108, 115–17
Ayres, Gillian, 205, 206

Bacon, Francis, 219, 220
Bacon, Roger (economist), 8
Ballad of Peckham Rye, The, 59
Ballard, J.G., 64, 88
Ballykissangel, 201
Balthazar, 56
Banks, Iain, 69
Barber, Anthony, 4
Barker, Clive, 86
Barker, Pat, 72
Barnes, Julian, 66
Barstow, Stan, 54
Barthes, Roland, 89
Baudrillard, Jean, 222
Bay City Rollers, 229
BBC, impact of ITV on, 177–81
BBC1, 193, 198, 200
BBC2, 193, 198, 200, 201
Beat Girl, 144, 149, 150
Beatles, 160, 225, 229
Beaufoy, Simon, 172
Beckett, Samuel, 104, 109
Bedroom Farce, 116
Bell, The, 59
Benjamin, Walter, 46
Bennett, Alan, 45, 105–6, 107
Berger, John, 63, 207
Berman, Ed, 104
Berwick Street Collective, 164
bestseller lists, 81
Betjeman, John, 38–9
Between the Lines, 201
Bhaji on the Beach, 173
bhangra, 233, 234, 236
Big Bang, 8
Billington, Michael, 115
Billy Cotton Band Show, 231
Billy Liar! (film), 159
Birt, John, 199–200
Black and White Minstrel Show, 231
Black British theatre, 119
Black, Conrad, 140
Black Dogs, 70
Black Lace (imprint), 83
Black Monday, 8

Blackwell, Chris, 234–5
Blair, Tony, 9, 259, 260, 266
Blake, Peter, 211
Bleasdale, Alan, 193, 194
Bloody Chamber, The, 67
Bloom, Clive, 76, 85
Blue Lamp, The, 144
blues, 226
Blunkett, David, 9
Blur, 225, 236, 261
Bolt, Robert, 110
Bond, Edward, 101, 104–5
Bond films, 157–8
book censorship, end of, 79
bookselling, 81–2
Boorstin, Daniel, 240
Bowie, David, 225, 229–30
Boxer, The, 173
Boys from the Blackstuff, 193–4
Braine, John, 15
Brass Eye, 201
Brassed Off, 171, 172
Bratby, John, 207
Braveheart, 173
Brechtian theatre, 109–10
Brenton, Howard, 102
bricolage, 31–2
Bridge on the River Kwai, The, 143, 158
Briefing for a Descent into Hell, 58
Briggflatts, 39, 40–1, 42
*British Art in the Twentieth Century –
   The Modern Movement* (exhibition),
   219–20
British Rail flotation, 9
British Telecom privatised, 8
Britishness, 12
Britpop, 236, 261–2
broadcasting *see* radio; television
*Broadcasting in the 90s: Competition,
   Choice and Quality* (White Paper),
   195–6
Brook, Peter, 103, 110
Brooke-Rose, Christine, 63
Brookner, Anita, 72
Brookside, 192

Brown, Gordon, 10
Brunsdon, Charlotte, 196
BSB (British Satellite Broadcasting), 197
Bunting, Basil, 39–42
Burgess, Anthony, 58
Burgin, Victor, 214, 215, 216
Burn, Gordon, 140
Busconductor Hines, The, 68–9
Byatt, A.S., 66
Byers, Stephen, 10

cable television, 197–8
Caine, Michael, 229
Callaghan, James, 3, 6
Calvino, Italo, 77
Campaign for Quality Television, 196
Capercaillie, 227
capital punishment abolished, 4
Captain Corelli's Mandolin, 71
Cardiac Arrest, 201
Cardwell, Donald, 243
Caretaker, The, 108, 110, 113, 114
Caribbean-derived music, 233–5
Carleton-Greene, Hugh, 181–2
Carlos Williams, William, 31
Caro, Anthony, 213
Carr, Robert, 4
Carry On films, 145, 155–6
Carter, Angela, 56, 66–7
Cartland, Barbara, 63, 80
Castle, Barbara, 3
Cathy Come Home, 184
Caughie, John, 149, 188, 193–4
Caulfield, Patrick, 211
celebrity fiction, 78, 80
Celtic bands, 227
Cement Garden, The, 70
censorship
  books, 79
  film, 152–3
  theatre, 100–1
Central TV, 199
Centre for Contemporary Cultural Studies, 18

Chada, Gurinder, 174
Chandra, Sheila, 234
Channel 4, 191–3, 198, 201
  films, 145–6, 167–70, 172
Channel 5, 198
Chariots of Fire, 164, 166–7, 168
Chas 'n' Dave, 225
Chatterton, 66
Chatwin, Bruce, 66
Chicken Soup with Barley, 106
Child in Time, The, 70
Children of Violence, 58
Christie, Agatha, 137
Churchill, Caryl, 102
cinema, 143–75
  attendance, 144, 163, 170, 190
Cinema Action, 164
City, 33, 34, 36
City of Spades, 61
Clapton, Eric, 234
Clark, Thomas A, 36
Clause 4, New Labour and, 9–10
cliché, in poetry, 25–8
Clifford, James, 33–4
Clockwork Orange, A, 58
Cocker, Jarvis, 261
Coelbeg, 227
Cohen, Bernard, 205, 206
Cohen, Stan, 232
Collings, Matthew, 218
Collins, Joan, 78
Comfort of Strangers, 70
commercial television, inception, 177–80
commercial theatre, 96
conceptual art, 215–17, 220–1
Connery, Sean, 157, 229
Conquest, Robert, 45
Conservative governments, 1, 2–3, 4–5, 6–8
constructions, 209–10, 211, 215
constructivists, 209–10
consumerism as culture, 19–21
control of technology, 239, 252–6
Cookson, Catherine, 63, 77, 78, 81, 83

Cool Britannia, 173, 259
Cops, The, 201
Cornwell, Patricia, 137
Coronation Street, 14, 83, 98, 179, 180, 182
Cosh Boy, 144
Cotton, Billy, 224
Cragg, Tony, 220
Craig-Martin, Michael, 215, 220
Crash, 88
Crichton Smith, Ian, 119
Croker, Arthur and Marilouise, 256
Crow, 26–8
Crying Game, The, 171
Cudlipp, Hugh, 125, 134
Culture Club, 236
culture *see* society
Curse of Frankenstein, 144, 152
Curse of the Werewolf, The, 152
Cut Pages, The, 35
cybernetics, 250–2, 255

Dad's Army, 183
Daily Express, 125, 126
Daily Mail, 125, 136, 137, 139
Daily Mirror, 125, 126, 128, 131–3
Daily Sketch, 126
Daily Star, 127
Daily Telegraph, 138
Dam Busters, The, 143, 158
dance bands, 226, 227
Dance to the Music of Time, A, 51
Daniel, Sarah, 98
Darkness Visible, 59
Darling, 159
Darling, Alistair, 10
Davie, Alan, 208–9
Davie, Donald, 38–9
Davies, Terence, 174
Days of Hope, 186–8, 189, 193
de Bernières, Louis, 71
de Man, Paul, 42–3, 46
Deacon, Richard, 220
Dead Babies, 71
Dead Man Upright, 86

Death of a Princess, 188
Death on the Rock, 197
Deighton, Len, 64
Delaney, Shelagh, 102
Denny, Robyn, 204–5, 206
Desperately Seeking an Audience, 87
detective fiction, 84–5
  and Yorkshire Ripper reporting, 135–9
devolution, 266
Diana, Princess of Wales, 259, 260
digital television, 202, 243
Dillons, 81
disco boom, 233
Diverse Reports, 192
Dixon of Dock Green, 179, 182, 189
Dockery and Son, 25, 28
Doctor at Large, 143
Doctor in the House, 143
Doctor Who, 183–4
Dodd, Ken, 227
Dolly the sheep, 247–8
Domestic Violence and Matrimonial Proceedings Act, 5
Donegan, Lonnie, 227
Dr Finlay's Casebook, 182, 183
Dr No (film), 157
Drabble, Margaret, 52, 57, 58
Dracula (film), 152
drama-documentary, 188–9
Driver's Seat, The, 59
Dunn, Nell, 184
Durrell, Lawrence, 55–6

East is East, 118–19
EastEnders, 98, 194–5
Eco, Umberto, 84
economic policy, 1–11
Edgar, David, 102
Edge of Darkness, 194
Elsaesser, Thomas, 170
Eltis, Walter, 8
Emigrants, The, 61
Empire Trilogy, 61
English Stage Company, 95

Englishman Abroad, An, 106, 107
Englishness, 12
Entertainer, The, 109
Entertaining Mr Sloane, 110–11
Equal Pay Act, 5
ethnography
  poetry, 33–4
  popular fiction, 77, 87
European Convention on Human
    Rights, 11
European Exchange Rate Mechanism
    (ERM), 9
Evans, Harold, 130
experimental novels, 62–3
Eye in the Door, The, 72

Faith, Adam, 227
Faith in Fakes, 84
farce, 111
Farrell, J.G., 61
fast-sellers list, 81
Fell, Alison, 72–3
feminism
  and novels, 52, 66–7
  and theatre, 102
fiction
  newspaper reports as, 127
  popular, 76–92
  writing, 51–73
Figes, Eva, 63
films, 143–75
First Love, Last Rites, 70
Fisher, Roy, 32–7, 46, 47
Flame in the Streets, 144, 150
Flanagan, Barry, 215, 217
Flaubert's Parrot, 66
Fleet Street, press move from, 131,
    133–4
Fleming, Ian, 126
Fluck, Winifred, 89
folk music, 226–7
Forrest-Thompson, Veronica, 26–8,
    46
Forrester, Helen, 83
Forster, E.M., filmed novels, 167

Forsyth, Frederick, 64, 77
Foster, Hal, 218, 220
Four Weddings and a Funeral, 171
Fowler, Bridget, 87
Fowles, John, 66
Francis, Dick, 81
free assembly rights, 11
Free Cinema movement, 143
Freeze (exhibition), 220–1
French Lieutenant's Woman, The, 66
Freud, Esther, 72
Freud, Lucien, 219, 220
Friday Alternative, The, 192
Fried, Michael, 212–13
fringe theatre, 96
From Russia with Love
  film, 157
  novel, 126
From the Frontier of Writing, 46
Frost, Terry, 208
Full Monty, The, 171, 172, 173, 260
Fullalove, 140
Fuller, Peter, 218–19
Fun'da'mental, 236
Funeral in Berlin, 64
Furnace, A, 34, 35, 46

G. (novel), 63
Galton, Alan, 97–8
Galton, Ray, 182
Garnett, Tony, 186, 200–1
Garrick Year, The, 57
Gasiorek, Andrzej, 65
gay theatre, 102
genetic engineering, 246–52
genetically modified foods, 247
genre novels, 63–4
Georgy Girl (film), 159
Ghost Road, The, 72
Gilbert and George, 216, 217
Girls of Slender Means, The, 59
glam rock, 229
Glasgow University Media Group, 189
Golden Notebook, The, 56, 57–8
Goldfinger (film), 157

Golding, William, 59
Goldsmiths' Art College, 220
Good Morning, Midnight, 62
Good Terrorist, The, 72
Gordon, Giles, 63
Gorgon, The, 152, 154
gothic movies, 144, 151–4
gothic writing, 85–6
Graham Bond Organisation, 234
Gramsci, Antonio, 18, 19
Granada TV, 199
Gray, Alasdair, 69
Gray, Simon, 107–8
Green, Peter, 234
Greenaway, Peter, 174
Greenberg, Clement, 204, 210,
    212–13, 222
Grove Family, 179, 180
Guardian, 131, 133
Guerillas, 62
Guyana Quartet, The, 56

Haines, Jim, 104
Hall, Stuart, 18
Hamilton, Alex, 81
Hamilton, Richard, 209–10
Hammer horror films, 144, 151–4
Hampton, Christopher, 109
Hancock, Tony, 97
Hancock's Half Hour, 97
Handsworth Songs, 169–70
Hard Day's Night, A (film), 157, 160
Hare, David, 102, 103, 106
Harriott, Joe, 234
Harris, Rolf, 227
Harris, Thomas, 86, 137
Harris, Wilson, 56
Hartoum, Mona, 221
Harvey, Marcus, 221
Harvey, Sylvia, 192–3
Hastings, Max, 129
Haw Lantern, The, 46
Hawksmoor, 66
health service privatisation, 9
Healy, Denis, 5

Heaney, Seamus, 46
Heartbeat, 199
Heath, Edward, 4, 5
Heathcoat-Amery, Derick, 2
Hebdige, David, 232
Hendrix, Jimi, 234
Hepworth, Barbara, 208, 209
heritage cinema, 167, 171–2
heritage television drama, 196–7, 200
Heron, Patrick, 206–7, 208, 212
Hideous Kinky, 72
Higgins, Jack, 80
Higson, Andrew, 163
Hill, Anthony, 209
Hill, John, 148
Hill, Susan, 79
Hilliard, John, 216
Hillsborough disaster, *Sun* coverage,
    127, 130
Hilton, Roger, 208
hip-hop, 233
Hirst, Damien, 221, 222, 259–60, 261
historical detective fiction, 84–5
Hitler diaries episode, 129
Hobsbawm, Eric, 217
Hockney, David, 211–12
Hodgkin, Howard, 219
Hoggart, Richard, 14, 18
Hollywood, and British film revival,
    156–7
Holocaust, and the novel, 58–60
Homecoming, The, 113
homosexuality decriminalised, 4
Hough, Graham, 16
Hound of the Baskervilles, The (film),
    152, 154
House for Mr Biswas, A, 62
house music, 233, 235
House of America, 173
Howard, Michael, 11
Howard, Philip, 119
Howard's End (film), 167, 171
Howe, Geoffrey, 7
Hoyland, John, 205
Hughes, Ted, 26–8

Human Genetics Advisory Committee, 249
Human Genome Project, 247
human rights, 11
Hume, Gary, 221
Hunt, Marsha, 234
Hutchings, Peter, 153, 154
Hutton, Will, 8
Hyland, Brian, 227

I'm Talking About Jerusalem, 106
ideology in popular fiction, 83–4
If... (film), 162
In Between the Sheets, 70
In Place of Strife, 3–4
Independent, 134
independent cinema, 162–5
Independent Film-Makers' Association, 164, 191
Independent Group (IG), 209–10
Independent Television (ITV), 177–86, 191–2, 198
Independent Television Commission, 196
Index 01, 216
Indi-pop, 236
Indo-Jazz Fusions, 234
information technology, 242–6
Insights series, 76
Inspector Morse, 98, 195
Insular Possession, An, 72
Interaction (theatre), 104
International Monetary Fund (IMF), 5–6
Internet, 243, 244–5
Ionesco, eugene, 104
irony in poetry, 45–7
Ishiguro, Kazuo, 72
Island Records, 234–5
ITV, 177–86, 191–2, 198

Jagger, Mick, 228
James Bond films, 157–8
James, P.D., 138–9
James, Susannah, 79

Jellicoe, Ann, 103
Jenkins, Roy, 3
Jethro Tull, 229
Job Seekers' Allowance, 10
John Mayall's Bluesbreakers, 234
Johnson, B.S., 63
Johnson, Paul, 253
Jones, Allen, 211
Jones, Jack, 5
Jones, Steve, 247
Jordan, Marion, 156
Justine (Durrell), 55

Kapoor, Anish, 220
Kelman, James, 68–9
Kennedy, A.L., 73
Keynesianism, 6, 11
Khan-Din, Ayub, 118–9
Kind of Alaska, A, 113–14
Kind of Loving, A
    film, 147, 157
    novel, 54
Kinks, 225
Kiss FM, 233
Kitaj, R.B., 211
Kitchen poems, 42
'Kitchen Sink' artists, 207
Knack, The, 157, 160–1
Kops, Bernard, 108
Kula Shakar, 234
Kureishi, Hanif, 168–9

Labour governments, 1, 3–4, 5–6
    see also New Labour
Lady Chatterley's Lover trial, 79
Laing, Jacqueline, 253
Lamb, Larry, 130
Lambert, Verity, 183–4
Lamming, George, 61
Lanark: A Life in 4 Books, 69
Lanyon, Peter, 208
Larch Covert, 37
Larkin, Philip, 12, 25, 26, 28–30, 35, 47
Late Capitalism, 78

Law and Order, 186, 188
Le Carré, John, 64
Lear (Bond), 104–5
Leavis, F.R., 15, 20, 81
Lee, Edward, 224
Legacy, The, 89–92
Legion Hall Bombing, The, 186, 188
Leigh, Mike, 174, 186
Lennon, John, 228
Les Miserables, 100
Lessing, Doris, 56, 57–8, 72
Lévi-Strauss, Claude, 31–2
Lide, Mary, 91–2
Life and Loves of a She-Devil, The, 70
Life support, 108
Light Programme (BBC), 230
Lisson Gallery, 220
literary criticism, 263–4
literature, 263–5
    and culture, 19–21
Littlewood, Joan, 102, 110
Lloyd, A.L., 226
Lloyd, Selwyn, 2
Lloyd Webber, Andrew, 100, 225
Loach, Ken, 174, 185, 186
local authority powers, 10–11
Lochhead, Liz, 119
London Fields, 71
London Film-Makers' Co-op, 164
London Trilogy, 61
London Women's Film Group, 164
Loneliness of the Long Distance Runner,
    The (film), 157
Long, Richard, 215, 216
Look Back in Anger
    film, 144, 147
    novel, 13, 53, 94–6, 105, 125
Loot, 104, 111, 112
Lord of the Flies, 59
Love Over Gold, 79
Lucky Jim, 12, 53
Lyotard, Jean-Francois, 217–18

MacColl, Ewan, 226
Macherey, Pierre, 17

MacInnes, Colin, 61
Macintosh, Cameron, 100
Mackenzie, Kelvin, 127
Macleod, Ian, 2
Macmillan, Harold, 2
Major, John, 9
Man for All Seasons, A, 110
management theory and language, 21
Mandel, Ernest, 78
Manderley, 79
Mann, Steve, 255
Marat/Sade, 103–4
Marley, Bob, 235
Marowitz, Charles, 104
Martin, Kenneth, 209
Martin, Mary, 209
Marxist structuralism, 17
mass culture, 15–16
Massive Attack, 236
Maudling, Reginald, 3
Maxwell, Robert, 127, 128, 130
McCartney, Paul, 228
McCracken, Scott, 76
McEwan, Ian, 70
McGrath, John, 186, 188
McLaren, Malcolm, 230
McLean, Bruce, 215
McLuhan, Marshall, 244, 254
Meadows, Shane, 174
Media Technology and Society, 240
Memento Mori, 59
men, portrayal in cinema, 146–7,
    153–4, 156
Mercer, David, 184
merchandising, books, 81–2
Merseybeat, 227–8
metamorphosis in poetry, 35–6
Middleditch, Edward, 207
Middleton, Stanley, 72
Midnight's Children, 52, 67
milk, free school, 4
millennium, 259–60, 265–7
Millennium Dome, 259, 260
Mills & Boon, 80, 82, 83
Minder, 195

miners' strikes, 4–5, 7
minimalists (art), 214
Minsky, Marvin, 249–51
Minton, John, 204–5
Mirror, see Daily Mirror
Mitchell, Julien, 108
Mo, Timothy, 72
mobile telephones, 244
Modern Painters, 218–19
modernism, 12, 13
  art, 212–15
Momma Don't Allow, 143
Monboit, George, 11
monetarism, 6–8, 11–12
Money, 71
Monk, Claire, 173
Monk, John, 255
Monocled Mutineer, The, 194
Monsanto, 247–8
Monty Python films, 163
Moorcock, Michael, 64
Moore, Henry, 213, 220
Morecombe and Wise, 225
Morris, Chris, 201
Mosco, Maisie, 83
Mountain Language, 115
Mountolive, 55–6
Movement, the, 12–14, 45, 53
movies, 143–75
Mr Love and Mr Justice, 61
multicultural society, 52
Mummy, The, 152, 154
Murdoch, Iris, 59
Murdoch, Rupert, 127, 128, 129, 130, 133–4
Murphy, Robert, 148
music hall
  and popular music, 225, 227
  and theatre, 109–10
music: popular, 224–37
musical comedy, 225
musical theatre, 100
Musicians' Union, 226
My Beautiful Launderette (film), 168–9

Naipaul, V.S., 61–2
Name of the Rose, The, 84–5
National Economic Development council, 2–3
National Health Service, 2, 9
national identity, 12
National Public Order Intelligence Act, 11
National Union of Seamen, 5
nationalism, post-Soviet, 260–1
Neaptide, 98
Nelson, Robin, 199
netmarketing, 244
Neuberger, Rabbi Julia, 85
New Labour, 9–11, 173, 259, 260, 266
New Lines, 45
New Poetry, The, 42, 59
new wave cinema, 143–4
Newman, G.F., 186
Newman, Sydney, 180, 182
News Corporation Limited, 78
News International, 129
News of the World, 127–8
News on Sunday, 128
newspapers, 125–40
newsprint rationing, and advertising, 126
Nicholson, Ben, 208
Night Mail, 29
Nights at the Circus, 67
No Man's Land, 115
nomadic radio, 255
Norman Conquests, The, 108, 116–17
North Sea oil, 6, 8
Northern Soul movement, 233
Nothing But the Best, 157
novels, 51–73
  popular fiction, 76–92
nuclear power privatisation, 9

O Dreamland, 143
Oasis, 236, 261
Observer, 125
Of Shade and Shadow, 36, 37

Ofili, Chris, 221
Oh Calcutta, 101
Oh What a Lovely War, 110
Old Country, The, 106
One Fat Englishman, 54
Open Space Theatre, 104
Open University, 4, 18
Opie, Julian, 220, 222
Oranges are not the Only Fruit, 72
Orton, Joe, 104, 105, 110–13
Osborne, John, 13, 53, 94–6, 105,
    109, 156
Other People, 71
Other Story, The (exhibition), 214
Oulton, Therese, 219
Our Friends in the North, 201
Owen, Alun, 180

painting, 204–9, 211–12, 220, 221
Palace of the Peacock, 56
Paolozzi, Edward, 210
Paradise Lost, A (exhibition), 220
Pargiter, Edith, 85
Party Time, 114, 115
Pasmore, Victor, 209
Passage to India, A (film), 167
Passion of New Eve, The, 67
pay policies, 2, 3
Pearson plc, 78
Peeping Tom, 152
Pennies From Heaven, 99
Pentangle, 227
Performance (film), 162
performance-related pay, 9
Peters, Ellis, 85
petit bourgeois culture, 12
Pevsner, Nikolaus, 12
Phantom of the Opera, 100
Phillips, Caryl, 119
photographs, in artworks, 216
Pilger, John, 128, 133
Pilkington Committee (on
    broadcasting), 180–1
Pillow-boy of the Lady Onogoru, The,
    72–3

Pincher Martin, 59
Pink Floyd, 229
Pinter, Harold, 104, 108, 110, 113–15,
    180
Play for Today (series), 186, 193
plays, 94–120
Pleasure of the Text, The, 89
Ploughman's Lunch, The, 70
    film, 168
Plunder, 111
pluralism in cinema, 173–5
Poe, Edgar Allen, 135–6
Poetic Artifice, 26
poetry, 25–47
Pogues, 227
police, Sheehy Committee on pay, 9
politics
    Conservative, 1, 2–3, 4–5, 6–8
    Labour, 1, 3–4, 5–6
    New Labour, 9–11, 173, 259, 260,
        266
    and newspapers, 129–31
    and television, 185, 187–92
    see also Thatcherism
Pollock, Jackson, 207, 208–9
pop art, 209–12
pop culture, in cinema, 158–62
pop music, 224–37, 261–2
Poplars, The, 36
popular culture, 15–16, 18
popular fiction, 76–92
popular music, 224–37
Possession, 66
post-structuralism, 17–18, 19–21
*Post-war British Fiction: Realism and
    After*, 65
postmodernism
    art, 217–18
    novels, 51, 53, 54–5, 64–8
    popular fiction, 78
Potter, Dennis, 99, 184, 186, 194
Potter, Sally, 174
Powell, Anthony, 51
Powell, Michael, 152
Pratchett, Terry, 64

press barons, 128–9
Prime of Miss Jean Brodie, The, 59
print unions, Murdoch and, 133–4
prisons privatisation, 9
Private Eye, 127, 139
privatisation, 7–8, 9
Profumo affair, *Daily Mirror* and, 132
progressive music, 229
provincial theatre, 97
provincial *vs* metropolitan values, 12–14
Prynne, Jeremy, 42–4
psychology and the novel, 58–60
psychopathology in fiction, 85
publishing industry, 77, 78–81, 82–3
Puffball, 57
Pulp (group), 225, 261
punk rock, 230
Pusztai, Arpad, 248
Pynchon, Thomas, 63

Quart, Leonard, 165
Quartermaine's Terms, 107–8
Quatermass Experiment, The, 144
Quatermass II, 153
Question of Attribution, A, 106

Race Relations Act, 11
Rachel Papers, The, 71
racism, cinema depictions, 144, 150–1
radical gay theatre, 102
Radio 1, 230
Radio 2, 231
radio and popular music 230–1
Radio Caroline, 230
Radway, Janice, 87
rail privatisation, 9
Raj Quartet, The, 60–1
rave subculture, 233
Ravenhill, Mark, 102–3
Raymond, Derek, 86
Reach for the Sky, 143
readers, popular fiction, 77, 87–9
realism in novels, 65
Rees-Mogg, William, 133
Regeneration, 72

reggae, 233, 234–5
Reisz, Karel, 143
Reith, John, 179
Remains of the Day, The, 72
Rendell, Ruth, 64, 80
Republic of Technology, The, 240
Rhys, Jean, 62
rhythm 'n' blues, 226–7
Rice, Tim, 100
Richard, Cliff, 227, 228
Richards, Jeffrey, 159–60
Richards, Keith, 228
Richardson, Jo, 5
Richardson, Tony, 143, 159, 160
Riley, Bridget, 206
Rob Roy, 173
robotics and genetics, 250–2
rock 'n' roll, 227
Rock Against Racism, 235
Rolling Stones, 132, 226, 228
  Daily Mirror and, 132–3
Rolls Royce, 4
romance fiction, 83
Room at the Top, 53, 54
  film, 144, 147
Room with a View, A (film), 167
Rosencrantz and Guildenstern are Dead,
  117
Roshier, Bob, 135, 139
Round and Round the Garden, 116–17
Rowett Research Institute, 248
Roxy Music, 225, 229–30
Royal College of Art, 204, 210
Royal Court Theatre, 95
Royal Opera House, 118
Royal Variety Command Performance,
  225
Royle Family, 201
Rudkin, David, 103–4
Runrig, 227
Rushdie, Salman, 52, 66, 67–8
Ruskin, John, 39

Saatchi, Charles, 259
Sandford, Jeremy, 184, 186

Sapphire, 144, 150–1
Satanic Verses, The, 67–8
satellite television, 197–8
Saturday Night and Sunday Morning, 53
    film, 147, 148
Saussure, Ferdinand, 16, 20
Savage Mind, The, 31
Saved, 101
Sawney, Nitin, 234
Schlesinger, John, 159
science, 239–56
Science and Technology, House of
    Lords Select Committee on, 8
science fiction, 64
Scientific American, 249
Scott, J.D., 53
Scott, Paul, 60–1
Scottish films, 172–3
Scottish writing, 68–9, 72–3
sculpture, 215, 220, 221
Seed, Richard, 248
Seige of Krishnapur, The, 61
Selecter (band), 236
Sensation (exhibition), 221, 259
sensationalism in newspapers, 127–9
Serpentine Gallery, 221
Severed Head, A, 59
Sex Discrimination Act, 5
sex in popular fiction, 83, 88
Sex Pistols, 230
Sexing the Cherry, 70
Shadow Dance, 66–7
Shame, 67
Sheila Chandra, 234
Sherwood, Adrian, 235
Shiva Nova, 234
Shock! Horror! The Tabloids in Action,
    139–40
Shopping and Fucking, 102–3
show business, news as, 127–9
Shrimpton, Jean, 229
sick building syndrome, 245–6
Siklos, Richard, 140
Silence of the Lambs, 86
    film, 137

Sillitoe, Alan, 53
Silver, Lee, 249, 253
Simon, Sir David, 10
Simpson, Alan, 182
Simpson, Ray, 97–8
Singapore Grip, The, 61
Singh, Talvin, 234
Singing Detective, The, 194
Sisterly Feelings, 116
Situation exhibition, 205–6
Six Day War, 3
Sixteen Sonnets, 36
Sketch for a Financial Theory of the Self,
    42–4
skiffle, 227
Sky TV, 197
Small Faces, 225
Smiley's People, 64
Smith, Anthony, 198
Smith, Austin, 249
Smith, David, 213
Smith, Dick, 204–5
Smith, Jack, 207
Snow, C.P., 12
Snowdon, Anthony Armstrong-Jones
    Lord, 229
So I am Glad, 73
Social Contract, 5
Social fund, 7
social policy, 1–11
social realism
    in art, 207
    in cinema, 143–4, 146–8
    in television, 180
society, 1–11, 265–7
    and cinema, 144, 149–51
    culture, conceptualised, 11–18
    economic character, 19–21
    and pop music, 228–9, 231–3
    and technological change, 240–2,
        245
    and theatre, 96–8, 117–20
Some Went Mad . . . Some Ran Away
    (exhibition), 221
Songlines, The, 66

Songwriters' Guild of Great Britain, 225–6
Sour Sweet, 72
Spark, Muriel, 55, 59
Special AKA, 236
Speight, Johnny, 97, 98
Spire, The, 59
Sport (tabloid), 127
Sport of My Mad Mother, The, 103
Spy Who Came in from the Cold, The, 64
Squeeze, 225
St Ives artists, 206, 208–9
Starmer, Thad, 255
statistics, book publishing, 81
Steele, Tommy, 228
STELARC, 256
Stephen Joseph Theatre, Scarborough, 116
Steptoe and Son, 97, 98, 182, 183
stock market crash, 8
Stoppard, Tom, 104
Storey, David, 54
Strawbs, 227
strikes, 4–5
structuralism, 16–17
Subculture: The Meaning of Style, 232
Success, 71
Suez debacle, 2
Summer Bird-Cage, A, 57
Summoned by Bells, 38–9
Sun, 125, 129, 131
  fictitious news, 127
  and Hillsborough disaster, 127, 130
Sun Hacks, The, 33
Sunday Sport, 127
Sunday Telegraph, 126
Sunday Times, 81, 125–6, 129, 130
Sweeney, The, 189–90
Swift, Graham, 66
Swinging London, 234
  and art, 205–6
  films, 161–2

Talbot, Mary, 76, 87–8
Tales from Hollywood, 109

Talking Heads, 45
tax policies, 6–8
Taylor, Martin, 10
Taylor, S.J., 139–40
techno music 233
technology, 239–56
teenager phenomenon, 231–3
telephones, 243, 244
television, 177–202, 243
  and books, 79, 83
  and cinema, 144–5, 163
  and newspapers, 126–7
  and popular music 231
  and theatre, 97–9
terrorism, definition widened, 11
text analysis, 89–92
Textermination, 63
Thames Television, 202
That Kind of Girl, 149, 150
That Was the Week that Was, 182
Thatcher, Margaret, 6–9
Thatcherism, 6–9
  and art, 218–19
  and cinema, 165–70
  and television, 190–2, 195, 197–8
  New Labour and, 10–11, 260–1
  and novels, 68–70
The Cheviot, the Stag and the Black, Black Oil, 186, 188
The Comforters, 55
The Uses of Literacy, 14
theatre, 94–120
Theatre and its Double, The, 104
Theatre of Cruelty, 103
This is Tomorrow (TIT) exhibition, 209–10
This Life, 201
This Sporting Life, 54
  film, 147, 162
Thomas, D.M., 59–60
Thompson, E.P., 214–15
Thompson Twins, 236
Thomson, Roy, 179
Thorneycroft, Peter, 2
Threads, 194

three-day week, 5, 185
Thurston, Carol M., 89
Till Death Us Do Part, 97
Time's Arrow, 60
Times, The, 130, 133, 136, 138
Titanic (film), 260
Tom Jones, 156–7, 159
Tomlinson, Charles, 30, 46
Tommy, 229
Top of the Pops, 231
Tosg, 119
tourism, and theatre, 100
Townsend, Pete, 228, 229
trade unions, 3–4, 5
Trainspotting, 72
  film, 172–3
Transport and General Workers'
  Union, 5
Travers, Ben 111
Traverse Theatre, 104, 119
Trilogy (Wesker), 106–7, 118
Troubles, 61
TUC (Trade Union Congress), 3, 4, 6
Turnbull, William, 205
Turner Prize, 220
Twiggy, 229
Tynan, Kenneth, 101

UB40 (band), 236
UK Gold, 202
Unfortunates, The, 63
universities, 262–3
Unnatural Nature of Science, The, 240
Up the Junction
  film, 159
  TV play, 184
Upper Clyde Shipbuilders, 4

V. (novel), 63
Victim, 144
Violent playground, 144

Wain, John, 12
Waiting for Godot, 109
Walker, Alexander, 160–1
Wall, Max, 109

Walters, Minette, 77, 85
Wapping, press move to, 131, 133–4
*War of Don Emmanuel's Nether Parts,
  The*, 71
Warwick, Kevin, 255
Wasp Factory, The, 69
Waterhouse, Keith, 159
Waterland, 66
Waterstones, 81
Waugh, Patricia, 11
Way of a World, The, 30
Ways of Seeing, 207
Wearing, Gillian, 221
Wednesday Play (series), 184–5
Weiner, Norbert, 25, 28
Weiss, Peter, 103–4
Weldon, Fay, 57, 83
Welfare and Pensions Bill, 10
welfare capitalism, 11–12, 13
Welsh, Irvine, 72, 172
Welthorpe, Mrs Edna, 110–11, 113
Wesker, Arnold, 15, 106–7, 118
Westwood, Vivienne, 230
What the Butler Saw, 111, 112
Where There is Darkness, 119
White Hotel, The, 59–60
Whitechapel Gallery, 209
Whitehouse, Mary, 184
Whiteread, Rachel, 221
Whitsun Weddings, The, 29, 30
Who, The, 228, 229
Wide Sargasso Sea, 62
Widows, 195
Wild and the Willing, The, 144
Willets, David, 218
Williams, Raymond, 13, 18, 76–7
Willis, Ted, 150, 180
Wilson, Harold, 3, 5
Winston, Brian, 240–1
Winterbottom, Michael, 174
Winterson, Jeannette, 52, 70, 72
Wise Children, 67
Wolpert, Lewis, 240, 242
women, portrayal in cinema, 146–8,
  149–50, 156, 159

Wonders of Obligation, 34–5
Woodrow, Bill, 220
working-class culture, 14–15
World Productions, 200–1
Wyndham, John, 64

X – The Unknown, 153

Yardbirds, 234
Yom Kippur War, 5

Yorkshire Ripper, newspaper
    reporting, 134–9
Yorkshire TV, 199
'You've never had it so good', 2
Young Contemporaries (exhibition),
    211
youth culture, 231–3

Z Cars, 182–3, 184
Zoom, 45